# Fields of Fire
## An Atlas of Ethnic Conflict

*Standard Edition*

www.ethnic-conflict.info

"And how can Man die better
Than facing fearful odds
For the Ashes of his Fathers
And the Temples of his Gods"

'Horatius'
Thomas Babington Macaulay

# Fields of Fire – An Atlas of Ethnic Conflict

**About the Author**

Stuart Notholt is a writer and business analyst with more than twenty years' international experience advising corporations and government agencies on the management of their communications and business risks. A graduate of Oxford University, he is a Fellow and Past President of the Chartered Institute of Journalists, a Fellow of the Royal Geographical Society and a member of the Royal African Society.

**Fields of Fire**
*An Atlas of Ethnic Conflict*
*(Standard Edition)*

ISBN: 978-1906510-473

© Stuart Notholt Communications Ltd
BM ATLAS, London, WC1N 3XX
United Kingdom
Tel/Fax: +44 (0)7092 071126
Email: atlas@ethnic-conflict.info
www.ethnic-conflict.info

The moral right of the author has been asserted.

*Apart from any fair dealing for the purposes of research or private study, or criticism or review, as permitted under the Copyright, Designs and Patents Act 1988, this publication may only be reproduced, stored or transmitted, in any form or by any means, with the prior permission in writing of the publishers, or in the case of reprographic reproduction in accordance with the terms of licences issued by the Copyright Licensing Agency. Enquiries concerning reproduction outside those terms should be sent to the publishers:*

Matador, 9 De Montfort Mews
Leicester LE1 7FW. United Kingdom
Email: books@troubador.co.uk
www.troubador.co.uk

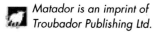
*Matador is an imprint of Troubador Publishing Ltd.*

*Neither maps nor commentaries in this Atlas should be taken as an endorsement of any territorial or political claim.*

This edition published July 2008.
Version: 4.2.

**Insurrections and inter-communal violence in which religious, linguistic, or racial divisions are a significant factor now form the majority of armed conflicts in the world today.**

This Atlas focuses on violent ethnic disputes that have been active since the fall of the Berlin Wall in 1989. Many of these have an earlier origin, and some have been resolved since 1989 – at least for the present. A small number of conflicts in which ethnicity does not play a significant role, but which have relevance either to individual population groups or to neighbouring disputes, are included for completeness. In each case, details of geographical extent, timeline, and ethnic composition of the relevant territory is included.

The Atlas provides a concise case-by-case summary of ethnic conflicts around the world. As many of these conflicts are unresolved, up-to-date information is often difficult to obtain and features of conflicts, including alliances and attempts at resolution, may be subject to rapid change.

**This Atlas accordingly has a dedicated website providing news, updates, and other information on current ethnic conflicts:**

## www.ethnic-conflict.info

Many of the resources on the website are available exclusively to Atlas owners.

Each page of the Atlas carries a version control number, which appears in the inside bottom margin. A version history of each page, as well as the most up-to-date edition for download, is available from the website.

This standard edition of this Atlas features black-and-white line maps. The Extended Edition has colour maps, flags of the belligerents, and an additional full-colour world maps section, which is also available as a separate publication. Details and on-line ordering options for the Atlas and its related publications appear at the website.

# Contents

*Entries in italics refer to text in panels.*

Contents .................................................iii
Key to symbols ........................................iv

Section 1

Introduction ..............................................1.01
Ethnicity and conflict............................1.03
Types of ethnic conflict......................1.06
*Birth of a nation*................................1.04

Section 2:
**Africa**

Africa (overview) ................................2.02
Algeria .....................................................2.06
Burundi....................................................2.26
Cabinda...................................................2.60
Casamance.............................................2.08
Central African Republic ....................2.16
Chad.........................................................2.10
Congo......................................................2.28
Cote d'Ivoire .........................................2.48
Darfur......................................................2.12
Eritrea......................................................2.18
Ethiopia...................................................2.18
Ghana .....................................................2.47
Guinea ....................................................2.45
Kenya.......................................................2.61
Liberia .....................................................2.41
Mano River region .............................2.40
Mauritania..............................................2.32
Namibia...................................................2.58
Nigeria.....................................................2.36
Ogaden....................................................2.22
Rwanda ..................................................2.24
Sierra Leone .........................................2.43
Somalia ...................................................2.20
South Africa ..........................................2.54
South Sudan.........................................2.14
Southern Cameroons ........................2.38
Tuareg.....................................................2.50
Uganda....................................................2.30
Western Sahara ..................................2.34
Zanzibar..................................................2.52
Zimbabwe ..............................................2.56
*Conflict interlinkage in Africa............2.05*
*The Eastern Front (Sudan).................2.13*
*Kenya's Kalashnikov economy............2.62*
*Oromo Liberation Front......................2.23*
*Secession in Somaliland .....................2.21*
*The Tutsi – a 'tribe' or not? ................2.27*

Section 3:
**The Americas**

Chiapas...................................................3.04
Colombia.................................................3.06
Guatemala..............................................3.10
Guyana....................................................3.12
Latin America (overview)...................3.02
North America (overview) ................3.14
Peru..........................................................3.08
*Canada's Quebec question................3.16*
*Guyanese border disputes..................3.13*
*The border with Belize......................3.11*

Section 4:
**Middle East**

Iraq...........................................................4.10
Islamic Caliphate .................................4.14
Israel........................................................4.16
Kurdistan.................................................4.08
Lebanon..................................................4.04
Middle Eastern Christians..................4.06
Palestine..................................................4.16
Sinai.........................................................4.13
Turkey......................................................4.02
Yemen .....................................................4.07

Section 5:
**Central and West Asia**

Afghanistan............................................5.22
Balochistan.............................................5.25
Central Asia ..........................................5.02
Chagos Islands .....................................5.17
India .........................................................5.08
Kashmir...................................................5.14
Nepal........................................................5.18
Pakistan...................................................5.22
Punjab......................................................5.10
Seven Sisters States ..........................5.12
Tamil Eelam ..........................................5.20
Tibet .........................................................5.04
Xinjiang....................................................5.06
*Minorities in China...........................5.07*
*NATO and 9/11 ..............................5.24*
*Nepal's Bhutanese refugees ..............5.19*
*Pakistan's political problems...............5.26*

Section 6:
**South East Asia and Oceania**

Aceh .........................................................6.08
Australia..................................................6.29
Bougainville ...........................................6.27
Burma (Myanmar)...............................6.02
Fiji.............................................................6.26
Indonesia ................................................6.06
Kalimantan (Borneo)..........................6.10

Indochina................................................6.24
Malaysia .................................................6.22
Mindanao...............................................6.18
Moluccas (Maluku) ............................6.14
Pattani .....................................................6.20
Solomon Islands...................................6.28
Timor Leste (East Timor) ..................6.12
West Papua...........................................6.16
*Ethnic conflict in Luzon......................6.19*
*Ethnic resistance to the Burmese state ..6.03*
*Indonesia's transmigration policy ........6.11*
*Nuclear conflict in the Pacific ............6.30*
*The dwifungsi policy..........................6.13*

Section 7:
**Europe**

Balkans....................................................7.25
Baltic states ..........................................7.06
Bosnia & Herzegovina .......................7.30
Chechnya...............................................7.22
Corsica....................................................7.38
Crimea ....................................................7.10
Cyprus.....................................................7.12
Dagestan ................................................7.24
Europe (overview) ..............................7.02
Euzkadi (the Basque Country) ...........7.08
Georgia....................................................7.14
Kosovo ....................................................7.32
Macedonia .............................................7.34
Nagorno-Karabakh..............................7.16
Northern Ireland ..................................7.36
Tatarstan.................................................7.20
Transnistra..............................................7.18
*Azeri separatists ................................7.17*
*Breakdown in Belgium? .....................7.04*
*Ethnic cleansing defined?...................7.29*
*Europe's 'other' minority – the Roma....7.05*
*The Kaliningrad question ...................7.07*
*Ukraine's struggle for independence....7.11*

Index.......................................................v

# Key to symbols

**Key data bar**

 This symbol indicates particularly harsh or arbitrary treatment by the state or its agents, including assaults on civilians, extra-judicial imprisonment, execution and torture.

This symbol indicates that religious conflict is a significant factor.

Death toll. It is notoriously difficult to get accurate figures for the casualties in ethnic conflicts. Figures published here represent the most likely tally.

Refugees. Refugee numbers may vary widely during a conflict, and may decline at its end when the refugees return home. The figures quoted here generally represent the refugee total at peak. Figures for IDPs – 'Internally Displaced Persons' (i.e., people who have been forced to leave their homes as a result of violence, but have not left their country) – are also shown where appropriate.

This symbol indicates that control of natural resources is a key driver for the conflict.

**Map legend**

Kisangani ● Town or city.

*(Towns and cities are included according to their relevance to the conflict; inclusion is not necessarily indicative of their size or overall significance.)*

 Refugee camp

**Croatia** Principal national or provincial names

Vojvodina Other regional names
Haute Casamance

*Fergana Valley* Geographical regions

 Main site of conflict

 Airfield

–·–·– International borders (including unrecognized or *de facto* borders)

--------- Provincial border

 Sea or other water feature

 River

 Mountain

iv  *Fields of Fire – An Atlas of Ethnic Conflict*  v4.0

# Introduction

"War," Winston Smith noted in Orwell's *Nineteen Eighty-Four*, "has changed its meaning." In the first years of the 21st century we might make a similar observation. The landscape of modern warfare appears fundamentally different from the bipolar certainties of the Cold War, or the catastrophes of the First and Second World Wars. Or perhaps human warfare has simply reverted to type?

From the French Revolution until the end of the Cold War in 1989, the tendency, at least in the English-speaking world, was to articulate global conflicts in universalist terms: they were struggles between 'freedom' and 'tyranny', whether the despot in question was Napoleon, Hitler or Stalin. This view masked our understanding that throughout history the parameters of conflict have usually been set by more primordial instincts. The basic need to define one's own people – whether by racial type, language or culture – and to ensure the tribe's survival and growth in the face of real or imagined challenges from others, has always been a compelling factor in urging groups towards violence. In other words, most wars have been what we would now call 'ethnic conflicts.'

Depending on one's viewpoint, this was also true of important aspects of the conflicts of the last century. The Second World War, from the German perspective, was very clearly a 'race war' both against the Jews and on the vital Eastern Front against the 'inhuman' Slavs. Even the USSR observed a racial hierarchy, ranging from the core Russian population down through various levels of reliability to groups such as the Chechens or the Crimean Tartars who were deported *en masse* for their alleged collaboration with the Nazis. Soviet racialism did not even, as its apologists claimed, arise solely under the stresses of the German invasion. During the first purges of the 1920s, those singled out for victimization were often identified in overtly racial terms, even if a 'class' veneer was applied. The slogan "if it's a Pole, it's a Kulak" sentenced hundreds of thousands to arbitrary arrest, deportation and extermination.

Of course, it is immediately necessary to add caveats. Most wars are also about preferential access to resources – land, food, fuel, money. And because the subject of ethnicity is subjective and frequently controversial, there are those who argue that there is no such thing as 'ethnicity' at all, let alone an ethnic war. To Marxists, the issue has a simple clarity: 'ethnicity' is a false consciousness, fuelled by political and other elites as a means of harnessing dissent and channelling it away from the essential class struggle. For liberals, ethnic quarrels are essentially the results of outmoded prejudices and ignorance, and can be overcome through education, rising living standards, and political tools such as multi-party democracy, or institutionalized programmes of respect for 'human rights'.

The Human Genome Project has established that, on a purely biological level, there is a less than one per cent genetic difference between all human population groups, and that in fact the genetic variations *within* populations are greater than those which distinguish them from their neighbours.

This discovery was seized upon enthusiastically by commentators, politicians, scientists and sociologists as 'proving' that the differences between humans are infinitely less than that which should unite us. Although this may be so, the 'race-is-dead' reasoning merely throws into stark relief the question of why, if ethnicity has no biological basis, it remains an extremely powerful motivator in human behaviour. Both Marxist dogma and liberal wishful thinking avoid the unpalatable reality that it is frighteningly easy for demagogues to mobilize populations by playing upon their fears and aspirations.

The implosion of the USSR and its attendant socialist ideology in the early 1990s was so sudden, and the 'victory' of the West so apparently complete, that many speculated whether the end of the long Cold War did not represent some fundamental sea-change in the affairs of Mankind.

This view was represented most provocatively by the historian Francis Fukuyama, who argued that the triumph of Western economic and political values marked nothing less than "the end of history". Fukuyama's vision was fundamentally an optimistic one – he believed that the onward march of modernity, in which he included open democratic systems and free markets, was irreversible, not least due to the failure of any sustainable alternatives to emerge. By this analysis, opposition to the Western model of society, whether violent or otherwise, was essentially a transient phenomenon: the death throes of obsolete ideologies doomed to failure and extinction.

Yet it is a sobering fact for modernists that, far from making ethnic conflict a throwback to some less enlightened age, aspects of 'modernization' actually highlight the perceived differences between groups and can thus be a contributor to tension and violence. Globalization imposes new stresses on possibly already vulnerable local cultures, traditions, and economic relationships, and is widely seen as benefiting primarily the internationally rich and powerful. The internet enables dissident voices, unchecked by any considerations of journalistic accuracy, to be universally broadcast. The creation of centralizing political blocs, such as the European Union, integrates formerly discrete economic communities and makes wealth and other disparities between them more visible, as well as promoting a sense of alienation between the citizen and the decision making centres. Finally, in a world that now wrestles with the problem of Islamic fundamentalism as well as the aspirations of rising powers such as China and India, the contention that there is no real alternative to Western liberalism seems markedly less credible than it did in 1989.

That the Cold War stayed, for the most part, cold, is a perverse testament to the stability of the post-1945 geopolitics. Both sides rattled sabres and armed proxies in the jungles of Vietnam, Angola or El Salvador, but, far from ushering in Armageddon, the limits to provocation (particularly after the near disaster of the Cuban missile crisis) were generally understood and respected. Violent ethnic contests over the control of national or regional assets, including superpower patronage, control of government, access to education, and, in the more kleptomaniac regimes, the State treasury itself, certainly did not cease during the Cold War. On the other hand, it is unlikely that either side would have permitted the dangerous vacuum resulting from the wholesale collapse of Somalia, Zaïre, or the Balkans that was witnessed in the 1990s.

Since 1989, ethnic conflicts have intensified and spread at an alarming rate. Old conflicts have re-ignited and new ones have emerged from the otherwise unlamented demise of the Soviet Union and Yugoslavia. India and Pakistan have come to the brink of nuclear-armed conflict over Kashmir, and Africa has seen the carnage of its 'first world war', in Congo, as well as the horrors of genocide in Rwanda and Sudan. Balefully hovering over this landscape is the new and additional danger of international Islamist terrorism from those seeking to impose their particularly narrow religious and social creed. This threat is not merely a physical one, but, equally importantly, carries with it the aim of dividing societies and creating hatred amongst and between peoples, religions and cultures.

Even in relatively benign democracies, the knee-jerk reaction of governments has involved the restriction of civil liberties in the name of domestic security. In harsher regimes, the 'war on terror' has been nakedly exploited to stifle legitimate dissent.

Globally, many countries face resource pressures, lack of democratic and other societal outlets for dissent, unfair and exploitative regional or social policies, the imposition of prescriptive social norms in religion, language, or dress code, and demographic changes such as unchecked immigration. All provide abundant scope for disadvantaged peoples to take up arms. And the point at which legitimate grievance becomes greed is a fine one.

In a world in which the majority of conflicts have strong religious, cultural, racial, or linguistic drivers, the failure of commentators and policy makers to factor in the ethnic dimension can, and does, have literally fatal results. Understanding the ethnic underpinnings of conflict also militates against the temptation to dismiss such violence as 'tribal', inexplicable, and therefore incapable of resolution. Only when Mankind makes a genuine celebration of difference, rather than pretending that such distinctions do not exist, or insisting that one standard must prevail, can we have a chance of going forwards instead of backwards.

# Ethnicity and conflict

An 'ethnic group' is a human population which self-identifies itself as such on the basis of shared traits such as religion, race, nationality, language, history or ancestry. Ethnicity can also be seen as reflecting the ongoing communication of shared cultural and other values from one generation to the next. Ethnic diversity has been the source and inspiration for great achievements in art, architecture, poetry and music. Unfortunately, such diversity comes at a price. It is a dangerously short jump from "my group is different" to "my group is better" or "my group is threatened." National or religious chauvinism, racial antagonism, the demonization of other groups, and ultimately, war, deportations, and genocide can then be among the consequences.

Most individuals have social and cultural affiliations that link them, whether consciously or not, to a specific ethnicity, however generalized. Equally, many examples exist of institutions, including political parties and sovereign political entities, that derive their legitimacy wholly or in part through their identification with an ethnic group. Nevertheless, because individual ethnicity is based on subjective belief, and may therefore have only very limited objective reality, many political scientists have wrestled with the whole concept, with some devising extravagant algebraic formulae purporting to plot the probability of ethnic conflict in a given scenario, while others have sought to reject altogether the value of ethnicity as a useful construct.

The issue has also been confused by the tendency to conflate 'ethnicity' with nationality or race. Undoubtedly, racial phenotypes such as skin colour, stature, and overall appearance have, throughout history, been key 'markers' for ethnic distinctiveness, but in contemporary ethnic conflict non-racial factors are frequently more immediate and important. In many current ethnic conflicts, not least those related to Islamic fundamentalism, religion is the central feature.

In other disputes, preserving linguistic distinctiveness has emerged as a critical issue, since language is not merely a set of different words for the same meanings and objects, but carries with it a whole raft of connotations surrounding the philosophy, history, and folklore of a people. Broader issues of cultural distinctiveness can cut across ethnic boundaries, while at the same time dividing groups that would not otherwise be thought of as two or more ethnicities. In contrast, the sometimes very great cultural differences that can exist between social classes, or even between generations, are rarely articulated in ethnic terms.

Ethnicity is thus a composite of a number of individually subjective 'identity markers' of which religion, language, race and nationality are generally among the more important. Since an individual can simultaneous subscribe to several such markers, it follows that, at different stages in their lives (or even during the course of a few hours) individuals may identify at different levels in a hierarchy of loyalties; with their family, workmates, sporting team, or clan, and so on up to their nation, race, or religion at the broadest level.

It can also be noted also that some of the attributes of ethnicity can be purposefully acquired. It is relatively easy to learn a new language, and possible to adopt a new religion (although social and cultural barriers often exist in practice). On the other hand, expensive cosmetic products and surgery aside, it is difficult to dramatically alter one's physiognomy, and impossible to alter one's genetic ancestry, although this may also be concealed.

The degree to which individuals, having made appropriate cultural, linguistic, religious, and other adjustments, are then accepted as full members of a group depends on whether the ethnicity in question is predicated primarily on notions of race and ancestry, and is therefore exclusive, or whether it is based on a more inclusive view.

This latter concept of ethnicity, which downplays aspects of identity based on heredity in favour of cultural integration and the formal attainment of citizenship, is in theory 'colour blind'. Examples exist where the assimilation of individuals from other racial groups was applied even in colonial situations. France, for example, accorded mainly urbanized Africans full citizenship, including representation at the National Assembly in Paris, and continues to strongly define French ethnicity in terms of adherence to French linguistic and cultural values rather than by race. While this has allowed non-European citizens to integrate into French society, it has very much been on the basis of their adopting 'Frenchness' and abandoning any distinctive features of their own original culture. Historically, the French state has also been reluctant to accommodate indigenous groups within its borders who differ from the national norm. Regional languages such as Occitan and Breton continue to suffer various forms of official discrimination, and it is hard to see, for example, France following the Spanish or British examples of regional devolution. More recently, the failure of Islamic immigrant populations to integrate has become an issue.

Mass immigration and the loss of religious and other signifiers of social cohesion have become key issues in many Western societies. Accordingly, most face variations on the French dilemma of how to square the circle between social integration and upholding the rights of individuals to maintain a group identity which is not that of the mainstream. The majority of Western states emphasize the legal equality of individual citizens and so have prohibited, in varying degrees, discrimination on the grounds of race or religion (and gender). However, they have simultaneously sought to embrace the concept of 'multiculturalism' under which different ethnic groups can co-exist while maintaining their separate identities. The problem is that multiculturalism at least implies a level of ethnically-based group rights, even if these are informal rather than legally enforced, which is in contradiction to the concept that the state's primary duty is to uphold *individual* entitlements. One logical end result of multiculturalism is not a uniform liberal pluralism, but a differential legal treatment of individuals as a consequence of their being a member of a distinctive ethnicity. *Apartheid* was one such system, as is the application of *sharia* law in countries that are, in theory at least, secular or non-Muslim. In countries where *sharia* law is admissible, the Muslim citizen has different civil rights, whether as plaintive or defendant, arising solely from their membership of a particular ethno-religious group. Ultimately, the success of a non-sectarian pluralism depends on the willingness of individuals in all groups, including immigrant populations, to identify with a common civic patriotism that transcends local or ethnic differences.

Modern ethnic conflicts stem from a variety of motivations, whether opposition to multiculturalism, political nationalism or separatism, promotion of indigenous rights, urban minority and other 'race relations' issues, and in religious revivalism.

Violent contests may arise from the perception that resources, including political power or patronage, are unequally shared between ethnic groups, or, alternatively, that one's own group, by virtue of its superiority, should have first claim on resources (which is the basis of imperialism and other forms of expansionism). In extreme examples, religious or racial sectarianism may lead one group to the conclusion that others are less than fully human, and thus fit for extermination or enslavement. A lack of any objective evidence for such views is rarely relevant. The 'resources' in question may not even be tangible, but may revolve around the co-option and interpretation of historical events, places names, and accessibility of religious sites.

Inevitably, groups are more likely to be able to sustain violence, whether essentially aggressive or defensive, if they have a regional base, a sufficiently large population, live in remote or difficult terrain, have 'kith and kin' in neighbouring countries, and if they receive external support. 'Conventional' wars, in which regular forces from internationally recognized states intervene in support of an ethnic group in another country, are, however, comparatively rare in modern conflicts. Most governments prefer to act through proxies, at least officially, and intervention, if it occurs, is usually linked to some broader vested interest. Examples include clashes between India and Pakistan over Kashmir, Rwandan intervention in support of the Congolese Tutsis,

and the NATO invasion of Kosovo, the latter being openly expressed in terms of 'humanitarian' intervention in favour of one ethnic group (the Albanians) over another (the Serbs). The US-led invasions of Afghanistan and Iraq, although they have subsequently involved the US and its allies in ethnic conflicts, were not initially expressed in ethnic terms.

Although the United Nations in theory upholds the right of self-determination for all nations and peoples, in reality, from 1945 until the early 1990s, the international doctrine was that the internal affairs of states were inviolable, and that internal ethnic and regional conflicts could only be solved by settlements within existing borders, rather than by secession

---

**Birth of a nation**

Since ethnicity is such a subjective concept, it is perhaps unsurprising that the processes by which new ethnicities are created (or create themselves) are incompletely understood.

The term used to describe the process by which distinctive ethnicities emerge – ethnogenesis – has itself been challenged as implying a quasi-organic process by which human populations spontaneously come to understand themselves as different from their neighbours. Clearly, the adoption of new religious practices, changes in culture through agricultural or technological innovation, the emergence of new languages, and genetic modifications to climate will all, given time and, usually, a degree of separation from other groups, produce 'new' human populations.

On the other hand, the creation of a new ethnicity can be a conscious political act. In the 1920s, for example, Soviet policy favoured the creation of a patchwork of states in Central Asia as a means of defusing any potential pan-Islamic threat. Soviet ethnologists worked to identify linguistic types, folk pathways and cultural signifiers in order to justify the new states and their extraordinarily convoluted borders. The result was a region in which national consciousness and identity remain uncertain. Similarly, the enforced use of the Cyrillic script to create the Moldovan language, as distinct from Romanian, was a conscious political act that, as in Central Asia, continues to have consequences.

The emergence of a new ethnicity, even if it does not engender open conflict, may be restricted by the politics of others. The concept of a 'Macedonian' ethnicity (as opposed to 'South Serb' or 'West Bulgarian') is comparatively new, having only found formal political expression with the creation of the Macedonian Republic in 1946 – and even today is controversial. Greek objections to the very name 'Macedonia' led to the cumbersome 'Former Yugoslav Republic of Yugoslavia' (FYROM) designation under which Macedonia joined the United Nations.

Nevertheless, whether artificially created or not, new ethnicities are constantly being born. The reverse side of the coin, of course, is that ethnic groups can die. This can occur through defeat in war, deliberate extermination, mass demographic changes, or through assimilation.

or partition. Secessionism has also been opposed on the grounds that ever smaller breakaway states would be economically unviable. Economic viability has never been a test for membership of the UN, however, as the admission of various post-colonial microstates demonstrates, and there is in any case no proven correlation between size and economic viability.

The general belief that peoples have a right to self-determination continues to inform many ethnic disputes today. The logical outcome of the universal application of the principle of self-determination would be for each ethnic group to have its own independent nation state, or at least to enjoy wide political and cultural autonomy within a state. The difficulty occurs, of course, where there is no clear geographical demarcation for such a state, or where more than one ethnic group lays historical claim to a given territory. In practice, modern states are very rarely coterminous with ethnic groups. While many groups continue to experience a divergence of political identities and interests from the mainstream of the states in which they reside – and there is no evidence that this is diminishing – ethnic conflict, and its resolution, will continue to be a pivotal issue in regional and global security.

# Types of ethnic conflict

Ethnic conflicts generally fall into three types: civil rights conflicts, ethnic rebellions and inter-communal violence. *(See next section for commentary.)* Civil rights conflicts and ethnic rebellions both focus on applying pressure on governments, either directly or on its agents. The degree of violence may alter during the course of the conflict, with initially peaceful civil rights protests, for example, turning violent and descending into full-scale confrontation. Whether this happens or not usually depends on the extent to which there are existing social and political outlets for dissent, as well as the willingness of the state and its supporters to use force. The nature of the challenge to government may vary. In civil rights conflicts it may be a call on government to reform, or become more inclusive. In full-scale rebellions, the objective generally becomes either the wholesale replacement of the government (civil war) or the creation of a separate state for a minority ethnic group (secessionism). Ethnicized contests over the control of government, even where they have not resulted in sustained political violence, can be seen as an intermediate form between civil rights conflicts and open rebellion.

In inter-communal violence, the immediate target for aggression is not directly the government, but members of another ethnic group. In these conflicts, the government may be a neutral bystander, policeman, or arbiter, or may be partisan towards one side or the other. Despite its sometimes random-seeming nature, inter-communal violence almost invariably has some underlying political or social agenda.

▓ Separatist conflicts (including irredentist and regionalist conflicts)
▥ Ethnic civil war
▨ Other civil war (ethnic conflict not the primary cause)
▦ Inter-state war
▧ Ethnicized political contests over control of government
▤ Civil rights disputes

✶ Significant inter-communal violence

(Map shows conflicts active since 1990.)

**1.06**  *Fields of Fire – An Atlas of Ethnic Conflict*  v4.0

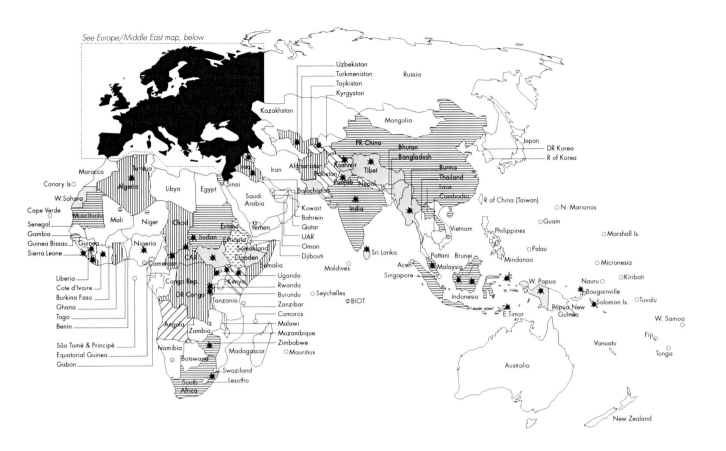
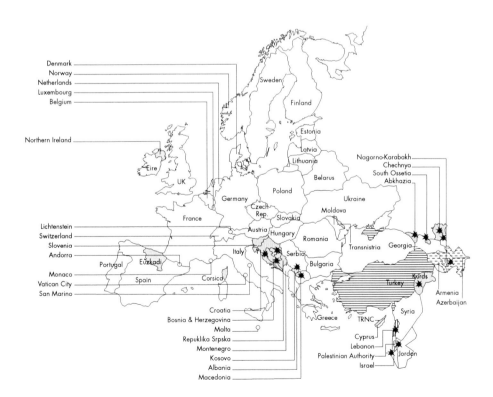

Fields of Fire – An Atlas of Ethnic Conflict

# Types of ethnic conflict

Ethnic conflicts can be divided into three broad categories: civil rights conflicts, ethnic rebellions, and inter-communal violence. These may co-exist or merge into other forms as the conflict progresses. Each type of conflict has its own own pathways to escalation and potential resolution, not all of the latter being benign or permanent.

---

**Escalation and resolution paths for ethnic conflicts**

**Civil rights conflicts**

*Escalation:*
- Strikes; passive resistance; demonstrations
- Hunger strikes; immolations by activists
- State repression; police/military brutality; rioting
- Extra-judicial imprisonments; torture; assassinations
- Ethnic rebellion *(see below)*.

*Potential resolutions:*
- Political concessions; economic measures
- Co-option of minority leaders
- Effective state repression

**Ethnic rebellions**

*Escalation:*
- Politically motivated banditry; kidnappings
- Terrorism
- Guerrilla attacks; counter insurgency
- Establishment of 'liberated territory'
- Secessionist war; civil war; coup d'etat

*Potential resolutions:*
- Political accommodation through federal or other structures
- International peacekeeping interventions
- Partition
- Seizure of power by opposition group
- Successful counter-insurgency

**Inter-communal violence**

*Escalation:*
- Political agitation and rabble-rousing
- Non-fatal assaults and harassment
- Individual murders; 'hate crimes'
- Violence by gangs; terrorism
- Anti-group riots; looting
- Full communal warfare; genocide

*Potential resolutions:*
- Intervention by anti-violence community leaders
- Political reinforcement of civil society and pluralist structures; economic measures
- Effective, non-partisan policing or peacekeeping
- Creation of self-defence forces by minority groups; informal segregation
- Physical separation of populations

---

## Civil rights conflicts

Civil rights conflicts occur when a group, which may or may not be the majority, feels it is denied access to state resources or to cultural rights. Civil rights contests may start with non-violent protests, demonstrations, strikes and political mobilization. Three paths to escalation can then occur, either individually or in combination. The demands may not be met, in which case the group may itself turns to violence. The state may instigate violence, including repressive or extra-judicial measures. Thirdly, retaliatory violence may be initiated by rival ethnic groups, particularly where these are aligned to the state. Civil rights conflicts can escalate, depending on the political geography, into full secessionist or civil wars.

The disadvantaged group may not necessarily seek the formal overthrow of the government or economic system (at least initially), merely the opportunity to participate fully in the life of the country. The US civil rights movement in 1960s is such an example, as was the anti-*apartheid* movement in South Africa, although the success of the latter required far more sweeping changes to the political landscape, and could easily have developed into a more general conflict.

## Ethnic rebellions

Ethnic rebellions take a number of different forms, depending on the goals of the belligerents and the nature of the governmental response to what may, in the first instance, be peaceful civil protest.

The majority of modern ethnic conflicts contain some form of separatist element, where an ethnic group seeks to detach or distance itself politically from the state in which it currently resides. Most separatists are nationalists, i.e., they seek ideally the establishment of an independent nation state, but some will settle for devolved or federal government as a compromise solution, while others merely seek a more equitable distribution of local or national wealth. Related to separatism is irredentism, where the ethnic group seeks union with a neighbouring state.

A number of conflicts are regarded (at least by the side seeking independence) as part of the 'unfinished business' of post-Second World War decolonization. Examples include Western Sahara, Cabinda, and East Timor, which gained internationally recognized independence in 2001. These disputes are generally regarded as secessionist conflicts by the 'metropolitan' government, which usually regards the 'colonial' region as an integral part of its territory.

The other main type of ethnic rebellion is the ethnically-predicated civil war. Unlike a secessionist or civil rights conflict, these represent a direct challenge to the central government, with the intention of its wholesale replacement either with a government drawn from a more pluralist ethnic constituency, or with one from a rival ethnic faction. Civil war may be initiated by disadvantaged ethnic groups either after all other options are eliminated, or as a more overtly factional power-grab. Coups d'etat also fall into this general category. Ethnicized political contests, such as those in Guyana and Kenya, may be regarded as an intermediate form, having the potential to lead either to inter-communal violence and/or to general insurrection.

### Inter-communal violence

Although often extremely vicious, inter-communal violence is rarely purely random or mindless. The participants will collectively recognize some real or perceived injustice against themselves, and these underlying sentiments will frequently be harnessed by political leaders for their own ends.Sustained inter-communal fighting without any broader political agenda or set of demands emerging is comparatively unusual.

The greatest death toll through inter-communal violence in the modern age has almost certainly been the millions of Hindus, Sikhs, and Muslims who died in the process of Indian partition in 1947-8. More recent example include anti-Chinese rioting in Malaysia and the conflicts between the Dayaks and the Melanese in Kalimantan. Government intervention in inter-communal fighting can range from even-handed policing to blatant support for one faction or the other. Revenge attacks, for example against the East Timorese community in reprisal for their successfully negotiating independence, or against Christian communities in Pakistan for alleged insults to Islam made by a cartoonist in Denmark, are another manifestation of inter-communal violence.

The incitement of an ethnic community to violently assault or persecute another may be a conscious strategy of political leaders, actual or aspiring. The most notorious example, of course, was the way in which the Nazis co-opted and inflamed already latent anti-Semitism in pursuance of broader political goals, but more recent instances can also be cited. The ethnic unrest in Kenya at the beginning of 2008, for example, involved a strong element of political manipulation by leaders on both sides in their contest for political control, even though most of the actual killings had no *direct* political objective.

In its more extreme manifestations, inter-communal violence may take the form of ethnic cleansing and outright genocide, and here again the distinction between political and apolitical motivation becomes increasingly blurred. Although the actual killings may be carried out in what seems to outsiders to be a blind frenzy, the instigators and promoters of the violence will usually have an understood political agenda.

### Conflict resolution

Resolution to ethnic conflicts, which may not always be equitable, can take three basic forms: political accommodation, physical separation of the two parties, or a comprehensive victory by one side over the other. Additionally, over time, assimilation may result in one or more ethnic groups merging – the American 'melting pot' being the classic example – although this usually entails the loss or abandonment of many of the distinguishing characteristics of the absorbed group. Assimilation is unlikely to occur, however, unless basic political and societal problems are resolved and is unlikely, therefore, to offer a short-term solution to an ongoing ethnic conflict.

Political accommodation can take a variety of forms. Where territorial or regional issues are at stake, the negotiation of devolved government or the establishment of federal structures may be an appropriate response. Where the conflict is essentially a civil rights one, laws and political structures can be modified to be more inclusive, while education and investment programmes may, given time, alleviate economic disparities and prejudices between groups. In cases of inter-communal violence, religious and other community leaders may intervene to stop the fighting, or citizens' groups may arise to demand its cessation, as happened with the Northern Ireland Womens' Peace Movement in the 1970s and the mass anti-terror demonstrations in Spain of the 1990s. Sadly, the success of such initiatives is all too rare or transient.

Overall, political resolution to ethnic conflict can proceed either by reducing the political inequalities between ethnic groups (by, for example, extending the franchise) or by institutionalizing ethnic differences. Lebanon, with its 'confessional' constitution, represents an example of the latter, as do Burundi and Northern Ireland, where political settlements are based on power sharing between the two main protagonists. Power sharing carries with it, however, the risk of renewed conflict at a later date if one of the parties comes to believe it is not benefiting satisfactorily from the arrangement. It may also exclude other groups who are not party to the deal, and stands in the way of the emergence of genuine cross-community institutions such as non-sectarian political parties, which, because they do not add to the quota of one side or the other, cannot be easily integrated into the political process. Once in position, it is often extremely difficult to modify a power sharing arrangement, and its inflexibility may make it vulnerable to changes in demography or broader political dynamics, as the breakdown of the political system in Lebanon demonstrates.

A further possibility for resolution is the physical separation of the antagonists. Although often unpalatable, segregation can prove to be the least costly solution in terms of overall loss of life. The 'green line' in Cyprus – politically offensive though it may be to many Cypriots – has nevertheless prevented serious communal violence between Greeks and Turks for over thirty years. Informal segregation, including the creation of urban quarters, or, in the more extreme cases, ethnic ghettoes, may also represent a solution, however imperfect, to inter-communal violence. Formal partition or secession may alleviate conflicts that have a regional aspect, although mutual consent to the separation will generally be a prerequisite for this to become a permanent solution.

Finally, there is the possibility of force succeeding. While at one level it is unacceptable to posit mass murders or deportations as a 'resolution' to any conflict, it has to be conceded that tactics such as ethnic cleansing have often proven to be ruthlessly effective in creating ethnically homogeneous societies. In the absence of any such 'final solution' ongoing state repression may keep ethnic conflict in check, however temporarily.

Even where the nature of one conflict appears similar to another the outcome may be very different, and solutions that work in one scenario may fail in the next. For example, many modern cases exist where government control has been vested in a very narrow ethnic group. Examples include Liberia under the Americo-Liberians, Chad under the Zaghara, and *apartheid*-era South Africa. Yet, despite the superficial similarities of the key issues, very different outcomes emerged in these three instances. The Americo-Liberian regime fell to a violent coup d'etat that was followed by a series of ethnic civil wars. Chad faces ongoing violence and the possibility of state collapse and/or outside intervention, while South Africa avoided civil war through timely political concessions. With so many human and other factors in play, plotting the trajectories of ethnic conflicts, let alone their resolution, remains an inexact science.

# Section 2: **Africa**

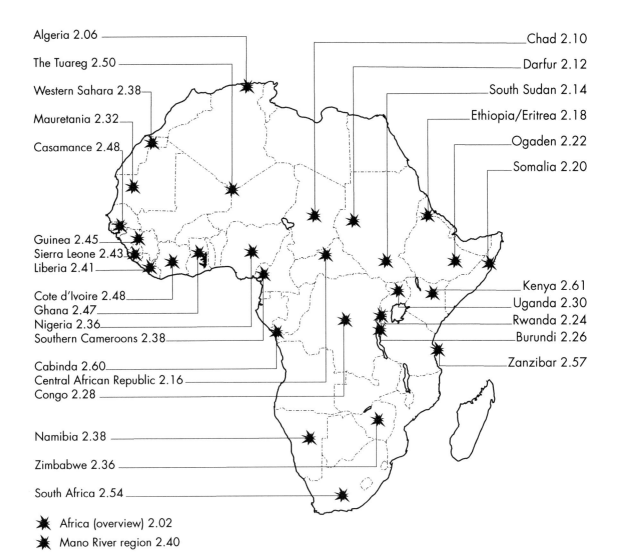

- Algeria 2.06
- The Tuareg 2.50
- Western Sahara 2.38
- Mauretania 2.32
- Casamance 2.48
- Guinea 2.45
- Sierra Leone 2.43
- Liberia 2.41
- Cote d'Ivoire 2.48
- Ghana 2.47
- Nigeria 2.36
- Southern Cameroons 2.38
- Cabinda 2.60
- Central African Republic 2.16
- Congo 2.28
- Namibia 2.38
- Zimbabwe 2.36
- South Africa 2.54
- Chad 2.10
- Darfur 2.12
- South Sudan 2.14
- Ethiopia/Eritrea 2.18
- Ogaden 2.22
- Somalia 2.20
- Kenya 2.61
- Uganda 2.30
- Rwanda 2.24
- Burundi 2.26
- Zanzibar 2.57

✶ Africa (overview) 2.02
✶ Mano River region 2.40

*Conflict interlinkage in Africa 2.05*
*The Eastern Front (Sudan) 2.13*
*Kenya's Kalashnikov economy 2.62*
*Oromo Liberation Front 2.23*
*Secession in Somaliland 2.21*
*The Tutsi – a 'tribe' or not? 2.27*

*Fields of Fire – An Atlas of Ethnic Conflict*

# Africa

With a population of nearly a billion, Africa, as befits the original home of mankind, is a continent of extraordinary ethnic diversity. The conventional continental-wide division of Africa is into five broad linguistic groups, Niger-Congo A, Niger-Congo B, Nilo-Saharan, Afro-Asiatic and Khoi-San. Within this simplified categorization, however, are several thousand individual ethnic groups often with their own distinctive languages, culture and social organization. Virtually all countries in Africa have significant ethnic diversity within their borders; some have several hundred ethno-linguistic groups.

A further fault line in Africa is between the largely Muslim north and the rest of Africa where Christianity and traditional African religions are the dominant cultural influence. *(See map opposite.)* Again, this division belies a much more complex situation in individual regions.

More than in any other continent, politicized ethnic conflicts are present throughout Africa. Ethnic conflict is fuelled by the harsh competition for resources and patronage in a region of the world which remains, for the most part, poorly governed, lacking technical and civic infrastructures, and marginalized from the world centres of economic and political power.

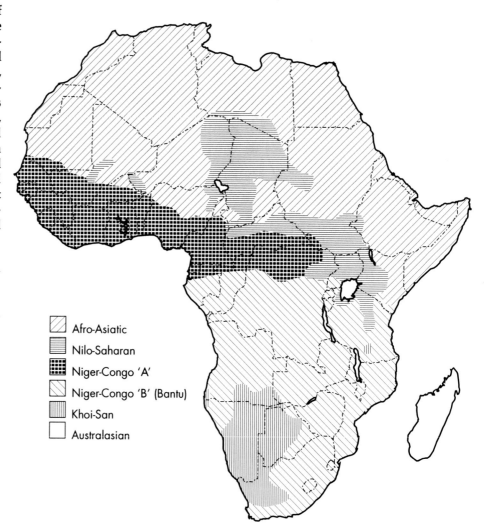

**Generalized ethno-linguistic map of Africa**

- Afro-Asiatic
- Nilo-Saharan
- Niger-Congo 'A'
- Niger-Congo 'B' (Bantu)
- Khoi-San
- Australasian

In much of Africa, competition for the control of state assets has been characterized by ethnic polarization at the expense of other issues, such as social class. This is a reflection in large part of the main criterion by which many Africans self-identify – i.e., by ethnicity rather than by occupation, socio-economic class or social status. In many African countries, the main ethno-cultural fault line is between traditional pastoralists and agriculturalists.

As the sudden explosion of violence in Kenya at the end of 2007 shows, latent political/ethnic tensions can easily erupt into violence even in countries regarded as relatively stable.

The physical barrier imposed by the Sahara desert and the lack of other overland routes to much of Africa have meant that for much of its history it has been convenient to divide the continent into 'North' Africa – with its strong historical links to the Mediterranean classical civilizations and to the Middle Eastern Muslim/Arab cultures – and 'Black' or Sub-Saharan Africa. Although the separation was never as stark as may be assumed, this continues to be a frequently useful division.

Africa is a continent of many contradictions, one being that, despite poor transport infrastructures, long-range migration by African populations is a common phenomenon. Seasonal migrations, cross-border travel in search of work, and refugee movements, all contribute to a local mixing of populations, potentially increasing tensions. Furthermore, the enforced migration of Africans through the Atlantic slave trade has resulted in a significant African diaspora in the Americas, especially in the Caribbean, where those of African descent form majority populations. In recent decades, African and Caribbean migration has resulted in African-descended populations becoming significant in many European countries as well.

In a relatively brief period towards the end of the 19th century and the

## Islam in Africa

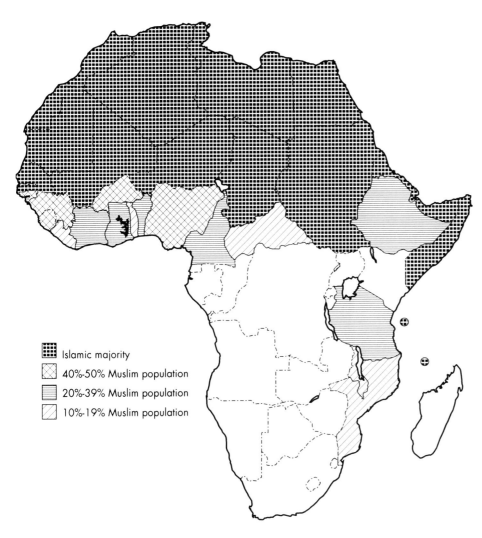

Islamic majority
40%-50% Muslim population
20%-39% Muslim population
10%-19% Muslim population

first decades of the 20th, virtually the whole of Africa was annexed by European powers during the 'Scramble for Africa', and divided in accordance with European notions of territorial ownership without, for the most part, regard to ethnic realities on the ground.

The role of colonialism in 'creating' tribalism, and by extension ethnic division, is subject to ongoing academic debate. Certainly, colonialists exploited and exacerbated existing ethnic differences by favouring certain groups and cultivating a 'divide and rule' policy. However, as with post-independence regimes, colonialists for the most part did not create communal tensions but rather harnessed them to political advantage. As in other parts of the world, 'real' ethnic tensions exist in Africa independently of the agendas of the political leadership.

Conventional European colonialism in Africa ended with the collapse of the Portuguese empire in 1975, leaving only three states, Rhodesia, Namibia and South Africa, under white rule. Although ethnic conflict in these countries was clearly, at one level, between black and white, both inter-black rivalries and the ability, albeit limited, of governments to co-opt non-white supporters, was also a feature of the political landscape.

In both Namibia and Zimbabwe (ex-Rhodesia) the black successor governments have had recognizably ethnic flavours – Ovambo in the case of Namibia and Shona in the case of Zimbabwe. In Zimbabwe, it has been left to the Shona dominated government to forcibly dismantle the civic structures inherited from Rhodesia. South Africa has thus far avoided this outcome, but its long term future may remain uncertain.

A key issue for Africa remains the fact that the colonial borders were rarely contiguous with ethnic divisions. As the colonial states became independent, their governments therefore faced an immediate challenge of nation building, not just in the economic sense but in the context of a lack, usually, of historical and social legitimacy for the state. In addition, the new states frequently found themselves with the challenge of accommodating the sometimes contradictory ambitions of the numerous groups within their borders. A radical solution would have been the wholesale re-drawing of borders or, even more radically, the merger of Africa into a single state as advocated by Pan-Africanists. Neither option was ever likely to be viable, and in 1964 the Organization of African Union closed the door on any significant re-adjustment by declaring the colonial border inviolable. This was presented as an attempt to dampen down the possibility of conflict either within or between states. The effective result was to give state governments *carte blanche* to clamp down ruthlessly on secessionist efforts within their borders, such as in Biafra/Nigeria in the late 1960s. No new African states emerged by partition (with the exception of the independent 'bantustans' created in South Africa) until the independence of Eritrea in 1993 – this being regarded as a special case since Eritrea had originally been a separate colony. Even this example set a limited, if so far internationally unrecognized, precedent in the form of the Somaliland independence declared in 1993, and forms the basis of nationalist claims in other territories, such as Southern Cameroons and Cabinda.

Those states which emerged as a result of protracted anti-colonial wars, such Angola, Mozambique, Algeria and Zimbabwe, tended to have 'liberation' movements that had forged, of necessity, a cohesive and disciplined ideology and structure. In the majority of cases, African independence (despite the subsequent rhetoric of its leaders) was attained by the peaceful consent, however unenthusiastically, of the metropolitan power. These states did not necessarily possess a mass nationalist movement nor a government with a firm ideology, beyond, in most cases, a vague adherence to socialism. For many post-independence governments, Marxism proved an inevitably attractive proposition. In addition to its ostensive rejection of colonialism and Western development models, Marxism offered a unifying non-racial ideology which could be used as the basis for nation building. Usefully (for elite groups at least) it also provided an ideological justification for the imposition of a single-party regime and the establishment of centralized state control over national economic and other assets. The convenient doctrine that a one-party state was necessary to avoid the social tensions arising from the emergence of ethnically predicated political parties was, for the most part, accepted uncritically by Western academics and donor organizations. Last and not least, the Soviet 'MiG diplomacy' of the 1950s and 1960s provided the necessary military hardware and expertise to keep restive local population groups in check. Even in states where the overt adoption of Marxism was limited, such as Milton Obote's Uganda, authoritarian, one party solutions tended to be the norm rather than the exception. In a number of countries, such as Rwanda and Burundi, these were overtly racially predicated.

The always implicit conflict between Marxist central planning and the familial, clan, or ethnically-based social and governance structures that command the loyalty of many Africans contributed directly to a number of conflicts. In Angola's long drawn out civil war, for example, part of the UNITA rebel movement's appeal came from its opposition to the *mestico* urban elites (UNITA had a largely Ovimbundu ethnic base) and from its support of 'Negritude' against the imported Marxist ideology of Angola's rulers. In Mozambique, efforts by the ruling FRELIMO party to crush 'primitive hut-habits' (and the traditional tribal authorities) contributed to the rise of the RENAMO resistance movement. Mozambique's first president, Samora Machel, expressed the issue in the starkest terms: "for the nation to live the tribe must die." FRELIMO sought to portray RENAMO as merely the creation of Rhodesian/South African imperialism, but was never able to explain the resistance movement's resilience, which stemmed directly from ideological and policy failings on the part of the government.

The collapse of the USSR in the 1990s resulted in the literal and ideological bankruptcy of the whole socialist experiment, at least so far as Africa was concerned. Since the collapse of Soviet Communism, donor aid to Africa – initially monopolized by Western governments and financial institutions – has supposedly been based on transparency, 'good governance' and other criteria. In practice this has meant the imposition of liberal/globalist economic models of dubious benefit to many Africans. In recent years the emerging role of China as an economic player in Africa has been the subject of much commentary, even leading to speculation surrounding a 'Chinese Scramble for Africa.' Although Chinese involvement may be seen as giving Africa an alternative economic model to the Western neo-liberal one, Beijing's less than scrupulous concerns over human rights and environmental rights, which may actually be an advantage in the eyes of some African elites, may emerge as a significant factor in future conflicts.

Africa's inherent weaknesses and its inability to propose, let alone implement, African solutions to African problems continues. The partial exception has been the re-emergence, post-*apartheid*, of South Africa as a diplomatic player on a continental basis. However, South Africa's willingness and ability to act as "Africa's policeman" is questionable. The only other sub-Saharan African state that could potentially fulfil that role is Nigeria, but given that country's own internal issues and unwholesome record for corruption, this is problematic. To date, therefore, distinctively African led solutions to regional or continental issues have met with only limited success.

The Cold War landscape of African conflict was characterized, however simplistically, as a power-play between US, Soviet (and occasionally Chinese) client groups. Post Cold War conflicts have been more overtly ethnic in composition and more complex, frequently involving conflict interlink between several states who may not even be geographical neighbours. The typical pattern is one of reciprocal funding, arming, and occasionally direct support, of ethnically-based rebel groups in opposing countries. Carried on over several borders, this process leads to a web of disputes of considerable complexity and geographical extent. The conflict in Chad for example, is linked in turn to that in Darfur, hence to South Sudan, Uganda, Rwanda, Congo and thus on to Namibia and Zimbabwe. *(See map opposite.)* Dispute resolution in such circumstances is extremely difficult.

One of the largest wars since the Second World War has been that in Congo (formerly Zaïre) which has involved multiple external participants as well as numerous internal factions and combatants. The genesis of this conflict is ethnic, surrounding the status of the Tutsi populations in eastern Congo and the Great Lakes region. The Congolese Tutsi, however, constitute well under 1% of the Congolese population. Perhaps no better example of the potency of ethnic conflict can be offered.

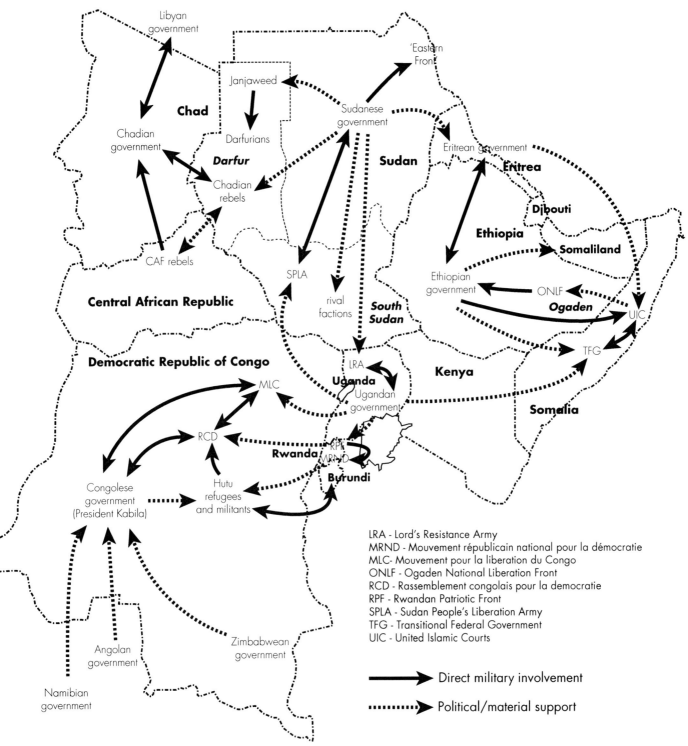

## Conflict interlinkage in Africa

This map demonstrates the complexity and extent of conflict interlinkage that has evolved in Africa, with separate conflicts in Chad, Sudan, the Central African Republic, the Horn of Africa and the Congo/Great Lakes region being ultimately connected through a chain of alliances between governments and rebel movements. The map does not depict the actual situation on any one date: not all these links are or were active simultaneously. The linkages in Congo broadly reflect the period during the second Congo War that arose when Congolese President Laurent Kaliba sought to expel his original Uganda and Rwandan patrons. (See 2.24.) Note also that Uganda and Rwanda, previously allies, fell out over the division of spoils in Congo, and this is reflected in the fighting between the MLC and RCD. Following their defeat at the hands of the RPF, the MRND (the previous government of Rwanda) regrouped among the Hutu population (both resident and refugee) in eastern Congo.

(See 2.44 for map of conflict interlinks in West Africa.)

# Algeria

**Principal protagonists**

Government of Algeria.

Al Qaeda in the Islamic Maghreb.

Kabyle (Berbers).

**Nature of conflict**

a) Islamist insurrection. b) Kabyle language and cultural/political autonomy issue. c) Civil war between government and Islamist insurgents, 1991-2002.

☪ Islamist versus moderate Muslim/secular government and civil society.
☠ 160,000 during 1990s civil war.

**Population/ethnic composition**

Algeria: 33m; Kabylie: 4m. Algeria ethnic composition: Algerian Arab 59.1%, Berber 23.2%, Arabized Berber 3%, Bedouin Arab 14.5%.

**Territorial extent**

Algeria: 2,400,000 km².

**Timeline**

5 Jul 1962: Algeria achieves independence from France.
10 Mar 1980: Start of 'Berber Spring'.
28 Dec 1991: Victory by the Islamist FIS in the first round of general election.
11 Jan 1992: The Algerian military stages a coup and cancels the elections, triggering civil war with Islamist forces.
1994-5: 'Satchel Strike' in Kabylie.
Jun 1998: Further protests in Kabylie, over compulsory use of Arabic for all official purposes.
2001: 'Black Spring' (severe rioting) in Kabylie.
2002: Islamist uprising defeated.
12 Dec 2007: Al Qaeda bombing kills over 60 people.

**Current status**

Sporadic Al Qaeda attacks. Political pressure for greater autonomy in Kabylie continues.

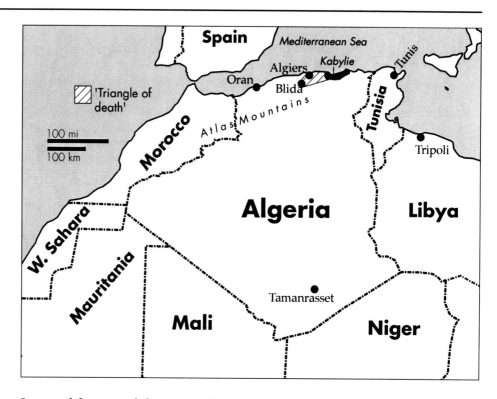

**In one of the most violent struggles of the decolonization era, Algeria threw off French rule in the war between 1954-1962 – a conflict which in many respects resembled a civil war not only in Algeria but, indeed, in metropolitan France itself. After independence, the victorious *Front de Libération Nationale* (FLN) maintained an increasingly authoritarian one-party rule until the early 1990s.**

Algeria's rulers faced calls for multi-party democracy from 1987 onwards and in 1988 there were widespread violent riots, against a background of economic stagnation, in which Islamist elements played a part. In the aftermath of the fall of the Soviet empire, Algiers came under enhanced pressure both from Islamists and from supporters of greater Berber linguistic and political autonomy. Corruption and general exhaustion amongst the 'old guard' who had run Algeria since independence were also factors in calls for reform. In 1989 the government conceded, allowing the legal formation of opposition parties and announcing elections for the end of 1991.

Algeria's initial attempt at introducing multi-party democracy proved to be a fiasco. The first round of the two stage electoral process, which took place in December 1991, appeared to show an appreciable majority for the Islamist *Front Islamique de Salut* (FIS) party, which, if carried through to the second stage, would have been sufficient to enable the FIS to modify Algeria's constitution. Although it had itself benefited from democratization, the FIS made no secret of its contempt for the democratic process, maintaining that the only basis for governance was the Koran. (The dilemma posed by the possibility of fundamentalist Islamic groups gaining power democratically has since been repeated elsewhere, most significantly in Palestine.)

Fearing that an FIS victory would lead to the establishment of an Islamic theocratic state, the Algerian military staged a coup on 11 January 1992 (with tacit approval from France and other Western powers), cancelling the electoral process. The FIS was banned and thousands of its supporters interned.

Islamist groups then quickly emerged to take up arms against the Algerian authorities. The FIS, forced largely underground, did not directly establish an armed wing, but an even more extreme group, the *Groupe Islamique Armé* (GIA), soon emerged and was to carry out most of the insurgency in what became a devastating civil war. In addition to targeting military and institutional targets, the GIA also attacked civilians. Women, and even schoolgirls, who deviated from the GIA's interpretation of Islamic propriety, were a particular target and a number of especially gruesome massacres of women and girls took place. In 1997, for example, in the notorious Rais and Bentalha massacres, pregnant women were sliced open, children beaten to death and girls kidnapped and raped. The GIA justified the killings as "an offering to Allah". Teachers, foreigners, journalists, popular singers and civil servants were also targeted by the GIA.

Although there was a steady stream of defections between the two organizations, the GIA disclaimed any connection with the FIS and declared war on the FIS after the latter opened negotiations with the government in 1994. On 26 August 1994 the GIA declared an 'Islamic Caliphate' for Algeria, although its territorial activity remained primarily limited to the 'triangle of death' south of Algiers where most of the GIA instigated massacres took place. Assassinations of FIS members by the GIA and fighting between the two became an additional feature of the conflict. The GIA was also, allegedly, heavily infiltrated by the security forces, and the extent to which some GIA activities, particularly the killing of FIS leaders, were at the instigation of the security forces remains a contentious issue.

GIA violence against civilians peaked around the time of the 1997 general election, which was won by the pro-army *Rassemblement National Democratique*. The pro-FIS *Armée islamique du salut* (AIS) opted for a unilateral ceasefire in the aftermath of the election, and an amnesty to guerrillas who 'repented' (the official term) was offered in 1999. The AIS officially disbanded in January 2000. The amnesty process neutralized the more moderate elements within the GIA, which itself split into several bitterly contested factions. The GIA, under pressure from the security forces, local militias, and from its own factionalism, had effectively been defeated by 2002, bringing an end to the war, although individual outbreaks of violence continued.

In 1998 the *Groupe Salafiste pour la Prédiction et la Combat* (GSPC) emerged as a split from the GIA. In 2003 the GSPC publicly aligned itself to Al Qaeda and in November 2006 merged with other Islamist organizations in Tunisia, Libya and Morocco to form 'Al Qaeda in the Islamic Maghreb'.

In March 2006 some 2,000 Islamic terrorists were released under a further amnesty programme; this was interpreted by most commentators as an indication of the confidence of the authorities that Islamist extremism was now under control. This optimism appears to have been premature, however, as in December 2007 Al Qaeda in the Islamic Maghreb launched a major attack against a United Nations target in Algers, killing 60, and raising fears of a general return to Islamist insurgency. Clashes in March 2008 in the east of the country left up to 20 soliders and 25 Al Qaeda fighters dead.

The other source of discord in post-independence Algeria, albeit one that has not thus far developed into sustained violence, is the conflict between Berber speakers over the suppression of their language and cultural rights. 'Berber' is a generic term for the heterogeneous ethnic groups who have inhabited much of north-west Africa for at least 12,000 years. Although the majority of the Algerian population are ultimately of Berber descent, most have become 'Arabized' and no longer speak Berber languages. Exceptions exist among the Berber population in the sparsely populated south of the country and among the four million inhabitants of Kabylie. Berbers, who in total number some 6.8 million of Algeria's population, also exist in neighbouring countries. Kabylie (also known as Kabylia) is not a political entity as such. It is situated in the Atlas Mountains in the extreme north of Algeria, along the Mediterranean coast and covers, wholly or in part, a number of the *wilayas* (administrative districts) of Algeria. 'Kabyle' is the Berber language spoken by the inhabitants, its use (or rather non-use) in official contexts being the main cause of conflict with the central authorities.

The Berbers contributed a disproportionately high percentage of the leadership, and the fighters, to the war against the French from 1954-62. As a consequence, the Berbers looked for recognition of their language and other rights. These hopes were dashed in the post independence period, President Ben Bella famously announcing in 1962 that "we are all Arabs now." Berbers have continued to protest against the exclusive use of Arabic in official and educational circles. Organized activism dates from 1963, when the *Front des Forces Socialistes* (FFS) was formed. (It remained illegal until 1989.)

1980 saw the arrest of Berber poet and activist Mouloud Mammeri and in the following months of the so-called 'Berber Spring' thousands of demonstrators marched, and were imprisoned, while a new movement, the *Mouvement pour la Culture Berbére* (MCB) came into being. The MCB worked for the development of a written version of the Berber language, transcribed in the Latin alphabet. The Algerian government refused to consider Berber demands, President Chadli echoing Bella by asserting that Algerians were "all Berbers Arabized by Islam." Further protests took place with the 'satchel strike' of 1994-5 when Berber pupils refused to attend school in protest at the exclusive use of Arabic in education. This protest was partially successful, in that proposals for teaching in Berber languages was accepted, however practical implementation was limited. More violence erupted in 1998 and 2001.

The new 1996 constitution rejected the core Berber demand that their language be acknowledged as an official language, alongside Arabic. Although since 2001 a somewhat more conciliatory rhetoric has been adopted by Algiers, the issue remains highly emotive.

# Casamance

**Principal protagonists**

Government of Senegal.

Casamance (Diola) people; *Mouvement des forces démocratiques de la Casamance* (MDFC).

**Nature of conflict**

Local autonomy/independence conflict, further fuelled by factional disputes in Guinea-Bissau. Widespread fighting between Senegalese/Bissauan forces and MDFC factions.

☠ 3,500+.
👥 17,000 IDP (2005); over 15,000, Gambia, August 2006

**Population/ethnic composition**

220,000. Majority from Diola people, who form 3.7% of Senegalese population.

**Territorial extent**

Casamance region of Senegal: c65,000 km².

**Timeline**

1880s: Senegal becomes part of French colonial empire. Unrest in Casamance continues until 1943.
20 Aug 1960: Senegal achieves independence from France.
1982: Arrest of local leaders sparks unrest in Casamance.
1990s: Conflict escalates with MDFC attacks on Senegalese military installations. Several ceasefires agreed but all fail.
1998-9: Senegal becomes embroiled in civil war in Guinea-Bissau.
Mar 2001: Peace agreement fails to halt fighting, but exacerbates tensions between political and military wings of MDFC.
30 Dec 2004: Ceasefire agreed.
Mar 2006: Fighting resumes between Southern Front faction of MDFC and Guinea-Bissau/Senegalese forces.

**Current status**

Unstable. Repeated failures of ceasefires and factionalism within the MDFC continue to bedevil chances for lasting settlement.

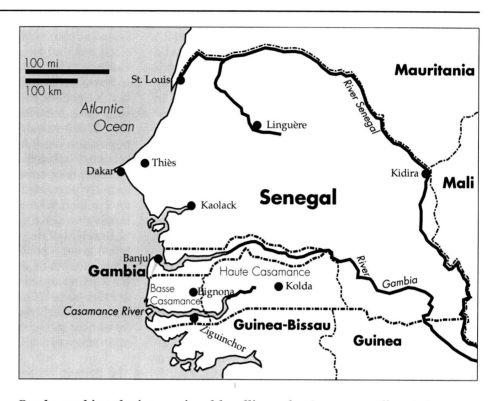

Rarely reaching the international headlines, the Casamance dispute is nevertheless one of the longest-running in Africa. It has resulted in over 3,500 civilian deaths and significant international regional tensions from 1982 to the present. Up to 4,500 Senegalese regular forces have at times been tied down in the conflict. It is a classic case of a post-colonial conflict involving a disadvantaged and geographically remote ethnic minority whose population straddles international (i.e., colonial era) borders.

Casamance is a fertile region of southern Senegal lying between Gambia (which effectively splits it off from the rest of Senegal) and Guinea-Bissau. The main ethnic group, the Diola (Jola), comprise only a small minority of the Senegalese population as a whole. Diola populations also live in Gambia and Guinea-Bissau.

The region is named for the Casamance River, which like Gambia to the north, divides the eponymous territory north-south. Formally, Casamance comprises two regions, Basse Casamance in the west and the larger Haute Casamance to the east. Senegalese regions are officially named after their capitals; Basse Casamance and Haute Casamance being, respectively, Ziguinchor and Kolda. Ziguinchor, with its population of 130,000, is the largest settlement, and as such is considered the capital of Casamance as a whole. It rose to prominence as a slaving centre during the 16th century and retains a Portuguese linguistic influence. (The name of the town is purportedly a corruption of the Portuguese *'cheguei e choram'* – 'I came and they cry' – an allusion to the slave trade.)

The Diola, an independently-minded people, have a long history of resistance to central authority. During the French colonial period, French administrators generally governed Senegal through local chiefs. The Diola, however, did not have such a formal hierarchical system of government, and attempts by the French to impose Mandinka chiefs to administer Casamance proved massively unpopular and counter-productive. Civil unrest flared repeatedly throughout the region. In 1943 a full scale uprising, led by a traditional priestess, Aline Sitoe Diatta, was suppressed. The imprisonment and subsequent death of Sitoe in a Timbuktu gaol created a national myth that "Casamance's Joan of Arc" would one day return to lead her people.

The current conflict dates from 1982, when a pro-independence demonstration in Ziguinchor by the *Mouvement des forces démocratiques de la Casamance* (MFDC) was violently suppressed and its leaders imprisoned. Sporadic tit-for-tat violence continued throughout the 1980s, and in 1990 the MFDC escalated the conflict with attacks on Senegalese military bases. The Senegalese Army responded with counter-attacks on MFDC camps in southern Casamance and Guinea-Bissau as well as with generally stricter civil security measures.

Throughout the Casamance conflict, Dakar has periodically accused Guinea-Bissau of giving formal support to the rebels. Despite Bissauan denials, there is no doubt that MFDC bases were frequently (according to Dakar, exclusively) located among their fellow Diola in Guinea-Bissau from where they could mount hit-and-run attacks on Senegalese targets. MFDC fighters were also involved (against a Senegalese supported faction) in Guinea-Bissau's civil war of 1998-9. Guinea-Bissauan soldiers displaced by their country's civil war have, in turn, fought alongside the MFDC in Casamance. Gambia has also, on occasion, become embroiled in the dispute, both as potential mediator and, allegedly, as harbourer of MFDC rebels. Both Guinea-Bissau and Gambia have received civilian refugees during the course of the conflict.

Intermittent attempts at peacemaking, including several ceasefires signed during the 1990s, failed to resolve the conflict. In March 2000, however, Abdoulaye Wade succeeded Abdou Diouf as President of Senegal, in part on a platform of ending the fighting, and concerted efforts were made to bring an end to the dispute. Wade's initial efforts – against a background of increased violence in Casamance and tangled factionalism in Guinea-Bissau – focused on Bissauan involvement in Casamance. These efforts were fuelled by the discovery of a dead Bissauan soldier and Bissauan equipment following a substantial cross-border MDFC attack in April 2000, but were, however, largely unsuccessful in moving the peace process forward.

Faced with the failure of his initiative, Wade opened direct negotiations with the MDFC and its veteran leader, the Catholic priest Father Augustin Diamacoune Senghor. (Unlike the rest of Senegal, which is predominantly Muslim, Casamance has a strong Catholic influence.) The two leaders signed a peace agreement in March 2001, which, while it allowed for humanitarian relief, minefield clearance and mutual prisoner exchanges, did not commit Dakar to autonomy for Casamance. This 'betrayal' heightened tensions between the military and political wings of the MDFC, and low intensity fighting (including between MDFC factions) continued.

Wade and Senghor signed a further peace agreement, with considerable ceremony, in Ziguinchor in December 2004, but further talks became stalled as it became apparent that the more moderate Zignuinchor-based MDFC leaders were unable to reign in the militants. In March 2006, however, with an anti-MDFC government once again in power in Bissau, the Guinea-Bissauan army attempted to eliminate the Southern Front (the more militant wing of the MDFC) who were based in northern Guinea-Bissau. After fierce fighting, the Southern Front fought their way into Casamance itself, re-igniting conflict throughout the region and driving thousands of refugees into Gambia. Further fierce fighting took place in September and October 2006.

Talks later resumed between Dakar and the MDFC, but in December 2007 the government's main envoy was assassinated by an unknown assailant. In view of the factionalism within the MDFC and the repeated failure of ceasefires to hold, the prospects for lasting peace in the region remain low.

# Chad

**Principal protagonists**

Zaghawa dominated government of Chad. French forces actively engaged.

Rebel groups, including those based in Darfur with Sudanese support.

**Nature of conflict**

Ethnic conflict over control of government patronage exacerbated by regional conflicts. Previous history of regional insurgency.

- Muslim/Christian disputes a factor in earlier conflicts.
- No accurate figure for casualties; death toll continuing to increase.
- 60,000 Chadian IDPs. 220,000 refugees from conflict in Darfur.
- Significant oil reserves in south of country.

**Population/ethnic composition**

9.7m. Sara 27.7%, Arab 12.3%, Mayo-Kebbi 11.5%. Politically dominant Zaghawa form only 2% of population. Religious mix: Muslim 55%, Christian 35%.

**Territorial extent**

Current conflict largely in eastern regions of Chad. Overlap with conflicts in Darfur (Sudan) and northern Central African Republic.
Total Chad area: 1,284,000 km².

**Timeline**

11 Aug 1960: Chad achieves independence from France.
1966: Full-scale civil war against northern (Muslim) factions.
23 Mar 1979: Northern-led government takes power.
Jan 2004 onwards: Thousands of refugees arrive fleeing fighting in Darfur.
Apr 2004: Conflict commences between Chadian army and Darfur-based rebels.
Jan-Jun 2006: Widespread incursions by Sudanese-backed rebels.
Oct-Nov 2006: Fighting renewed with onset of dry season. State of emergency declared November 2006.

**Current status**

Unresolved. Widespread conflict continues; significant danger of wholesale state collapse.

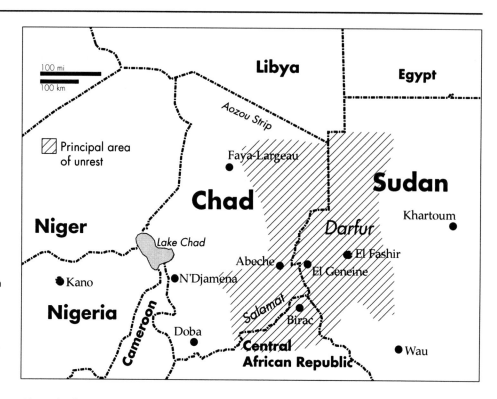

**Since independence from France in 1960, Chad has been characterized by extremely weak central government and widespread ethnic unrest. Both internal and cross-border insurgencies have been a regular feature of Chad's modern history. Neighbouring states – most recently Sudan – have also used Chad's internal factionalism to promote dissent. What little central authority exists has been bolstered by the permanent presence of French forces, which have been repeatedly obliged to intervene to prevent the collapse of the Chadian state.**

Chad presents a classic picture of a state in which access to government, and thereby to patronage, is concentrated in an extremely tight ethnic/familial group. At the broadest level, Chad is split between Muslim and Christian communities, which roughly reflect a north-south geographical divide within the country. Governmental power is currently held by Idriss Déby, of the Zaghawa people, a largely Muslim group that comprises barely 2% of the total population. Zaghawa currently dominate all significant government and military positions of authority at all levels. Even within this very narrow ethnic base, however, Déby rules through a small clan/family clique, and this has resulted in opposition from excluded Zaghawa elements. These even include some from Déby's own extended family, who feel they have lost out in the allocation of the exploitation of Chad's Doba oilfield in the south of the country. Perhaps unsurprisingly, Chad comes bottom of the Corruption Perceptions Index produced by the monitoring organization Transparency International.

The Zaghawa are not in fact themselves a unified people, but rather a collection of clans and septs scattered across northern and eastern Chad and also – crucially in the current conflict – over the Sudanese border in Darfur province. Outside the ruling faction, other ethno-religious groups are progressively removed from the possibilities of power and patronage. With little other recourse, the response from excluded groups has generally been to attempt to seize power militarily. In a very centralized and sparsely populated country this, to all practical purposes, has necessitated taking the capital N'Djamena, and a repeated characteristic of Chadian politics has been rebel groups attempting motorized dashes to the capital, before, usually, being stopped and destroyed by French ground and air attacks.

Chad's first post-independence President, Francois Tombalbaye, was from the southern Christian community. His policies led to unrest in the largely Muslim north, which by 1966 had developed into full-scale civil war. France intervened in support of Tombalbaye, who was nevetheless deposed and killed in a coup by a southern rival, Felix Malloum, in 1975. In 1977, Libya annexed the disputed Aozou strip in the north of the country and in 1979 Malloum was deposed in favour of a largely Muslim northern coalition under Goukouni Oueddei. Fighting in the north continued, however, and despite Libyan support for Oueddei he was in turn deposed by Hissène Habré in 1982. In fierce clashes in 1987, Chadian and French forces drove Libyan troops from much of the disputed northern territories, but not from the Aozou strip itself, which remained occupied by Libya until international arbitration in 1994 awarded the territory to Chad. Habré lasted until 1990 when he was defeated by Idriss Déby, who at that time had support from both Libya and Sudan, and from Zaghawa on both sides of the Sudanese border. Déby has remained in power ever since, with his office being confirmed by general elections in 1995, 2001 and 2006.

In May 2004, Zaghawa opponents of Déby organized a coup against him. The attempt failed, and the rebels established bases in Darfur against the backdrop of worsening unrest and accelerating humanitarian catastrophe in that region. *(See 2.12.)* Khartoum, with an eye on achieving control over Chad's oil resources, supported the rebels while simultaneously engaging in a campaign of ethnic cleansing of non-Arabic groups in the region, including the Zaghawa. The chief Chadian rebel groups in Darfur each had an ethnic base. The largely Zaghawa *Rassemblement des forces démocratiques* (RAFD) was led by two nephews of Déby, Tom and Timan Erdimi, who were originally aligned with Déby but subsequently fell out of favour. The *Rassemblement pour la démocratie et les libertés* (RDL) was similarly led by a former Déby ally, Nour Abdelkerim. Unlike the RAFD, however, the RDL drew its support largely from the Tama ethnic group. Nour split with Déby in 1994 when it became obvious that power was being allocated solely to the Zaghawa. In 2005 he formed the RDL with Sudanese assistance. In December 2005, Nour formed a coalition group called the *Front uni pour la changement* (FUC) which included the RDL but not the RAFD. FUC staged an unsuccessful attack on Chad in April 2006, operating from bases both in Darfur and the Central African Republic.

Closely aligned to Khartoum, Nour's forces were accused of assisting the Sudanese-backed *Janjaweed* militia in the ethnic cleansing of Zaghawa in Darfur. In return for this support, *Janjaweed* forces were involved in the cross border insurgency, attacking Zaghawa villages in eastern Chad. In 2007, Nour defected back to the Déby camp but a FUC-successor organizaion, the *Union des forces pour la démocratie et le développement* (UFDD) continues to be active, as does another faction, the *Rassemblement des forces pour le changement* (RFC).

On 3 May 2006, presidential elections were held, which saw Déby re-elected for a third term against a factionally and ethnically divided opposition. The election 'campaign' was marked by a full-scale invasion attempt by rebels from bases in Darfur; these were repelled by the French. Over 50,000 people were forced to flee their homes during the fighting. October 2006, and the start of the dry season, saw the resumption of widespread hostilities. Rebels briefly occupied a number of towns. Some of the attackers were described as being Arabs on horseback – a general identifier for the pro-Khartoum *Janjaweed* militia in Darfur. The main victims were black Dadjo-speaking Chadians. Fighting continued throughout the rest of 2006, including clashes between Arabic Darsalim people and the non-Arab Kibele in the Salamat prefecture, which borders both Darfur and the Central African Republic, particularly around the regional capital, Am Timan. These two groups have a long-standing history of violent conflict over land and grazing rights. In December 2006 hundreds were reported killed in the region of Abeche between government troops and the UFDD and in April 2007 the first direct fighting between regular Chadian and Sudanese forces was reported. Fierce fighting resumed in November 2007 after the failure of a brief ceasefire, with the conflict reaching N'Djamena itself in February 2008 before the rebels were repelled. A March 2008 peace agreement between Chad and Sudan collapsed after the Sudanese accused Chad of facilitating rebel attacks on Khartoum, and in June Chadian rebels were once more reported as advancing.

Chadian rebels also operate in the lawless northern regions of the Central African Republic. *(See 2.15.)* The Central African rebels are in alliance with Sudan on the basis that if they back pro-Sudanese rebels in Chad they will receive Khartoum's backing in their own struggle. Secessionist factions in the politically marginalized south of Chad are an additional potent factor.

The French maintain over 1,000 troops in Chad, plus air support, which includes a squadron of fighter jets. The French presence was increased in 1986, when the main territorial threat to Chad arose from the conflict over the Aozou strip. Both France and the US have oil interests in Chad, as well as a broader interest in preventing Chad from becoming a failed state. A potentially significant rivalry exists between Western interests in Chad and the rising Chinese presence in Africa. Beijing is a close ally of Khartoum, with China being the main export destination for Sudanese oil. For many years, Chad maintained diplomatic relations with the Republic of China (Taiwan), only recognizing the Peoples' Republic in 2007.

Exacerbated (although not caused) by the unrest in Sudan and the Central African Republic, Chad's military and political position is perilous. There is little doubt that without the continued direct intervention of French forces the government in N'Djamena (whether headed by the ailing Déby or a successor) would simply collapse. This would lead to the likely emergence of 'warlordism' on the Somali model, with little or no central authority and the probability of regional players, such as Sudan, taking full advantage of the chaos.

# Darfur

**Principal protagonists**

Government of Sudan; *Janjaweed* and other state-sponsored militias.

Sudanese Liberation Movement/Army (SLM); Justice and Equality Movement (JEM); various other groups and factions. United Resistance Front umbrella group.

Chadian government forces and rebel factions also engaged. *(See 2.10.)*

**Nature of conflict**

Racial conflict primarily between 'Arab' and 'African' ethnic groups. Water and land access rights are important issues.

† Systematic human rights abuses including bombing of civilian targets and massacres by state-sponsored *Janjaweed* militias.
☠ 400,000
👥 2 million IDP, further 200,000 in Chad.

**Population/ethnic composition**

Darfur: 7.4m (pre war). Over 30 ethnic groups including 'Arab' Abbala Kizeigat and Baggara, and 'African' Fur, Zaghawa and Massaleit.

**Territorial extent**

Darfur: 493,180 km².

**Timeline**

1916: Darfur occupied by British; incorporated into Sudan.
1 Jan 1956: Sudan independent.
23 Feb 2003: Rebel attacks trigger current conflict.
6 Jul 2004: AU troop deployment begins.
5 May 2006: Darfur Peace Agreement between Khartoum and SLM fails to halt fighting.
31 Aug 2006: UN approves peacekeeping force. Deployment prevented by Khartoum.
1 Jan 2008: Joint AU/UN force deployed.

**Current status**

Unresolved. Massive humanitarian emergency continues.

*See 2.14 for map of Darfur and for commentary on South Sudan.*

**Described by the United Nations in 2006 as the "world's worst humanitarian disaster" Darfur – 'home of the Fur' – is a huge sparsely inhabited region in western Sudan. One of the last territories to come under European rule during the partition of Africa, Darfur remained an independent Sultanate until 1916, when, fearing expanding Turkish influence during the First World War, it was occupied by the British. Resistance to central rule has been a consistent feature of Darfurian history, and continued after Sudan achieved independence in 1956, with a low-intensity war continuing until the early 1970s. The modern history of Darfur has in general been one of political and economic marginalization.**

Unlike the war between north and south Sudan, which is at one level a religious conflict between Muslims and Christian/Animist populations, the fighting in Darfur is essentially along racial and cultural lines, with the 'Arab' population of camel-herding Abbala Rizeigat and Baggara pastoralists pitted against the 'African' Fur, Zaghara, and other peoples who are largely settled agriculturalists. Both groups are Muslim, although not necessarily of the Salafist variety favoured by Khartoum. Land rights issues, including access to valuable grazing and watering rights, are a powerful contributor to the violence.

The current conflict in Darfur escalated from 2003 onwards, ironically at a time when the war between south and north Sudan showed signs of resolution under the Inter-Governmental Authority on Development (IGAD) peace talks. *(See 2.14.)* Darfurian dissident groups were both encouraged by the south's ability to negotiate a favourable peace deal with Khartoum, and at the same time aggrieved by their exclusion from the talks and from the broader picture of ensuring nationwide security and equality throughout Sudan.

The principal insurgent groups in Darfur are the Sudanese Liberation Movement/Army (SLM) and the Justice and Equality Movement (JEM). In February 2003, the SLM and JEM launched a joint attack against government targets, thereby igniting the current war.

Initially, the rebel attacks were highly successful and included an assault on a regular army and air force installation in the provincial capital, al-Fashir, which resulted in the destruction of a number of Sudanese air force bombers and helicopters. Rebel forces also started in infiltrate further east, into Kordofan.

Faced with the failure of conventional forces to stem the uprising, the Khartoum government transferred responsibility for the prosecution of the war to Sudanese Military Intelligence, backed up by air power. From this stage of the conflict onwards, the war was increasingly characterized by the indiscriminate use of bombing against civilian targets and violent assaults by 'Arab' *Janjaweed* ('devils on horseback') militias, who are generally understood to be operating with the connivance and support of Khartoum against 'African' settlements. The *Janjaweed* attacks were accompanied by the systematic rape of women, destruction of property, enslavement, and the organized denial of food, medical and other relief supplies so as to promote deaths by 'natural' causes. (The region was experiencing the worst drought for a generation.) On 9 September 2004, US Secretary of State Colin Powell described the Darfur conflict as a 'genocide', acknowledging both its scope and its racial underpinnings.

Elements of the *Janjaweed* are of Chadian origin, and the Darfur conflict has increasingly interlocked with that in Chad. *(See 2.10.)* Both Darfur and eastern Chad have similar ethnic makeups – Chad's President Idriss Déby is himself as Zaghawa, as is most of his ruling clique – and both sides have accused the other of aiding rebel groups. In December 2005 Chad declared that a state of war existed between Chad and Sudan, and Chadian regular forces were engaged against Khartoum-backed rebels on both sides of the Chad/Darfur border. Sudan similarly accused Chad of providing support for an audacious JEM attack on Khartoum in May 2008.

Throughout the conflict, the Khartoum regime has consistently restricted access to international humanitarian and peacekeeping forces in the Darfur region. In July 2004, however, an African Union force, initially of only a few hundred but eventually numbering 7,000 troops, was deployed in the region. The authority of the AU force was flagrantly flouted by Khartoum and its allies, and the AU force itself came under direct attack, as well as having aviation fuel confiscated by the Sudanese Air Force for use in counter-insurgency operations. Although overall its record has been one of, at best, only limited success, the AU force claims some positive results in reducing attacks against civilians.

In May 2006, the Khartoum government signed the Darfur Peace Deal with elements of the SLM and other movements, in Ajuba. If anything, fighting increased after this 'agreement', however, and in August 2006, the United Nations approved the intervention of a 17,000-strong UN peacekeeping force to supersede the AU force. Khartoum refused to allow its deployment. Instead, in September, 10,000 Sudanese troops started moving into Darfur with the ostensive intention of suppressing those dissidents who had not signed the Darfur Peace Agreement. Faced with the Sudanese refusal to allow the UN peacekeeping mission, the AU agreed to continue to maintain its presence in the country. UN forces finally started arriving in January 2008.

Aid organizations report ongoing lawlessness and problems in operating in the region. Increasing fragmentation among the rebel movements has also hindered local security. Meanwhile, several hundred thousand people remain in refugee camps in Sudan, Chad, and the Central African Republic under generally appalling conditions. Underlying the racial elements to the fighting is the conflict to be found in many societies between settled agriculturalists and nomadic or semi-nomadic peoples over scarce land and water resources. The discovery, in July 2007, of a massive underground lake in northern Darfur opens up the possibility of alleviating the region's chronic water shortages. However, the danger is that Khartoum will limit availability of the new assets to its client ethnic groups, thereby heightening, rather than reducing, ethnic conflict in the region.

**The Eastern Front**

In addition to the better-known conflicts in Darfur and South Sudan, Khartoum has also been confronted with an ethnic insurgency from the Beja of the east of the country.

The Beja – the 'Fuzzy-Wuzzies' immortalized as courageous and honorable opponents by Kipling – number around 2.2 million. The Beja are subdivided into clans, speak several different languages, and practise a form of Islam heavily influenced by the appeasement of *jinn*, or spirits. Many of the Beja continue their historical nomadic lifestyle.

As in Darfur and South Sudan, the Beja complain of being marginalized by the central government in Khartoum, while simultaneously being highly suspicious of outside influence and interference. The Beja Congress was formed in the 1960s and took up arms in the 1990s. In 1989 the Beja Congress joined with 12 other parties in forming the National Democratic Alliance to oppose the post-coup Islamist regime in Khartoum. In 2000, Beja fighters claimed to have attacked oil industry assets on the Red Sea coast, although little damage appears to have been inflicted. Sporadic attacks continued throughout the early 2000s. Khartoum has accused the Eritrean government of supporting the insurgents, who have an office in the Eritrean capital, Asmara.

When the Khartoum government entered into comprehensive talks with the Sudan People's Liberation Movement, with the focus being primarily on the future of South Sudan, activists both in Darfur and the 'Eastern Front' felt themselves excluded and marginalized by the process. In January 2004 the Darfur-based Sudanese Liberation Movement and the Beja Congress announced an alliance aimed at promoting their shared objective of a federal constitution for Sudan. On 14 Oct 2006 a peace agreement was signed between Khartoum and the Beja Congress aimed at bringing a reduction in violence, but the situation in Sudan's east remains highly volatile.

# South Sudan

**Principal protagonists**

Government of Sudan.

Sudan People's Liberation Movement/Army; various other groups and factions.

**Nature of conflict**

Racial, religious, and self-determination conflict.

- Systematic human rights abuses including massacres by state-sponsored militias.
- Muslim/Christian and Animist.
- 1.9m.
- Up to 4m refugees.
- Very significant reserves of oil.

**Population/ethnic composition**

Sudan: 41.2m. Sudanese Arab 49.1%, Dinka 11.5%, Nuba 8.1%, Beja 6.4%, Nuer 4.9%, Zande 2.7%, Bari 2.5%, Fur 2.1%. Religious mix: Sunni Muslim 70.3%, Christian 16.7%, traditional beliefs 11.9%.
South Sudan: 11m. Dinka c40%; numerous other groups. Most of the population are Animists or Christians of the Episcopal Church of Sudan or Roman Catholic.

**Territorial extent**

Sudan total: 2.5m km².
South Sudan: 589,745 km².

**Timeline**

1 Jan 1956: Sudan gains independence.
1955-72; 1983 onwards: Civil war between north and south.
May 1983: Sudan People's Liberation Army formed.
30 June 1989: National Islamic Front seizes power with military help.
9 Jan 2005: Naivasha Agreement signed.

**Current status**

Unstable. Clashes continue.

**The long-running war between north and south Sudan is usually characterized as a racial and religious conflict between the southern, non-Arab Christian and negro populations and the northern, Arab-dominated Islamist government in Khartoum. In recent years the south's rich oil reserves have added a potent economic rationale to the fighting.**

Under the British, the northern and southern provinces of Sudan were originally administered separately. The south was held to be similar to Britain's east African colonies such as Kenya and Uganda, while northern Sudan was held to be more akin to Arabic states such as Egypt. Trade and movement between the two regions was limited. In 1946, however, the British amalgamated the two areas and Arabic was made the language of administration throughout the country. Southern administrators, trained in English, bitterly resented these changes. After decolonization, power was seen to be increasingly concentrated among the northern elites based in Khartoum, causing unrest in the south.

In 1955, southern resentment at northern domination culminated in a mutiny among troops in the southern Equatoria Province. The uprising centred on demands that a federal structure – which had purportedly been agreed to with the British as a pre-condition for decolonization – be introduced. Fighting continued until the signing of the Addis Ababa Accords, under which the south achieved a degree of autonomy, in 1972. However, in 1983, the Khartoum government, which had been steadily introducing *sharia* Islamic law in the areas under its direct control, formally abrogated the Addis Ababa agreements following the declaration of a state of emergency.

The Sudan People's Liberation Army was formed in 1983 in opposition to the Islamization of the country. (A political wing, the Sudan People's Liberation Movement, was developed later.) Although the SPLA nominally sought a change in the character of the national government in Khartoum, it soon became the vehicle for southern secessionists. Fighting rapidly escalated, and what became known as the second Sudanese Civil War developed into one of the bloodiest conflicts since 1945, with around 1.9 million fatalities and, at peak, 4 million internally displaced persons and refugees.

In 1986 the Sudanese government of Sadiq al-Madhi opened negotiations with the SPLA and agreed the framework for a constitutional settlement in 1988. Before this could be implemented, however, the al-Madhi government was overthrown in a military-led coup and replaced by a hard-line Islamist regime dominated by the National Islamic Front (NIF). Fighting resumed, and in 1991 the government further extended the application of Islamic law, as well as replacing all non-Muslim judges in the south with Muslim appointees. Widespread atrocities, including slave taking and the bombing of civilian targets, began to be reported. The SPLA faced its own internal challenges, with breakaway factions clashing with the main SPLA forces.

Sporadic attempts at securing a negotiated end to the hostilities started as early as 1993, when regional governments promoted the Intergovernmental Authority on Development (IGAD). Although the Khartoum government, after losses to the SPLA in 1997, agreed to the IGAD principles, it was not until January 2005 that a lasting ceasefire, the Naivasha Agreement, was brokered. As part of the peace deal, the long-standing SPLA leader John Garang became a Vice President of Sudan. His death in a helicopter crash in March 2005, in what appears to have been a genuine accident, robbed both the SPLA and Sudan generally of a capable potential leader. Under the proposed settlement, South Sudan is to hold a referendum on full independence in 2011.

The south has significant oil fields, and oil revenues make up about 70% of Sudan's export earnings. Influence by the oil lobby has on occasion led to partiality towards the Khartoum regime on the part of Washington, despite Khartoum's Islamist credentials. (The Khartoum regime has made efforts to distance itself from its former alliance with Osama Bin Laden, whose pronouncements in support of the Sudanese regime and against Western intervention in the Darfur conflict nevertheless tend to confirm that he still regards Khartoum as an ally.) In recent years Chinese influence has become very significant. Sudan is seen as a key ally for Beijing in the so-called 'Chinese Scramble for Africa'. Chinese companies hold around a 40% holding in Sudanese oil exploitation, and Sudan is viewed by Beijing both as a key source of supply as well as a potential lever against US interests.

The south is home to numerous ethnic groups of which the Dinka, with around 40% of the population, is the largest. The political and economic astuteness of the Dinka has on occasion caused resentment among other southern groups. An internal civil war between the Nuer and Dinka peoples flared in the south for many years and factionalism within the SPLM/A remains a significant issue.

A key milestone in the 2005 agreement was the completion of a comprehensive national census, seen as essential for the establishment of constituencies and determining the power-sharing ratios in central government. This was undertaken in May 2008 (involving 60,000 enumerators at a cost of over $100m). The exercise was boycotted in Darfur and the South announced that it would not be bound by the results.

To all practical purposes, the South Sudanese government is increasingly operating as a sovereign entity, and has even made forays into the field of international diplomacy, such as its facilitation of talks between the Ugandan government and the Lord's Resistance Army insurgents. *(See 2.30.)* In the run up to the 2011 referendum, one security fear is that Khartoum will seek to manipulate southern factionalism in order to provoke domestic unrest, which it can then intervene to stop in the name of 'restoring order.' An intriguing possibility is that a southern SPLM candidate could, given the unpopularity of the Khartoum regime, win nationwide elections scheduled for 2009, which might in turn lead to a softening of SPLM enthusiasm for South Sudanese independence. Meanwhile, clashes continue between South Sudanese factions, and with the Sudanese government and its surrogates. In March 2008, fighting erupted between the SPLA and the Messiria people (part of the Baggara Arab ethnic group) in the disputed (and oil-rich) Abyei border region. A 'road map' intended to resolve the border dispute was initialled in June 2008, but several key 'African' regions, such as Nuba, are either outside the territory of South Sudan or still undemarcated, and insurgency by irredentists seeking to join South Sudan is a distinct possibility in these regions.

# Central African Republic

**Principal protagonists**

Central African Republic government; French interests actively engaged; Chadian government.

'Northern' ethnic groups; Union des Forces Démocratiques pour le Rassemblement (UFDR) umbrella group and others; Chadian rebels and pro-Khartoum Sudanese factions.

M'bororo ethnic group.

**Nature of conflict**

Ethnic conflict over control of government exacerbated by regional conflicts.

- Widespread violence against civilians by military reported.
- Unknown, but rising.
- 20,000 refugees to Cameroon; 50,000 to Chad. Up to 100,000 refugees from Darfur to CAR, particularly around the south-eastern town of Mboki. 150,000 CAR IDPs.

**Population/ethnic composition**

4.3m. Gbaya 33%, Banda 27%, Mandjia 13%, Sara/Kaba 10%, M'bororo 5%, Yakoma 4%. Religious mix: Traditional beliefs 35%, Roman Catholic 25%, Protestant 25%, Muslim 15%.

**Territorial extent**

Central African Republic: 622,984 km².

**Timeline**

13 Aug 1960: Central African Republic independent from France.
4 Dec 1976: Country remained 'Central African Empire'.
20 Sep 1979: 'Emperor' Bokassa deposed in French-instigated coup.
1 Sep 1981: André Kolingba seizes power.
9 Sep 1993 Ange-Félix Patassé elected.
15 Mar 2003: François Bozizé seizes power.
2004 onwards: Security situation deteriorates.
13 Apr 2007: Peace agreement between UFDR and Bangui government.

**Current status**

Unstable and highly dangerous.

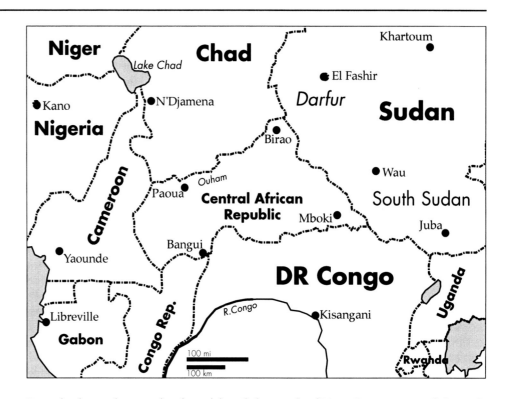

Largely dependent on foreign aid and the work of Non-Governmental Organizations (NGOs) to provide essential services, the Central African Republic is a state in which the central government barely functions and which is frequently unable even to pay civil servants, teachers, and – crucially – soldiers. Since independence in 1960, France has maintained a dominant political and military presence in the country, which, despite mineral and other assets, remains one of the poorest in the world.

The main ethnic fault-line in the Central African Republic is between the southern 'riverine' people who live in the Ubangi and Chari river basins, and the northern savanna peoples. The 'southerners' include the Yakoma, while the 'northerners' include the Gbaya (the largest single ethnic group), the Kaba and the M'bororo. The eastern region of the country was largely depopulated by Arab slavers in the 1890s-1910s and remains sparsely inhabited. More recently, Arabic or Hausa speaking Muslim immigrants have become significant.

The sectarian use of ethnic power-bases for candidates seeking to monopolize control of the government and the state's natural assets has been the norm throughout most of Central Africa's period of independence. Dangerously, these domestic disputes now align geographically with international conflicts, most prominently the crises in Darfur/Chad. Congolese and Ugandan elements have also been involved in support of factional interests.

No presidential appointment in Central Africa has been made without tacit approval, and sometimes overt support, from Paris. This has rarely resulted in good governance and has on occasion been mired in controversy and outright corruption, most notoriously the friendship between Jean-Bédel Bokassa (who seized power in 1966) and French President Valary Giscard d'Estaing, who accepted a valuable gift of diamonds from the Central African leader. In 1972, in a lavish $40m ceremony based on that of his hero, Napoleon, Bokassa crowned himself emperor, and the impoverished country was re-named the 'Central African Empire.' Eventually Bokassa's excesses became too much even for French sensibilities and he was deposed in a French-organized coup in 1979, in favour of the previous incumbent, David Dacko, who was little more than a French puppet.

The hapless Dacko was ousted for a second time in September 1981 by André Kolingba. The Kolingba period saw a systematic accumulation of power in the hands of a narrow ethnic base, the 'southern' Yakoma group, who total only 4% of the population overall. This process was sharply reversed when Kolingba was in turn deposed by Ange-Félix Patassé, a Kaba, who won CAR's only truly democratic election to date in 1993. Patassé evicted many of the Yakoma from their positions of authority but as a consequence his period of office was marred by frequent coup attempts and unrest in the armed forces until, in October 2002, the Armed Forces Chief of Staff, François Bozizé, a former close ally, seized power while Patassé was abroad. Bozizé, who had lived in exile in Chad for a while, was a close ally of Chadian President Idriss Déby, who probably directly aided the coup. In March 2005, Bozizé's presidency was legitimized in a general election that he won with 64% of the vote.

A Gbaya, Bozizé is a northerner from Ouham Prefecture, from where he launched his successful coup attempt, but later aligned himself with southern factions to maintain his grip on power. As a consequence, various rebel factions, including former Presidential Guards loyal to Patassé, and disaffected former Bozizé supporters, have been active in the increasingly lawless northern regions of the country. Since 2004 the security situation has deteriorated steeply as the factionalism in Central Africa has been aligned with, and exploited by, sectarian interests in Chad and Sudan. At the end of 2006, the various rebel groups were reported as operating under a loose umbrella organization, the *Union des Forces Démocratiques pour le Rassemblement* (UFDR), in alliance with Chadian rebels and pro-Khartoum Sudanese forces.

In October 2006 the UFDR launched a major attack, backed by Chadian rebels and, allegedly, Sudanese elements, seizing the town of Birao. The assumption is that the Chadian rebels hoped to use their incursion into Central Africa to bypass strong Chadian forces in the eastern part of Chad and so seize the Chadian capital, N'Djamena, from the south. Following Bozizé's coup, Chad and CAR signed a mutual assistance agreement that in practice allows Chadian government forces to intervene in CAR, against both Chadian and CAR rebels. Sporadic fighting continued throughout 2006, with Chadian forces staging several operations in northern CAR. France also committed both ground and air power to the conflict. The incursion severely shook the Bangui government, which had publicly maintained (and may even have believed) that the violence was the isolated work of bandits and gangs.

The semi-nomadic M'bororo people of the north-western region (also known as the 'Bush Falani') have been the specific target of attacks. Land scarcity issues have resulted in attacks on M'bororo communities in Nigeria and Cameroon (where 15,000 M'bororo were forced to flee their homes in mid-2007) as well in CAR. In CAR, political unrest and specific issues (such as the failure of the government to pay soldiers' salaries) have exacerbated the problem. Regarded as comparatively wealthy, the M'bororo have been targeted for banditry and the kidnapping of children and women for ransom; repeated attacks of this nature have resulted in many of the M'bororo being forced to sell their entire stocks of cattle with devastating consequences for their financial sustainability. An estimated 10,000 M'bororo fled to Cameroon in 2007, where they potentially face further dangers. A suspicion exists among commentators that the looting of M'bororo communities is tacitly approved by the government, as a means of defusing the issue of unpaid soldiers' wages; many of the 'bandits' being former Bozizé troops. Thousands of M'bororo and other Central African refugees have also fled over the border into southern Chad, where reception facilities are rudimentary.

In April 2007 a peace agreement was signed between the Bangui regime and the UFDR, amid the ruins of Birao. Under the agreement, UFDR fighters were to be incorporated in the regular army and the UFDR was recognized as a political party. Attacks by other rebel factions continued, however. By the end of 2007, international concern over Darfur, frustrated by Sudanese lack of co-operation, has, if only by default, partially switched to Chad and CAR. The deployment of a French-led UN/EU force to CAR was agreed in December 2007, mainly with the intention of securing the porous border between CAR and Darfur.

# Eritrea/Ethiopia

**Principal protagonists**

Republic of Eritrea.

Federal Democratic Republic of Ethiopia.

**Nature of conflict**

Border war, 1998-2000, underlain by nationality and other ethnic issues in both countries.

 Accusations of forced deportations levelled against both sides.
 100,000.
 1 million refugees, IDPs and people rendered stateless.

**Population/ethnic composition**

Eritrea: 4.8m. Tigrayan 51.8%, Tigre 17.9%, Afar 8.1%, Kunama 3%. Ethiopia: 74.8m. Oromo 31.8%, Amhara 29.3%, Somali 6.2%, Tigrayan 5.9%, Walaita 4.6%, Gurage 4.2%, Sidamo 3.4%.

**Territorial extent**

Ethiopia: 1.1m km²;
Eritrea: 117,600 km².

**Timeline**

1 Jan 1890: Italian rule proclaimed over Eritrea.
15 Sep 1952: Eritrea federated with Ethiopia.
1961: Armed agitation for Eritrean independence commences.
14 Nov 1962: Eritrea annexed by Ethiopia.
21 May 1991: Fall of *Derg* (Communist) regime.
23-25 Apr 1993: Referendum overwhelmingly endorses Eritrean independence.
2 May 1993: Ethiopia recognizes Eritrean independence. UN follows on 14 May.
13 Apr 2002: Boundary Commission publishes its rulings. Ethiopia refuses to recognize border demarcation.
Nov 2004: Ethiopia accepts 'in principal' Border Commission proposals, but progress remains stalled.

**Current status**

Unresolved and extremely tense.

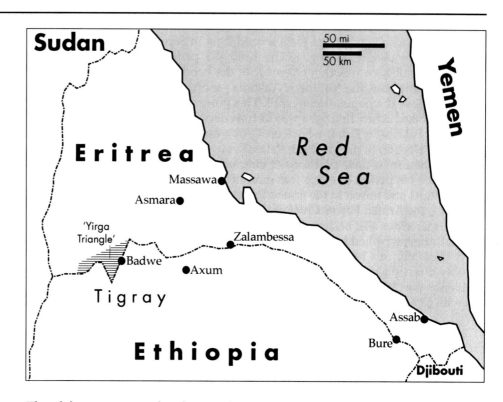

**The vicious 1998-2000 border war between Ethiopia and Eritrea was regarded as inexplicable by outside commentators ignorant of the deep-seated national and ethnic tensions which fuelled the conflict. The fighting was all the more tragic as the leaders of the governments of Eritrea and Ethiopia were formerly firm friends and allies.**

During the protracted war against the Communist *Derg* regime in Addis Ababa the Tigrayan People's Liberation Front (TPLF) formed and dominated the Ethiopian People's Revolutionary Democratic Front (EPRDF) – a coalition of ethnically-based liberation movements – and was closely aligned to the Eritrean People's Liberation Front (EPLF) which conducted a thirty-year struggle for Eritrean independence, first against the Emperor and latterly against the Communists. After the overthrow of the *Derg* in May 1991, close relations continued. The EPRDF-led Transitional Government pledged to uphold the right of self-determination of all Ethiopia's peoples and approved Eritrean plans for a referendum on independence. Under UN supervision, a poll was held on 23-25 April 1993. More than 90% of Eritreans voted and 99% of these supported independence. Ethiopia was one of the first countries to recognize the new state.

The new Federal Democratic Republic of Ethiopia meanwhile established new provinces for Ethiopia on an ethnic basis. The constitution of Ethiopia is unusual in that it recognizes the right of the provinces to self-determination, including potential independence. Ethiopia continued to share a currency union, open cross-border movement and many other elements of close intergovernmental co-operation with Eritrea. In June 1996, Eritrean President Issavas Afewerki told an Ethiopian newspaper that the border between the two countries was becoming 'meaningless'. Sadly, this was to prove far from being the case.

An unintended consequence of the close relations between Ethiopia and Eritrea was that many practical issues – including the details of border demarcation and the national status of Eritreans living in Ethiopia (and vice-versa) – were simply left unresolved. Ethiopian law, unlike Eritrean, did not allow dual Ethiopian/Eritrean nationality, but this issue was rarely tested in practice. In 1996, a joint commission was established to enable citizens to choose their nationality, but no practical progress was made on the issue. As relations soured between the two nations these oversights acquired a new and more dangerous significance as potential flashpoints.

Ethiopian discontent with Eritrea gradually crystallized over a number of issues. Through Eritrea independence, Ethiopia lost its coastline, and although Eritrea guaranteed Ethiopia generous access to the ports at Assab and Massawa, this reliance on Eritrean goodwill proved a source of increasing irritation and hurt pride on the part of Ethiopians, who started developing alternative export routes via Djibouti. Ethiopia also reacted negatively to Eritrean demonstrations of independence, such as shifting the calendar from the Julian system, still used in Ethiopia, to the Gregorian calendar (used everywhere else) and Eritrea's adoption of a new currency, the n*afka*, which weakened Ethiopian fiscal influence.

Furthermore, many Ethiopians came to be resentful of the economic and political prominence allegedly held by ethnic Tigrayan Eritreans within Ethiopia itself. This tension needs to be viewed against the background of ethnic sensitivities within Ethiopia, particularly between the Tigrayan ethnic group and other peoples. Having overthrown the Amharic domination of the Empire and the *Derg*, many Ethiopians resisted what they saw as the imposition of a new ethnic hegemony by the Tigrayan-dominated EPRDF. (Ethiopian Prime Minister, Meles Zenawi, a Tigrayan, is also chairman of both the TPLF and the EPRDF.) Hostility towards the Eritreans may be seen in part, therefore, as a cipher for wider issues of resentment and resistance by marginalized groups. From 1997 onwards, tensions increased markedly with calls for the government to declare the Eritreans as aliens.

In 1998, border flashpoints including Badwe in the west (claimed by Tigray province), the central Tsorona-Zalambessa area, and Bure in the south-east came to dominate the deteriorating relationship between the two countries. According to the Eritrean view, tensions in the Badwe area were exacerbated by Ethiopian immigration and settlement by former liberation fighters, and expulsions of the Eritrean population. In May 1998 the simmering discontent exploded into a military confrontation in Badwe as Eritrea sent in troops to expel Ethiopian soldiers and, allegedly, the settlers. Clashes on all three border fronts continued until June 1998, and resumed again in February 1999 when Ethiopia expelled Eritrean forces from the Badwe region. The Eritreans did, however, halt an Ethiopian offensive in the central region before the onset of the rains in June 1999 brought an overall cessation to hostilities.

The border over which the two sides are in dispute – a conflict described as 'two bald men fighting over a comb' – was originally demarcated in 1902 between the Ethiopians and the Italian colonial authorities, who occupied Eritrea in 1890. In 1935, Italy invaded Ethiopia and occupied it until expelled by British forces in 1941. After the Second World War a number of options were considered for Eritrea. In 1952 the country was federated with Ethiopia, but in 1962 Addis Ababa broke the terms of this agreement by annexing Eritrea as Ethiopia's 14th province. From 1962 until after Eritrean independence in 1993 the detailed demarcation of the border thus became largely irrelevant. Its modern resurgence as an issue owes much to the psychology of both nations, and interlocks with other regional conflicts in Sudan, Uganda, and Somali – with both Addis Ababa and Asmara backing the other's opponents in a pattern all too typical of Africa. *(See Conflict interlinkages, 2.05.)* Under Italian rule, Eritrea – which had never before been unified – developed not only a national consciousness but a relatively sophisticated infrastructure. This process of nation forming was reinforced by the discipline established by the EPLF during the long liberation war. The comparatively advanced socio-economic development of Eritrea is jealously resented by some Ethiopians, who are in turn accused by their neighbours of having a 'superiority complex' arising from Ethiopia's 3,000-year history of independence.

Eritrea, as a new nation, has vigorously sought to assert its identity and prestige. One consequence is that since independence Eritrea has had border disputes with all its neighbours – Yemen, Ethiopia, Sudan and Djibouti, with which Eritrea clashed in June 2008. In general, the EPLF has not easily made the transition from liberation movement to political party, despite its name change to the People's Front for Democracy and Justice in 1994, and the country's record on religious minority and other rights remains poor. Former EPLF fighters occupy virtually all senior government positions. Eritrean society remains militarized and cynics note that the war with Ethiopia has done little to diminish this.

Both governments sought to use the border conflict to garner domestic populist support. With the outbreak of war, Ethiopia asserted that all those who had voted in Eritrea's independence referendum had thus declared themselves Eritrean citizens. Tens of thousands of 'Eritreans' thereby became potentially stateless, in defiance of international conventions which endorse the concept of nationality as central to the effective exercising of individual civil rights. De-naturalized persons were subsequently deported, with their passports stamped 'Not to Return.'

The major Ethiopian offensive of June 2000, conducted along a wide front, displaced up to a million Eritreans. Eritrea, in turn, retaliated by deporting Ethiopians citizens living in the capital, Asmara, and elsewhere in the country. Tacit recognition of the scale of the deportations, on both sides, was given by the establishment in October 2000 of safe passage routes for civilians expelled across the border.

A peace agreement was signed in December 2000 and in 2002 both sides agreed to submit to the arbitration of a Border Commission, which published its results on 13 April. This awarded the 'Yirga Triangle' and, crucially, the town of Badwe, to Eritrea. Ethiopia refused to accept this verdict, and although it did concede ground in 2004, the implementation of the border settlement remains stalled.

# Somalia

**Principal protagonists**

Transitional Federal Government; Ethiopian forces actively engaged; African Union peacekeeping force.

United Islamic Courts.

Republic of Somaliland. *(See 2.21.)*

Linked conflict with Ogaden separatists opposed to Ethiopian central government. *(See 2.22.)*

**Nature of conflict**
State collapse through ethnic in-fighting.

☠ 350,000 since 1991.
   2,000 since 2007.
👥 1,000,000 IDPs. Unknown total number of refugees (figures masked by large scale Somali out-migration). 320,000 refugees reported since upsurge in violence in December 2006.

**Population/ethnic composition**
c8.8m. Somali 92.4%, Arab 2.2%, Afar 1.3%. Virtually all the population is Sunni Muslim.

**Territorial extent**
Somalia area officially 637,657 km².

**Timeline**
1 Jul 1960: Somali Republic formed.
23 Jul 1977-15 Mar 1978: Ogaden War between Ethiopia and Somalia.
23 May 1986: Onset of Somali civil war.
18 May 1991: Somaliland secedes.
Jul 1991: Effective collapse of central authority. UN declares Somalia to be 'without a government'.
9 Dec 1992: US-led UN intervention.
4 May 1993: Withdrawal of US/UN forces.
2004: Transitional Federal Government formed.
mid-2006: United Islamic Courts establish control in Mogadishu and elsewhere.
Dec 2006: Ethiopian forces expel UIC.

**Current status**
Unresolved and highly unstable.

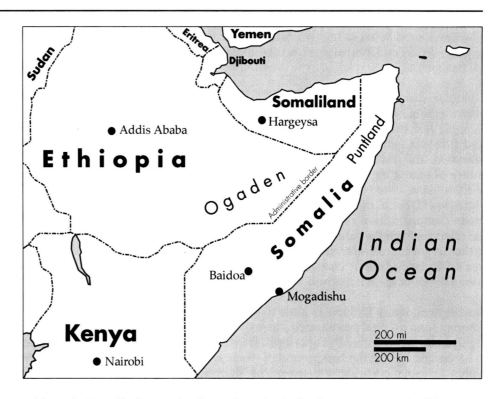

**Although Somalia is nominally quite ethnically homogeneous (unlike most African countries), the country has for years been torn apart by sectarian violence. The meaningful ethnic breakdown is not between Somalis and other groups, but in the clan sub-divisions of the Somalis themselves. Each clan is in turn divided into a bewildering array of castes, familial groupings and septs, many of which are numerically significant in their own right and that have their own systems of loyalties and historical antagonisms.**

In addition to a widespread international diaspora, there are significant Somali minorities in Kenya, Djibouti and Ethiopia. The Ethiopia/Somalia border is largely undemarcated and the Ogaden region of Ethiopia has been the scene of repeated conflict between the Ethiopian government and Somali separatists/irredentists on both sides of the border. *(See 2.22.)* The Ogaden War of 1977-8 saw conventional forces engaged on both the Ethiopian and Somalian sides and resulted in a major regional power shift. Prior to the conflict both states were clients of the Soviet Union, but as a consequence of the fighting the USSR abandoned its support for Somalia in favour of backing Ethiopia. This enabled Ethiopia to win the war and pushed Somalia into the American sphere of influence.

Following the Ogaden War and the loss of Soviet support, the security situation in Somalia deteriorated throughout the 1980s with the emergence of clan-based militias only loosely under central control. In 1986 President Siad Barre launched attacks using his 'Red Beret' special forces against the clan militias, but following his injury in a car accident of 23 May rivals both within the government and the clans took the opportunity to attempt to seize power.

With the country rapidly degenerating into civil war, Siad Barre ordered a violent security clampdown in Mogadishu. This, however, had the effect of causing Barre's squeamish Washington backers to start distancing themselves from his regime. The Barre government finally fell in July 1991, whereupon the country splintered into competing factions. Repeated attempts to get the factions and warlords to co-operate in a new national government failed. A US-led United Nations intervention in 1993 ended in disaster, with the notorious 'Black Hawk Down' incident in which two US helicopters were shot down and the bodies of killed Marines paraded through the streets. Traumatized by this incident, US policy towards Somalia has seen been largely reactive and not integrated into any larger regional strategy.

In 2004, in the fourteenth attempt to create a unified Somali government, a Transitional Federal Government (TFG) was established, initially in Nairobi and later in the Somali town of Baidoa, from where the 'government' was unable to exercise much practical authority. The US, while theoretically supporting the TFG, also sponsored the creation of a client coalition of warlords, the Alliance for the Restoration of Peace and Counter terrorism, which failed to live up to its name.

In mid-2006 a coalition of Islamic courts, which had originally arisen spontaneously to provide some degree of law and order in the urban areas, succeeding in ousting the clan warlords from Mogadishu and extended their control over much of southern and central Somalia. The emergence of the United Islamic Courts (UIC) inevitably prompted US concern at the potential creation of a Taliban-style regime in Somalia. In fact, the United Islamic Courts were by no means homogeneous and included moderate as well as extreme factions. Ethiopia had its own security concerns as well: they accused the UIC of backing the Ogaden National Liberation Front, the Omoro Liberation Front and the *al-Itihaad al-Islamiya* terrorist group responsible for a number of bombings in Addis Ababa. Ethiopia also accused Eritrea of having 2,000 troops in Somalia in support of the UIC. The UIC, for its part, declared a *jihad* against Ethiopia.

In December 2006, with US air support, Ethiopia intervened massively and decisively against the UIC, ousting them from Mogadishu. Although this allowed the Transitional Federal Government to base itself in Mogadishu for the first time, the overall security situation in the capital actually deteriorated, with ongoing violence against the Ethiopian 'occupiers'. To support the TFG the African Union has committed a peacekeeping force, of which the first contingent – 1,500 troops from Uganda – arrived in March 2007. The fragility of international relations in the region was revealed when Eritrea immediately condemned the Ugandans' arrival as provocative and the Ugandans came under attack from insurgents in November 2007. In June 2008 a peace deal was signed between the TFG and the Alliance for the Re-liberation of Somalia, and opposition coalition headed by ex-UIC chairman Sheikh Sharif, but Islamist groups vowed to continue their insurgency.

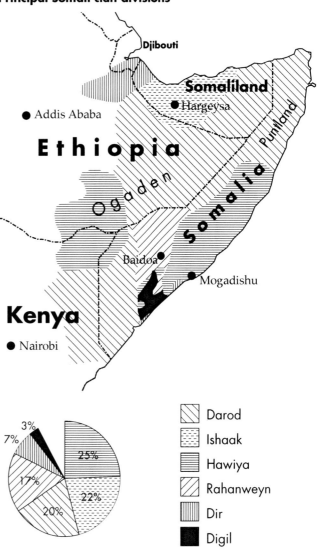

**Principal Somali clan divisions**

- Darod
- Ishaak
- Hawiya
- Rahanweyn
- Dir
- Digil

**Secession in Somaliland**

Modern Somalia was created out of two former colonies: Italian Somaliland and, in the north, British Somaliland. The latter was, in fact, separately independent for five days (26 June-1 July 1960) before joining the new Republic of Somalia. On 18 May 1991, after the collapse of the central government in Somalia, the territory of former British Somaliland re-asserted its independence as the Republic of Somaliland.

Somaliland has a hybrid system of governance combining traditional and Western institutions. Clans are allocated representation in the upper and lower houses proportionately, while district councils are elected under a system of multi-party democracy.

Somaliland's political and economic stability is in stark contrast to the rest of Somalia. The emergence of the United Islamic Courts and the subsequent conflict between the UIC and the Somali interim government has not yet significantly affected Somaliland. Nevertheless, Somaliland has been thus far been denied recognition by an international community still insistent on resurrecting the failed Somali state.

# Ogaden

**Principal protagonists**

Government of Ethiopia.

Ogaden (Somali) people; Ogaden National Liberation Front/Army.

**Nature of conflict**

Separatist conflict. Ethiopian/Somalian border demarcation an issue, as is current Ethiopian intervention in Somalia. (See 2.20.)

- Systematic human rights abuses alleged against Ethiopian forces.
- c40,000 in 1977-8 conflict, several hundred since.
- 1,500 to Kenya, November 2007.

**Population/ethnic composition**
Somali region of Ethiopia: c4.3m. Somali 96.25%, Oromo 2.25%.

**Territorial extent**
Principally Somali region of Ethiopia: 279,252 km².

**Timeline**

Jun 1897: Agreement between Britain and Ethiopia assigns Ogaden to Ethiopian sphere of influence.

3 Oct 1935: Italian invasion of Ethiopia; Ogaden region occupied by end 1935.

10 Jun 1940-27 Nov 1941: East African Campaign between Italian and British forces.

17 Mar 1941: Occupation of Ogaden by British forces largely complete.

24 Sep 1948: Britain withdraws from Ogaden in favour of Ethiopia.

1 Jul 1960: Somali Republic formed.

1963: Ogaden Liberation Front formed.

23 Jul 1977-15 Mar 1978: Ogaden War between Ethiopia and Somalia.

15 Aug 1984: Ogaden National Liberation Front formed.

2005: Peace talks proposed, but do not take place.

Dec 2006: Ethiopian forces invade Somalia.

**Current status**

Ongoing low-level conflict continues.

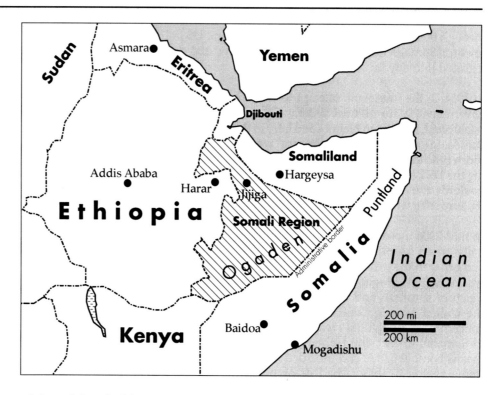

Although inevitably closely intertwined with conflict in neighbouring Somalia, the Ogaden conflict has its own history and dynamic. The vast majority of inhabitants of the Ogaden region are Muslim Somalis, and the region remained politically independent until the end of the 19th century. In the 1890s, colonial rivalries between Italy, France and Britain resulted in the creation of European colonies in Somali lands around the Horn of Africa. At various stages, all three powers tacitly supported the maintenance, or even extension, of Ethiopian independence as a bulwark against the ambitions of their European rivals.

In 1896, Britain came to an agreement with the Ogaden Somalis, which was thought (by the latter) to be a guarantee of Ogaden independence. Britain, however, continued to support Ethiopian ambitions in the region. In 1887, Ethiopia occupied the strategic Muslim city-state of Harar and in 1897 Britain recognized Ethiopian claims over the entire region, including the Ogaden. In June 1897 British and Ethiopia formalized the border between Ethiopia and British Somaliland. The majority of the border (with Italian Somaliland) remained undefined, as it does to the present day.

Central governmental control over Ogaden remained marginal, however, until the Italian invasion of 1935, after which all of Ethiopia, including Ogaden, fell under Mussolini's control. The Italians were, in turn, expelled in 1941 by the British who directly ruled the Ogaden region until 1948.

Although there are some suggestions that the British favoured separating Ogaden from the rest of the Ethiopia and joining it with their own holding in British Somaliland, this proved untenable and in 1948 they handed most of the region back to Ethiopia (the remainder being handed over in the mid 1950s).

The basis of Ogaden nationalist claims, therefore, rests on the 1896 agreement, the claim that Ogaden was never an historical part of Ethiopia, and that following British occupation during and after the Second World War they should have been allowed the right to separate self-determination.

The creation of an independent Somali state in 1960 complicated matters from the Ogaden perspective. Somalia was formed from a merger of the formerly British and Italian Somalilands and the new state had openly expansionist claims, under the title 'Greater Somalia', upon Somali regions in modern Djibouti, Kenya, and Ogaden. In 1963 the Ogaden Liberation Front was formed with the intention of progressing Ogaden claims on the basis of union with Somalia. This enabled Ethiopia (as well as Greater Somalia proponents in Mogadishu) to portray the conflict in terms of a dispute between two nations, Somalia and Ethiopia, over an ill-defined border, rather than a separate self-determination issue. The Somalis, furthermore, created the Western Somali Liberation Front to operate alongside the OLF in Ogaden.

Following the collapse of Emperor Haile Selassie's regime in 1974 and its replacement with a Communist state, Somalia sought to capitalize on Ethiopian weakness by attempting to occupy the Ogaden. Full-scale conflict between Ethiopia and Somalia in 1977-8 resulted, however, in Ethiopian victory and the withdrawal of Somali forces.

In 1984 the Ogaden National Liberation Front (ONLF) was created to press for Ogaden independence from both Ethiopia and Somalia. Although criticised as being too narrowly ethnically based – drawing most its support from the Ogaden clan – the ONLF consolidated its support in the region, particularly as Communist power declined during the long Ethiopian civil war. In December 1992, as the Communist regime collapsed, the ONLF won, with 84% of the vote, overwhelming support in the Somali District Five (as the Somali/Ogaden region was then officially known).

Under the post-Communist government, Ethiopia was formally reorganized in a number of ethnically based regions, the Somali Region (covering the bulk of the Ogaden region) being geographically one of the largest. The ONLF joined with the post-Communist government, but lost ground to the Somali Peoples' Democratic Party (which it accused of being a government front organization) and fighting eventually resumed between Ethiopian forces and the ONLF. In 1994 the Ethiopians launched a large-scale military offensive against the ONLF. Peace talks proposed by Ethiopia in 2005 failed to materialize.

In November 2006, as relations between Addis Ababa and the United Islamic Courts regime in Mogadishu declined, the ONLF threatened that it would not allow Ethiopian troops to transit through the Somali Region into Somalia. Ethiopian forces massively intervened in Somalia anyway in support of the Somali Transitional Federal Government, displacing the United Islamic Courts occupying Mogadishu. In subsequent fighting, the Ethiopians claimed (probably accurately) that the ONLF had been in receipt of support from Eritrea and the UIC, and that, more generally, the ONLF is a terrorist organization. In April 2007, the ONLF attacked a Chinese-run oilfield killing over 70 civilians in what Addis Ababa condemned as "Ethiopia's 9/11". Attacks by the ONLF against Ethiopian targets (and vice versa) continue, with Ethiopia using air power and additionally being accused of denying relief efforts into rebel-held areas (a claim previously made against the Communist *Derg* regime during Ethiopia's drought crises of the 1980s). Overall, the Ogaden self-determination claim has once again been clouded by outside events and international manoeuvring.

**Oromo Liberation Front**

Ethiopia faces an ongoing conflict in the Oromo Region of the country against elements calling for greater Oromo self-determination or outright independence. With over 30% of the population, the Oromo are the largest ethnic group in Ethiopia.

A distinctive Oromo nationalist voice has existed since at least 1973 when the Oromo Liberation Front was created to 'oppose Ethiopian colonial rule.' The OLF fought against the Communist *Derg* regime and was a part of the first post-Communist government but, in common with a number of other separatists groups, later came to believe the successor government to be overtly Tigrayan-dominated. The current Ethiopian state is divided into autonomous regions, primarily on an ethnic basis, but it accused by its opponents of placing limits on the practical expression of self-determination.

OLF elements were allegedly armed and supported by Eritrea for action against Ethiopian forces during the Ethiopian-Eritrean war from 1998-2002, but OLF action declined after 2002. In 2005, during the fraught Ethiopian election campaigns, the OLF was accused of massacring 400 Oromo who opposed their stance.

The OLF was allegedly linked to the United Islamic Courts in Mogadishu and is claimed by Ethiopia to be a terrorist organization lacking widespread support from the Oromo population.

# Rwanda

**Principal protagonists**

Rwandan Patriotic Front (government of Rwanda from 19 Jul 1994); Tutsi people.

*Mouvement républicain national pour la démocratie et le développement* (MRND); (government of Rwanda until 19 Jul 1994); extremist Hutu elements.

**Nature of conflict**

Ethnic civil war and genocide.

☠ 800,000 killed in genocide of 1994.
👥 Approximately 400,000 Tutsi refugees 1993-4; 2 million Hutu refugees, mainly to DR Congo, 1994.

**Population/ethnic composition**

8,648,248. Hutu 85%, Tutsi 14%, Twa 1% (2002). Tutsi losses in the 1994 genocide have to an extent been balanced proportionately by subsequent Hutu out-migration.

**Territorial extent**

Rwanda: 26,338 km².

**Timeline**

Aug 1884: German protectorate established.
20 Jul 1922: Part of League of Nations mandated territory of Ruanda-Urundi under Belgian control.
1 Jul 1962: Independence from Belgium under Hutu-dominated government.
Oct 1990: Rwanda Patriotic Front begins insurgency from Uganda.
2002-3: Arusha Peace Accords negotiated.
6 Apr 1994: Juvénal Habyarimana assassinated. Pre-planned massacres of Tutsis by Hutu extremists commence.
3 Jul 1994: Kigali falls to RPF.
19 Jul 1994: RPF forms provisional government.
21 Aug 1994: Following French withdrawal, RPF in control of entire country.

**Current status**

Currently stable.

In 1904 the twentieth century's first genocide took place in Namibia, when German colonists attempted to exterminate the Herero people. (*See Namibia, 2.58.*) Ninety years later, Africa was the stage for the last genocide of a particularly blood-stained century, with the previously obscure central African country of Rwanda briefly occupying the world's headlines as the scene of the murder, within a few weeks, of up to 800,000 men, women and children.

Prior to German occupation in 1884, Rwanda existed as a centralized kingdom ruled by a cattle-holding minority, the Tutsis, and an agriculturalist underclass, the Hutu. After the First World War, as part of Ruanda-Urundi, Rwanda (together with what is now Burundi) became part of a Belgian League of Nations Mandate. Both the Germans and the Belgians operated through the existing Tutsi power structures in both Rwanda and Burundi. (*See Burundi, 2.26.*) In 1959, however, as the country moved towards self-government, a Hutu rebellion erupted that resulted in the massacre of 20,000 Tutsis and the first of a wave of Tutsi emigration to Uganda that was to have powerful consequences over forty years later. In 1962, Rwanda became independent under the militant Hutu-led government of Gregoire Kayibanda. Kayibanda was deposed in 1973 in favour of President Juvénal Habyarimana and a single dominant party, the *Mouvement républicain national pour la démocratie et le développement* was established. Persecution – and outward migration – of Tutsis continued until the 1990s.

In 1985, Tutsi exiles in Uganda formed the Rwandan Patriotic Fund (RPF) and five years later invaded Rwanda, provoking fierce fighting in the northern border regions. By 1993, the internal situation had deteriorated to the extent that the Habyarimana government was obliged to negotiate with the rebels. The result was an internationally brokered power-sharing agreement, the Arusha Peace Accords.

On 6 April 1994, with the negotiations in their final stages, an aircraft carrying both President Juvénal Habyarimana

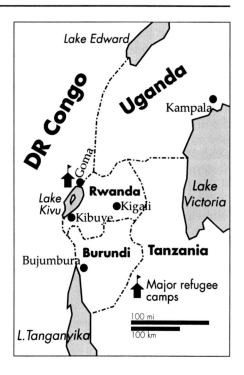

and his Burundan opposite number was brought down over Kigali airport by a surface-to-air rocket, both leaders being killed. Fierce controversy persists over the identity of perpetrators of the double assassination. Circumstantial evidence points to elements of the RPF, which had been allowed to station around 3,600 armed supporters in the capital as part of the Arusha Accords. The theory goes that this faction, with or without the connivance of the RPF leadership, calculated that the RPF was capable of seizing overall control of the country (which, in fact, the RPF did go on to do) and so had little to benefit from power sharing. Others contend that the attack was the work of Hutu *agent provocateurs*.

What is not in doubt is that the assassinations were the prelude to horrific atrocities.

The day after the assassinations, ten Belgian peacekeepers were kidnapped and tortured to death by government soldiers, precipitating a wholesale withdrawal by Belgian and other UN peacekeeping forces. In what was clearly a pre-planned operation, leaders of the Tutsi community in Kigali were liquidated by the Presidential Guard and recruits dispatched to all parts of the country to eliminate both the Tutsis and any moderate Hutus who supported them. Local 'Hutu Power' militia called the *Interahamwe* ('those who attack together') quickly joined the fray. Participants, in addition to being whipped into a killing frenzy by nakedly racist propaganda, were frequently given incentives that ranged from the free handouts of the machetes used to kill their neighbours, to cash and the promises of expropriated Tutsi land. Businessmen, regional officials, and even priests were among the perpetrators. Intermarriage between Hutu and Tutsis being by no means uncommon, instances of one spouse killing their partner and children were reported. In a number of verified cases, Catholic priests deliberately encouraged Tutsi members of their flock to seek sanctuary in churches instead of fleeing, thereby facilitating their massacre.

Even assuming the RPF was responsible for the downing of Habyarimana's flight it is clear from the speed and violence of the response by Hutu extremists that a wholesale extermination of the Tutsi population had long been planned. *Radio Télévision Libre des Mille Collines*, the main 'Hutu Power' propaganda vehicle, began broadcasting in July 1993 using government facilities, and contributed significantly to the atmosphere of paranoia among Hutus. The radio station described Tutsis as 'cockroaches' – originally an allusion to the RPF's 'scuttling away' after hit-and-run attacks but later used to characterize all Tutsis as vermin to be destroyed.

The 'international community', with its attention focused on Bosnia and the transition to majority rule in South Africa, found the 'tribal bloodletting' of the Rwandan massacres to be conveniently incomprehensible and intractable, but international bodies did call for an immediate ceasefire – which, as commentators pointed out at the time, was somewhat like asking the Jews to negotiate a ceasefire with the Nazis. The only significant foreign intervention, Operation Turquoise, was by the French – and that was primarily in support of the Rwandan regime, which enjoyed a close relationship with Paris.

In around six weeks of killing the genocide left around 800,000 people dead, and spurred the RPF into full military action aimed at seizing control of the country and halting the massacres. In July 1994 the RPF captured Kigali, and on 19 July, the RPF set up a Transitional Government of National Unity that included the participation of other parties under a Hutu president, Pasteur Bizimungu. The immediate consequence of the RPF victory was a massive humanitarian emergency, with 2 million panic-stricken Hutu refugees – including the perpetrators of the genocide – fleeing into Congo and other neighbouring countries.

In the aftermath of the genocide, the new government faced the huge task of reconstructing a civil society deeply traumatized by the experience of neighbour killing neighbour, and the loss not only of Tutsi administrators and skilled personnel, but the flight or arrest of the 47,000 Hutu administrators implicated in the genocide. The inexperienced judiciary faced a challenge, daunting by any standards, of meting out justice to the 700,000 people accused of genocide related crimes. A new constitution was agreed in a referendum of May 2003, and elections for a regular government, which the RPF won with over 70% of the vote, took place in August/September 2003, with RPF leader, Paul Kagame, a Tutsi, being elected President.

Faced with a deluge of cases, Rwanda turned to the traditional local *garara* courts to gather information about perpetrators of the genocide and to try offenders. While these have had some success in clearing the backlog of cases, particularly at the local or junior level, the *garara* courts have also been prone to accusations of inexperience and failure to follow procedural rules. The appeals procedure is particularly weak, and the overall result has been a massively overcrowded prison system. Around 60,000 low-ranking '*génocidaires*' have been released by the government, but this policy is understandably controversial.

Internationally, the new Rwanda soon became involved in sectarian conflict in the Democratic Republic of Congo (then Zaïre; *See Congo, 2.28*). Initially, Rwandan involvement centred on legitimate security concerns arising from cross border raids by supporters of the previous regime, who had re-grouped among the Hutu refugees in Congo. Rwanda also intervened in support of the Congolese Banyamulenge (Tutsi) population.

In 1996, the well-drilled Rwandan army intervened in force against the disintegrating Zaïrean state, installing a Rwandan client, Laurent Kabila, in place of long-standing Zaïrean dictator Mobutu Sese Seko. Kabila subsequently fell out with Rwanda, which attempted a second 'regime change' in 1998. Against a background of Angolan and Zimbabwean intervention this was unsuccessful, and Rwandan conventional forces withdrew in 2002. Rwanda also fell out with Uganda over the spoils of their respective Congolese adventures, with Rwandan and Ugandan regular forces and their proxy local factions fighting each other in Kisangani in 1999 and 2000. *(See Conflict interlink in Africa, 2.05.)*

In recent years, Kigale has come under censure for its increased authoritarianism. Tutsis have progressively tightened their grip on the country's political life. Officially, the Rwandan government dismisses the ethnic division between Tutsi and Hutu as a false creation of colonialism, maintaining that all citizens are now simply 'Rwandan'. Because in theory this means that no figures exist for the respective numbers of Tutsi and Hutu in public life, this policy has in practice facilitated minority hegemony, with foreign commentators noting ironically that most holders of senior posts just happen to have the light, fine features and thin noses of the typical Tutsi. Such criticism is firmly suppressed internally, with an array of measures aimed at targeting 'divisionism' (a term only loosely defined legally) and 'genocide ideology.' Against this criticism of the government must be measured the considerable strides it has taken, with only limited resources, to re-build a shattered country.

# Burundi

**Principal protagonists**

Government of Burundi. (*Conseil National pour la Défense de la Démocratie-Forces de Défense de la Démocratie* [CNDD-FDD].)

Hutu radicals.

Tutsi radicals.

**Nature of conflict**

Civil war (1993-2003) predicated on racial conflict. Post-civil war disputes.

- Extra-judicial imprisonment, executions, and forced deportation of refugees alleged against government since 2005.
- 150,000 Hutu in massacres of 1972.
  300,000 in civil war of 1993-2003.
- Up to 420,000 refugees in Tanzania and Rwanda at peak.

**Population/ethnic composition**

8 million. Hutu 80.9%, Tutsi 15.6%, Lingala 1.6%, Twa 1%.

**Territorial extent**

Burundi: 27,830 km².

**Timeline**

1903: Becomes a German colony.
20 Jul 1922: Part of League of Nations mandated territory of Ruanda-Urundi under Belgian control.
1 Jul 1962: Burundi independent from Belgium under a Tutsi-dominated government.
13 Aug 1972: Gatumba massacre.
10 Jun 1993: Melchior Ndadaye becomes first Hutu president.
21 Oct 1993: Melchior Ndadaye assassinated in failed Tutsi coup attempt. Civil war starts.
16 Nov 2003: Peace agreement signed.
28 Feb 2005: New constitution agreed by referendum.
4 Jul 2005: CNDD-FDD led government elected.

**Current status**

Clashes continue with rebel factions.

*See 2.24 for map of Burundi.*

**Burundi has a similar geographical and ethnic mix to Rwanda, and like its neighbour was originally a German colonial territory before being transferred to the Belgian League of Nations mandate at the end of the First World War. However, the trajectory of ethnic conflict in Burundi has been markedly different to that in Rwanda – so much so that the two countries have been christened 'the false twins' by some observers.**

As with Rwanda, national politics has historically been dominated by often violent disputes between the Tutsi minority and the Hutu majority. Unlike Rwanda, which gained independence under a Hutu majority government, in Burundi the Tutsi were able to maintain political hegemony into the 1990s under a series of dictatorial governments.

In August 1972, 160 Tutsis were murdered in Gatumba camp near the Zaïre border. In a mirror image of the genocide of Tutsis in Rwanda 30 years later, Tutsis used the massacre as a pretext for a well-organized slaughter of Burundan Hutus. Up to 150,000 Hutus were murdered in a matter of a few weeks.

In 1993, Burundi held its first democratic elections. These were won by the Hutu-dominated Front for Democracy in Burundi (FRODEBU). Melchior Ndadaye became Burundi's first Hutu President, but in October 1993 he was assassinated by a group of Tutsi army officers during a failed coup attempt. For Tutsi dissidents, the main trigger for rebellion was a move by the FRODEBU government to reduce Tutsi control over the army. The Tutsi minority has long viewed effective control of Burundi's armed forces as the 'court of last resort' for the protection of Tutsi rights. The assassination of President Mechior Ndadaye in 1993, and the subsequent death of his successor Cyprien Ntaryamira in the same plane crash which killed Rwandan leader Juvénal Habyarimana *(See 2.24)*, plunged Burundi into over a decade of civil war which repeated attempts at international mediation failed to halt. A peace accord was finally signed in Dar es Salaam on 16 November 2003.

By 1994, the *Conseil National pour la Défense de la Démocratie-Forces de Défense de la Démocratie* (CNDD-FDD; the CNDD being the political wing and the FDD the military) had emerged as the main group in escalating multi-factional civil strife. Later transforming itself into a registered political party, the CNDD-FDD went on to win generally peaceful parliamentary elections in 2005. CNDD-FDD leader Pierre Nkurunziza was elected President of Burundi on 19 August 1994.

In stark contrast to Rwanda, where the post-genocide government insists on refusing to recognize racial differences, the CNDD-FDD led Burundan government explicitly accepts ethnic realities. This power sharing agreement requires that there be a disproportionately high number of Tutsis in government and civil appointments, as well as formal representation for the Twa minority. The constitutional provisions allow for a top-up mechanism to rectify any ethnic imbalance should the first round of elections not produce the requisite racial mix. Against the wishes of Tutsi militants, individual Tutsi members of Hutu-majority parties count towards the Tutsi total in parliament. This has had the effect of reducing, although not eliminating, the ethnic partisanship of Burundan political parties. A South African-style Truth and Reconciliation Commission was also established to candidly examine Burundi's recent past. Finally, although measures have been put in place to increase the numbers of Hutu soldiers in the previously Tutsi-dominated Burundan army, a tacit arrangement exists whereby Tutsis will preserve their majority at senior level, thereby giving Tutsis confidence that, in the last resort, their equal position in society as whole can be defended by armed force.

Despite much political progress since the formal end of the civil war, political problems continue. The CNDD-

FDD won a largely fair general election in 2005, but has since used state institutions to maintain and consolidate its hold on power. Relations with Rwanda have deteriorated, not least because Kigali sees the partial success of Burundi's openly racially based power-sharing arrangement as an implied threat to its own 'colour blind' policy, which in reality has been used to extend Tutsi control of the government.

On the positive side, over 21,000 former combatants have been demobilized since 2004. Burundi's judicial system has, however, proven largely incapable of meeting the admittedly considerable challenges placed upon it. Burundi has also been criticised internationally for the high numbers of child soldiers employed both by state forces and by other combatants. Internally, Burundi faces problems of widespread corruption, continuiong clashes with rebel factions, and lack of press freedom. It has also been accused of forcibly repatriating refugees from Rwanda in violation of international standards. Despite these limitations, a return to the widespread violence of the past appears unlikely.

### The Tutsi – a 'tribe' or not?

When European explorers and colonists arrived in the Great Lakes region of Africa they discovered in the Tutsi an elite ruling class of cattle owners and warriors. The Tutsi evidently made a positive impression on their visitors, with some early anthropologists going so far as to proclaim them to be one of the 'lost tribes' descended from Ham, Noah's son in the Bible. (Seeking lost Biblical tribes gave rise to the largely discarded general term 'Hamitic' for Afro-Asiatic population groups in northern Africa.)

Controversy exists as to whether the Tutsis, who share a common language, religion and overall culture with their Hutu neighbours, are a 'genuine' ethnic group or merely a social caste whose position was codified and consolidated by colonialism. The 'average' Tutsi is tall, thin, light skinned and with a long, thin nose. Physiologically, this would suggest a Nilotic origin for the Tutsis and a Bantu origin for the Hutu. But interbreeding and individual variations in physiognomy mean that such stereotypes are not reliable. Similarly, while traditionally the Tutsis were cattle owning (whereas the Hutu were agriculturalists) the relationship between the two is complicated by the fact that it was apparently possible for a Hutu to 'become' a Tutsi by acquiring ten or more head of cattle.

The area that now comprises Rwanda and Burundi came under German colonial influence towards the end of the 19th century. The Germans maintained a form of indirect rule that consolidated the Tutsi position as the local overlords over the majority Hutu population; the Tutsi, needless to say, were not adverse to the status this policy accorded them. (It is somewhat ironic that the Tutsi-dominated government in Rwanda is now among the loudest proponents of the 'tribalism is the creation of colonialism' theory.) From 1916, when the Belgians occupied the region, identity cards classified people into Hutu, Tutsi or Twa. Eighty years later, similar national identity cards were used by Hutu extremists to identify Rwandan Tutsis for extermination in the 1994 genocide.

In reality, whether the Tutsi are a 'genetic' ethnicity or one created out of historical class divisions, while doubtless of interest to academics, is entirely irrelevant to the situation on the ground. Distinctive groups of Tutsis (populations recognized as such both by the Tutsi themselves and their neighbours) exist in Rwanda, Burundi, Uganda and Congo. In whichever community they live, they comprise a small and often resented minority. At various times in Rwanda, Congo and Burundi, politicians have used the 'Tutsi problem' to whip up local resentment, while conflict between Hutus and Tutsis has flared into all-out slaughter in 1959, 1963, 1970, 1972, 1988, 1994 and 2007. Clearly, whether the Tutsis are a 'real' ethnic minority or not matters little to the perpetrators of violence, or to their victims.

# Democratic Republic of Congo

**Principal protagonists**

Government of DRC, supported by Angolan and Zimbabwean (and Namibian) forces. Heavy UN involvement (MONUC).

Mainly Tutsi rebel/opposition groups, historically backed by Uganda (*Mouvement pour la liberation du Congo* [MLC]) and Rwanda (*Rassemblement congolais pour la democratie* [RCD]).

Hutu factions, including refugees from 1994 Rwandan fighting.

Past secessionist conflicts, including Katanga (1960-3) and South Kasai (1960-2).

**Nature of conflict**

Regional general war, characterized by outside intervention in pursuit of commercial/political advantage. Ethnic underpinnings to conflict, particularly in relationships between Tutsi and other groups.

- 3.8 million..
- 400,000 still in exile in 2007.
- Huge reserves of gold, copper, cobalt and other resources. Total value estimated at US $24 trillion.

**Population/ethnic composition**

62.66 million. Luba 18%, Kongo 16.1%, Mongo 13.5%, numerous others. No accurate figures exist for Tutsi/Hutu populations.

**Territorial extent**

Democratic Republic of Congo: 2,344,858 km².

**Timeline**

1 Jul 1885: Congo Free State formally established.
15 Nov 1908: Annexed by Belgian state.
1 Jul 1960: Independence from Belgium.
(Continued overleaf.)

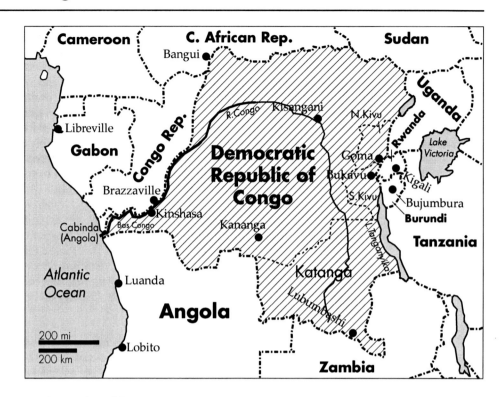

**Christened "Africa's First World War" the conflict in Congo (formerly Zaïre) which raged from 1996-2002 has been one of the most destructive, both in terms of human life and infrastructural damage, since 1945.**

An entirely artificial construct of the Scramble for Africa in the late 19th century, Congo was unusual in that was initially the personal fiefdom of one man – Leopold, King of the Belgians. The excesses of his 'Congo Free State' eventually prompted international outrage, and obliged the Belgian state to take control of the massive territory in 1908. Congo has huge mineral and other resources. The ongoing tragedy for the peoples of the region is that this wealth has always been exploited for the benefit or others, be they external colonizers or internal despots.

Home to over 250 different peoples, Congo has unsurprisingly failed to establish genuine national unity. Granted precipitate independence in June 1960, Congo immediately faced a challenge to its territorial integrity through the secession, in July 1960, of copper-rich Katanga, a move backed by Belgian and other Western commercial interests. Although the Katangese secession was quelled in 1963 (largely by the intervention of UN 'peacekeepers') further insurrections flared throughout the 1960s and 1970s (including an attempt to set up a breakaway state in South Kasai province) and as recently as 1995 Katangese politicians made a formal appeal that Katanga be allowed to secede on the grounds of its 'right to self-determination'. With a population of around 4 million, Katanga is home to the politically active Bemba and other peoples who have closer ethnic links to kin in Zambia than to the rest of Congo.

In 1965 Lieutenant-General Mobutu Sese Seko seized power and, in an Africanization process, later renamed the country (and the eponymous river) 'Zaïre'. Mobuto soon acquired a reputation for personal financial aggrandisement extraordinary even by the standards of other African dictatorships. But in the post-Cold War environment, the geopolitical imperative (for the West) of keeping anti-Communist leaders like Mobutu in power, regardless of domestic incompetence, repression or kleptomania, evaporated. With the health of its leader also failing, the Zaïrean state itself had all but collapsed as a functional entity by the mid 1990s. Regional and ethnic power-politics now intervened to fill the vacuum. For Rwanda and its (then) Ugandan ally, a key aim was the elimination of ex-Rwandan Hutu militia groups, members of which had been responsible for the 1994 Rwandan genocide, from their bases in eastern Zaïre. *(See 2.24.)* A secondary aim was to provide support to local Tutsi populations (locally known as Banyamulenge) living mainly in South Kivu province, who were under pressure from Hutu and other Zaïrean groups. (As in other parts of the Great Lakes region, the Tutsis are resented by other groups for their 'clanishness', entrepreneurial success and alleged snobbery.) In November 1996 the Zaïrean government issued an edict demanding that all Tutsis leave Zaïre on penalty of death. Instead, backed by Rwanda, Uganda and Burundi, they rose in rebellion. By 16 May 1997, the Tutsi rebels and their backers were in Kinshasa, and the Mobuto regime fell, replaced by a new government headed by Laurent Kabila.

Buoyed by this rapid success, Kampala and Kigali seized the opportunity for an all-out resource grab in the newly re-named Democratic Republic of Congo. Both established proxy forces, Uganda the *Mouvement pour la liberation du Congo* (MLC) and Rwanda the *Rassemblement congolais pour la democratie* (RCD). As an unintended consequence, this rivalry over the spoils of war was to shatter the formerly close political and military relationship between Uganda and Rwanda. Some indication of the relative weakness of the Congo state by this time may be judged from the fact that by the end of 1998, either directly or through its RCD surrogate, tiny Rwanda controlled a territory approximately fifty times its own national area.

The Rwandan/Ugandan intervention was deeply resented by Congolese as a whole and this in turn contributed to the instability of the new Kinshasa regime, which quickly sought alternative allies. These were swift to offer themselves: The Angolan MPLA-PT regime saw both the opportunity to eliminate any vestigial Congolese rear-bases controlled by UNITA rebels and the chance for profit. Robert Mugabe's Zimbabwe similarly saw the potential for unfettered economic exploitation of the collapsed Congo state. Namibia also joined the renewed conflict, albeit on a minor scale. By 1998 the Kinshasa government was essentially the puppet of Angolan and Zimbabwean military and commercial interests.

On 26 July 1998, the Congolese government demanded the withdrawal of Rwandan and other foreign troops, immediately precipitating a second Congolese war. During this conflict, local ethnic militia, collectively known as Mai-Mai, were formed (mostly in North and South Kivu) to fight the Banyamulenge and their allies. The war raged unchecked until a ceasefire proposal of 1999 agreed a *de facto* partition of the country between Angolan/Zimbabwean/Kinshasa and Rwandan (RCD)/Ugandan (MLC)/Burundan spheres of influence.

In January 2001 Laurent Kabila was assassinated, apparently in a failed coup attempt, the motives for which remain unclear. He was succeeded by his son, Joseph, who continued his father's policy of close alliance with Harare and Luanda.

The 1999 ceasefire was never fully implemented and fighting continued until a South African brokered Inter Congolese Dialogue in 2002 produced a 'Global and Inclusive Act on Transition' paving the way for the restoration of functional state institutions. As part of this process, which involved the withdrawal of Rwandan and Ugandan forces and an ambitious schedule of voter registration and preparations for elections, Congo was effectively placed under UN trusteeship, the *Mission de l'Organisation des Nations-Unies au Congo* (MONUC) becoming, with 17,000 deployed military personnel, the largest UN operation in the world.

Successful elections took place in August 2006, which were won by a coalition supporting the incumbent, Joseph Kabila. The runner up, with 42% of the vote, was Jean-Pierre Bemba of the MLC. Although the smooth progression of the election allowed the next steps in the creation of national institutions to proceed, it did highlight significant regional tensions. Kabila polled well in the largely Swahili-speaking east of the country, whereas Bemba's vote, very low in the east, was much higher in the mostly Lingala-speaking western regions (which include the capital, Kinshasa). In the immediate aftermath of the election, fierce clashes, including the use of heavy weaponry, broke out in Kinshasa between the army and supporters of the MLC, forcing Bemba to flee the country. (He was later arrested in Belgium for alleged war crimes relating to his involvement in the civil conflict in the Central African Republic. *[See 2.16.]*) In March 2008 a hundred people were killed in Bas Congo region as government forces fought with supporters of the Kongo ethno-cultural *Bundu dia Kongo* movement, which was subsequently banned. Meanwhile, a vicious triangular conflict between the Congolese army, Banyamulenge rebels and ex-Rwandan Hutu factions continues, especially in the North Kivu region from which 400,000 refugees fled in 2007 alone. In general, any meaningful identification between the Congolese citizen and the state remains an unfulfilled aspiration.

---

**Timeline** *(continued from previous page).*
11 Jul 1960-14 Jan 1963: Katangese secession.
8 Aug 1960-Jul 1962: South Kasai secession.
24 Nov 1065: Mobutu Sese Seko seizes power.
27 Oct 1971: Country renamed 'Republic of Zaïre'.
Jul 1994: Following Rwandan civil war, up to 2 million Hutus flee Rwanda to camps in Zaïre.
Nov 1996: Start of first Congo war.
17 May 1997: Renamed Democratic Republic of the Congo at conclusion of first Congo war.
2 Aug 1998: Start of second Congo war.
17 Dec 2002: Peace agreement ends second Congo war.

**Current status**
Unstable. Factional and inter-ethnic conflict continues.

# Uganda

**Principal protagonists**

Government of Uganda.

Mainly Acholi Lord's Resistance Army.

(See Kenya's Kalashnikov Economy, 2.62, for commentary on ethnic banditry in Uganda/Kenya border region.)

**Nature of conflict**

Regional insurgency.

☠ 12,000.
🚶 2m, including IDPs at peak of LRA insurgency in 2002.

**Population/ethnic composition**

27.6m. Baganda 18.1%, Ankole 10.7%, Basoga 8.2%, Acholi 4.4%.

**Territorial extent**

Primarily northern regions of Uganda, c80,000 km². (Total Uganda area: 236,040 km².)

**Timeline**

9 Oct 1962: Uganda independent from Britain.
15 Apr 1966: Milton Obote takes power.
25 Jan 1971: Obote deposed by Idi Amin.
13 Apr 1979: Amin deposed.
17 Dec 1980: Obote becomes President for second time.
27 Jul 1985: Obote deposed by Tito Okelo.
29 Jan 1986: National Resistance Movement takes power.
1986: Acholi insurgency. Holy Spirit Movement formed.
1987: Lord's Resistance Army formed.
March 1991: Major government offensive against LRA; 'Arrow Groups' created.
24 Jul 1993: Traditional kingdoms restored (except Ankole).
2001-4: Height of Lord's Resistance Army insurgency.
14 July 2006: Negotiations commence between LRA and Ugandan government.

**Current status**

Unresolved. Negotiations continue against a background of low-level violence.

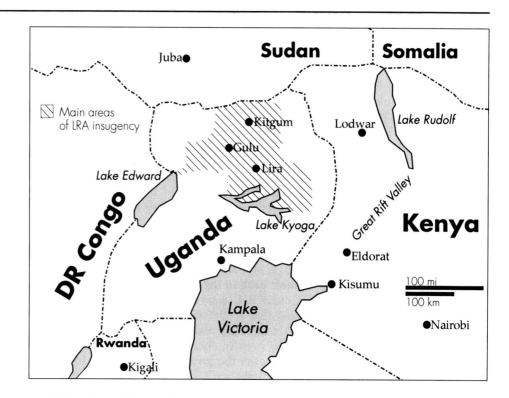

**In Africa, the soldiers of defeated regimes and insurgencies rarely fade away. Frequently, both they, and their armaments, are re-cycled in later conflicts. Uganda, with a history of civil strife and proximity to neighbours whose conflicts have spilled over into her territory, is awash with arms.**

The roots of the current conflict in Uganda may be traced to the rivalry between northerners, particularly the Acholi people, and rulers or movements from other parts of the country. Following the ousting of the dictator Idi Amin in 1979, Uganda saw the return (after a succession of short-term presidencies) of its previous ruler, Milton Obote, an Acholi. Although less flamboyant than Amin, Obote's regime was no less tyrannical. In 1985, Obote was deposed by another Acholi, Tito Okelo, who himself fell a year later to the present incumbent, Yoweri Museveni and his National Resistance Movement/Army (NRA). The NRA largely drew its support from the south-west of the country.

Obote's defeated army, the Uganda National Liberation Army (UNLA) retreated into its northern heartland, where the Acholi people feared retribution from the NRA for the excesses of previous Acholi-led regimes. Fighting continued between the Uganda People's Democratic Army (the successor to the UNLA) and the NRA throughout 1986. In the same year, an Acholi spirit medium called Alice Auma started receiving messages from a spirit called 'Lakwena' ('messenger') who called upon her to form a 'Holy Spirit Movement' (HSM), which would redeem the Acholi people (and incidentally take political power). After initial successes, the Holy Spirit Mobile Units' guerrillas overstretched themselves in their advance on Kampala. HSM warriors were assured they were immune from gunfire, but the artillery of the new Ugandan army cruelly disabused them of this belief. Discredited, Auma/Lakwena was accused of being a witch and forced to flee to Kenya, where she died early in 2007.

The mantle of 'Lakwena' now transferred itself to another Acholi spiritual leader, Joseph Kony, who combined syncretic Acholi beliefs with fundamentalist Christianity and a practical basis in guerrilla tactics inherited from the UPDA. Kony developed an eclectic theological base for his new "Lord's Resistance Army". Dissatisfied with the traditional ten Christian commandments, he introduced twenty. This eccentric mix of edicts included, for example, the requirement that all men have the correct number of testicles (two, fortunately).

The LRA initially gained appreciable support from the Acholi, despite its practice of abducting civilians for military service. The LRA was aided by the heavy-handed approach of the Museveni government in the Acholi region. In 1991, the Acholi minister responsible for ending the conflict, Betty Bigombe, initiated 'Arrow Groups' for local defence. The bows and arrows of these militia proved ineffectual against the Kalashnikovs of the LRA, but served to alienate Kony, who concluded that the Acholi people had betrayed his movement. From 1991 onwards, the LRA engaged in attacks, abductions and atrocities against the Acholi, who were, like civilian peoples in many other ethnic conflicts, caught between the rebels and the government. In 1996, still unable to halt the conflict, the government started concentrating civilians in deeply unpopular 'protected villages.' The conflict also acquired an international dimension with the Sudanese government supporting the LRA in retaliation for Kampala's support of Southern Sudanese rebels. LRA rebels also sought sanctuary in the Democratic Republic of the Congo.

In 2001 a *rapprochement* took place between Kampala and Khartoum and this, together with Ugandan disengagement from the Congo war, enabled the Ugandan army to launch 'Operation Iron Fist' against LRA bases in southern Sudan. The LRA retaliations into northern Uganda reached unparalleled levels of brutality. Only by 2004 was the level of violence significantly reduced. In 2005, the International Criminal Court (ICC) issued warrants for the arrest of Joseph Kony and several of his lieutenants for crimes against humanity.

Since July 2006 a series of meetings have been held, under the chairmanship of South Sudanese regional Vice President Riek Machar, with a view to ending the conflict. Having long argued that it was impossible to negotiate with the LRA because it has no recognizable political agenda, the LRA initially startled Ugandan government representatives with a comparatively detailed manifesto, calling for, among other features, regional autonomy and tax breaks for Acholiland. The ICC warrants have proven unhelpful in overall dispute resolution; Kony and his delegates consistently refusing to sign a peace agreement unless they were granted immunity from prosecution, an undertaking that, under modern interpretation of international law, Kampala cannot give. More recently new objections, including to Machar's chairmanship, have emerged from the LRA camp. For its part, the Uganda government has repeatedly threatened military strikes against LRA bases in Congo. Desultory talks continue.

# Mauritania

**Principal protagonists**

Beydane (Arab and Berber) racial group; Government of Islamic Republic of Mauritania.

Haratine population group.

Black Mauritanian population groups, especially in south of country.

**Nature of conflict**

Racially-based conflict centring on control of governmental patronage. Slavery an important human rights issue. Land use pressures also significant. 1989-92: regional violence between Senegalese and Mauritanian communities used as *raison d'etre* for ethnic cleansing of black Mauritanians.

☠ At least 500 civilian casualties, 1989-92.
   Up to 500 black soldiers executed by regime, 1987-9.
👥 1989-92: 120,000 refugees to Senegal. Approximately 12,000 remain.

**Population/ethnic composition**

3m. Beydane 30%, Haratines 40%, Black African 30% (mostly Wolof, Tukulor, Soninke and Fulani).

**Territorial extent**

Mauritania: 1m km².

**Timeline**

28 Nov 1960: Independence from France.
10 Jul 1978: Military coup overthrows Ould Daddah regime.
12 Dec 1984: Ould Taya seizes power.
Nov 1987: Coup attempt, allegedly by black army officers, results in purge and assassinations.
1989-92: Land use dispute with Senegal leads to ethnic cleansing of southern black groups.
Jun 2003: Coup attempt against Taya regime prompts wholesale purge of security forces.
3 Aug 2005: Coup deposes Ould Taya regime.

**Current status**

Elections held in November 2006, but issues relating to slavery remain. unresolved.

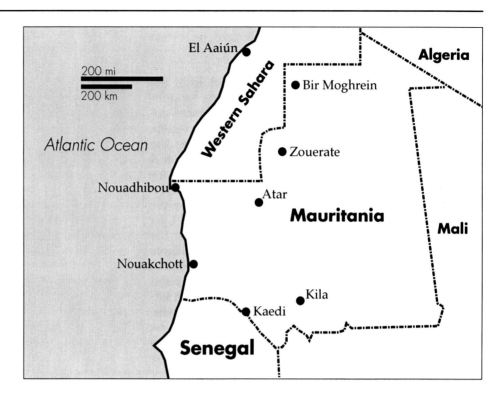

**Mauritania is a country deeply divided on racial lines, with the continuing widespread prevalence of chattel slavery and the exclusion of all but a limited ethnic clique from effective participation in government. Although the majority of the Mauritanian population professes Islam, the religion has not been a unifying factor in the country, two thirds of which is desert.**

Mauritania is divided into three main ethnic groups. The 'white Moors' or 'Beydane' are drawn from the original nomadic Arab and Berber population of the desert north of the country and identify strongly with the broader Arab world. Beydane society is hierarchical with the approximately 150 tribes linked by family alliances and divided by often deep-seated hereditary rivalries. Comprising something under one third of the population, the Beydane dominate all aspects of Mauritanian society. Beydane political hegemony has enabled past Mauritanian regimes to characterize the country as a 'Arab' one and to pursue a policy of Arabization in public life.

The second group, the largest, is the 'black Moors' or 'Haratines' who are the mixed-race descendants of enslaved black Africans, many thousands of whom remain in conditions of virtual slavery.

The third group, the 'black Mauritanians' live largely in the south of the country, along the Senegalese and Malian borders. They are drawn from the Wolof, Bambera, Fulani and Soninké peoples and total around a third of the population. The south of the country is the only truly fertile region, and sustains corn and sorghum agriculture as well as cattle herding.

The continuance of slavery is a noteworthy, although sadly far from unique, feature of Mauritanian racial politics. A feature of Mauritanian slavery is that the same family often holds slaves for several generations. Born into slavery, with no education or alternative employment opportunities, and systematically brutalized, many slaves are effectively reduced to the level of domestic animals. Religious and linguistic assimilation, as well as enforced interbreeding between black female slaves and their masters, has also tended to limit Haratine cultural autonomy. Slavery was first officially abolished (by the French) in 1905, and this was confirmed at independence in 1961. In 1981, slavery was yet again abolished, by proclamation. However, the ordinance, which granted compensation to slave holders (but not their victims) was ambiguous in that it was unclear from where the money was to be sourced, and made no provision for enforcement. In 1982, the London Anti-Slavery Society estimated that there were 400,000 people held in slavery. Although by 1994 this figure had fallen to 90,000, the vast majority of the 'freed' slaves were found to be still serving their former masters through economic or psychological dependency. Attempts by Haratine activists to attain greater civil rights have been met with outright rejection by successive Mauritanian regimes. In 2002, for example, the Action for Change party, which campaigned for greater rights both for black Mauritanians and the Haratine, was simply banned by the government.

The first post-independence government, headed by Ould Daddah, sought to keep in balance the underlying ethnic tensions within the country while retaining Beydane hegemony. However, in 1975 the Daddah regime became embroiled (with Morocco) in the occupation of Western Sahara *(See 2.34)* and this led to attacks on the country's infrastructure by Western Saharan POLISARIO guerrillas. Weakened economically and militarily, the Daddah regime fell in a bloodless military coup in 1978, after which Mauritania withdrew from its portion of Western Sahara. Mauritania did not achieve internal stability, however, until Colonel Ould Taya, then army Chief of Staff, seized power in December 1984. The Taya regime blatantly used regional, tribal and racial rivalries to maintain control.

Desertification and drought have long placed pressure on the northern Beydane communities and encouraged land use conflict with the agrarian black populations of the south. In 1989, taking advantage of a dispute with Senegal between Senegalese farmers and Mauritanian cattle herders, the Taya regime took the opportunity to deport 120,000 black Mauritanians, whose 'vacated' land was then occupied by settlers from the north. In what became a full-scale regional war, Taya also took the opportunity to purge the army of black officers (who had previously been accused of a coup attempt in 1987) and replaced them with Arab speakers. Between 300-500 black soldiers were executed, including 28 who were publicly hanged to 'celebrate' Mauritania's independence day in November 1990. Approximately 12,000 black Mauritanians remain in exile as refugees in Senegal. Black Mauritanian exiles have organized themselves into the African Liberation Forces of Mauritania (FLAM); this has thus far achieved only a limited underground presence in Mauritania.

From 2000 onwards, Taya sought increasingly to align the country, diplomatically and financially, with the Maghreb countries to its north. Mauritania withdrew from the west African regional grouping, ECOWAS, in 2000, apparently to limit black African criticism of the marginalization of the non-Arab population.

Following the 9/11 attacks on the United States, Taya sought to re-define himself as a supporter of the US against Islamic terror, even allowing a US military presence in the north of the country against alleged Islamist insurgents from Algeria.

The Taya regime ruled through a tight-knit 'grand compromise' of families and tribal factions centred on his own Smassides clan. Members of the 'compromise' – including members of Taya's own extended family – enjoyed monopolistic control of Mauritania's economic and parastatal institutions. Vast government resources were expended in either suppressing or co-opting opposition. In parcelling out control to his key allies, however, Taya made two classic mistakes. The first was that, in any system of patronage, there have to be sufficient spoils to dole out to prospective supporters. General economic failure increasingly, however, fuelled disenchantment within the inner circle. In June 2003 an unsuccessful coup attempt prompted Taya's second error: he purged elements of the very security apparatus upon which his regime's stability depended and moved elite troops, whose political reliability might be suspect, to remote areas. Following the 2003 coup attempt, opponents of Taya (particularly non-Smassides) were openly plotting against him. The officer corps, having been purged by Taya himself, was too weak and demoralized to arrest this process. In August 2005, while Taya was attending the funeral of King Fahd of Saudi Arabia, a bloodless coup was carried out by his own presidential guard, the *Battalion autonome de sécurité présidentielle* (BASEP).

Inasmuch as it removed an increasingly corrupt and incompetent regime, the coup was welcomed by many Mauritanians. The strong suspicion exists, however, that Taya was regarded as incapable of sustaining the social and political hegemony of the groups he relied on for his continued rule (and which he in turn rewarded through patronage) and was therefore simply jettisoned by members of the elite clique. In November 2006 multi-party parliamentary elections were held, followed by a Presidential election in March 2007. These were, on the face of it, positive signs for Mauritania, however the willingness and ability of the new government to address the country's underlying racial divisions will be a key test of its democratic credentials.

In August 2007, in a unanimous vote, Mauritanian parliamentarians finally agreed effective sanctions against slave owners. Slave ownership became punishable by up to ten years' imprisonment, and being an 'apologist' for slavery by two years. Anti-slavery organizations welcomed the measure, but pointed out that no reparations for former slaves were proposed and questioned how effectively the law would be applied.

# Western Sahara

**Principal protagonists**

Government of Morocco.

Saharawi people; Saharan Arab Democratic Republic/POLISARIO.

**Nature of conflict**

Long-standing self-determination issue. Invasion by Morocco, 1975. Low intensity violence since 1999.

- Illegal detentions and repression of human rights activities both in Western Sahara and Morocco reported.
- c10,000.
- 200,000 Saharawi refugees in Algeria.
- Major reserves of phosphates. Also fishing and potentially offshore oil.

**Population/ethnic composition**

Disputed (see text).

**Territorial extent**

Western Sahara: 284,000 km².

**Timeline**

1884-1904: Spanish occupy territory now known as Western Sahara.
1956: Morocco achieves independence from France.
1965: Major phosphate deposits discovered in Spanish Sahara.
18 Oct 1975: International Court of Justice confirms that self-determination for the Saharawi people should proceed.
6 Nov 1975: Morocco stages 'Green March' invasion of Spanish Sahara.
27 Feb 1976: Saharan Arab Democratic Republic proclaimed.
Aug 1979: Mauritania withdraws in favour of SADR.
1981-91: Morocco expands effective occupation of Western Sahara.
1991: Ceasefire agreed.
1999: Saharawi 'intifada' starts.
2003: 'Baker II' plan adopted.

**Current status**

Unresolved. Desultory talks continue.

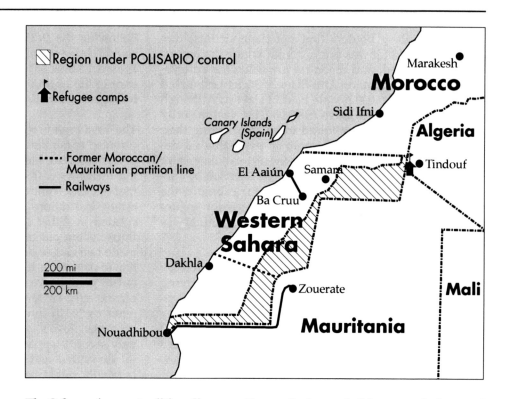

The Saharawis are a traditionally nomadic people descended from an admixture of Sanhaj Berbers, Bedouin Arabs, and Africans. Although largely absorbed by Arab culture from the 15th century onwards, the Saharawis continue to speak a distinctive Arabic dialect, Hassanlya, and practise a moderate form of Islam. Climatically, Western Sahara is hot and extremely arid, with cold offshore currents producing fog and heavy dew along the coast. Only about 5% of the land is arable.

Following their defeat of the Moroccans in 1860, the Spanish established a protectorate over Rio de Oro in 1884, and the northern part of what is now Western Sahara, Saguia el Hamra, in 1904. Interest in the fog-bound desert territory remained slight until, in 1965, massive reserves of phosphate were discovered at Ba Cruu. The tragedy of the Saharawi people is that this considerable economic asset was discovered before independence, thereby attracting the acquisitive interest not only of the Spanish metropolitan power, but the territory's neighbours.

In May 1973 the *Frente Popular Para la Liberación de la Saguia El Hamra y Rio de Oro* (POLISARIO) was founded to press for independence from Spain. Madrid sought an opinion on the status of the territory from the International Court of Justice. The ICJ, while acknowledging pre-colonial ties between Western Sahara, Morocco and Mauritania, found no grounds for denying self-determination to the Saharawi people. Despite this ruling the Spanish, Moroccans and Mauritanians signed the Madrid Accord on 13 November 1975, dividing the territory while safeguarding Spanish economic rights. A week earlier, Morocco had staged the 'Green March' – effectively an unarmed invasion by 350,000 Moroccans. The Spanish offered no resistance and withdrew completely by early 1976, leaving Western Sahara partitioned (along the old border line between Rio de Oro in the south and Saguia el Hamra) between Mauritania and Morocco. Tens of thousands of Saharawi were driven from their homes in a military campaign by Morocco which, according to the International Red Cross, included the use of napalm.

POLISARIO continued a guerrilla war against both Morocco and Mauritania, operating throughout Western Sahara and from rear bases in Algeria, which supported Saharan independence. On 27 February 1976, the Saharan Arab Democratic Republic (SADR) was formally proclaimed. Mauritania's rail link to its iron ore reserves at Zouerate proved particularly vulnerable to attack, and in 1979 Mauritania, after a domestic coup prompted by the cost of the war, recognized the SADR and withdrew from its portion of Western Sahara, which was subsequently occupied by Morocco. In November 1984 the SADR achieved a major diplomatic coup when it was recognized by the Organization of African Union in a controversial majority vote. As a consequence, Morocco withdrew from the OAU and is today the only major African territory not a member of the African Union (the OAU successor body). The SADR is recognized by over 60 countries.

From the late 1980s onwards, however, POLISARIO suffered a series of military reverses, in part because of a warming of relations between Morocco and Algeria. In a series of sweeps, Morocco progressively extended its occupation from the 'useful triangle' of the capital, El Aaiún, the town of Semara, and the phosphate mines at Ba Cruu, to take control of 80% of the territory. At over 1,000 miles long (including an extension into Morocco itself) Morocco's defensive wall (the *berm*) is the longest unbroken wall in the world. The SADR nominally administers the 'liberated territory' to the east of the wall, which is in reality only very sparsely inhabited. A UN operation, the UN Mission for a Referendum on Western Sahara (MINURSO) comprising only around 220 personnel, theoretically separates the two sides.

Around 200,000 Saharawis (the majority of them women and children) continue to live in refugee camps in the extreme south-west of Algeria, which has a 45 km long common border with Western Sahara. The refugee camps (the main four camps, or *wilaya*, are named after Western Saharan towns) are located approximately 30km from the Algerian town of Tindouf. The discipline with which the camps are run cannot disguise the extremely marginal nature of refugee life. Water supplies are inadequate and the desert is characterized locally as *hammada* – a region always extremely hot or cold.

From 1976 onwards, the UN General Assembly passed several resolutions calling for an end to the occupation of Western Sahara and re-affirming the rights of the Saharawi people to self-determination. Peace negotiations were also initiated by the Organization of African Unity. In May 1991 a UN-brokered ceasefire, the 'Settlement Plan', was agreed which envisaged a referendum on independence to be held in 1992. This poll was never held, and, with no diplomatic or military imperatives at stake, progress over the Western Saharan issue has been painfully slow. Low intensity violence resumed in September 1999 when an '*intifada*' was initiated by Saharawis living within the Moroccan-held portion of the territory.

The key stumbling blocks to a settlement continue to be the wording of any referendum to be held on the future of the territory (Morocco opposing the inclusion of any possibility of independence) and the composition of the electoral roll. The SADR continues to insist on the last Spanish census (conducted in 1974) as the basis for electoral eligibility; Morocco, which has moved 170,000 settlers into Western Sahara since 1975, demands a wider franchise, which presumably would favour an integrationist solution. In 2000, the UN published a provisional list of 86,000 voters. Morocco immediately filed appeals on behalf of 130,000 potential voters, thereby overwhelming the registration process and bringing the referendum process to a halt. In total, Morocco has attempted to add 250,000 names to the electoral roll on the basis of 'other ties' to the territory. POLISARIO, naturally, objects to their inclusion.

In 1997, the former US Secretary of State, James Baker III, was appointed UN Special Envoy, subsequent proposals being known as the 'Baker Plan.' Baker succeeded in re-activating talks between the two parties and secured agreement to resume voter identification and registration. However, his initial proposal, a 'framework agreement' envisaging a 5-year period of Saharawi autonomy followed by a referendum in which anyone who had lived in Western Sahara for a year could vote, was dismissed as wholly unacceptable by POLISARIO. The subsequent 'Baker II' plan of July 2003 set out the autonomy proposal in more detail and restricted the franchise. Baker II was accepted, albeit unenthusiastically, by POLISARIO, but rejected by Morocco. In May 2004, in a hardening of the UN position, the Security Council adopted Baker II as the basis for a political settlement, explicitly 'disallowing' Morocco's rejection of the plan. In June 2004, however, James Baker resigned and impetus was once again lost. Since 2004, the UN has also canvassed the option of a 'third way' involving autonomy within Morocco. These proposals are, naturally, supported by Morocco but vigorously opposed by POLISARIO as representing a significant retreat from the principle of self-determination for the Saharawi people.

Moroccan occupation continues to carry with it significant commercial benefits both for Rabat and its allies. Phosphate mining is carried out by the Phosboucraa corporation, in which the Spanish state holds a 35% stake. Morocco is the world's largest exporter of phosphate and, although it has declined from its 1970s peak, Ba Cruu production still accounts for 2 million tonnes out of Morocco's total production of around 21 million tonnes. The cold, fertile currents off the Saharan coast also make Western Sahara a lucrative fishing ground, accounting for half of Morocco's total catch. In May 2006 the European Union signed a fisheries deal with Morocco, the legality of which is disputed, for the exploitation, mostly by Spanish vessels, of Western Saharan waters. Offshore oil reserves may also become significant, but with little diplomatically or militarily at stake, there is little incentive for the 'international community' to move Africa's last major colonial issue towards a lasting and just solution.

# Nigeria

**Principal protagonists**

Government of Nigeria.

Muslim (mainly Hausa) community, especially in northern Nigeria.

South-east regional autonomists/separatists (mainly Igbo); Niger Delta Frontier Force; Movement for the Emancipation of the Niger Delta.

**Nature of conflict**
a) Self-determination and resource allocation issues, especially in south-east. b) Religious conflict in north.

☦ Violence against Christians especially in northern Nigeria.
☠ 15,000 since 1999.
⛽ Very significant reserves of oil.

**Population/ethnic composition**
131.8m. Yoruba 17.5%, Hausa 17.2%, Igbo (Ibo) 13.3%, Fulani 10.7%, Ijaw 10%. Numerous others. Religious mix: Christian 45.9%, Muslim 43.9%.

**Territorial extent**
Nigeria: 923,768 km².

**Timeline**
1809: Islamic caliphate of Sokoto established in what is now northern Nigeria.
1 Feb 1852: British declare a protectorate over Lagos.
1 Jan 1914: Colony and Protectorate of Nigeria established by Britain.
1 Oct 1960: Nigeria independent.
30 May 1967: Republic of Biafra declared
12 Jan 1970: Biafra suppressed.
29 May 1999: Restoration of democracy.
27 Jan 2000: Zamfara state adopts *sharia* law. Others follow.
2006: Separatist violence (aimed against oil assets) in Niger Delta region.

**Current status**
Unstable. Security situation declining in south east.

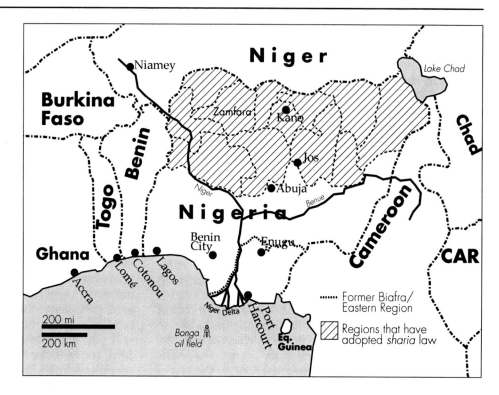

Nigeria is Africa's most populous nation, and (after South Africa) its largest economy. With over 130 million inhabitants, Nigeria is home to an enormous variety of ethnic groups speaking 395 languages and innumerable dialects. Three main ethno-linguistic groups – the Hausa, Yoruba and Igbo – predominate in the north, west, and south-east respectively of the country. Religion provides a further important line of ethnic alignment, with the largely Hausa north being predominantly Muslim. Nigeria has roughly 3% of the world's reserves of oil and is seen as a vital alternative to the Middle East as a source of supply to the West. Oil reserves are geographically concentrated in the south-east.

Nigeria has been the scene of ethnic violence during most of its history as an independent state, with regional, racial and, especially in recent years, religious divisions providing ample grounds for disharmony, particularly as they are coupled with regional disparities in wealth and resource availability.

Nigeria was segmented into Northern, Western and Eastern Regions upon independence in 1960 and a further Mid-West Region was created in 1963. Politics in the immediate post-independence era focused on tensions both between north and south, and east and west. The first significant flashpoint was over political power and the resource allocation between the relatively developed oil-rich south-east and the rest of the country. The south-east is dominated by the Igbo (Ibo) people, who, because of their general sophistication and mercantile skills, have been called 'the Jews of Africa' and, like the Jews, have been subjected to persecution as a consequence. In 1967 anti-Igbo riots in the north killed thousands. Anti-Igbo violence escalated, and on 30 May 1967 Nigeria's erstwhile Eastern Region declared itself independent as the Republic of Biafra.

The prevailing international political orthodoxy at the time was that colonized nations had the right to independence – but only within the constraints of the artificial borders created by the colonial powers. The Organization of African Union had, in 1964, declared that the African colonial borders (which had been drawn up with precious little concern for local ethnic or physical geography) could not be substantively altered. Thus Biafra – in contrast to the considerable military aid proffered to Nigeria by Britain and the Soviet bloc – received little official support in its struggle for self-determination. Only four African states, Gabon, Côte d'Ivoire, Tanzania, and Zambia (plus Haiti) broke ranks and recognized the fledgling republic.

In the absence of official recognition of Biafra's plight the eventual outcome was never seriously in doubt. However, the desperate resistance of the Biafrans, coupled with military ineptitude on the part of the Nigerians, meant that the war dragged on for three years and rapidly turned into a humanitarian disaster. For the first time in the emerging TV age scenes literally never seen before shocked the world. A massive humanitarian airlift, conducted illegally by Church and other groups and operated with great courage by mercenary pilots from the Portuguese island of São Tomé, saved many lives. Nevertheless, over a million people, the vast majority Biafran civilians, perished before Biafra was finally beaten into submission on 12 January 1970.

Nigeria has repeatedly been under military rule, with periods of civilian rule in fact representing the exception. Civilian governments have operated only from 1960-65, 1979-83 and from 1999 to the present. Formal politics in Nigeria continues to be closely aligned to race, region and religion. In addition, widespread informal and unconstitutional forms of discrimination exist against ethnic groups deemed not to be 'indigenous' to their region of residence. In addition to discrimination, overt racial violence has been a feature in many regions, since as the 2001 inter-tribal warfare in Benue state, which resulted in thousands being internally displaced, and the clashes between the Ijaw and Itsekiri in the Delta region in August 2003.

In recent years, tensions between Christians and Muslims have become a significant cause of ethnic violence. The period since the return of democracy in 1999 has been projected as one of relative stability for Nigeria. Nevertheless, over 15,000 people have died during this period, mostly in inter-religious violence between Muslims and Christians. Instances of violent oppression of Christians have become routine. In October 2001, hundreds of Christians were murdered during rioting in the city of Jos, and in 2002 over 100 people were killed in Lagos in fighting between Muslim Hausas and Yorubas. Religious violence has been frequently been fuelled by the extreme sensitivity of Nigerian Muslims towards perceived sleights. Over 200 died in rioting during controversy over the staging of the proposed Miss World Contest in Nigeria in November 2002, and a State of Emergency was declared in Plateau State after 200 were killed in clashes in Yalwa city. Further rioting occurred in 2006 after Pope Benedict XVI made remarks purportedly insulting to Muslims. Muslims in the city of Dutse, capital of Jigawa state, went on the rampage destroying the Anglican cathedral and twelve other churches. In March 2007, in a single example, a Christian teacher was beaten to death by a mob of Muslim students after allegedly 'insulting' the Koran while invigilating an exam.

In recent years, ethnic/religious tensions have crystallized around the adoption of Islamic *sharia* law by predominantly Muslim northern states. Poverty, land competition, unemployment and rising crime in the north have fuelled the *sharia* movement. 'Shariaization' started in the northwest of the country, with its adoption by Zamfara state in January 2000. By the end of 2002, a belt of 12 states across the northern portion of the country had declared *sharia* law. Outbreaks of violence in Kano and Kaduna following their adoption of *sharia* law in 2000 and 2002 respectively caused thousands of casualties. As in other countries where *sharia* law has been introduced, *sharia* in theory applies only to Muslims. However, the ability of Muslims to apply for trial under *sharia* law, where evidence from non-Muslims is effectively inadmissible, leads to manifest injustices in cases where one party is a non-Muslim.

Despite attempts by local Islamist activists, *sharia* law has not been introduced in any state with a Muslim minority. The 'Middle Belt' states are strongly Christian and have resisted Islamist pressures since independence, as have the Yoruba in the west (many of whom practice variants of traditional animist religions). The view of the openly secessionist Yoruba O'edua People's Congress is that the spread of *sharia* law is proof that Nigeria as a single entity is no longer tenable. Since the initial fervour surrounding the introduction of *sharia*, however, some of the heat appears to have gone out of the issue in recent years as its implied economic, as well as moral, benefits have failed to materialize.

The south of Nigeria is home to a particularly vigorous variant of the world's fastest growing religion, evangelical Christianity. Many in the largely Christian south are now openly questioning why their oil wealth should be shared with a north so openly hostile to their values. Regionalist sentiment has re-emerged in the south-east with a variety of activist websites calling for the 'restoration' of Biafra. A number of groups in the Niger Delta region have turned to various forms of violence in pursuit of criminal and/or secessionist objectives, including the Niger Delta Frontier Force which in October 2006 kidnapped a group of British oil workers to publicise their demands. Militants of the Movement for the Emancipation of the Niger Delta started attacking oil pipelines and installations in 2006 and in December 2007 murdered an Exxon oil worker. In January 2008, thirteen people were reported killed when gunmen attacked a police station and a hotel in Port Harcourt. High-profile kidnappings of Britons and other foreign nationals connected to the oil industry are now a major security concern in the south-east. By mid-2008, oil production in Nigeria was said to be down 25% as a result of sabotage and attacks on oil workers, and in June 2008 MEND for the first time attacked an off-shore oil installation, Shell's Bonga platform, some 80 miles off the coast. Nigerian offshore oil fields had hitherto been regarded as immune from attack, and the temporary disabling of the Bonga field, which supplies 10% of Nigeria's oil, was seen as a significant escalation of the conflict.

# Southern Cameroons

**Principal protagonists**

Government of Cameroon; Francophone population.

Anglophone Southern Cameroons population; Southern Cameroons National Council (SCNC); Liberators of Southern Cameroon People.

**Nature of conflict**

Self-determination and linguistic rights.

☠ c30.
⛏ 70% of Cameroon's natural resources, including oil reserves, are located in Southern Cameroons.

**Population/ethnic composition**

2.1m. Cameroon is home to over 200 ethnic groups; the main cleavage between Southern Cameroons and the rest of the country is on language and cultural lines. The total Cameroon population is 17.3m.

**Territorial extent**

Northwest and Southwest Provinces of the Republic of Cameroon: 42,383 km².

**Timeline**

20 Jul 1922: German colony of Kamerun partitioned between Britain and France under a League of Nations mandate.

1 Jan 1960: French Cameroun becomes independent as Republic of Cameroun.

11 Feb 1961: Southern Cameroons votes for federation with Cameroun.

1 Jun 1961: British Northern Cameroons united with Nigeria.

1 Oct 1961: British Southern Cameroons joins Republic of Cameroon to form Federal Republic of Cameroon.

2 Jun 1972: Federal structure abolished. United Republic of Cameroon formed.

31 Dec 1999: Independence of the 'Federal Republic of Southern Cameroons' proclaimed by SCNC.

**Current status**

Unresolved. Discrimination against Anglophone community continues.

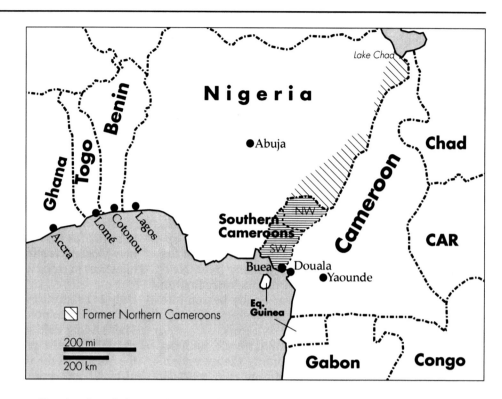

**Following her defeat at the end of the First World War, Germany's colonies were assigned to the victors as League of Nations Mandates. The former German colony of Kamerun, in West Africa, was partitioned between France, which took around four fifths of the territory, and Britain, which was awarded a relatively narrow strip contiguous with its existing Nigerian colony.**

Technically, the League of Nations Mandated territories were not colonies, but were to be ruled with the needs of the indigenous peoples uppermost. Wherever possible, moves were to be made to guide the territories towards independence. In reality, little was done on the latter (at least as regards the African mandates) until after the Second World War when the United Nations inherited the trustee mantle from the now defunct League, and sought decolonization for the remaining mandated territories.

The former French Cameroons became independent on 1 January 1960 as the Republic of Cameroun, and the question then arose of the future status of the British Cameroons. From 1954, when they were separated administratively from Nigeria, these were run as two regions, Southern Cameroons (hence the rather confusing name of the region, which is actually in the north-west of the modern Cameroon republic) and two non-contiguous regions comprising Northern Cameroons. The latter, which had a mainly Muslim population, opted in a referendum to join Nigeria. Southern Cameroons, in contrast, voted to join the newly independent Cameroun republic on the basis of federation. The new Federal Republic of Cameroon was thus created on 1 October 1961.

In 1972, however, a unitary state was imposed with the creation of United Republic of Cameroon. Although English remains nominally an official language, in practice French is predominant in politics, commerce and education, to the exclusion of the Anglophone Southern Cameroons population. Southern Cameroons separatists thus demand either the restoration of a federal structure, in which the rights of English-speaking citizens are respected, or full independence from Cameroon. Each year on the 1 October anniversary of unification with Francophone Cameroon, demonstrators gather throughout the English-speaking Southwest and Northwest provinces (the areas which formally constituted the British Southern Cameroons) to demand greater political and cultural autonomy.

Southern Cameroons nationalists consider the Republic of Cameroon to be an extension of French colonialism, and have adopted a vehemently anti-French rhetoric. In April 1993, Anglophones met to discuss means of advancing their cause at the first 'All Anglophone Conference', and the leading nationalist organization, the Southern Cameroons National Council (SCNC), emerged in the mid 1990s. In 1995 nationalists organized a local referendum in which they claimed a 99% support for independence, although the veracity of this claim cannot be confirmed. In the face of severe repression domestically, the SCNC has struggled to get its voice heard in Cameroon itself, although it staged a minor coup in December 1999 when armed members captured a regional radio station from which they broadcast a declaration of independence.

Southern Cameroons expatriate groups are active, and in 2004 a 'government in exile' was created. Some nationalists use the name 'Republic of Ambazonia' as the title of their putative independent state. Nationalists maintain that the separate historical status of the British Cameroons, allied to their Anglophone linguistic culture, mean they have an entitlement to separate decolonization. They maintain that the 1961 plebiscite, which was sponsored by the United Nations, was flawed in that it only offered the possibilities of union with Nigeria or with Cameroon and not the third option of independence.

Interestingly enough, the 'British' historical connection was itself exploited by the Cameroon government in its application to join the Commonwealth, which took place in 1995. Cameroon thus became the first Commonwealth country in which English is not the principal language of commerce and government. (The other exception is Mozambique, which also joined in 1995 and was never, even partially, part of the British Empire.)

Between 1994-6 Nigeria and Cameroon fought a localized war over the oil-rich Bakassi peninsula. In 2006 an international court ruling awarded sovereignty of the area to Cameroon, and Nigerian forces officially withdrew in August. Southern Cameroons nationalists claim the peninsula as part of their territory, and fighting broke out between the Cameroonian authorities and displaced Nigerian residents in June 2008.

Although protests continue, the potential for outright ethnic warfare in the region appears limited, not least because the government security apparatus, which is one of the most brutal in the world, is currently well able to quash dissent. However, in November 2007 a previously unknown group called the 'Liberators of Southern Cameroon' was reported as having killed 21 government troops in clashes in the Bakassi peninsula region.

# Mano River region

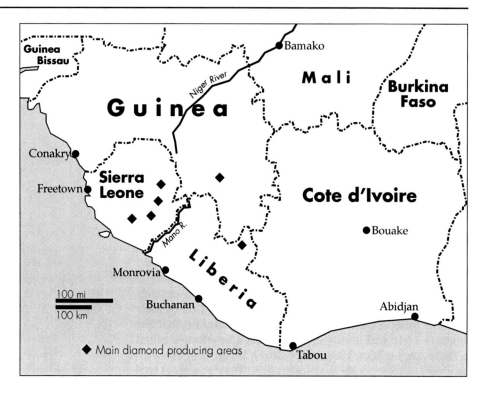

The Mano River, which forms the border between Sierra Leone and Liberia, lent its name in 1973 to the Mano River Union between the two countries. Guinea joined in 1980. The Union was expected to facilitate hydroelectricity, transport and other areas of regional co-operation. Instead, by 1990, the three countries were embroiled in a series of interlocking regional wars and rebellions of bewildering complexity. Côte d'Ivoire and Burkina Faso were also drawn into the conflict, as were powers from outside the region, most notably Nigeria, Britain and France.

As in much of Africa, party politics in West Africa has traditionally fractured along ethnic lines. This in turn has tended to mean that the governing party is drawn from a narrow ethnic base, sometimes (as in Liberia during the Americo-Liberian period) from just a few leading families.

Patronage, the ability to dispense governmental jobs, the management of natural resources, and seniority in the armed forces, has similarly encouraged familial and ethnic factionalism. For smaller ethnic groups, the only possibility of access to patronage is either to seek co-option to larger groups (which is likely to be opposed by vested interests within the ruling clique) or the violent seizure and retention of government.

The key issue for combatants in the region has been the control of Sierra Leone's extensive diamond producing areas. However, although the conflicts in West Africa in the 1990s-2000s had the control of government and thereby resources at their heart, they also, with the partial exception of Sierra Leone, had ethnic overtones. In general, the Liberian conflict appears to have a more overtly racial base than the uprisings in either Sierra Leone or Côte d'Ivoire (where religious divisions are more significant).

The power politics of Libya and its leader, Colonial Muammar Gaddafi, also have much to answer for in the region. At the time, Gaddafi maintained a strong interest in exporting his brand of revolution to the West African region. Future rebels, including Charles Taylor and Foday Sandoh, were trained by Libya, as were the leaders of Burkina Faso's revolution. Taylor's support for rebel groups in Sierra Leone created enormous hardships throughout the region, as well as encouraging the arming of Liberian rebel groups by Guinean or Sierran Leonean host governments.

Both Sierra Leone and Liberia joined the unenviable list of the world's failed states in the 1990s with no functioning central government and ineffectual intervention by regional and UN forces. Under close international supervision, both countries are now making slow progress towards normality.

*See the following sections for details of the conflicts in Liberia, Sierra Leone, Guinea and Côte d'Ivoire.*

# Liberia

**Principal protagonists**

1997-2003 Charles Taylor regime; Sierra Leonean Revolutionary United Front.

Opposition factions; Guinean government.

Nigerian-led ECOMOG intervention force.

**Nature of conflict**

Ethnically predicated civil wars over control of government and patronage, 1989-2003.

- Muslim/Christian tensions a secondary issue.
- 200,000.
- At least 500,000.
- Rubber, and proxy control of Sierra Leonean diamonds.

**Population/ethnic composition**

3.3m. Kpelle 18.9%, Bassa 13.1%, Grebo 10.3%, Gio 7.4%, Kru 6.9%, Mano 6.1%, Loma 5.3%, Kissi 3.8%, Krahn 3.7%, Americo-Liberians 2.4%.

**Territorial extent**

Republic of Liberia: 111,369 km².

**Timeline**

12 Apr 1980: Samuel Doe seizes power.
24 Dec 1989: Civil war begins with invasion by Charles Taylor's forces from Côte d'Ivoire.
10 Sep 1990: Samuel Doe murdered by Prince Johnson rebel faction.
19 Jul 1997: Charles Taylor wins election.
Apr 1999: Dissidents from Guinea stage invasion. Other incursions follow.
17 Jun 2003: Ceasefire agreed between LURD, MODEL and Taylor government.
4 Aug 2003: ECOMOG intervention in Monrovia.
11 Aug 2003: Charles Taylor steps down as President.
Dec 2003-5: Gradual political progress under UN auspices. Ellen Johnson-Sirleaf wins internationally supervised election.

**Current status**

Stable, but fragile, peace under UN supervision.

*See page 2.40 for map of Liberia.*

**Founded by freed American slaves, and becoming an independent republic in 1847, Liberia rapidly descended into a plantocracy in which the ruling Americo-Liberian clique, aping the dress codes and mannerisms of the antebellum South, lorded it over the 'aboriginals'.**

The development of the rubber industry effectively concentrated power in the hands of a few families, plus large scale American backers, most significantly the Firestone corporation. This remained the situation until 1980 when Master Sergeant Samuel Doe, from the indigenous Krahn people, staged a coup. The ministers of the previous government were shortly thereafter executed on the beach at Monrovia to the tune of 'Those were the days.' Both Côte d'Ivoire and Burkina Faso subsequently harboured grudges against the Doe regime, since the murdered President Tolbert was the son-in-law of Côte d'Ivoire President Felix Houphouet-Boigny and his widow subsequently married Captain Blaise Compaore, Burkina Faso's head of state.

Doe's regime was not an improvement on its predecessor. In 1989 Charles Taylor and his National Patriotic Front of Liberia, drawing support primarily from the Mano and Gio peoples, launched an uprising against Doe and his Krahn-dominated government. (Taylor himself is of mixed race, having had an Americo-Liberian father and an indigenous African mother.) By 1990 central authority, never very stable, had all but collapsed. In September the leader of a breakaway faction headed by Prince Yormie Johnson occupied the government quarter of Monrovia, capturing Doe in the process. Johnson then proceeded to torture the former President on video in an attempt to get him to disclose the whereabouts of the national treasury, before leaving him to bleed to death in the bathroom of the presidential mansion. (Johnson later fled to Nigeria.) Assorted peace agreements, power-sharing governments and the presence of peacekeeping troops of doubtful impartiality, failed to prevent Liberia joining the ranks of failed states in the 1990s.

In 1997 a thoroughly terrified and war-weary population voted Charles Taylor formally into office with a vote of over 70%. Taylor had campaigned under the memorable slogan "He murdered my Ma, he murdered my Pa, but I'll vote for him."

Charles Taylor targeted the mainly Muslim Mandinko population, as well as the Krahn, for particular persecution, these being the two groups most closely identified with the Doe regime. As it gained strength, the Guinean-backed Mandinko ULIMO-K group and other opposition factions reversed this process, attacking churches and persecuting Christians in the areas it controlled.

The long-term backer of the Sierra Leonean rebel Revolutionary United Front (which also on occasion acted as the surrogate for Taylor in clashes with Guinea), Monrovia nevertheless announced, in May 2000, that its troops would be joining the Economic Community of West African States Military Observer Group (ECOMOG) force attempting to keep the peace in Sierra Leone. Liberia was far from being an impartial observer to the crisis – not only was it the backer of the RUF but was, more importantly, enthusiastically committed to the continued control of illicit diamond trading that this alliance facilitated. In 1998, in the same year that Sierra Leone, previously a major diamond exporter, reported a paltry 8,500 carats export of legal diamonds, Liberia, with a supposed capacity of only 150,000 carats, nevertheless managed to export a staggering 770,000 carats. Most of these 'conflict diamonds' were in fact extracted by the RUF in Sierra Leone and routed to Liberia through middlemen in Burkina Faso. Liberia's contribution to the ECO-

MOG force did little to enhance either its credibility or effectiveness and the United Nations subsequently banned the export of diamonds from Liberia.

Taylor's regime, always chaotic, continued to face armed challenges and in 2003 full-scale war broke out once again with two new rebel groups staging attacks from the north and east of the country. Liberians United for Reconciliation and Democracy (LURD) formed from long-standing opponents of the Taylor regime and supported by Guinea and Sierra Leone, seized the northern third of the country before attacking Monrovia. This group drew its largely Muslim support base from the Krahn and Mandinko groups. MODEL (the Movement for Democracy in Liberia) split from LURD in March 2003 and, backed by Côte d'Ivoire, occupied the southern third of the country, capturing the port city of Buchanan at the end of July. MODEL was a largely Krahn group which resented the influence of the Mandinko in LURD.

A ceasefire was agreed in June and almost immediately collapsed. In early August, ECOMOG secured Monrovia, but the rest of the country remained in chaos. Under huge international pressure, Charles Taylor stepped down as president on 11 August 2003. (He was placed on trial at The Hague for war crimes in June 2007.) At the end of 2003 a UN Mission to Liberia (UNMIL) started disarming the combatants. Under UN auspices, some degree of political stability was restored and in November 2005 Ellen Johnson-Sirleaf became Africa's first elected female president after an internationally supervised election. Liberia's slow recovery continues.

# Sierra Leone

## Principal protagonists

Government of Sierra Leone; British-led UN stabilization force (UNAMSIL); anti-RUF Civil Defence Forces.

Revolutionary United Front (Liberian-backed rebel movement); Armed Forces Revolutionary Council.

Nigerian-led ECOMOG intervention force.

## Nature of conflict

Control over government/resource exploitation. Civil wars, 1991-2002.

- At least 50,000.
- 2,500,000 refugees and IDPs at height of conflict.
- Very large reserves of diamonds.

## Population/ethnic composition

5.5m. Mende 26%, Temne 24.6%, Limba 7.1%.

## Territorial extent

Republic of Sierra Leone: 71,740 km². Fighting especially concentrated in eastern diamondiferous regions.

## Timeline

1991: Revolutionary United Front (RUF) founded. Sporadic insurgency follows.
25 May 1997: AFRC coup ousts President Kabbah. RUF subsequently invited into government, which is not internationally recognized.
1998: Hundreds of thousands of refugees flee into Guinea.
Jan 1998: ECOMOG intervention. Kabbah restored to power in March.
19 May 2000: British-led United Nations Assistance Mission to Sierra Leone (UNAMSIL) intervenes.
18 Jan 2002: Official end to conflict.
May 2002: Tejan Kabbah re-elected.

## Current status

Gradual re-construction since 2002.

*See 2.40 for map of Sierra Leone.*

**Prior to the 1990s, ethnic division within Sierra Leone traditionally focused on the rivalry between a northern group of peoples, the Temne and their allies the Limba, who together comprise around 30% of the total population, and a southern group, the Mende and their allies the Serbro, Kissi and Gola peoples.**

The Temne have a reputation for a strong if somewhat humourless work ethic, such that they have attracted the nickname 'the Germans' from other Sierra Leoneans. The small but influential Krio (Creole) population of 60,000 is descended from the former freed slaves who established Sierra Leone under British tutelage in the 19th century. They are largely centred on the capital, Freetown. Krio is the second language throughout most of Sierra Leone.

As in other African countries, ethnic loyalty remained an important factor in government appointments and patronage. This inevitably led to charges of corruption and nepotism. Nevertheless, ethnicity does not appear to have been a significant initial factor in the civil wars from 1991 onwards although the Civil Defence Forces *(see below)* which emerged during the war evolved out of pre-existing tribally-based societies. Capture and control of the country's valuable diamond producing areas proved a much stronger motivation for violence.

In 1982 the *Ndogboyosoi* ('bush devil') conflict in the southern Pujehun District was fought between supporters of rival political parties. This is seen by some commentators as the genesis of the 1991-2002 war; disaffected survivors of the conflict going on to join what became the main rebel group, the Revolutionary United Front (RUF). Beyond a general pan-African rhetoric, the RUF does not appear to have had any evolved ideological or racial agenda. Led by Foday Sankoh and backed by the Taylor regime in Liberia, the RUF rarely enjoyed much genuine support. (A political successor organization, the RUF Party, polled a derisory 2.2% of the vote in the 2002 elections, gaining no parliamentary seats.)

In May 1997, a coup led by a group calling itself the Armed Forces Revolutionary Council (AFRC) seized power in Freetown, deposing President Tejan Kabbah. The proximate cause of the coup was dissatisfaction within army ranks at poor and indifferent pay, and senior officer corruption. The RUF were not directly involved in the coup. The AFRC, foolishly (as it later admitted) invited the RUF into government, thereby conceding to the RUF a legitimacy that its failure in the field did not accord it. The Kabbah government, meanwhile, decamped to a disused Chinese restaurant in Conakry, Guinea, from where it continued to enjoy international recognition.

A Nigerian-led ECOMOG (Economic Community of West African States Military Observer Group) force occupied Freetown in 1998, restoring Kabbah to power, but hundreds of thousands of refugees (including former AFRC and RUF supporters) fled to Guinea and Liberia. In the case of the latter, rebel elements among the refugee population were supported and armed by the Liberian authorities. By the end of the year RUF elements had re-infiltrated Freetown and the security situation in the capital was once against perilous. A peace agreement was signed between the RUF and President Kabbah's government in 1999, but as of mid-2001 the RUF still controlled the diamond fields in the east of the country.

The RUF acquired a reputation for viciousness extreme even by African standards. Fuelled by alcohol and drugs, RUF fighters indulged in mass rape and systematic mutilations. Entertainment included betting on the sex of a pregnant woman's child before slitting her open to discover the result. Lacking an ethnic, geographical or popular power-base, the RUF's only recourse was extreme violence, with campaigns of terror against the civilian population under titles such as 'Operation No Living Thing.'

In the absence of a functioning state, local anti-RUF self-defence units were drawn from traditional ethnically-based hunting societies. These included the *Kamajohs* (Mende) *Kapras* (Temne) *Tamaboros* (Koranko) and *Donsos* (Kono). Collectively brought together and legitimized as the Civil Defence Forces, and trained initially by Sandline (a British security/mercenary firm) and later by the British Army, these militias proved an effective counterweight to the RUF.

On 19 May 2000 the United Nations Assistance Mission to Sierra Leone (UNAMSIL), led by the British, was established. At an eventual complement of 13,000, this grew into the largest single UN peacekeeping mission in the world at the time. From mid-2000 onwards, Sierra Leone was, to all practical purposes, under British control.

Under the terms of the 7 July 1999 Lomé Peace Accord between the government and the RUF, Sankoh, who had fled to Nigeria, was allowed to return (and placed in charge of the ministry responsible for diamond exploitation). In 2000, however, the RUF again rose in revolt, capturing 500 UN peacekeepers and holding them hostage until their release was negotiated by Charles Taylor of Liberia. Sankoh was subsequently captured by an angry mob and handed over to the British, who indited him for war crimes. Sankoh died of natural causes, however, before he could be brought to trial.

On 18 January 2002 the war officially ended with the signing of a 'Declaration of the End of the War' by all parties. The RUF and other insurgents were successfully demobilized by the British, as were the Civil Defence Forces. In May 2002 Tejan Kabbah was re-elected president. By this stage the UN reported only 12,000 internally displaced persons in the country, down from a peak of 2.5 million – or half the population – in the late 1990s.

**Cross border interventions in West Africa, 1989-2004**

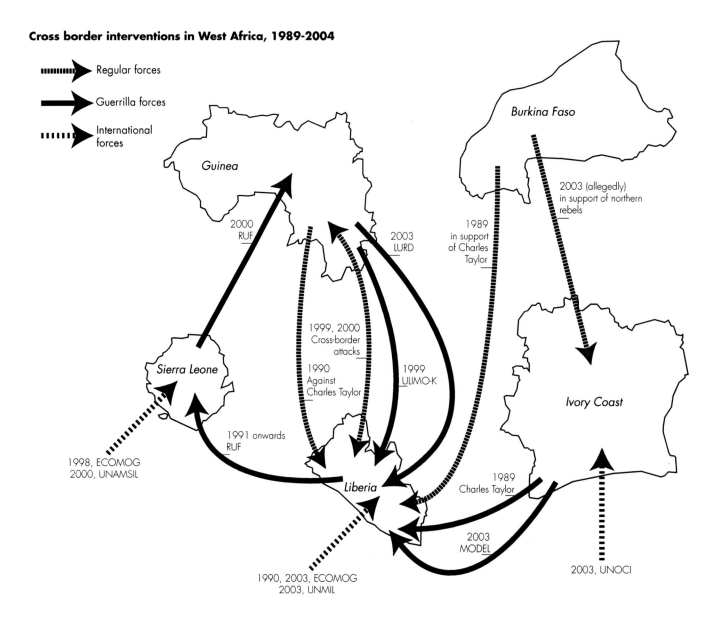

# Guinea

**Principal protagonists**

Guinean government; Guinean-backed Liberian rebels.

Liberian government (Charles Taylor regime); Revolutionary United Front (Sierra Leone).

**Nature of conflict**

Primarily refugee crisis from Liberian and Sierra Leonean (and, later, Ivoiran) conflicts. Domestic rebellion, Guinean support for Liberian factions, and consequent retaliations were also factors. 1999-2004 clashes between Guinea/Guinean-sponsored Liberian rebels, and Liberia/Liberian-sponsored Sierra Leonean rebels. Also (2004) Guinean inter-communal violence.

☠ c1,000.

👥 Up to 500,000 refugees from Liberian/Sierra Leonean conflicts. 100,000 Guinean IDPs by 2001. Up to 100,000 Guinean refugees from Côte d'Ivoire, 2003-4.

**Population/ethnic composition**

9.4m. Fulani 38.6%, Mandinko 23.2%, Susi 11%, Kissi 6%, Kpelle 4.6%.

**Territorial extent**

Primarily the south eastern regions of Guinea, notably the "Parrot's beak" area. Total Guinea area: 245,857 km².

**Timeline**

1998-2004: Massive refugee crises caused by overspill from wars in Sierra Leone, Liberia and Côte d'Ivoire.

1999-2001: Cross-border raids and incursions by Guinean and Liberian forces, and their respective allies.

2003: Liberian LURD group uses Guinea as base for invasion of Liberia.

2004: Guineans flee Côte d'Ivoire. Civil unrest in south eastern Guinea.

Post 2003: Peace agreements in Sierra Leone and Liberia allow general return of refugees.

**Current status**

Refugee issues reduced with end of wars in neighbouring countries. Possibility of domestic ethnic unrest.

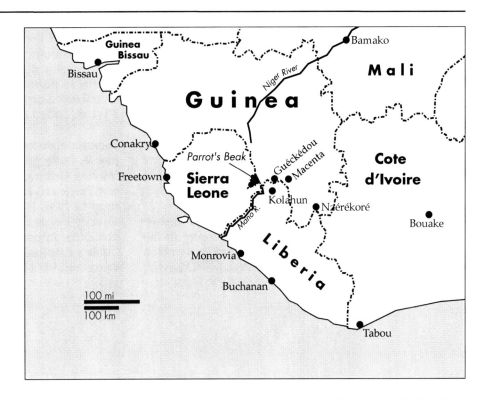

Guinea is deeply divided ethnically between the Fulani, Mandinko, Susi and numerous smaller groups. Religion, however, provides a degree of unifying force, as 85% of the population is Muslim. Perhaps for this reason, Guinea has been spared much of the direct ethnic violence that has plagued other nations of the region, most notably Liberia, but has nevertheless suffered hugely from mass refugee immigration and cross-border violence during the various interlocked West African conflicts of the 1990s-2000s. Despite significant reserves of bauxite and diamonds, Guinea generally remains poor and ill-governed with significant internal problems.

The multiple refugee crises sparked by the civil wars in Sierra Leone and Liberia (See 2.40-2.44) spilled into Guinea, placing intolerable strains on local resources particularly in the south-eastern Forest Region. By 2002 up to 500,000 refugees were in Guinea, many trapped in the Parrot's Beak region where Guinea abuts into Sierra Leone. From there they could neither return home, nor, because movement was prevented by the Guinean Army, could they move further into Guinea. Simultaneously attacked by rebels and accused by the Guinean authorities of collaboration, the state of the refugees was desperate.

Guinea also played a direct role in the Sierra Leonean and Liberian conflicts both by sponsoring rebel groups sheltering in Guinea, and by direct military intervention. Guinea supported the opponents of Charles Taylor in Liberia, thereby gaining his enmity and that of his Sierra Leonean Revolutionary United Front allies. In 1999 the Liberian government launched a series of raids into Guinea, attacking Liberian dissidents of the Joint Forces of Liberation of Liberia (JFLL) movement at Macenta. Meanwhile, Taylor's RUF allies were responsible for the re-capture of the Liberian town of Kolahun, which had been briefly taken by the JFLL.

Later in 1999, rebels of the Mandinko-based ULIMO-K faction attacked the northern Liberian town of Voinjama, Charles Taylor's regime accusing the Guineans of being behind the assault. In 2000 Liberian forces once again attacked Macenta, this time targeting ULIMO-K, launching a massive cross-border attack to dislodge the insurgents.

Throughout 2000-1 fighting between the government and Liberian-backed rebels caused over 1,000 Guinean deaths and resulted in over 100,000 Guineans being displaced. The RUF also waded in with an attack on the Guinean town of Gueckedou. The poor security situation forced the postponement of legislative elections scheduled for 2000.

By 2003 the Liberian war had again flared up, with Guinea this time lending support to the largely Muslim Liberians United for Reconciliation and Democracy movement (LURD) which attacked northern Liberia from Guinean territory.

In July 2004 there were major inter-communal disturbances between the Malinke and Guerza peoples in the south-eastern town of Nzérékoré. In related incidents, a number of LURD supporters were arrested, LURD having fallen out of favour with the Guinean authorities following accusations that it was forcibly recruiting locals. The demographic upheavals caused by the continuing presence of an estimated 10,000 refugees from Liberia, as well as 100,000 Guinean returnees fleeing the chaos in Côte d'Ivoire, added to the general tension.

The peace processes in Sierra Leone and Liberia, although fragile, have greatly diminished the refugee crisis confronting Guinea, but domestic concerns remain. The current President, Lansana Conte, seized power in a military coup in 1984. In February 2007 riots broke out between security forces and demonstrators calling for his resignation. Now in poor health and with no obvious successor, Conte's eventual demise may bring instability, with power being contested between the three main racial groups.

# Ghana

**Principal protagonists**

Dagomba people

Konkomba people

**Nature of conflict**
Primarily a land use dispute.

☠ 15,000 in 1994 'Guinea Fowl War.'.

**Population/ethnic composition**
Northern Region, 1.8m. (Dagbon Traditional Area: 650,000.) Dagomba 33%, Konkomba, 20%. Numerous others.

**Territorial extent**
Northern Region (70,384 km²) especially Dagbon Traditional Area, a region of some 13,000 km².

**Timeline**
1994: "Guinea Fowl War."
Mar 2006: Further fighting between Dagomba and Konkomba.

**Current status**
Relatively stable although underlying tensions remain.

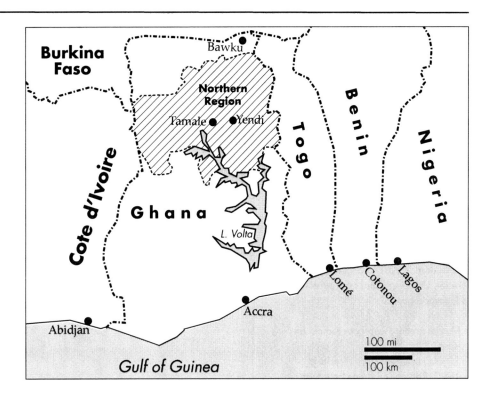

Ethnic disputes in Ghana tend to take the form of highly localized disputes over clan inheritance and land ownership issues, particularly in the north of the country. In 2001, for example, 28 people were killed in Bawku in fighting between the Kusasi and Mamprusi communities, and a further outbreak in 2008 necessitated army intervention.

A protracted dispute exists in the north of the country between the Dagomba and Konkomba peoples. This has flared into fighting on numerous occasions. In the most extensive outbreak, in 1994, 15,000 people were reported killed in violence that also embroiled other local groups, who largely aligned themselves against the Konkomba minority. The fighting, which spread throughout the eastern part of Ghana's Northern Region, was locally christened the 'Guinea Fowl War' as it allegedly arose from a dispute over the price of a guinea fowl. In addition to the death toll, several thousand Ghanians were forced to flee their homes.

The Dagomba have traditionally claimed suzerainty over the Konkomba, who have never been regarded as the owners of the land on which they have settled. An acephalous people, the Konkomba have no central authority, and this lack of a negotiating partner has made dispute resolution difficult. In March 2006 fighting between the Dagomba and Konkomba broke out in the town of Yendi, which is situated in the Dagbon Traditional Area. Twenty-eight people were reported killed in the 2006 outbreak, and the fighting became sufficiently serious for the government to declare a local state of emergency and send in troops to control the unrest.

The Konkomba are largely nomadic and are accused by other ethnic groups of being rootless bandits, despite in many cases having lived in Ghana for several generations. They claim kinship links with peoples over the Togo border, and the Togolese have been accused of supplying the Konkomba with weapons and sanctuary. Although the dispute therefore has the potential to acquire an international dimension, it is currently essentially a Ghanaian domestic issue that, although unpleasant, is unlikely to result in general regional unrest.

# Côte d'Ivoire

**Principal protagonists**

Government of Côte d'Ivoire.

*Forces Nouvelles*; northern rebel groups.

French-led United Nations Operation in Côte d'Ivoire (UNOCI).

**Nature of conflict**

Regional tensions over access to government fuelled by religious divisions and large-scale immigration. 2001-2004 insurgency by northern rebels against government. Civil disturbances in Abidjan. Clashes between UN forces and both rebels and government.

Muslim conflict with government an issue.

50,000 refugees from Liberia in 1990. Refugee/IDP numbers from 2003 civil war not reliably recorded.

**Population/ethnic composition**
18.1m. Akan 42.1%, Gur 17.6%, Northern Mandes 26.5%, Krous 11%, Southern Mandes 10%. Religious mix: Muslim 38.6%, Christian 30.4%. (70% of foreign workers are Muslim.)

**Territorial extent**
Côte d'Ivoire: 322,463 km².

**Timeline**
7 Dec 1993: Death of President Felix Houpouét-Boigny.
24 Dec 1999: Military coup.
22 Oct 2000: Laurent Gbagbo's *Front Populaire Ivoirien* (FPI) wins election.
19 Sep 2002: Uprising by northern troops triggers civil war.
Feb 2003: Riots against French and other foreign interests in Abidjan; foreigners evacuated.
Feb 2004: French-led UNOCI force mandated.

**Current status**
March 2007 peace agreement may lead to resolution.

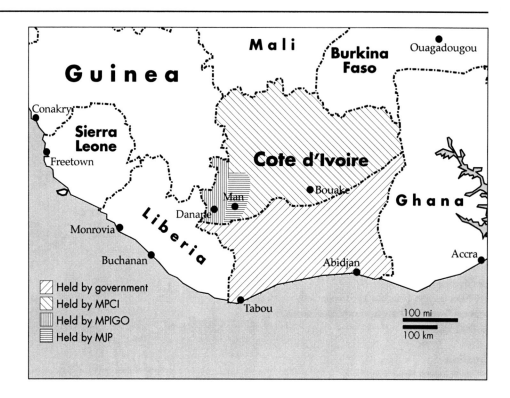

**The long rule of Cote d'Ivoire's founder-president Felix Houpouét-Boigny served to disguise both ethnic divisions in the country and underlying economic collapse. With his death in 1993, his successor, Henri Bédié, attempted less successfully to hold the country together and increasingly resorted to anti-foreigner (and religiously partisan) rhetoric to hide his government's failure to address a declining economic situation.**

The contemporary problems in the country were triggered by disputes surrounding the status of immigrants to Cote d'Ivoire, including naturalized foreigners, some of whom had in fact lived in the country for two or three generations. (Even indigenous Ivoiran migrants – called *allogene* – are viewed with suspicion by local communities.) By the mid-1990s, over a quarter of the population was of foreign origin. Burkina Faso, with 56% of the immigrants, was the main source country with many of the migrants being confined in ironically named 'Welcome Centres.' An underlying north-south division of the country along religious lines compounded these difficulties with the northerners, primarily the Dioula-speaking Mande and the Burkinabé immigrants professing Islam, whereas the southerners tend towards Roman Catholicism. Houpouét-Boigny was a Christian from the Akan group. In the west of the country, tension focuses on conflict between the Burkinabé *'etrangers'* and the local Gur people.

The term *ivoirity*, originally coined by Bédié to signify the *common* nationality of all Ivorians, rapidly acquired overtones of ethnic exclusivity from which the Burkinabé and other immigrants were implicitly excluded. In 1995, racially motivated riots, involving a number of deaths, took place at Tabou, with Burkinabé being the main victims. Increasingly open discrimination against the Burkinabé led to fears in Burkina Faso of a forced mass exodus.

At the end of 1999, Bédié was deposed in a coup by army commander General Robert Guéï, who promised elections for 2000. Immediately prior to the 2000 election legislation was enacted requiring not only individual candidates to have been born in Côte d'Ivoire but both of their parents as well. This was widely seen as aimed against the northern Muslim candidate in the presidential race, Alassane Ouattara. Following the October 2000 poll Guéï attempted a second coup against Laurent Gbagbo's *Front Popu-*

laire Ivoirien (FPI) which had triumphed in the election. This attempt failed, and the new FPI government's policies continued the xenophobic tendencies initiated by the Bédié regime.

On 19 September 2002 northern troops, apparently operating with Burkinabé support, mutinied against the government and within hours took control of the northern half of the country. (Ouattara did not benefit from the uprising; his home was destroyed and he was forced to seek refuge in the French Embassy.) On 22 September French troops stationed in the country intervened to stop the rebel advance on Abidjan. The northern party, the Muslim-dominated *Mouvement Patriotique de Côte d'Ivoire* (MPCI) did however, capture a number of northern towns and cities, most notably Bouaké, which became their *de facto* capital. The MPCI drew its racial base from among the Dioula and Senoufo peoples. Another rebel group, the *Mouvement Populaire Ivoirien du Grand Ouest* (MPIGO) appeared in late November 2002 in the west of the country. The MPIGO was ethnically based, drawing support from the Youcouba group, which has close ties to the Gio in Liberia. A third group, the *Mouvement pour la Justice et la Paix* (MJP) also emerged in the west, the MPIGO and MPJ controlling, respectively, territories around the cities of Danane and Man. In 2003 the three rebel groups forged an uneasy alliance, the *Forces Nouvelle*, antagonistic both to the Gbagbo government and foreign stabilization forces.

Serious splits then emerged between the French, who favoured a negotiated settlement, and the government of President Gbagbo, who considered the uprising to be a consequence of Burkinabé destabilization and sought a purely military solution. In February 2003 serious disturbances against French interests, and in support of President Gbagbo, took place in Abidjan by a militia calling itself the Young Patriots of Abidjan. Nevertheless, a formal end to the conflict was declared on 4 July. A French-led UN civilian protection mission, United Nations Operation in Côte d'Ivoire (UNOCI) was mandated in February 2004. On 4 November, the Ivoiran air force, allegedly employing Belarusian mercenary pilots, attacked Bouaké, hitting the French base on 8 November. The French responded by destroying much of the Ivoiran air force on the ground.

The Mande, who straddle both sides of the *de facto* partition line, are predominantly Muslim and their loyalty to the central government is doubtful. A peace agreement signed in March 2007 proposed the re-unification of the country and in April a transitional government was established with representatives from the major rival parties. As part of this process, the French agreed with local factions a December 2007 deadline for the withdrawal of foreign troops from the buffer zone. Rebel disarmament commenced in May 2008.

# The Tuareg

**Principal protagonists**

Governments of Niger and Mali.

Tuareg people. *Mouvement des Nigériens pour la justice* (MNJ). *Alliance Touareg pour le Changement (Nord Mali)* (ATNMC).

**Nature of conflict**

Autonomy issues exacerbated by pressures on land use and, more recently, by Islamic insurgents from Algeria.

☠ Several thousand, 1990-5.
💰 Niger: Significant uranium reserves.

**Population/ethnic composition**
Niger: 12,525,000. Hausa 53%, Djerma 21.2%, Tuareg 10.4%.
Mali: 11,716,800. Bambara 30%, Senufo 10.5%, Fula 9.6%, Soninke 7.4%, Malinke 6.6%, Tuareg 7%, Dogon 4.3%. Other Tuareg communities exist in Algeria, Libya and Burkina Faso.

**Territorial extent**
Primarily northern Niger and Mali. Total area of Tuareg inhabitation c2.4m km².

**Timeline**
c1000 AD: Tuareg credited with founding of Timbuktu.
1917-22: Tuareg fight a war of resistance against French colonialism.
20 Jun 1960: Mali becomes independent from France.
3 Aug 1960: Niger becomes independent from France.
1990-1995: Tuareg in armed revolt against Mali (until 1992) and Niger.
1995 onwards: Periodic outbreaks of violence continue.
2006: Tuaregs clash with Islamist groups, primarily from Algeria.
2007 onwards: rising levels of insurgency.

**Current status**
Unstable. Tuareg aspirations generally unresolved.

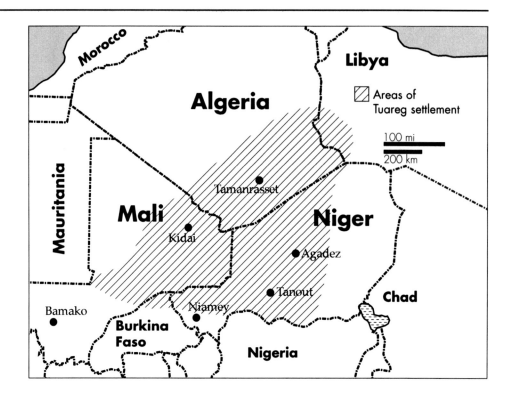

**The Tuaregs, an ancient desert people distantly related to the Egyptian and Semitic peoples, and who speak a language related to ancient Egyptian, have long had a hostile relationship with the peoples to their immediate south.**

Historically, the Tuareg, also known as the 'blue men' from their blue veils (in contrast to other Islamic societies, men wear veils, women do not) were centred on the famous city of Timbuktu, which they are credited with founding in around 1000 AD. From this base, their caravans dominated the vitally important trans-Saharan salt trade. An essentially nomadic people, their struggle for survival in an extremely harsh environment has led to an isolationism and a self-reliance that has not endeared them either to colonial administrators or to post-independence governments.

In Niger, where the majority of Tuareg live, the Tuareg are concentrated in the northern Adagez region of the country, where their settlement predates the arrival of the Arabs in the 8th century. During the colonial period, the Tuareg region was divided between the various elements of the French empire. The Tuareg vigorously resisted the French, fought a war against them in 1917, and were not entirely subdued until 1922, when Niger became a French colony.

Divided by colonial borders, the Tuareg, populations of which exist in Mali, Niger, Algeria and, in limited numbers, elsewhere in western Africa, have never in modern times had a state of their own. National governments tend to be suspicious of nomadic peoples in general and post-independence governments, especially that of Niger, have sought on occasion to mobilize racial antagonism towards the 'white' Tuareg. The Tuareg, for their part, have a history of raiding settled communities for cattle and, on occasion, slaves.

Socially, geographically, and politically isolated from the national governments' centres of power to the south, the Tuareg have found themselves increasingly marginalized. In Niger, this process was exacerbated by deliberate government discrimination including the banning of the use of Tamasheq, the Tuareg language, from public use. The Niger army is officered by Hausas, with the majority of troops being drawn from the Djerma and Songhai peoples. All these groups have traditionally been hostile to the Tuareg.

In 1990 the Tuareg rose in full scale rebellion against the Nigerien and Malian governments. Their grievances included under-representation in government, discrimination, and a lack of government interest in their concerns, which included drought and other land use pressures arising from desertification. The Tuareg of Niger have a relatively strong tradition of political organization (albeit highly factionalized) but those in Mali have generally been characterized as being less well organized. The immediate trigger for the 1990 revolt was the return of a number of Tuareg émigrés from Libya, where they had been recruited by Colonel Gaddafi into his 'Islamic Legion' for service in Libya's ongoing conflict against Chad. Periodically in the 1980s, Libyan radio broadcasts sought to incite the Tuareg in both Mali and Niger into revolt. With the resolution (in Chad's favour) of this conflict at the end of the 1980s, the Tuareg, many of whom had military training and experience, returned home.

Ceasefires, brokered by France and Algeria, led to peace agreements in 1992 and 1995 with the Malian and Nigerien governments respectively. Both agreements recognized the principal of 'cultural autonomy' for the Tuareg as well as proposing practical measures for the integration of the Tuareg into the security forces and civil service. However, the Tuareg have periodically claimed that government discrimination and indifference have continued and that the peace agreements have not been implemented. Periodic outbreaks of violence occurred throughout 1996 and a further full-scale conflict with the Nigerien government broke out in September 1997. As a result of this violence, a new timetable for the implementation of the peace accords was agreed, and the remainder of 1997 and 1998 passed relatively peacefully. In April 1999 Nigerien President Mainassara was assassinated in a coup d'etat and replaced with Major Daouda Wanke, who attempted a more conciliatory attitude towards the Tuareg.

In 2002 and 2003 fighting over the use of scarce water and grazing rights broke out between the Tuareg and Toubou in Niger and in April 2006 further clashes were reported between the Tuareg and the Malian government. In August 2006 a Tuareg group calling itself the Revolutionary Armed Forces of the Sahara kidnapped two Italian tourists in Niger. A further outbreak of fighting in the northern region of Agadez was reported in July 2007 with attacks by supporters of a new organization, the Tuareg *Mouvement des Nigériens pour la Justice* (MNJ). The Movement claims to control a large area of Agadez and to have two thousand fighters, including US-trained counter-insurgency forces who have defected from the Nigerien Army. Around 50 government soldiers were killed in clashes during 2007. In January 2008, the MNJ launched an attack on the town on Tanout, kidnapping the mayor, and in June they kidnapped (and later released) four French uranium workers during fighting that led to 17 fatalities. High-profile abductions have emerged as a conscious strategy on the part of Tuareg organizations as a means of forcing dialogue with the authorities. Meanwhile, in Mali, Tuareg guerrillas looted an army weapons store barely 150 miles from Bamoko, the nearest to the capital they have operated. (The attack was allegedly facilitated by the base's Tamasheq-speaking commander, who deserted a few days earlier.)

The 2002 defeat of Islamic fundamentalist forces in Algeria forced a number of Islamic militants south into Mali and Niger where they have sought to re-group. There have also been related allegations that Al Qaeda recruits from Algeria and West Africa are being trained at mobile bases in the Sahara. *(See Algeria, 2.06.)* These developments have brought Islamic extremists into collision with the Tuareg, who fear both unwanted Governmental attention in their activities and direct competition with the Islamists over opportunities for smuggling and general banditry. On the other hand, Tuareg antipathy to the Islamists has brought them into rare common cause both with the governments of Mali and Niger and with the United States, which has provided training support to the Malian armed forces. Tacit support has been given to the Mali-based Tuareg Democratic Alliance for Change in their attempts to dislodge Islamist fighters of the Algerian-based 'Al Qaeda in the Islamic Mahgreb'. In October 2006 fierce fighting broke out between the Democratic Alliance for Change and the Islamists near the northern town of Kidai, which had been, in May 2006, the scene of renewed Tuareg agitation against the Malian government.

The risk for the Tuareg is that the governments of Mali and Niger may use this confused situation as a pretext for a general security clamp-down, ostensibly aimed at combating Islamist activities (and thereby gaining tacit or active support from Washington) but in reality aimed at suppressing Tuareg dissent as well. On the other hand, Algeria has in the past supported the Tuareg cause, and their shared interest in suppressing the Islamists may provide the opportunity for an Algerian-brokered agreement with the Niger and Malian governments.

# Zanzibar

**Principal protagonists**

Government of Zanzibar; Government of Tanzania.

Zanzibari separatist and opposition groups. (Primarily Civic United Front.)

**Nature of conflict**

Separatist/ethnic dispute.

※ Human rights abuses by Tanzanian authorities against opposition and separatist leaders reported.
☠ 17,000 in 1964 coup.

**Population/ethnic composition**

c1m. Shiraz c60%, 'Africans', c35%.

**Territorial extent**

Zanzibar (inc. Pemba): 2,460 km².

**Timeline**

1505: Zanzibar becomes part of Portuguese empire.
1698: Zanzibar becomes part of Omani sultanate. Capital of sultanate moved from Muscat to Stone Town in 1840.
1873 onwards: Royal Navy enforces closure of slave market.
1890: Heligoland-Zanzibar treaty assigns Zanzibar to British sphere of influence.
9 Dec 1961: Tanganyika independent from Britain.
10 Dec 1963: Zanzibar independent from Britain.
12 Jan 1964: Coup overthrows the Sultan.
26 Apr 1964: Tanganyika and Zanzibar merge to form Tanzania.
28 May 1992: Civic United Front formed.
Oct 1995 poll produces narrow (and contested) victory for ruling CCM party.
Oct 2000: Multi-party elections held; results contested.
26 Jan 2001: At least 27 protesters killed by police.
30 Oct 2005: Multi-party elections held; results contested.

**Current status**

Unresolved. General political discontent continues; matters likely to come to head at next Tanzania/Zanzibar general elections.

**Zanzibar's romantic reputation and popularity as a tourist destination belie a violent past and an uncertain future.**

The racial mix on Zanzibar is complex. The majority population, collectively known as the Shiraz, although primarily black, draw a distinction between themselves and 'Africans' who are more recent immigrants from the mainland. In addition, there are small populations of Arabs, Indians and Pakistanis, immigrants from the Comoro Islands, and Zanzibaris of mixed race. Most of the population is Sunni Muslim.

Vasco da Gama's visit to the region in 1499 marked the beginning of European influence, with Zanzibar formally becoming part of the Portuguese empire in 1505. The Portuguese were displaced by the Omani sultans in 1698, who moved their capital from Muscat to Stone Town in 1840. In addition to the islands of Zanzibar and Pemba, the Omanis possessed a number of holdings on the mainland (the last of which was not officially surrendered until 1963). Indeed, the Arabic name *Zinj el Barr* – 'land of blacks' – originally referred both to the islands and the mainland holdings. The majority of Tanzania's Muslim population – about one third of the total – is to this day concentrated along the formerly Omani coastal regions.

The Omanis developed Zanzibar as a major *entrepot* for the vicious and extensive Arab slave trade throughout East Africa. The Arabs also established slave plantations on Zanzibar itself to service the profitable clove industry. From the 1870s onwards the British asserted control over the region, establishing a functioning protectorate over Zanzibar in 1896 following the Royal Navy's victory in the world's shortest war (4 minutes) which enabled the British to establish a pliant Sultan in preference to a pro-slavery claimant to the title. Although officially Omani rule was not revoked, in practice power now passed to the British Resident, whose "advice was to be sought and acted upon" on all issues relating to the good governance of the territory.

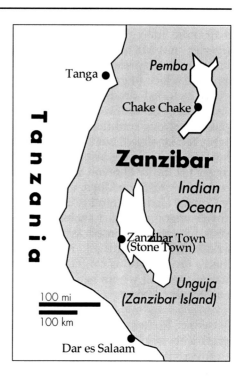

The British essentially regarded Zanzibar as an Arab state; the Sultan retained nominal power and recruitment to government and the civil service favoured the Arabs. A legislative assembly was established in 1926, but did not include Africans until 1945. The census of 1948 classified the population as Shirazi, Arabs, Indians and 'other Africans.'

In 1934 an African Association was formed among the immigrant population and this was followed five years later by the establishment of the Shiraz Association. The Arab Association and Indian Association similarly represented their population groups. In 1957 the African and Shiraz Associations merged to form the Afro-Shiraz Union (ASU) presenting a common front against both the British and the Sultan, while the Zanzibari National Party (ZNP) was formed to represent the Asian minorities. Ethnic and regional tensions within the Afro-Shiraz Union forced a split in December 1959, with a largely Shiraz party, the Zanzibar & Pemba People's Party (ZPPP) breaking away. The 'African' wing of the ASU became the Afro-Shiraz Party (ASP).

On 10 December 1963 Zanzibar became independent with the Sultan, Jamshid ibn Abdullah, as head of state and a government led by the

ZNP and its allies, including the ZPPP. This outcome was bitterly resented by the Afro-Shiraz Party, and on 12 January 1964 a violent left-wing coup was launched against the Sultan's government. (A similar coup took place on Pemba on 18 January.) The Sultan was forced into exile, and all parties other than the Afro-Shiraz Party were banned. The ASP government played up the common 'African' ancestry of all Zanzibaris, which increased tensions with many Shiraz but which was in line with the pan-African policies of Julius Nyerere's regime in Tanganyika. (It is widely accepted that Tanganyika was behind the Zanzibar coup.) In April 1964 Zanzibar and Tanganyika merged to form Tanzania. The Afro-Shiraz Party and the Tanganyika African National Union (TANU) later also merged, in 1977, to form the *Chama Cha Mapinduzi* (CCM), the party that continues to dominate Tanzanian politics. Under the terms of the Union, Zanzibar was allowed its own President and to have its own government responsible for insular affairs. Secessionist dissent continued in Zanzibar, however, to such a degree that in 1989 Nyerere felt obliged to issue an official warning that discussion of the future of the Union was not permissible.

Economic and political failure throughout Tanzania eventually forced the abandonment of one-party socialist rule in the early 1990s. In May 1992, a new political party, the Civic United Front (CUF) was formed out of a merger of two existing pressure groups. Although, as is required by Tanzania electoral law, the CUF is officially a Tanzanian-wide organization, it draws the bulk of its support from Zanzibari Muslims. It is committed to greater autonomy for Zanzibar; officially (and necessarily) its policy stops short of outright independence. In 1993, tensions increased when Zanzibar announced it was joining the Organization of Islamic Conferences. (Membership was later abandoned.)

The first multiparty elections, held in 1995, were widely regarded as flawed by international observers. The CCM officially gained 62% of the mainland vote, but on Zanzibar the CUF claimed a narrow victory. In a pattern that has become established in subsequent polls, this result was disallowed by the Zanzibari Electoral Commission, which announced a 50.2% vote in favour of the CCM incumbents.

The 2000 Tanzanian election was, especially in Zanzibar, surrounded by widespread allegations of vote-rigging, media bias and intimidation. The CUF boycotted the Zanzibari election, which Commonwealth observers described as 'a shambles'.

In January 2001 at least 27 protesters were killed by police in Zanzibar. Later in 2001, the CCM and the CUF signed a political accord aimed at reducing tensions, but with minimal results. The 2005 elections were, like the 2001 polls, chaotic, with the CUF claiming blatant rigging by the CCM to deny them victory in Zanzibar. It seems clear that the Tanzanian/Zanzibari political establishment will not permit the free election of a regime in Zanzibar which could lead to independence, and talks aimed at a longer term resolution of power-sharing arrangements floundered in April 2008.

The political atmosphere in Zanzibar remains tense and charged with racial and religious undertones. More trouble can be expected when Zanzibaris next go to the polls, especially if (as is likely) the opposition again claims to have been robbed of a fair result.

# South Africa

**Principal protagonists**

African National Congress (government of South Africa).

Potential for coercive measures to reduce White influence in commercial and land ownership. Racial tensions between Xhosa and Zulu, Indian, Coloured and regional minority groups. Violence against immigrants.

**Nature of conflict**

Resource accessibility and race relations issues.

☠ c12,000 in political violence, 1948-1994.
👥 Refugee pressure an issue. (4m Zimbabwean refugees/immigrants.)
🌱 Very significant agricultural and mineral resources; sophisticated banking and financial sector.

**Population/ethnic composition**

44m. Zulu 23.8%, Xhosa 17.6%, Pedi 9.4%, Tswana 8.2%, Sotho 7.9%, Tsonga 4.4%, Swazi 2.7%, White 9.6%, Coloured 8.9%, Asian 2.5%.

**Territorial extent**

Republic of South Africa: 1,221,037 km².

**Timeline**

7 Apr 1652: Earliest European colony (Dutch Cape Colony) established.
11 Jan-4 Jul, 1879: Zululand annexed by Britain at conclusion of Anglo-Zulu war.
11 Oct 1899-11 Apr 1902: Boer republics of Transvaal and Orange Free State annexed by Britain during Second Boer War.
31 May 1910: Independent Union of South Africa within British Empire.
4 Jun 1948: National Party elected. Start of *apartheid* era.
10 May 1994: Nelson Mandela elected President of South Africa in first full multi-racial elections.
Apr-May 2008: Widespread violence against Zimbabwean and other immigrants.

**Current status**

Ethnic tensions may surface as significant issues in the future.

Prior to the mid-1990s it is inconceivable that a volume on ethnic conflict would not need to devote a considerable section to the threat of major violence in South Africa. Following the dismantling of the *apartheid* system and elections on a full adult franchise of all races in 1994, South Africa has thus far evaded the dire predictions for race war which on occasions in its recent history seemed all too likely. After years of political and economic exclusion from the world mainstream, South Africa has rapidly regained both its continental leadership role and its status as the regional financial and economic powerhouse. Nevertheless, a number of ethnically related issues, which may flare into more serious problems in the future, should be highlighted.

South Africa was one of the first African countries to be settled in large numbers by Europeans, who initially came mainly from the Netherlands where, as 'Boers' ('farmers') they established remote autonomous communities and became the only European colonists to evolve their own language, Afrikaans. After the Napoleonic wars, the British established themselves in the Cape region and in Natal, in the north-east. Both Boers and British periodically fought wars of territorial expansion against the local Black nations, most famously the Anglo-Zulu war of 1879.

Following the Second Boer War of 1899-2, the UK annexed the Boer republics of Transvaal and Orange Free State and united them with Britain's colonies of Cape Colony and Natal. In 1910, South Africa achieved independence as a Dominion under the British crown. From the outset, race relations dominated the politics of the new state – both in terms of rivalry between Boers and British, and between White 'Europeans' and the Black population. In 1912 the African National Congress (ANC) was formed to press for political and land ownership rights for the 'native' population. (The 1913 Land Act prevented Blacks from buying land outside established Native Reserves.) The 1948 election of the National Party ushered in the era of *apartheid* – 'separate development' – and legislation designed to physically separate the races both in residency and, through the Sexual Immorality Act, in the bedroom. In the early 1960s, the ANC, having resorted to violence, saw its leaders, including Nelson Mandela, either imprisoned or exiled.

*Apartheid* was condemned for its economic inefficiencies and bureaucratic absurdities as well as its basic inhumanity, while many of the day-to-day restrictions of 'petty *apartheid*' – such as separate public toilets and travel facilities – simply served to insult and demean the majority of the population. Despite the artificial constraints imposed on society by *apartheid*, South Africa was a politically and economically freer society (for citizens of all races) than the majority of African states, but this did not disguise the basic injustices of the system. Nevertheless, a crucial distinction can be drawn between South Africa and many other African states. Even under *apartheid*, South Africa had democratic institutions – multiple political parties, a free press, a functioning civil service and a relatively free judiciary. What was denied was full access to those institutions by all citizens. To that extent, South Africa's ethnic conflict more resembled the 1960s civil rights movement in the US – i.e., a demand for inclusion in the existing civic institutions of the state – albeit on a larger scale.

Under *apartheid*, a series of homelands (the so-called 'bantustans') was created for the various Black ethnic groups. Four states – Transkei, Bophuthatswana, Ciskei and Venda – became independent under this system, but were not internationally recognized. The long term aspiration of the *apartheid* planners was a 'constellation' of ethnically predicated states, theoretically equal in status, but in which in practice the core White South African state would be pre-eminent.

Throughout the 1980s and early 1990s the tenability of *apartheid* was eroded against a background of largely cosmetic sanctions by the outside world and by domestic civil unrest. In 1990 the ANC and other militant organizations were legalized and Nelson Mandela released after 27 years of imprisonment. Mandela subsequently led the ANC to victory in South Africa's first truly multi-racial elections in 1994. The ANC has held power ever since, with Thabo Mbeki succeeding Mandela as President in 1999.

Thanks in no small measure to the moderating influence of Nelson Mandela, the ANC did not succumb to the temptations either of wholesale ethnic retribution nor of outright Marxism. Nevertheless, the post 1994 perception amongst many of South Africa's Whites – and to an extent this is shared by elements of the Coloured (mixed race) and Indian communities – is one of rapidly rising crime, corruption, and declining standards in the face of vigorous 'Affirmative Action' and official Black Economic Empowerment (BEE) programmes designed to accelerate the appointment of Blacks into all fields of commercial, academic and political life. Faced with what many regard as institutionalized racial discrimination against Whites in the fields of employment, promotion opportunities, and access to higher education, a fifth of the White population has left South Africa since 1994, taking valuable skills and commercial resources with them.

In the mid-1990s, fierce fighting between Zulus and Xhosan ANC members threatened to derail the democratization process. Although a 'compromise' was established whereby the mainly Zulu Inkarta Freedom Party retained local control over the KwaZulu-Natal province and a stake in national government, tensions persist between Xhosas and Zulus. Jacob Zuma, elected in December 2007 as president of the ANC and thus (corruption charges notwithstanding) likely to the next President of South Africa, openly played on his Zulu credentials during his populist election campaign.

The Vhavenda, in the north of South Africa, are another group to cite grievances over the protection of indigenous religious sites, intrusive mining, and traditional land ownership. The Venda homeland was one of the four to accept independence under the *apartheid* system and the Vhavenda feel they are being punished for that decision. The Coloured population continues to occupy the somewhat anomalous position they held during the *apartheid* era: strongly religious and Afrikaans-speaking, they have little in common with the secular, English-speaking ANC. The Indian population, concentrated in Durban and the east coast, continues to occupy a disproportionately large space in the commercial, legal and civil service spaces, and this may breed, as in other societies, resentment from the Black population.

The deteriorating situation in neighbouring Zimbabwe *(See 2.56)* prompted a refugee emergency that was the trigger for the most serious inter-communal violence in South Africa since 1994. Over 40 deaths and up to 70,000 displacements resulted from rioting in April 2008 that also targeted Somali, Mozambican, and other immigrants. Troops had to be deployed in Johannesburg and Cape Town, and the Western Cape province declared itself a disaster area.

In September 2006 Archbishop Desmond Tutu – a long-standing critic of *apartheid* – voiced his alarm at the direction being undertaken by the new South Africa, speaking of his fears not only at corruption but at the possibility of ethnic unrest. While in the immediate future such fears may seem over-stated, they reflect a genuine undercurrent of concern. For South Africa, longer term, the key question is whether the general pragmatism which has prevailed since 1994 will continue or be eroded by sectarian demands from groups who feel they have not sufficiently benefited from the transition to democracy.

# Zimbabwe

**Principal protagonists**

Government of Zimbabwe; ruling Zimbabwe African National Union-Patriotic Front (ZANU-PF); rural Mashona support base.

Opposition groups; urban/Matabele support base; White farming minority.

**Nature of conflict**
Manipulation of ethnic division by government for political ends.

- Widespread human rights abuses reported.
- 20,000 mostly Matabele in 1983-4; 5,000 since 2000.
- Up to 4 million, mostly to South Africa.
- Valuable commercial farming land.

**Population/ethnic composition**
12.2m. Shona 67.1%, Matabele 13%, Chewa 4.9%, White 3.5%.

**Territorial extent**
Zimbabwe: 390,757 km².

**Timeline**
11 Feb 1888: British South Africa Company annexes Matabeleland.
29 Oct 1889: British South Africa Company annexes Mashonaland.
24 Jan 1901: Matabeleland and Mashonaland united as Southern Rhodesia.
1 Oct 1923: Southern Rhodesia becomes a British Crown Colony, with internal self-government.
1 Aug 1953-31 Dec 1963: Federation of Rhodesia and Nyasaland.
11 Nov 1965: Rhodesia unilaterally declares independence.
17 Apr 1980: Internationally recognized independence as Zimbabwe.
1984-87: *Gukurahundi* campaign against Matabele.
Feb 2000: Farm occupations begin.
25 May 2006: 'Operation *Murambatsvina*' begins.
29 Jun 2008: Robert Mugabe re-elected President, in flawed election.

**Current status**
Uncertain. Probability of further political repression and violence.

In pre-colonial times the region now known as Zimbabwe was dominated by a cattle-owning elite, the Matabele (an offshoot of the Zulu nation) who claimed ascendancy over their Mashona neighbours. In the 1890s, the region came under the control of Cecil Rhodes' British South Africa Company. Formal British colonial rule was established in 1923, at which time, uniquely in a British colony, Southern Rhodesia was granted wide internal self-government, albeit on a largely White franchise. White rule continued uncontroversially until the early 1950s, when a constitutional and economic experiment, the Federation of Rhodesia and Nyasaland, sought to unite modern-day Zimbabwe, Zambia and Malawi. After the failure of the federation, Britain speedily advanced Northern Rhodesia and Nyasaland to independence (as Zambia and Malawi respectively) under Black majority governments. The Southern Rhodesian government resisted these changes, however, and on 11 November 1965, under the leadership of Ian Smith, Rhodesia unilaterally declared itself independent.

Rhodesia failed to gain official international recognition and came under increasing pressure from Black nationalist groups, who waged a bush war aimed both at Black civilians (who constituted the majority of casualties) and White Rhodesians. Two factions, the largely Mashona Zimbabwe African National Union (ZANU, later ZANU-Patriotic Front) and the largely Matabele Zimbabwe African People's Union (ZAPU) came to dominate the militant struggle. Both operated their own guerrilla forces; ZANU the Zimbabwe African National Liberation Army (ZANLA) and ZAPU the Zimbabwe People's Revolutionary Army (ZIPRA). Tensions, although publicly suppressed during the bush war, existed between these two forces throughout the conflict.

Following the failure of an internal solution in 1979, which created a Black government for the new state of Zimbabwe-Rhodesia under the leadership of the moderate Bishop Abel Muzorewa, talks under British auspices resulted in a peace settlement, the Lancaster House Agreement, and the holding of a general election in 1980. Claims of voter intimidation by ZANU were widespread, and equally widely suppressed, and ZANU's leader, Robert Mugabe, emerged as the leader of an independent Zimbabwe in February 1980.

An immediate post-independence priority for the incoming regime was the elimination of the potential Matabele political power base, the only force realistically capable of opposing the new government. As early as October 1980, Mugabe held talks with the North Korean government that resulted in an agreement that North Korea would train troops to 'combat malcontents' – an illusory threat at the time. The resulting force, Fifth Brigade, was effectively Mugabe's private army, reporting directly to him and bypassing the conventional military chain of command.

Throughout the first eighteen months of Zimbabwean independence, relations gradually soured between ZIPRA and ZANLA. Both forces, together with the Rhodesian Army, were to be incorporated into the new Zimbabwe Defence Force. However, Matabele recruits complained of lack of preferment for promotion and general ill-treatment at the hands of ZANLA cadres. Pitched battles took place between ZIPRA and ZANLA troops in November 1980 and again in February 1981, which were only quelled by the intervention of former Rhodesian forces. The violence provided the government with the pretext for a major security clampdown, particularly after the discovery of alleged ZIPRA arms caches in early 1982. From March 1983, the 3,500 ex-ZANLA troops now comprising Fifth Brigade were unleashed in Matabeleland, where they engaged in a general campaign of terrorism against the civilian population under the code-name Operation *Gukurahundi* – a Shona term which has the rough English connotation of 'sorting the wheat from the chaff.' Violence continued until 1987 when a thoroughly cowed and frightened Matabele leadership sued for peace. Under the terms of a 'Unity Accord', ZAPU leader Joshua Nkomo agreed to 'merge' ZAPU into ZANU-PF in December 1987, whereafter ZAPU disappeared as an independent political force. A general ordinance was signed granting 'pardon' to 'dissidents' who laid down their arms – but which also provided amnesty for ZANU-PF members guilty of the violence.

The elimination of ZAPU, and the 1987 constitutional amendments abolishing the 20 parliamentary seats reserved for Whites under the independence settlement, effectively rendered Zimbabwe a one party state. This situation continued until, in February 2000, Mugabe unexpectedly lost a referendum which would have further amended the constitution and that also provided for the confiscation of farming land without compensation. Land alienation had been a key issue both before and after independence. At independence, the agreed policy of 'willing seller, willing buyer' allowed the mainly White land-owning class to stall on land reform. Successful whittling down of the rights of landowners progressively enabled the government to compulsorily purchase land at the market value and, later, without effective compensation or legal recourse. The actual policy of land redistribution was mired in corruption, however, with farms being transferred to the ownership of ZANU-PF party members lacking the skills to develop their new properties. Many Zimbabweans felt frustrated at the slow pace of reform, but equally many deplored the cronyism with which land distribution was conducted. Despite widespread voter intimidation, the opposition Movement for Democratic Change (MDC) did well in the general election of June 2000, winning nearly half the contested seats, including virtually all those in Matabele-dominated areas.

Stung by his defeat in the 2000 referendum, Mugabe launched an openly racist campaign against White 'settlers' – many of whom had in fact come to Zimbabwe since independence – British 'colonialists', and their 'stooges' in the MDC. Within days of the poll defeat, 'War Veterans' (many patently too young to have seen active service) began occupying White farms in moves that the police and the courts did little to prevent. In 2005 all land was nationalized, and former owners denied legal recourse. In 2006 legislation was passed forcing banks to finance Black peasants now occupying formerly White-held farms. The inevitable result was a wholesale collapse in the farming industry, an exodus of the White farmers and other experienced entrepreneurs, and a fatal loss of confidence in the financial sector. The 2002 general election, which Mugabe won, was conducted in an atmosphere of open violence and repression.

Undeterred by international criticism, which was in any case lukewarm, Mugabe then embarked on a campaign called 'Operation *Murambatsvina*', which has been generally translated as 'taking out the trash.' This was supposedly aimed at informal traders and settlements in the towns and cities. Although not overtly ethnic in its targeting, the fact that the political opposition largely draws its support from urban areas, while Mugabe's rural Mashona power base was largely unaffected, means that the campaign had a disproportionate impact amongst urban Matabele. The campaign left whole districts in ruins, and was christened "Zimbabwe's *tsunami*". Over four million Zimbabweans have fled abroad, triggering violent rioting in South Africa. *(See 2.55).*

With Zimbabwe, once the regional breadbasket, barely able to feed itself, and hyper-inflation of over 100,000%, Zimbabweans voted in Presidential and Parliamentary elections at the end of March 2008. Despite widespread voter intimidation by ZANU-PF, the opposition MDC emerged as the largest parliamentary party, and also claimed victory in the Presidential poll. Against a background of overt violence, however, the MDC Presidential candidate, Morgan Tsvangirai, was forced to withdraw from the Presidentlal run-off, allowing Mugabe to claim victory.

# Namibia

**Principal protagonists**

Ovambo-dominated Government of Namibia; South West African People's Organization (SWAPO).

Caprivi African National Union; Caprivi Liberation Front/Army.

Rehoboth Basters.

**Nature of conflict**

Land alienation and regional self-determination issues.

☠ Up to 75,000 in Herero war (1904-7);
13,000 (1966-90); c10 in Caprivi 'uprising' (1988-9).
👥 2,500 Caprivi refugees, 1988-9
⛏ Very significant mineral reserves.

**Population/ethnic composition**

2m. Ovambo 34.4%, Coloured 14.5%, Kavangos 9.1%, Herero 5.5%, White 6%, Damara 7%, Nama 4.4%, Caprivian 4%, San/Bergdama 7%, Kwambi 3.7%, Baster 2%.

**Territorial extent**

Namibia: 825,418 km². (Rehoboth: 14,000 km²;
Caprivi Strip: 19,532 km².)

**Timeline**

7 Aug 1884: German South West Africa established.
15 Sep 1885: Rehoboth self-government recognized by Germany.
12 Jan 1904: Start of Herero uprising.
2 Oct 1904: 'Extermination order' issued against the Herero.
9 Jul 1915: Occupied by South Africa. Subsequently (1919) awarded to South Africa by Treaty of Versailles.
21 Mar 1990: Namibia independent (from South Africa) under SWAPO rule.
1998-9: Secessionist tensions in Caprivi.

**Status**

Largely peaceful, although with some underlying ethnic tensions.

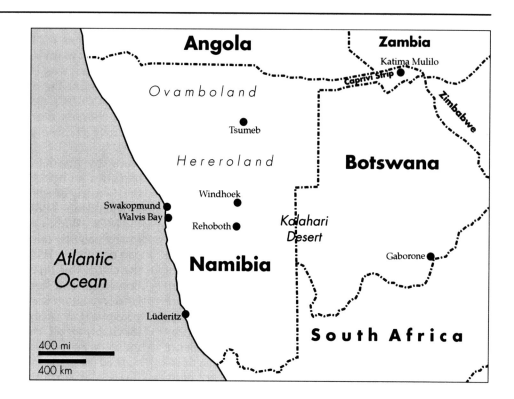

**Occupied late in the Scramble for Africa (by Germany, in 1884) Namibia (South West Africa) has had a troubled racial history. It was the scene of the first organized genocide of the 20th century: the massacre of the Herero by German forces. Under South African rule from 1919 until 1990 South West Africa/Namibia was subject to Pretoria's *apartheid* philosophy and an often brutal insurgent war. Post-independence, Namibia has been largely stable, but a number of ethnic tensions remain.**

A cattle-raising people whose language contains over a thousand words for the colour and markings of cattle, the Herero were a politically and economically advanced people with a long history of trade and interaction with European missionaries and settlers. To this day, Herero women's costumes are based on 19th century European fashions, albeit more colourful. The largest ethnic group in the region at the time, the Herero bitterly resented the German colonial view of the African populations as inferior (although it was apparently common for German officers to take the light-skinned Herero women as mistresses) and the practical effects of discrimination and illegal land confiscations. In January 1904 the Herero rose in revolt, destroying German held farms in Hereroland and killing the settlers. The uprising was joined by other tribes, such as the Nama, but not, for the most part, by the Ovambo. (Ovamboland, in the north of the territory, had barely been penetrated by Europeans at the time and indeed remained beyond the effective reach of European administration until 1916 when it was occupied by the Portuguese from Angola during the Allied invasion of German South West Africa during the First World War.)

German reinforcements failed to halt guerrilla attacks and on 2 October 1904 the German Commander in Chief, Lothar von Trotha, issued his infamous 'extermination order' under which the Hereros and their allies, regardless of gender, age, or military status, were to be expelled wholesale into the Kalahari desert and shot if they attempted to return. Over 60,000 perished and the remnants reduced to virtual slavery. The slaughter permanently altered the demography of South West Africa in which the Ovambo, rather than the Herero, were now the largest group.

In 1915, Germany South West Africa was occupied by South African forces; South Africa subsequently receiving the territory, as a League of Nations

Mandate, in 1919. In 1966 a low intensity insurgency, lead by the South West African People's Organization (SWAPO) started against South African rule and lasted until 1990, when the territory became independent as Namibia. SWAPO won the election before independence with around 60% of the vote.

Despite being declared the 'sole authentic voice of the Namibian people' by the United Nations in 1976, SWAPO was, and is, a largely Ovambo party. (It was originally called, in fact, the Ovambo People's Organization.) Under SWAPO rule, Ovambos, who comprise a third of the population overall, are in dominant positions in the government, economy and military. This has led a number of minority groups to claim discrimination.

Unlike Zimbabwe, mineral extraction rather than commercial agriculture represents the mainstay of the economy, and for this reason land redistribution has not developed into the major issue that it has become in Zimbabwe. Nevertheless, the Namibian government has applied pressure on White farmers, who owned the majority of Namibia's commercial farms. In 2003 the government demanded White farmers apologise for *apartheid*-era crimes and register land ownership history data. Perhaps significantly, the government has not supported Herero claims for compensation from Germany for the Herero massacre and the confiscation of Herero land. Herero legal claims, involving a complex use of 18th century US legislation which supporters maintain allow tort claims to be lodged in the US against non-American third parties, are being fronted by a private Herero association. The Namibian government has, in contrast, sought to maintain a 'special relationship' with Germany, encouraging the use of generous German financial and infrastructural aid. A suspicion exists among the Herero that should forcible land redistribution ever become the policy of the Namibian government, the beneficiaries, as in Zimbabwe, will be government supporters (i.e., Ovambos) rather than the historically displaced Herero and Nama populations. Political and cultural tensions exist between the Ovambo/SWAPO and the Herero, many of whom support the opposition Democratic Turnhalle Alliance (DTA).

In the post-independence period, ethnic violence has flared in the remote Caprivi Strip region, the poorest part of the country. The Caprivi Strip is a colonial creation granted to Germany to allow German South West Africa access to the upper Zambezi – which in fact proved impracticable. Throughout the 1970s and 1980s the region was heavily militarized and used by the South Africans as a base for attacks upon SWAPO insurgents in Namibia and Angola as well as for supporting the UNITA rebel movement in Angola.

The Lozi people of Caprivi are ethnically distinct from the rest of Namibia, having ties with Lozis in Zambia, where the majority of the Lozi population live. Centred in their ancestral region of Barotseland, the Zambian Lozi have long chaffed under rule from Lusaka, and the Barotseland Liberation Front has been active in pressing for autonomy or independence for the region.

After Namibian independence elements of the SWAPO government questioned the loyalty of Caprivians to the new state, noting that a majority in the region had supported the DTA. Caprivians formed the Caprivi Liberation Front/Army, which had links to the Bartoseland Liberation Front, in 1994. In 1996 the Caprivi African National Union, which had originally been formed in 1963 before merging with SWAPO in the 1960s, was revived. In clashes in 1998 some 2,500 Namibians fled to Botswana and in August 1999 a state of emergency was declared in which 600 dissidents were arrested following a number of attacks on government buildings in the Caprivian capital, Katima Mulilo. The Namibian government accused the Caprivi Liberation Army of being allies of UNITA in Angola, long-term enemies of SWAPO.

In October 2002 the Caprivi African National Union declared the independence of the 'Free State of Caprivi Strip/Itenge' at a London conference, but to little practical effect. In August 2007 ten leaders of the 1999 'uprising' received long jail sentences in a trial in Windhoek after being found guilty of treason charges.

Another group which claims it has suffered under the post-independence Namibian government are the Rehoboth Basters, a distinctive and tight-knit community south of Windhoek. The Rehoboth Basters are an Afrikaans speaking people who are descended from intermixing between Europeans and the indigenous Khoisian peoples – the name 'Baster' means 'bastard' in Afrikaans. Like other 'Coloured' communities in South Africa the Basters occupied an anomalous position in society, being accepted neither by the Afrikaner community (despite linguistic and religious affinities) nor by the Black population. In the late 19th century the Basters migrated to South West Africa where they purchased land in the Rehoboth region south of Windhoek from local tribes. (German rule had yet to be established in the region.) The Rehoboth Basters developed their own agricultural communities and system of self-government under an overall elected leader or 'Captain.' Baster autonomy was recognized both by the German colonial administration and, subsequently, by South Africa, although a degree of land alienation took place from the 1920s onwards. In July 1979 the Basters were formally granted self-government by the South African government, but this was seen by opponents of South African rule as being in the context of *apartheid* attempts to create independent Black homelands or 'bantustans.' Following Namibian independence Baster self government was perfunctorily revoked and traditional land confiscated by the new SWAPO government. The new parliamentary constituencies for Namibia also cut across Baster lands, thereby effectively denying Baster representation in parliament. These measures continue to be the basis of deep dissatisfaction and mistrust of the government among the Basters, who number some 35,000 people.

# Cabinda

**Principal protagonists**

Angolan government.

*Frente de Libertação do Enclave de Cabinda* (Various factions.)

**Nature of conflict**

Nationalist, self-determination issue. Invasion by Angolan forces with Cuban support, 1975. Sporadic insurgency, including acts of terrorism.

☠ Unknown.
⚐ 100,000 to Congo-Brazzaville reported, 1975
💰 Very significant offshore oil reserves.

**Population/ethnic composition**

300,000. Majority from the Bakongo people. The minority Mayombe live in eastern Cabinda.

**Territorial extent**

Angolan-held enclave of Cabinda: 7,283 km².

**Timeline**

1885: Kakongo kingdoms become a Portuguese protectorate under the Treaty of Simulambuco.
1963: *Frente de Libertação do Enclave de Cabinda* formed.
25 Apr 1974: Left-wing coup in Lisbon heralds dismemberment of Portuguese empire.
1 Aug 1975: Cabinda declares independence.
11 Nov 1975: Angola independent.
Nov 1975: Cabinda invaded and occupied by Angolan (MPLA) and Cuban forces.

**Current status**

Low-level insurgency continues, although largely suppressed. No likelihood of resolution.

Often dismissed as a post-colonial anomaly, Cabinda's claim to nationhood does, in fact, have a sound historical grounding. Exploring the west African coast in the 15th century, Portuguese traders and missionaries came into contact with three kingdoms, collectively known as the Kakongo, which, though nominally subject to the Bakongo kings, were effectively independent. In 1885 the Treaty of Simulambuco was concluded between the local rulers, who were anxious to secure outside protection, and the Portuguese.

Cabinda's southern border was originally the mouth of the Congo River, but this was moved north at the 1885 Congress of Berlin, thereby separating Cabinda from Angola proper and allowing the Congo Free State (as it became) access to the sea.

Although a nationalist movement, *Frente de Libertação do Enclave de Cabinda*, emerged in the early 1960s, Cabinda saw little nationalist unrest until the fall of the authoritarian Lisbon regime in 1974 heralded independence for Portugal's colonies. Cabinda's claims to separate independence were ignored both by the new Portuguese government and by Angolan nationalists. On 11 November 1975, Angola became independent and the *Movimento Popular de Libertação de Angola* movement, which went on to win Angola's civil war, invaded and occupied the territory, overthrowing the fledgling FLEC government, which had declared Cabindan independence on 1 August.

By the late 1990s, with Angolan intervention in the civil wars in both Congo-Brazzaville and the Democratic Republic of Congo, FLEC was cut off from previously supportive neighbouring countries and supply routes, forcing the insurgents into the jungle hinterland. The 2002 demise of Jonas Savimbi, leader of the Angolan rebel UNITA movement (which had sided with FLEC) brought an effective end to Angola's long-running civil war and further marginalized the Cabindans. Furthermore, with Cabinda emerging as a major supplier of oil – up to 700,000 barrels a year – Luanda found increasing common cause

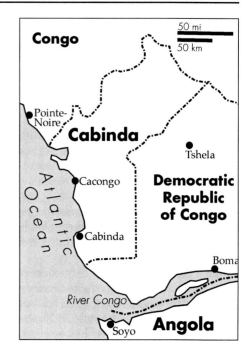

with Western oil purchasers, which removed the possibility of overseas diplomatic or material support for FLEC. Finally, FLEC itself was riven with factionalism between the FLEC-Renovata and FLEC-*Forças Armadas de Cabinda* (FLEC-FAC).

Faced with these problems, the insurgents were forced into an increasingly desperate response, including acts of banditry, urban terrorism and economic sabotage. The strained logic of the nationalist position is that, as the Treaty of Simulambuco has never been revoked, Portugal is under an obligation to intervene by temporarily taking over the territory prior to a poll on independence. In order to highlight this claim, FLEC-FAC has on occasion directed its activities against Portuguese interests, including the kidnapping of Portuguese oil workers. In 2006, Angola announced, despite evidence to the contrary, that FLEC-FAC, the more militant of the factions, was defunct. Un-coincidentally, a hitherto unknown movement, the "Cabindan Forum for Dialogue," emerged as a claimed negotiating partner with the Luanda government and a 'memorandum of understanding' was signed on 1 August 2006. FLEC-FAC denounced the Forum as having no authority to speak for the Cabindan people. Little progress appears to have been made on the issue of autonomy, which Luanda is currently under little pressure to grant.

# Kenya

**Principal protagonists**

Government of Kenya; elements of Kikuyu population.

Opposition Orange Democratic Movement; Luo and other ethnic groups

(See Kenya's Kalashnikov economy, 2.62, for commentary on ethnic banditry in the Uganda/Kenya border region.)

☠ Up t0 1,000. (c50,000 in Mau Mau uprising.)
𐂂 70,000 IDPs reported, January 2008.

**Nature of conflict**
Ethnic conflict over control of government resources and patronage.

**Population/ethnic composition**
34.7m. Kikuyu 22%, Luhya 12.4%, Luo 10.6%. Numerous others.

**Territorial extent**
Kenya: 580,367 km².

**Timeline**
20 Oct 1952-Dec 1959: Mau Mau uprising.
12 Dec 1963: Kenya independent from Britain.
1963-7: 'Shifta' war.
10 Nov 1964: Merger of KANU and KADU creates de facto one party state.
22 Aug 1978: Daniel arap Moi becomes President.
1 Aug 1982: Attempted coup by air force officers.
30 Dec 2002: Mwai Kibaki elected President.
21 Noc 2005: New constitution rejected by voters.
27 Dec 2007: General election held.
30 Dec 2007: Ethnic violence breaks out after elector commission confirms Kibaki victory.

**Current status**
Unstable. Violent clashes continue.

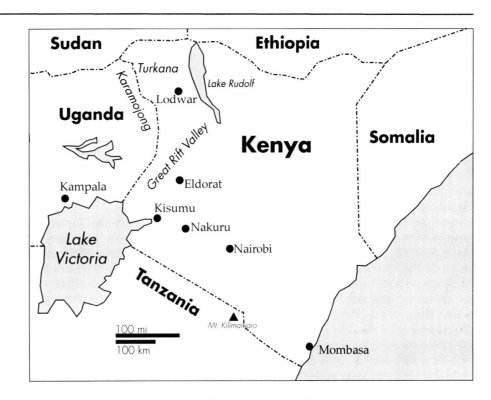

**Regarded by observers unfamiliar with its ethnic tensions as inherently stable, Kenya has a history of political violence and an undercurrent of ethnic partisanship that has marred the country's development both before and after independence. Land alienation, the dispossession of Africans in favour of European settlers, came to be a critical grievance in the late colonial period.**

As early as 1924, the collision between European commercial farmers and Kikuyu and other indigenous agriculturalists resulted in the formation of the Kikuyu Central Association, headed by Jomo Kenyatta, which later evolved into the Kenya African National Union political party. Measures introduced at the behest of the influential commercial farming lobby, such as the 'hut tax' and the banning of the production of coffee by Africans were hugely unpopular, and in the 1950s simmering discontent exploded into violence with the Mau Mau uprising.

Focusing on the Kikuyu population, Mau Mau drew upon traditional Kikuyu blood oaths to bind its supporters. The campaign was marked by atrocities on both sides and, in particular, Mau Mau attacks on non-Kikuyus and against 'traitors' who had broken their oaths. On 25 October 1952 a State of Emergency was declared. Twenty thousand regular British and African troops, backed up by the Royal Air Force, were deployed.

In countering the insurgency, the British, who viewed the uprising largely as a Kikuyu tribal disturbance, deployed a number of counter-insurgency techniques evolved during the 1948-60 Malay Emergency. Chief amongst these was the use of 'loyalist' Home Guard forces, drawn both from non-Kikuyu and from reliable or 'de-oathed' Kikuyus. The latter were organized into highly successful 'psuedo gangs' who infiltrated Mau Mau ranks, feeding back intelligence and carrying out sabotage and black propaganda functions. The British also initiated a policy of mass internment and of 'villagization': the concentration of Kikuyu populations into government-controlled settlements. Both the infiltration techniques and the fortified village strategy were used, with varying degrees of success, in later counter-insurgency wars, including by the Rhodesians and by the Americans in Vietnam.

Although militarily a victory for the British, the uprising entered Kikuyu national mythology as a great nationalist victory, and Kenya achieved independence under Jomo Kenyatta, a Kikuyu, and his Kenya African National Union (KANU) party in 1963. From 1963-7 the new state fought the '*shifta*' ('bandit') war in the Northern Frontier District against Somali irredentists demanding union with Somalia, who were defeated.

KANU was widely seen as a Kikuyu-Luo alliance, but shortly after independence, Kenyatta negotiated the 'merger' of KANU with the opposition Kenya African Democratic Union, headed by a Kalenjin, Daniel arap Moi. While this had the ostensive effect of broadening the ethnic power-base of the KANU government, it also eliminated opposition voices and resulted in a *de facto* one party state which persisted until the 1990s. Following the 1966 resignation of the Vice President, Luo chief Jaramogi Oginga Odinga, and the banning of his Kenya Peoples' Union, Luo influence in government sharply declined. Moi succeeded Kenyatta as President upon the latter's death in 1978, seeing off a challenge from the 'Kiambu Mafia' (the core group of Kikuyu beneficiaries of Kenyatta's rule). In 1982, Moi defeated a coup attempt by junior Luo officers in the air force, who allegedly had Odinga's backing. Moi remained in power, against a backdrop of economic stagnation and rising corruption, until the end of December 2002, when he was defeated in an election by Mwai Kibaki, a Kikuyu, and his National Rainbow Coalition.

Throughout the Moi period, poverty and marginalization in the Great Rift and Lake Victoria regions deepened, and the Kibaki government was seen, particularly among the slum dwellers of Nairobi and other cities, as doing little to widen economic opportunity, while at the same time being allegedly partisan towards its Kikuyu core support base.

In 2005, an attempt by the Kibaki government to introduce a new constitution was voted down by electors. Although the core issues in the new constitution surrounded Presidential power and land ownership issues, its rejection was largely a protest vote against the unpopularity of the government.

In the December 2007 general elections, Raila Odinga (son of Jaramogi Oginga Odinga) led his Orange Democratic Movement – orange having been the colour of the 'no' vote in the referendum – against Kibaki's newly created political vehicle, the Party of National Unity. Initial results showed a modest Odinga lead, but on 30 December the Kenyan Electoral Commission declared in favour of Kibaki. Within hours ethnic violence had broken out among the slum dwellers of Nairobi and rapidly spread to other cities, with violence in Nakuru, Kisumu, Odinga's home town, and Eldoret, where 50 Kikuyu, including children, were burned to death in a church. Both sides accused the other, with some justification, of inciting racial violence. On 28 February 2008 a power-sharing agreement was concluded that saw Kibaki retaim the Presidency and Odinga becoming Prime Minister, but with clashes continuing, Kenya is a salutary reminder of how rapidly underlying ethnic issues can rise violently to the surface.

### Kenya's Kalashnikov economy

The north-west region of Kenya has been nicknamed the 'Kalashnikov economy' – one in which bullets are used as currency. Cattle rustling, struggles over water accessibility, and armed banditry are regular occurrences in the semi-lawless Kenya/Uganda border country. In 2000, drought pressures in the region contributed to an attack by Karimojong warriors on Pokot pastoralists that left 60 dead, including women and children. Over 5,000 head of cattle were stolen. Such incidents, although generally smaller scale, are not uncommon; during the drought of 2006 tens of thousands of Pokot sought to move into Uganda in search of water and pasture, and clashes with the Karimojong and other groups were commonplace.

Traditionally, cattle rustling has been an almost acceptable means of wealth redistribution in times of environmental hardship as well as a means for young men to acquire the dowries required to buy a bride. However, the ready availability of assault rifles, left over from assorted wars, has given the practice a more lethal dimension. The size of inter-ethnic and cross-border raiding parties has increased to, in many cases, several hundred – totally outnumbering local security forces. Amongst the Karimojong of the remote north-eastern part of Uganda, both the state's failure to provide security and the recruitment of tribal warriors from the former Uganfa National Liberation Army has encouraged a heavily armed society. *(See 2.30.)* The Turkana people, over the border in Kenya, have similarly acquired weapons left over from fighting in Sudan and Somalia.

Security in the region has been encouraged by the creation of Local Defence Units in Uganda and Police Reservists in Kenya, but poor conditions of service and ethnic factionalism have meant that this system remains open to abuse. In 2003, for example, 600 members of the Police Reservists were disarmed in the Tana district. In May 2007 three game wardens and four alleged poachers in the region were killed in a firefight. Remoteness, severe land use pressures, and the continuing availability of small arms, are likely to see a level of ethnic violence continuing.

# Section 3: **The Americas**

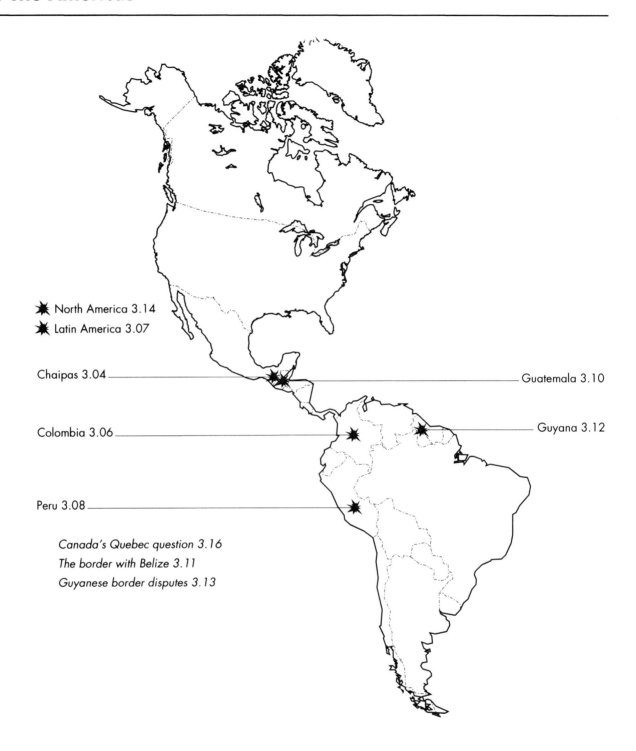

North America 3.14
Latin America 3.07

Chaipas 3.04
Colombia 3.06
Peru 3.08

Guatemala 3.10
Guyana 3.12

Canada's Quebec question 3.16
The border with Belize 3.11
Guyanese border disputes 3.13

# Latin America

Stretching from Mexico to the near-Antarctic regions of Terra del Fuego, Latin America displays a number of unifying features arising from shared history, culture and religion. Unlike Africa, which experienced highly fragmented colonization by a number of European players, Latin America (with the exception of those northern states which, in effect, form a mainland extension of the Caribbean) was divided between two blocs, Portuguese and Spanish. Moreover, the common Iberian roots of the main colonizers brought additional unifying features such as Roman Catholicism, Spanish/Portuguese as widespread common languages, and Iberian social systems of centralized government and estate-based agriculture dominated by a small number of landowners who were both wealthy and politically influential.

This Iberian economic and political heritage meant that independent Latin America experienced, for the most part, long periods of authoritarian rule (as indeed did Portugal and Spain themselves). Similarly (and again in contrast with Africa and Asia) both colonization and decolonization took place much earlier in history, for the most part being complete by the first half of the 19th century. A further common feature, albeit a negative one, is that virtually all Latin American countries have unresolved territorial claims against their neighbours. Although many of these are now dormant, disastrous wars were fought over border issues until the middle of the 20th century and as recently as 1982, Argentina and Britain went to war over the Falkland Islands.

All that being said, very considerable differences exist across the continent whether measured in terms of economic development, political participation and the rights of minorities, the nature of local conflicts, and the national ethnic mix.

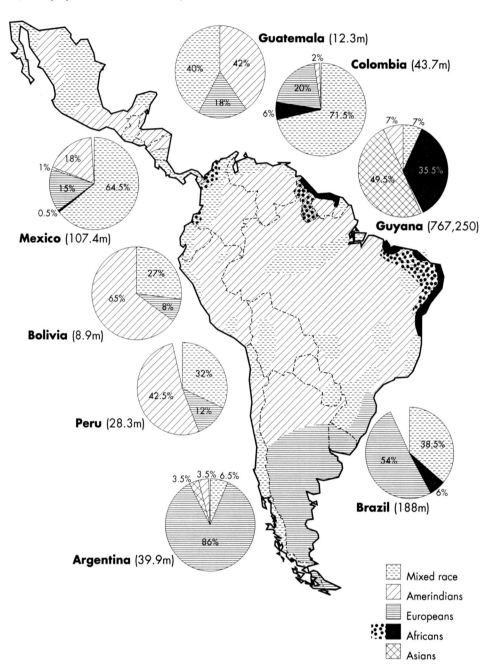

Generalized ethnic map of Latin America, with breakdown of selected countries (total population in brackets).

The underlying base population of Latin America is formed of Amerindian peoples who originally migrated from Eurasia across the Bering Straits. Never particularly numerous (estimates of the pre-colonial population suggest a total Latin American population of only 12 million) the Amerindian population was severely adversely affected by colonization through miscegenation, enslavement, disease and dispossession. Population shortages led to the very large-scale importation of African slave labour, particularly to north-eastern Brazil and the Caribbean-facing states. Today, the percentage of national populations who are 'pure' Amerindian varies widely from country to country.

A distinction also needs to be made between the advanced agrarian cultures of peoples such as the Incas, the Aztecs and the Mayans, and the primitive forest dwellers of the vast Amazonian basin, who either have no formal agriculture or who operate at a largely subsistence level. In many regions, particularly in those countries along the Caribbean/Atlantic coast, 'Bush Negroes' – the descendents of escaped (or freed) slaves who fled into the hinterland – established communities based on African cultural and agricultural models. In some areas, interbreeding between Africans and Amerindians to form 'zambo' populations is demographically significant. Guyana and Suriname, with their basically Caribbean history and outlook, form an exception to the demographic pattern in the rest of the continent, with their high East Asian populations. Asian immigrant communities, of Chinese, Japanese, and, more lately, Koreans, exist throughout the continent where they have in some cases gained economic and political importance, most notably in Peru, where the former President, Alberto Fujimori, is of Japanese extraction. In addition to the main Iberian European population, some countries, particularly Paraguay, Argentina and Uruguay, have experienced significant levels of European immigration from Italy, Germany and Britain.

A characteristic of Latin America (and the Caribbean) is the extent to which the population has become miscegenated. The Mestizos, admixtures of European and Amerindian populations, are significant in many Latin American countries and in some states form the economically and politically dominant group.

Throughout Latin America's modern history, conflict over land use has been a key feature. The widespread *hacienda* system of plantation agriculture, with its patterns of tied labour, conformed with the semi-feudal *latifunda* back in Iberia, and was eminently suitable for a colonial economy. With its emphasis on large-scale monocultures, this system has been closely aligned, from the colonial era to the present, with the interests of local elites, governments keen to promote commercial export crops, and with foreign capital. Extensive cultivation of cash crops such as coffee, and, more recently – albeit illicitly – coca, has been encouraged throughout the region as has ranching and, in some regions, sheep rearing. In contrast, the Amerindian agricultural patterns native to the region tend to emphasize local market needs, diversity and smallholdings.

In considering regional ethnic conflicts, it is significant that many, if not all, of the land use issues in Latin America have a significant racial component, with Iberian and/or Mestizo land owners (who are generally also the social political elites) pitched against Amerindian and/or Bush Negro populations. In most cases, governments and foreign capital have tended to support the large-scale agricultural and industrial exploitation of Latin America hinterlands, particularly the vast Amazonian basin. The desire of Latin American governments to develop their hinterlands, while understandable, has rarely gone hand in hand with considerations of sustainability or of local aspirations. The impact on the forest dwellers in countries such as Brazil has in many cases been a highly negative one. Both legally and informally subjected to various forms of discrimination and political exclusion, forest dwellers have suffered displacement as the direct effects of land expropriation, environmental degradation as a result of primary industries such as logging and mineral extraction, and from the associated development of transport structures. Indirect consequences have included exposure to foreign diseases, such as measles and influenza to which they have no natural immunity, pressure to move to urban areas in search of paid work, and associated problems of alcoholism, prostitution and cultural disorientation. Although in recent years more attention has been paid, both by national civil rights groups and internationally, to the needs and rights of Amerindian populations, the practical results have been incomplete and uneven.

In each of those countries where land use issues have erupted into full-scale fighting a distinctive ethnic element to the conflict can be traced. However, the exact relationship between each conflict and its ethnic underpinnings varies considerably. In identifying conflicts where the racial element is the most overt, Guatemala is probably the most straightforward: Ladino land owners (backed by local and foreign interests) versus Mayan indigenous farmers. In Peru and Mexico, conflict has been viewed, not least by the belligerents themselves, largely in Marxist terms of class and ideology. This approach has not always worked to the benefit of marginalized groups nor, for that matter, of guerrilla movements themselves. The Shining Path movement in Peru, in particular, managed to alienate its potential ethnic base by insisting on adherence to Marxist ideology inappropriate to the genuine needs of local populations, In contrast, Colombia, where analysis of conflict has been complicated by the emergence of 'narcoterrorism' as an issue, the main protagonists do not appear to have a significant ethnic base, although ethnic minority groups have been among the main victims of the fighting.

# Chiapas

**Principal protagonists**

Government of Mexico.

Indigenous peoples of Chiapas state; *Ejército Zapatista de Liberación Nacional* (EZLN).

**Nature of conflict**
Indigenous peoples rights' issues; autonomy demands by EZLN.

☠ c1,000.
🏠 Land ownership a central issue.

**Population/ethnic composition**
4.3m. Mestizos 55%, Amerindian 40%. c25% of population wholly or partly Mayan.

**Territorial extent**
Chiapas: 74,211 km².

**Timeline**
c400 BC: Start of continuous human inhabitation.
1500s: Conquered by Spain.
1823-1880s: Annexed by Mexico.
17 Nov 1983: EZLN founded.
1 Jan 1994: Armed uprising by EZLN.
16 Feb 1996: San Andrés Accords signed.
5 Dec 2000: COCOPA Law proposed.
14 Aug 2001: Heavily modified COCOPA Law, omitting regional autonomy proposals, passed by Mexican Congress.
Aug 2003: Autonomous government declared by EZLN.

**Current status**
Ceasefire agreements generally holding, Autonomous control of 32 local municipalities in Chiapas by EZLN.

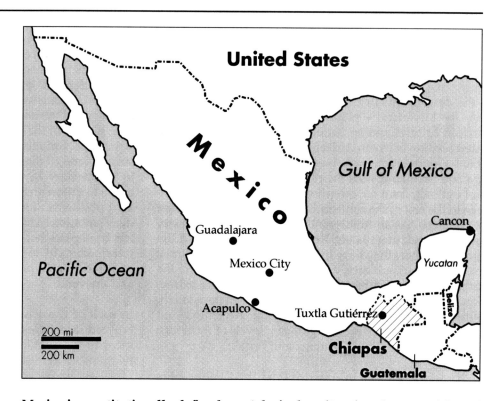

Mexico is constitutionally defined as a 'pluricultural' society, in recognition of the wide ethnic diversity within its borders. Sixty-four groups of Amerindian 'indigenous peoples' are recognized, with classification largely on a linguistic basis. Although most Amerindians are fully integrated into Mexican culture, and do not speak an indigenous language, several states have overtly identified themselves with the pre-conquest history of their regions, examples including Yucatan (with the Mayan civilization) and Tlaxala with the Tlaxcaltec people.

The Mexican constitution grants indigenous peoples the right to self-determination, although this has not always been upheld in practice. As in many other Latin American countries, land ownership has been a key issue, with a largely Hispanic elite controlling land rights over indigenous peons or peasant farmers. Following the 1917 Mexican revolution, the new national constitution enshrined, under Article 27, the right of indigenous peoples to *ejido* or communal land, and by the 1980s land reform was largely complete. Programmes of bilingual education and the official recognition of indigenous language were also introduced. Despite these efforts, under-development of indigenous communities continues to be a significant issue in Mexico, with continuing rural poverty and the migration of Amerindians to major Mexican cities and to the USA.

Left very much behind in the developmental process was the southernmost province of Chiapas, scene of unrest as far back as 1868 (when a full scale Amerindian revolt erupted) and where indigenous farmers long harboured a grievance that they were being ignored in the land reform process. Debt peonage and absentee landlordism continued to be issues. This is coupled with general poverty in the region, including the highest level of malnutrition in the country.

Forty per cent of the population of Chiapas is Amerindian, with around a quarter of the population claiming pure Mayan descent. The region thus has a high level of ethnic identification, reinforced by the fact that a relatively high percentage – over a third – of the Amerindians do not speak Spanish.

Matters came to a head at the beginning of 1994, with Mexican accession to the North American Free Trade Area (NAFTA). Seen by many as an exploitative extension of liberal economic expansionism – i.e., 'globalization' – the NAFTA agreement required Mexico to abandon the constitutional provision of communally-owned *ejidos* land for rural indigenous communities.

On 1 January 1994, to coincide with the coming into force of the NAFTA agreement, the *Ejército Zapatista de Liberación Nacional* (EZLN, or 'Zapatistas') rose in armed rebellion. As the name implies, the EZLN challenge was to the national government and their aim was an armed march on Mexico City in defence of indigenous rights and more generally against globalization. In practice, the Zapatista core strength remained among the Maya and other indigenous communities in the Chiapas region, although it did secure some backing from urban students and intellectuals, as well as considerable sympathy from international activist groups.

After some initial military successes by the EZLN, the Mexican army found little difficulty in confining the Zapatistas to their rural strongholds. A ceasefire was brokered by local church leaders on 12 January, although much of the land occupied by the Zapatistas remained in their possession until early 1995, when the army asserted its control more thoroughly over the region. In 1996 the government and the EZLN agreed the San Andrés Accords which made provision for regional autonomy, These provisions were largely ignored by the Mexican government, however, and sporadic fighting continued, including attacks by pro-government paramilitaries, culminating in the Acteal massacre of 1997, in which hundreds of Amerindian refugees attending a church service were killed.

In 2000 the EZLN renewed its offensive, with the aim of pressurizing the newly elected government of Vicente Fox Quesada, who had ousted the Institutional Revolutionary Party regime that had ruled Mexico for over seventy years. Quesada proposed the *Comisión de Concordia y Pacificación* (COCOPA) Law – actually a constitutional reform rather than a law – which again promised local autonomy. This was heavily watered down by Congress, however, before being passed in August 2001.

In response to the slow progress of government reform, the EZLN consolidated the process, started in 1994, of establishing 'Juntas of Good Government' at local municipal level in the regions under their control. In 2003 these were declared 'autonomous' by the EZLN, although not formally independent of Mexico. The creation of these juntas has, in practice, been tolerated by the Mexican government. The lead decision making body in the EZLN is the *Comité Clandestino Revolucionario Indígea* – or 'Revolutionary Indigenous Secret Committee' – but local government is devolved to representatives of the municipalities who are elected on a rota basis.

The Zapatistas, aligning as they do with an international movement of underlying concern at economic liberalization, environmental degradation, and the lack of self-determination of local communities, have garnered widespread support and sympathy from international anti-globalization protesters and campaigners. This has been supported by effective use of the internet and other modern communications techniques. The issues confronting the Chiapas are neither unique within Mexico nor in the wider world and serve to emphasize the ongoing tension between global trends, state governments, and local ethnic aspirations.

# Colombia

**Principal protagonists**

Government of Colombia; *Autodefensas Unidas de Colombia* (AUC).

Left-wing rebels, especially *Fuerzas Armadas Revolucionarias de Colombia* (FARC).

Amerindian and Black communities.

**Nature of conflict**

Overlapping conflicts over political patronage and resource exploitation, particularly of narcotics. Violence between government and rebel groups continues to affect ethnic minority communities.

- No reliable statistics on death toll.
- Up to 3 million, including IDPs, of which 750,000 from ethnic minority communities.
- Large scale production and trafficking of illegal drugs. Forestry and other natural resources also significant.

**Population/ethnic composition**

Total population: 43.7m, of which 4.8m Black and Amerindian.

**Territorial extent**

Colombia: 1.14m km².

**Timeline**

20 Jul 1810: Independence from Spain proclaimed (recognized 1819).
1946-58: *La Violencia* civil unrest claims 300,000 lives.
1964-5: FARC and other left-wing armed rebel groups created.
1983-1993: 'Narcoterrorist' wars against drug cartels.
1990s: Height of FARC insurgency. Rightist paramilitaries also active.
7 Aug 2000: Election of Álvaro Uribe as president.
2002 onwards: Conflict reduced, although not wholly suppressed.

**Current status**

Ethnic minority groups remain highly vulnerable to violence and human rights abuses both by militants and government.

**Colombia has been inhabited for at least 13,000 years, with the evolution, by the time of the Spanish conquest in the 1500s, of a number of organized agricultural cultures. Today, the majority of Colombians are Mestizos of mixed white and Amerindian ancestry. Blacks, the descendants of imported slaves, form a distinct ethno-cultural group organized into autonomous farming communities. Around 1% of the population is comprised of indigenous Amerindians, some in extremely remote Amazonian territories in the east of the country. In total, Colombia is home to over 80 ethnic groups and as many languages.**

Throughout much of its history the country has suffered violent civil unrest, and the majority of Colombians, particularly those from ethnic minority groups, have had little direct input into political life. Marginalized communities have suffered disproportionately during these conflicts.

Ideological conflict dates back to the country's formation in 1810. The creation of the Liberal and Conservative Parties in the 1850s consolidated these divisions, which continue in Colombian politics today, although in recent years greater political plurality has emerged. The differences between the two have frequently owed more to access to patronage than significant ideological differences. Shared access to patronage has led to corruption and tacit co-operation between the parties. In 1946 full-scale fighting – the period known as *La Violencia* – broke out. This continued for over ten years and cost 300,000 lives before the Conservatives and Liberals bonded together to form the National Front. While this had the effect of reducing the violence, it also excluded other political forces, with patronage being shared out between the political elites.

One response to this process was the establishment in 1965 of the *Ejército de Liberatión Nacional* (ELN) and the *Ejército de Liberatión Popular* (EPL) – the former claiming some Cuban support and the latter professing Maoism. A year later, the *Fuerzas Armadas Revolucionarias de Colombia* (FARC) was established to defend semi-autonomous Communist controlled rural areas of the country. FARC subsequently became the largest of the guerrilla groups with, at peak, some 12,000 fighters. With the exceptions of the small Quintín Lame Command group and a number of other small factions, the left-wing groups have rarely sought to recruit members of the Amerindian communities. Although FARC purports to protect peasant farmers against landowners in the areas they control, this would appear to be as much out of self-interest as any genuine consideration for local rights.

The National Front formally ended in 1974, but the tradition of presidents inviting opposition leaders to hold government posts (and thereby share in the division of the political spoils) continued into the 1990s. In an environment of generally weak, self-motivated and factional government, minority groups have suffered at best neglect and at worst open discrimination and abuses such as land alienation. The response of native peoples has either been to move to towns to seek work or, alternatively, retreat into the more remote areas. The needs of the Black communities to secure land ownership have been ignored by the government, which has used displacements forced upon the population by rebel/paramilitary activity as an opportunity to impose centrally planned monocultures.

The long-standing political conflicts were exacerbated by the emergence of the cocaine drugs traffic as a significant motivator for violence that resulted in the 'narcoterrorist' wars of 1983-1993. Possessed of vast wealth from their activities, the drugs cartels pursued a policy of *plata o plomo* (silver or lead) to either bribe or eliminate opponents at all levels of society. Although the Medellín and other cartels were broken up by the government in 1993, Colombia remains the world's leading coca producer. FARC activities continued to grow throughout the 1990s, as the group exploited the benefits of the drugs trade, including protecting coca growers from the government (and FARC itself) in return for 'taxes'. FARC has also directly attacked indigenous groups, either taking over their land and/or forcing them to grow coca. In 1999 three US Indian rights activists were kidnapped and murdered by FARC.

In the 1990s, rightist paramilitary groups, most of whom came to be united under the *Autodefensas Unidas de Colombia* (AUC) banner, emerged to combat the spate of kidnappings and assaults by leftists. Subsequently, the paramilitaries became military players in their own right and have, like their left-wing counterparts, been accused of complicity in the drugs trade as well as widespread human rights abuses. 2000 saw the election of the Conservative Álvaro Uribe on a mandate to clamp down hard on the left-wing rebels. This Uribe did, and also demobilized the paramilitary AUC groups, with a pledge to re-integrate these militia into civilian life. Civil unrest (whether ideological or drugs related) has declined somewhat since 2002, but Colombia remains a highly unstable and crime-ridden country.

During the various conflicts, Black communities, particularly in the Chocó region, organized autonomous councils to fill the vacuum left by the collapse of central authority. This has brought these communities into conflict both with irregular groups and with the government. In 2005, for example, the government disallowed Black collective ownership of some 10,000 hectares of land to the east of the Atrato River, which had been vacated by the local communities following killings by paramilitary groups. The vacated land was subsequently used for large-scale oil palm plantations, which both the government and the AUC claimed were a source of employment.

In summary, the minority communities, while rarely direct combatants themselves, have been regularly caught in the crossfire between government forces, rightist paramilitaries, drug barons, left-wing rebels – or assorted combinations of these factions, which often overlap. In November 2005, a conference organized by the Inter-ethnic Solidarity Forum of Chocó (representing 300 community and indigenous groups) sent open letters to government, the various rebel groups, and the paramilitaries, insisting on their neutrality in the conflict and demanding that their land ownership and other rights be respected. The indigenous groups condemned the cultivation and trafficking of drugs in their territories and the forcing of local communities to grow coca. However, they were also critical of the more heavy-handed governmental responses to the problem that have included the wholesale use of defoliants, which can damage legitimate crops. The government-sponsored alternative to the coca trade, which focuses on monoculture palm oil production, has also been criticised as being ecologically unsustainable. A further area of contention is the Colombian government's determination to close the so-called 'Darién Gap' – the break in the Pan-American Highway between Colombia and Panama. Critics allege that the construction and development work associated with the highways programme will damage local communities and ecologies. (The region is home to the Waurana and Emberá peoples as well as to around 700,000 Black farmers.) The government's 2005 forestry bill has similarly been criticized as opening up vulnerable forest regions to large scale logging operations.

The most vulnerable indigenous and Black communities are those in the Sierra Nevada de Santa Marta and Chocó regions but communities throughout the country remain exposed. In July 2006, for example, 1,700 Awá villagers in the southwestern Nariño region were forced to flee their homes after fighting broke out between government and rebel forces. This was just one of a series of displacements which have plagued the Awá since the early 1990s. The government has also sought to establish battalions of locally recruited 'peasant soldiers', who numbered some 15,000 by 2006. Although this has in some areas enabled local populations to defend themselves, it has also on occasion left the communities at increased danger of revenge attacks by rebel groups.

Particularly tragic has been the fate of nomadic and other forest groups in remote regions. The Nukah, for example, have only had contact with the wider world since 1988. Since then, around half the population of 1,000 has died from diseases such as influenza and FARC rebels drove the remainder from their lands in 2005. Several members of the community, including the tribal leader, are reported as having committed suicide in despair at their situation. Unless there is a comprehensive and lasting peace agreement, combined with a more flexible approach by government to the needs of minorities, such tragedies are likely to continue.

# Peru

**Principal protagonists**

Government of Peru; *Comités de auto defensa*

*Sendero Luminoso* (Shining Path) and other guerrilla movements.

**Nature of conflict**
Widespread regional insurgency, 1980s. Also inter-ethnic disputes.

☦ Violence, including massacres, perpetrated by security forces, especially the National Intelligence Service.
☠ 25,000.
⚥ 50,000 IDP, mostly from minority groups.

**Population/ethnic composition**
28m. Quechua 47%, Mestizo 32%, White 12%, Aymara 5.4%

**Territorial extent**
Peru: 1.85m km².

**Timeline**
1542: Inca civilization defeated by the Spanish.
28 Jul 1821: Peruvian independence proclaimed. (Not officially recognized by Spain until 1879.)
1970: Shining Path formed.
18 May 1980: Start of Shining Path insurgency.
1980-1992: Principal period of Shining Path insurgency.
12 Sep 1992: Capture of Shining Path leader Abimael Guzmán marks effective end of cohesive Shining Path activity.

**Current status**
Guerrilla activity significantly reduced since 1999. Sporadic outbreaks continue.

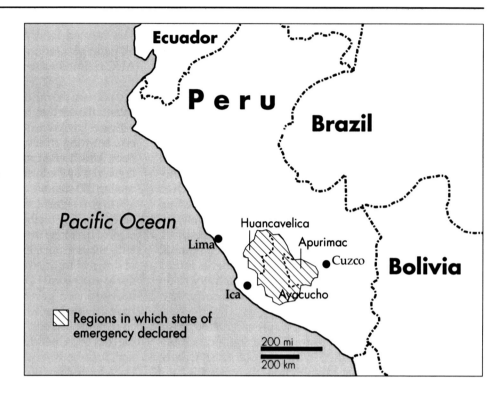

**Historically home to the advanced Inca civilization, Peru had fallen to Spanish control by 1542. Modern Peru is split ethnically between the Amerindian population, mostly Quechua, the mixed race Mestizos, Europeans and other smaller ethnic groups.**

Hispanic Europeans have traditionally dominated political and economic life, generally to the exclusion of other groups. Ethnic and political violence began in the 1950s and accelerated in the 1970s with the growth of the Communist Party of Peru, better known as *Sendero Luminoso* or Shining Path, which was formed in the late 1960s.

Shining Path drew its support primarily from the Quechua and Mestizo populations, in opposition to the Hispanic social and political elite. Despite its ideological veneer, the conflict therefore has essentially ethnic roots. Shining Path initially drew genuine popular support from elements of the Quechua population, particularly in the Andean highlands, where it attacked unpopular landowners, estate managers and cattle rustlers. By the mid-1980s Shining Path was in effective control of a number of regions, aided in part by a lacklustre military response to the movement from the government, which initially underrated its significance. However, disillusionment with Shining Path soon set in, largely through its attempts to impose an ideological overview to the struggle. Most peasants were indifferent to Marxism and hostile to Shining Path's opposition to indigenous cultural practices. Shining Path's Maoist ideology guided its belief that a rural revolution could choke the urban elites, but the movement's forced closure of rural markets serving the cities simply alienated its erstwhile supporters. Shining Path also clashed with other groups, such as the Túpac Amaru Revolutionary Movement (which took its name from the last Inca ruler).

Deep hostility exists, moreover, between the Quechua and other indigenous peoples, and this was manifested in Shining Path attacks on minority groups, for example the Ashaninka, the largest ethnic group in Peru's forest region. The Ashaninka live in constant conflict with Quechua settlers from the mountain regions. They have long been vulnerable to the aggressive expansion of the Quechua and the expulsion of Shining Path from its original core central and southern mountain valley areas pushed the organization and its supporters into the central forest region, and thus into collision with local peoples. In addition to exploiting long-standing conflicts between the Quechua and the forest peoples, Shining Path has also been accused of forcing local communities to grow coca for the illicit drugs trade.

Faced with Shining Path violence, local communities in some regions formed *rondas* or 'peasant patrols' which were later legitimized by the government as *Comités de auto defensa* ('Committees of Self Defence').

From 1990 onwards, the Peruvian government had progressive successes against the faltering Shining Path insurgency, although the process was marred by human rights abuses and judicial irregularities. In 1992, the founder and leader of Shining Path, Abimael Guzmán, was captured. Other leaders, including Guzmán's successor, were rounded up in 1999. Subsequently the movement splintered and in November 2004 the leaders of the remaining Shining Path factions offered a ceasefire in exchange for an amnesty. Sporadic attacks by splinter groups are likely to continue, but at nowhere near the level of previous insurgencies.

# Guatemala

**Principal protagonists**

Ladino population; Government of Guatemala; pro-government paramilitaries; Civilian Defence Patrols.

Maya population; *Unidad Revolutionaria Nacional Guatematelca* (URNG) and other movements.

**Nature of conflict**

Ethnically predicated land use conflict. Full-scale civil war, 1954-1995.

⚔ Systematic attacks on Maya civilian targets by government and paramilitaries, especially in 1980s. (According to the UN-sponsored Truth Commission, 90% of all human rights violations during the war were committed by government/pro-government forces.)

☠ 200,000.

👥 1 million.

🌾 Agricultural resource exploitation a key issue.

**Population/ethnic composition**

13m. Ladino 40%, Mayan 42%.

**Territorial extent**

Guatemala: 109,000 km².

**Timeline**

1954: CIA-backed coup against Jacobo Arbenz Guzmán government.
23 Mar 1982: Coup results in the rise to power of Rios Montt.
1982: A number of left-wing movements merge to form the *Unidad Revolutionaria Nacional Guatematelca*.
8 Aug 1983: Coup against Rios Montt government marks gradual return to civilian rule.
7 Apr 1995: Peace accord marks official end of civil war.

**Current status**

Peace agreements holding, although government corruption and slow progress towards social reform remain problems. Since 2002 there has been a significant worsening in the security situation.

As in all Latin American societies, profound differences in wealth and social and political influence exist in Guatemala. Similarly, although to varying degrees, all Latin American societies experience an overlap between social status and ethnic origin. In Guatemala, however, the linkage is particularly stark, such that the country's social unrest – although also having an economic motivation – had a clearly racial basis.

The major population groups are the Ladino (mixed race Mestizos) who comprise 40% of the population, and the indigenous Maya, who are the largest ethnic group in Guatemala. Although both groups are primarily Roman Catholic, a small percentage of the Maya continue to practise their traditional religious beliefs.

Since colonial times the Maya have been subject to both legal and informal social and educational discrimination, with land use being the principal centre of dispute. Traditional Mayan agriculture centres on the cultivation of beans and maize, two staple crops essential to Mayan subsistence and deeply engrained in their culture. Guatemala's national economy, however, is heavily dependent on commercial crops such as bananas, coffee and sugar, as well as beef production. Plantation and land owners are generally from the Ladino population, who for centuries have sought to displace the Maya in order to grow commercial export crops, generally with governmental backing. A clear socio-ethnic demarcation thereby exists between the two population groups. This is exacerbated by the fact that many of the Maya do not speak (or read) Spanish. From the Ladino point of view, this facilitates the use of Spanish as a 'language of control' with, for example, legal documents being written in Spanish, which the Maya do not understand. The Maya themselves are resistant to learning Spanish, believing that this will undermine their culture.

In 1944, following many years of military rule, the 'October Revolutionaries', a group of reformist army officers with liberal civilian support, overthrew the previous military dictatorship and replaced it with a civilian presidency which initiated land reform and other social changes. However, in 1954 the Guatemalan army, with CIA support, staged a coup against the reformist government of President Jacobo Arbenz Guzmán, the proximate cause of the coup being the expropriation of lands owned by the US-based United Fruit Company. Following a failed counter-coup attempt in 1960, left-wing movements, drawing support from the Mayan population, organized in armed opposition to the new regime, and full-scale civil conflict started.

The guerrillas gained a considerable base of support in the countryside, but were broken up by a major government counter-insurgency campaign in 1966. Thereafter the guerrillas concentrated their attacks on urban targets, including a number of high-profile assassinations, one of whom was the US ambassador.

Throughout much of the conflict, the Guatemalan military has enjoyed close logistical, financial and *materiel* support from the United States. With the exception of the years 1977-82, the United States provided Guatemala's armed forces with training and equipment until the 1990s. In the early days of US support, Guatemala in turn provided training grounds and airbases for the US-based Cuban émigrés who went on to stage the failed Bay of Pigs invasion of Cuba in 1961.

As the war progressed, its racial undertones became increasingly apparent, with Mayan villages and populations being systematically targeted. More than 450 Mayan villages were destroyed during the conflict, which resulted in over one million refugees. In the Baja Verapaz region, the post-ceasefire Truth Commission concluded that the Guatemalan state intentionally engaged in a genocidal policy towards targeted ethnic groups. Frequently, villages were razed simply on suspicion of harbouring the guerrillas. The guerrillas, in turn, took revenge on villagers suspected of supporting the government or joining the government-sponsored Civilian Defence Patrols.

Military activity reached a peak in 1982 following the coup which brought to power the hard-line Efrain Rios Montt regime. Montt initiated a combination of military action and economic reforms under the slogan 'rifles and beans'. In 1982 the various left-wing movements merged to form the *Unidad Revolutionaria Nacional Guatamatelca* (URNG), but this was more an expression of weakness than strength. Montt's policies were successful in crushing much of the insurgency, although at a fearful cost in civilian lives, and by the end of 1982 the guerrillas were largely reduced to staging hit-and-run raids. Further pressure was applied by right-wing paramilitaries and vigilante groups, which, together with the Civilian Defence Patrols, enjoyed open government support. In 1983 Montt was himself deposed by Defence Minister Oscar Mejia Victores who, with the military situation largely secured, was able to initiate a managed return to democratic rule.

Throughout the latter stages of the war a clear demarcation had arisen between urban areas, which the army controlled, and rural areas in which the URNG maintained a strong presence. The resulting stalemate propelled both sides towards UN-mediated negotiations. On 7 April 1995, the government and the guerrillas concluded a peace accord, which among other measures specifically undertook to protect the rights of Amerindian peoples. Under the peace terms, some 3,000 guerrillas were disbanded, along with up to 200,000 paramilitaries and elements of the regular forces. A subsequent agreement signed in September 1996 required the military to concentrate solely on external security threats.

Although incidents have been reported throughout the 2000s, significant armed unrest in Guatemala is no longer currently an issue. Civilian rule appears to be holding, with generally free elections being held. However, underlying problems of governmental corruption and slow progress towards land and social reform remain. During 2002, Guatemala experienced a significant decline in the security situation with a spate of assassinations, kidnappings and drug-related violence. The poor security situation, although not yet marking a return to the full-scale war of previous years, has obliged the government to rely increasingly on the military (effectively overturning the 1996 agreement) and limiting its ability to carry out social reform.

### The border with Belize

Guatemala has a long standing claim over the entire territory of the neighbouring country of Belize, the existence of which denies Guatemala an effective eastern seaboard. The dispute delayed Belizean independence, which was somewhat reluctantly gained (from Britain) in 1981. The potential for annexation by Guatemala necessitated a continuing British military and air force presence in the country. Guatemala did not recognize Belize until 1991. In 2005 the two nations agreed a series of "confidence-building measures" aimed at the peaceful resolution of the dispute. While not formally resolved, therefore, the border issue may be considered effectively dormant.

Belize is a highly ethnically diverse but generally racially tolerant country, with English (including a vibrant Creole variant) tending to act as a unifying influence. (Belize is the only English-speaking country in central America.) As with Guatemala, Belize was historically home to the Mayan civilization. Land tenure issues exist in Belize, as in Guatemala, but have never broken out into significant violence. In 2005, however, civil unrest, including rioting, broke out over proposed tax increases.

# Guyana

**Principal protagonists**

Indo-Guyanese population.

Afro-Guyanese population.

*(See boxed text opposite for description of the territorial disputes between Guyana and Venezuela/Suriname.)*

**Nature of conflict**

Racial tensions reflected in voting patterns.

**Population/ethnic composition**

751,000. Indo-Guyanese 49.4%, Afro-Guyanese 35.6%, mixed race 7.1%, Amerindian 6.8%.

**Territorial extent**

Republic of Guyana: 214,969 km².

**Timeline**

1616: Dutch settlement. Importation of African slaves to man plantations.
1815: Former Dutch Guyanese colonies ceded to Britain.
1831: British Guyana founded.
1834: Abolition of slavery; inward migration of Indian and Asian labour commences.
1917: Indian/Asian immigration discontinued.
1 Jan 1950: First political party, the People's Popular Party, founded.
30 May 1953: PPP wins election. British intervention to prevent Communist takeover. PPP splits, with formation of largely Afro-Guyanese People's National Congress.
12 Dec 1964: PNC forms government.
26 May 1966: Independence gained from Britain.
9 Oct 1992: PPP regains power.

**Current status**

Largely peaceful, although racial tensions continue.

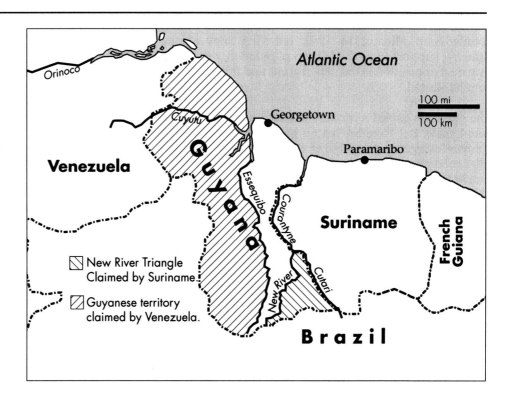

**Although race has only rarely resulted in sustained open conflict, ethnic rivalries have been the principal factor in Guyanese politics since before independence in 1966, and continue to be the main determinant of voting patterns, with the two main political parties being largely racially based.**

The principal ethnic division is between 'Afro-Guyanese', the descendants of the original negro slave population, and the 'Indo-Guyanese'; Indian and other Asian indentured labourers imported to work the sugar and rice plantations after the abolition of slavery in 1834. These two groups currently comprise around 35% and 50% respectively of the Guyanese population. A small Amerindian population, comprising some 7% of the total population, and itself divided between several ethnic groups, lives in communal settlements in the interior.

A large proportion of the Afro-Guyanese population is urbanized whereas the Indo-Guyanese tend to be rural, although there are commercially influential minorities in the towns.

Religion also generally follows racial lines, with the Afro-Guyanese (and mixed-race Guyanese) following Christianity, and the Indo-Guyanese professing Hinduism. Islam is practised by around 10% of the population. Historically, however, religion has not been a strong defining characteristic in Guyanese ethnic conflict.

More than 90% of Guyanese live along the northern coastal strip and culturally, Guyana, the only English-speaking country in Latin America (except for Belize), is more closely aligned to the Caribbean than it is to Latin America. Guyana is part of the Caribbean Community, a member of the Commonwealth, and plays cricket as part of the West Indies team.

The British occupied the region during the Napoleonic wars, bringing to an end Dutch expansionism in the area. In 1815 the Dutch colonies of Essequibo, Demerara and Berbice were ceded to Britain at the Congress of Vienna. In 1831 these were consolidated into one holding, British Guyana.

Political emancipation began after the end of the Second World War and this led to the creation, on 1 January 1950, of the People's Progressive Party (PPP) led by Forbes Burnham and Dr Cheddi Jagan, two figures who were to dominate Guyanese politics for many decades. The PPP announced a platform of independence from Britain and a 'just socialist society'. It won 18 of the 24 seats available at the 1953 election. Just five months after the election, however, the British intervened militarily in the colony, asserting that the PPP was seeking the establishment of a Communist state.

Although both Burnham and Jagan professed Marxism, Burnham saw in the British intervention the opportunity to break with Jagan. He formed the People's National Congress (PNC) with a largely Afro-Guyanese base, while Jagan's PPP thereafter drew support from the Indo-Guyanese population. The lasting racial/political fault line in Guyanese politics was thereby established. The PPP won both subsequent elections and, in 1961, Dr Jagan became the first Premier of Guyana.

The period 1962-64 saw the first significant violent conflict between the Indo- and Afro-Guyanese when tensions erupted into widespread inter communal rioting. In 1963, the British announced a timetable for Guyanese independence, with one condition being the introduction of an electoral system of proportional representation that was widely interpreted as favouring the Afro-Guyanese electorate, and thus the PNC. In the pre-independence election, in 1964, the PNC did indeed emerge as the largest party, although not with an overall majority. Nevertheless, with the support of minor parties, Forbes Burnham was able to form a government and become the first Prime Minister of independent Guyana.

In part because of the weakness of his political base, Burnham ruled Guyana in an increasingly authoritarian manner, while continuing to win elections by suspiciously increasing majorities. The polls of 1980 and 1985 were regarded as particularly suspect. Widespread formal and informal discrimination against the Indo-Guyanese was routine. This Dr. Jagan condemned as reducing them to 'second class status'. Allegations of human rights abuses and the assassination of political opponents further marred Guyana's international standing. In August 1985, Forbes Burnham died and his successor, Desmond Hoyle – who was confirmed in the office of President in the election of December 1985 – sought to reverse both Burnham's authoritarianism and his socialist ideology.

In October 1992, in a remarkable comeback, Dr. Cheddi Jagan was elected President, the PPP having won 53.5% of the votes in the first poll since independence to be generally regarded as free and fair. Like the PNC, the PPP officially renounced Marxism. Dr. Jagan remained in power until his death in 1997. The PPP remains the governing party, and has sought to claim that the racial element in Guyanese politics has been overstated, while (in contradiction) blaming the Afro-Guyanese PNC for many years of discrimination against the Indo-Guyanese.

While the potential for ethnic conflict clearly exists in Guyana, the country has in recent years escaped serious violence. Demographic changes tend to favour the expansion of the Afro- and mixed-race Guyanese, at the proportional expense of the Indo-Guyanese. Large-scale emigration, particularly to the United States has also been a feature, although less so in recent years. Whether new political organizations will reflect these changes, and whether the PPP is prepared to willingly relinquish power should the electoral demographics turn against it, represent the key internal challenges for Guyana.

---

**Guyanese border disputes**

Guyana is subject to two significant territorial claims by its neighbours. The claims by Venezuela and Suriname, while not necessary ethnic in nature, could, should they become active, have critical consequences for the future of the Guyanese state.

The dispute over the Essequibo basin, which, at around 140,000 km$^2$, covers two thirds of Guyana's land territory, dates back to the interpretation of the 1648 Treaty of Münster which ended the war between the Dutch and the Spanish. Former Spanish possessions in the Essequibo region were recognized as Dutch. The British, in turn, gained the territories in 1815. Neither the Venezuelans nor the Guyanese, therefore, are the original parties to the dispute.

In 1895, under American pressure, Britain agreed to arbitration over the issue and an International Arbitration Tribunal was convened in 1899. In making its 'full, perfect and final' settlement, the Tribunal awarded the upper Cuyuni basin to Venezuela, but the majority of the disputed territory to Guyana. A full border survey was conducted with the participation of the Venezuelan government shortly afterwards.

The dispute with Suriname similarly concerns a riverine border. The Courantyre is accepted as the border between Suriname and Guyana but controversy exists as to whether the New River or the Cutari is its principal southern tributary. The Guyanese would appear to have the stronger case, as the Cutari basin is bigger than the New River's.

In 1962 Venezuela announced that it no longer recognized the 1899 award, and re-stated its claim to the territory. Upon independence, Guyana therefore inherited a position where nearly three quarters of the national territory were claimed by its neighbours. Guyana was initially denied entry into the Organization of American States because of a Venezuelan veto prompted by the border issue. Venezuelan maps routinely show the area as 'territory to be reclaimed'.

In 1970 a 12-year cooling off period was agreed with Venezuela, but this was allowed to lapse without any progress having been made.

The Essequibo dispute continues to have practical consequences for maritime demarcation between the Orinoco and Essequibo Rivers and in November 2007 Venezuela was accused of destroying two gold-mining dredgers in the disputed area.

# North America

**Social segregation, racial antagonism, and issues relating to minority rights and 'race relations' continue to be potent issues in North America. Although it is the continent in which the chances of wholesale ethnic warfare are lower than elsewhere in the world, the region has by no means been immune to past racial conflict.**

Through disease, conflict, miscegenation and forced integration, the European colonization of North America had the effect of all but exterminating the indigenous population of the region, so that today just over 1% of the population of USA, and 3.4% of the population of Canada, is American Indian. ('American Indian', although not without detractors, is the term most widely favoured by indigenous people themselves. In Canada, the term 'First Nations Peoples' is used.)

Throughout the early colonial period in North America, there was no consistency in the relationship between settlers, whether British, French or Spanish, and the indigenous American Indians.

Local politics, including inter-tribal rivalries, resource pressure, and, doubtless, individual personalities, all played a part in determining whether settlers and the indigenous inhabitants co-existed, traded, or fought. In many cases settlers and local tribes forged initially amicable relationships that later broke down into violence. Initially more damaging to native populations than overt conflict were the new diseases the Europeans brought with them: as in Latin America, it has been estimated that in some regions 80% of the population succumbed to chicken pox, measles and smallpox, to which they had no immunity.

During the American Revolutionary War many American Indians sided with the British, seeing this as the best means of preventing further westwards encroachment by settlers. In the peace treaty of 1783 Britain ceded vast areas, without consulting the local tribal inhabitants, to the new United States. The Americans thus initially treated the American Indians as a defeated people who had lost their land and their rights. This policy ultimately proved untenable, and the United States thereafter sought to achieve western expansion by treaty arrangements and land purchase agreements with indigenous nations. The Indian Removal Act of 1830 authorized the exchange of lands west of the Mississippi for those east of the river. Although the population transfer of Indian Americans to the west was supposedly voluntary, in practice considerable pressure, and in some cases open coercion, was applied.

American Indian resistance to treaties which were patently unequal (and frequently ignored or abrogated anyway by the US government) led to the 'Indian Wars' of the second half of the 19th century. Although individual Indian nations scored some famous victories against the US Army, the long term result was never in doubt and on 31 January 1876 the US government ordered all surviving American Indians to move onto reservations. Not until 1924 was American citizenship granted to American Indians. Today, some 563 tribal governments are recognized by the United States. These have wide-ranging autonomy, including their own flags, the right to make treaties as between sovereign powers between each other and with the US government (but not with other powers), to enforce local laws, to raise taxes and license casinos and other often lucrative activities. Nevertheless, social problems, including alcoholism and youth delinquency, are rife in many reservations. The largest American Indian populations are to be found in California, Arizona, and Oklahoma. Only in South Dakota, Montana and Oklahoma do American Indians account for more than 5% of the population. 16% of the population of Alaska is native Alaskan: in this state conflict issues have mainly centred around land ownership and consequent oil exploitation rights.

In what is now Canada, the treatment of the indigenous population initially followed broadly the same lines as in the United States. The 1876 Indian Act established reservations for Canada's Indian population and regulated the Canadian government's powers in establishing treaties with tribal nations. Widespread conflict broke out in the 1880s with Canada's westwards expansion. In 1996 the Royal Commission on Aboriginal Peoples proposed the creation of a First Nations government with which the federal Canadian government would treat on a bilateral basis. This was intended to replace the previous arrangements whereby First Nations matters were dealt with under the jurisdiction of the office of Indian and Northern Affairs. In 1999 a new territory, Nunavut, was created. Out of a sparse population of some 29,500, some 22,500 in the territory identify themselves as Inuit (Eskimo).

The second significant racial question to have divided the United States has been the legal and social status of the Afro-American minority, an issue compounded by the issue of slave ownership that persisted until 1865. From 1700 until the early 1800s, African slaves were imported to service the needs of the plantation economies of the southern United States, the enslaved population reaching 4 million by 1860.

The increasing economic and social divisions between northern and southern states (and also, to a lesser degree, between east and west) imposed increasing strains on the US throughout the 19th century, while defining the exact relationship, and distribution of power, between central and state governments was to give rise to America's bloodiest and most tragic war, the Civil War of 1860-5. In 1860, South Carolina, followed by a number of other Southern states, seceded from the Union to form the Confederate States of America. Facing the dismemberment of the United States, and following the forcible seizure of Federal military installations and assets by the Confederacy, the central government in Washington resolved to crush the 'rebellion' by force.

The American Civil War can be classed as an ethnic conflict on a number of levels. Most fundamentally, the South believed it was fighting not just for 'states rights' but for the preservation of a different culture and way of life – in other words, for its ethnic identity. Secondly, although the conflict was fundamentally a crisis between the central Washington government and the Southern state capitols as to where sovereign power resided, the particular 'state right' that was the

**Ethnic composition of the United States and Canada (total population in brackets).**

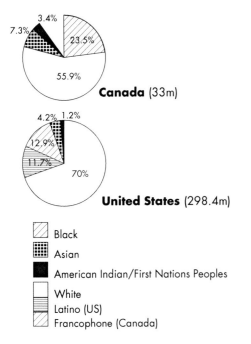

Canada (33m): 3.4%, 7.3%, 23.5%, 55.9%

United States (298.4m): 4.2%, 1.2%, 12.9%, 11.7%, 70%

- Black
- Asian
- American Indian/First Nations Peoples
- White
- Latino (US)
- Francophone (Canada)

primary catalyst for the war was the continuation of the institution of slavery by the Southern states.

To suggest, however, as some commentators have attempted, that the Civil War was primarily a struggle to free the slaves is at best simplistic. Only a minority of Southerners were slave owners, and the popular initial enthusiasm for the conflict among Southern Whites, the majority of whom were economically quite poor, could not have been sustained throughout five years of horrific fighting if the war had been merely to preserve the privileges of a narrow economic group. Initially, the North did not articulate the war in terms of emancipation either. Lincoln famously declared his indifference to the slavery issue by stating that if he could save the Union by *not* freeing the slaves he would do so. It was only when the propaganda, as well as the moral, values of abolitionism became apparent in Washington that moves were made towards emancipation. This was in large part to head off putative recognition of the Confederacy by Britain and France, a possibility that receded once the conflict had been aligned to the issue of abolition. The Confederacy did, although admittedly only once the war was all but lost, start arming negroes and even offered emancipation provided Southern independence could be preserved. These moves came too late not just to avert the military outcome but because the core political issue – state sovereignty – was not about slavery and could not be resolved save by military victory by one side or the other. This was achieved by the North, albeit at huge cost in human lives, in 1865.

Post war 'reconstruction', while advancing Afro-American civil liberties, did not embed equality. Until the 1960s, blacks in the South continued to be subject to the *apartheid*-style 'Jim Crow' laws that segregated them in schools, transport and leisure, and largely excluded them from the political process.

There were two consequences to the Jim Crow laws. The first was a mass migration of blacks to cities in the northern USA. The second was the rise, in the 1960s, of a civil rights movement that was largely successful in removing the more overt discrimination. Ethnic segregation (indicative of unresolved racial antagonisms and tensions) remains at a very high level in many US cities. Ironically, statistics suggest the issue is greater in northern cities than in the formerly deeply segregated south. Race relations continues to be a key domestic issue for American politics (especially after the 9/11 terrorist attacks) and on occasion, racial tension continues to flare into all-out violence, such as the rioting that disfigured Los Angeles in 1992 and Cincinatti and Seattle in 2001.

In recent years, attention has focused on the emergence of the numerically increasingly significant Latino or Hispanic ethnic group. (The US census enumerates racial rather than ethnic groups, and accordingly Latinos are classed as 'White' in census returns.) Latinos, with an official population of 35 million (a figure that may be under-enumerated through illegal immigration) now represent the second largest ethnic minority in the United States. Four US states, California, Texas, Hawaii and New Mexico are currently 'minority majority' states, in which non-Hispanic Whites are not the majority population. On current demographic trends, non-Hispanic Whites will cease to be the majority population of the United States overall by 2050.

From the 1970s onwards, the time-honoured American socio-ethnic model of the 'melting pot' (under which ethnic minorities, whether immigrants or not) were to integrated into American social, political and cultural norms, gradually mutated into a model of 'multiculturalism' under which the distinct cultures of ethnic groups were to be advanced as being equal to that of the 'white' mainstream. Most other countries in the Western world adopted this model, some, such as Canada, going so far as to officially declare themselves multicultural societies – despite, in Canada's case, an overwhelmingly white majority. In the 21st century, the effectiveness of the multicultural model has been challenged for its moral relativism as well as its practical ineffectiveness in creating stable plural societies. Nevertheless, various forms of 'affirmative action' (which critics dismiss as reverse racism) remain the norm in many walks of American life (particularly in ethnic quotas for higher education) as a means of redressing perceived social injustices.

---

**Canada's Quebec question**

Originally part of the French colony of New France, Quebec was conquered by the British during the Seven Years' War in the middle of the 18th century, and officially annexed to Britain by the 1763 Treaty of Paris. The region continues to differ markedly from the rest of Canada, being primarily Roman Catholic in religion, and largely French-speaking linguistically.

Within Quebec a body of political sentiment has long favoured independence from the rest of Canada, with the nationalist *Parti Québécois* periodically emerging as the governing party in the province. In 1994, in the second of two referendums held on the subject, a narrow majority voted against independence. A clear majority of French-speaking Quebecers (who constitute 82% of the population overall) voted for independence. Nationalism remains a potent and unresolved issue for Quebec, and, by extension, for Canada generally.

In an attempt to appease Francophone sentiments, French was declared an official language in Canada, alongside English, in 1989. The equal status of the two languages is not mirrored in Quebec, however, in which French is the sole official language. The state of Quebec actively intervenes to promote the French language in many sectors of public life, a process whose legality continues to be challenged by English speakers.

# Section 4: **Middle East**

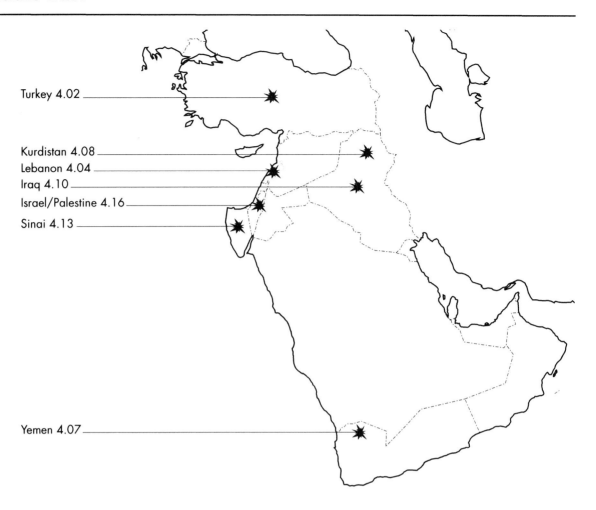

Fields of Fire – An Atlas of Ethnic Conflict

# Turkey

**Principal protagonists**

Turkish republican/secular traditionalists; Turkish Army.

Islamists; elements in parliament and government; elements in *Adalet ve Kalkınma Partisi* (AKP).

Kurds; *Partiya Karkerên Kurdistan* (PKK). (See also Kurdistan, 4.08.)

**Nature of conflict**

a) Nationalist issue (Kurdistan). b) Conflict between secular and religious elements in society.

- Widespread human rights abuses reported against authorities.
- Muslim/secular conflict a key potential flashpoint.
- 40,000 in Kurdish conflict.

**Population/ethnic composition**

70.4m. Turkish 65.1%, Kurdish 18.9%, Crimean Tatar 7.2%. Religious mix: Sunni c67%, Shia c30%.

**Territorial extent**

Republic of Turkey: 783,562 km².

**Timeline**

1307: Ottoman Empire established.
10 Aug 1920: Treaty of Sevres formally abolishes Ottoman Empire.
28 Oct 1923: Ataturk becomes President. Turkish republic declared next day.
1984 onwards: PKK leads armed uprising in Kurdish south east.
18 Nov 2002: *Adalet ve Kalkınma Partisi* (AKP) elected.

**Current status**

Insurgency and Turkish military action continues in Kurdish south-east (including cross-border incursions into Iraq).

Modern Turkey faces ethnic problems on a number of levels. The first concerns the accommodation of minorities within Turkey's current borders – most notably the Kurds, who have fought a long-standing guerrilla war against Ankara for an independent state. The second is one ultimately internal to Turks themselves, but one which has crucial implications for the country's future international role – how, and as what, do Turks view themselves? Self-realization and the actualization of that vision is a crucial question for all ethnic groups, and it may be that Turkey is at a very dangerous crossroads.

Historically a great power, by the 16th century Turkey had, under the Ottomans, established an empire with a foothold in three continents. The Ottoman rulers developed a complex Koranic-inspired system for accommodating the *dhimmi*, or non-Islamic populations, in the Islamic Ottoman state. Under this doctrine, which still serves as the template for many Islamists today, non-Muslims were reduced to the legal status of minors, or 'protected' persons, who were therefore deemed unfit, in most cases, to present evidence in a court of law or hold positions of social responsibility.. Although exempt from military service and other duties, the reality was the majority of Christians and Jews were subject to, at best, petty and humiliating restrictions on worship, trade, and forms of dress, and at worst overt exploitation, discriminatory taxation, and slavery. Sporadic pogroms took place against Greek, Bulgarian and other minorities and in 1915 up to 1.4 million Armenians were murdered in the Armenian Genocide – an historical event about which Ankara, to this day, is in denial. (In 2005, Turkish-Armenian journalist Hrant Dink was prosecuting for 'insulting Turkish identity' after raising the issue of the Armenian genocide. He was assassinated a year later.) As a consequence, the legacy of Turkish occupation has undoubtedly left a swathe of suspicion and resentment throughout much of south-eastern Europe, which more recent actions – most notably the Turkish invasion of Cyprus in 1975 – have done little to assuage.

Turkey has faced the threat of sporadic bombing campaigns by Armenian militants as well as the much more serious conflict in Turkish Kurdistan, where the majority of the 20 million Kurds live. Since the 1970s Kurdish separatists, led by the *Partiya Karkerên Kurdistan* (PKK) have mounted an insurgency against Turkish rule. Intense rivalry and divide-and-rule tactics by all governments in the region have limited overall Kurdish effectiveness, but the turmoil in neighbouring Iraq and the emergence of an autonomous Kurdish state in that country have set alarm bells ringing in Ankara. *(See Kurdistan, 4.08, and Iraq, 4.10.)*

The conflict escalated markedly in October 2007 after the Turkish parliament authorized Turkish military incursions into Iraqi Kurdistan against the PKK. Over 30 Turkish soldiers were killed in two weeks of violence that Ankara blamed on PKK elements crossing the border from Iraq. (The PKK, while not denying its presence in northern Iraq, claims to have fighters based permanently on Turkish soil.) In retaliation, the Turkish air force attacked PKK bases in Iraq, claiming 34 PKK insurgents were killed. Further Turkish incursions continue, and in May 2008 Turkey claimed that 150 guerrillas had been killed in an air attack on a PKK base in the Qandil mountains of northern Iraq.

The defining moment in modern Turkish history came after its defeat in the First World War and the collapse of the Ottoman dynasty, when Mustafa Kemal Ataturk declared Turkey a secular republic. Secularism has continued to closely inform Turkish political life until the present day, but in recent years has come under increasing pressure as the conservative and religious Turks have voted for more openly Islamic orientated political parties.

In May 2007 the ruling *Adalet ve Kalkınma Partisi* (AKP), which is accused by opponents of having an Islamist 'hidden agenda', sought to appoint the Foreign Minister, Abdullah Gul, to the presidency. Gul was accused by his opponents of having an 'Islamist past' and as therefore be inappropriate to occupy the position first held by Ataturk. Gul narrowly failed to be elected in the first round of voting by parliamentarians. To resolve the crisis, the Prime Minister, Recep Tayyip Erdogan, called a general election for July 2007, some months ahead of previously scheduled, which the AKP won. In March 2008 Turkey's chief presecutor brought a case, to the heard by the country's Constitutional Court, that would have the effect of banning the AKP for 'undermining secularism'.

The broader challenge facing Turkey is to how the nation sees itself, and in turn is seen by others. The questions of whether Turkey is a European or Asian power, and whether it is secular or Islamic, are crucial both for the country's internal stability and for its economic relationships with the wider world, including the long-running and vexed question of Turkish admission to the European Union.

# Lebanon

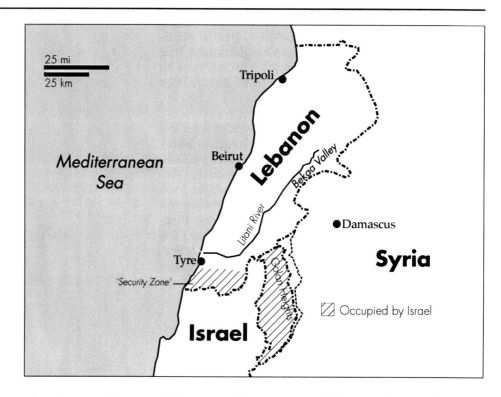

**Principal protagonists**

Government of Lebanon; Mainly Sunni 14 March Coalition, which also includes Druze and Christian factions.

Mainly Shia opposition groups Hizbollah and Amal; Free Patriotic Movement (mainly Maronite); Palestinian factions. (Opposition generally pro-Syrian.)

Periodic Israeli and Syrian intervention.

**Nature of conflict**

Religious conflict (primarily intra-Muslim) exacerbated by general Middle Eastern conflict and foreign interventions.

- Sunni/Shia; Muslim/Christian conflicts are issues.
- 150,000 since 1975.
- 370,000 Palestinian refugees. Upwards of 50,000 refugees from 2006 fighting.

**Population/ethnic composition**

3.8m. Arab 71.2%, Palestinian 12.1%, Armenian 6.8%, Kurd 6.1%, other 2.6%. Religious mix: Shia 34%, Sunni 21.3%, Maronite 19%, Greek Catholic/Melakite 4.6%, Orthodox 11.7%, Druze 7.1%. (Offical figures.)

**Territorial extent**

Lebanon: 10,452 km².

**Timeline**

22 Nov 1943: Lebanese independence recognized.
2 Nov 1975: Syrian occupation begins.
14 Mar 1978-13 Jun 1978: Southern Lebanon occupied by Israel.
23 Mar 1978: UNIFIL deployment begins.
6 Jun 1982: Southern Lebanon occupied by Israel.
22 May 2000: Israeli withdrawal.
25 Apr 2005: Syrian withdrawal.
22 Jul 2006-1 Oct 2006: Israel/ Hizbollah conflict.
May 2007 onwards: Fighting between Lebanese Army and Palestinian factions.

**Current status**

Political situation remains highly unstable.

**Since independence in 1943 the need to preserve a balance of power between Lebanon's religious communities has informed the doctrine of 'confessionalism' under which certain posts in government are reserved for members of particular groups. Under the terms of Lebanon's constitution, the President must be a Maronite Catholic Christian, the Prime Minister a Sunni Muslim, the Deputy Prime Minister an Orthodox Christian, and the Speaker of the Parliament a Shia Muslim. A confessional balance is also maintained in government appointments and in the distribution of parliamentary seats.**

Traditionally articulated in terms of easing dissent between the Christian and Muslim communities, in recent years the potential for intra-Muslim conflict between Sunnis and Shias has increasing come into focus, with Shias invoking the confessional doctrine as a means of highlighting their perceived marginalization.

Although unwieldy and resulting in the institutionalization of religious divisions, the confessional system nevertheless provided Lebanon with a surprisingly long period of relative stability and a strong record in the fields of tourism, banking and agriculture until 1975 – an achievement made all the more remarkable by Lebanon's geographical position at the heart of the Middle East conflict. The increasing downside was its inevitable tendency to encourage weak and divided central governmental institutions and to promote intense factionalism and political horse-trading between the various groups, particularly influential minorities such as the Druze, who are a distinctive offshoot of Ismaili Islam.

In 1975 the consensus collapsed and Lebanon descended into civil war. Calls by Muslim groups for a new census – the last one had been taken in 1932 – were seen by the Maronite Christians as likely to undermine their disproportionate influence in governmental structures. Compromise proved impossible, and all factions began forming militias. The ability of the central government to contain this situation was severely limited both by its own inherent weakness and by the disintegration of the Lebanese army through the defection, to the militias, of many of its Muslim troops. (The army has traditionally been officered by Maronites.)

Although the underlying divisions in Lebanon provided the raw fuel for the conflict, external factors and regional power politics were to have a devastating effect in inflaming the conflict. Since its defeat in the Jordanian civil war in 1970, the Palestinian Liberation Organization (PLO) had moved the bulk of its fighting force to Lebanon, where, together with local allies, it effectively occupied much of southern Lebanon and a number of districts in Beirut. This ultimately led to Israeli intervention, both directly and via local surrogates. Syria and other Arab powers in turn backed local factions.

The initial phase of the civil war saw conflict mostly between the Christian Phalange and the Muslim Lebanese National Movement (LNM). By mid-1976 the latter had gained the upper hand, but, following an appeal by Lebanon's Maronite President, Syria reversed its previous tacit support for the LNM/PLO factions and occupied much of the country. Syrian intervention stabilized the situation in the Bekaa Valley and East Beirut, but left southern Lebanon and the West Beirut in the hands of the PLO. One long-lasting consequence of the civil strive has been the creation of a 'state-within-a-state' in south Lebanon, alternately under pro-Israeli and pro-Palestinian forces, but rarely under the authority of Beirut.

PLO attacks into Israeli prompted Israeli invasion in March 1978. Although Israeli forces withdrew later in the year, they retained a 12 mile deep 'security zone' along the border and sponsored a Christian/Shia militia, the South Lebanon Army, to act as its regional proxies. In 1982, Israel once again intervened in force against the PLO, occupying southern Lebanon and, with the support of Maronite factions, East Beirut. In August 1982, the PLO withdrew from Lebanon under international supervision. Following the PLO withdrawal, Phalangist elements moved into the refugee camps of West Beirut where, in the notorious Sabra and Shatila massacres, they killed an estimated 3,000 Palestinians.

In September 1983, Israeli forces withdrew from Beirut (creating a power vacuum which prompted further killings) but remained in southern Lebanon, in defiance of UN Security Council resolutions, until 2000, whereupon the South Lebanon Army collapsed. For much of the rest of the decade, sectarian violence continued in Lebanon, this period also seeing the rise of the largely Shia Hizbollah movement, which found inspiration (and practical support) from the Iranian Islamic revolution of 1979. Successive peace efforts failed until Syria imposed a settlement, the Ta'if agreement of November 1989, which marked the formal end of the civil war and secured effective Syrian suzerainty over Lebanon. This continued until 14 February 2005 when, in what proved to be a pivotal moment in recent Lebanese history, former Prime Minister Rafik Hariri, an opponent of Syria, was assassinated. Amid huge rallies protesting against the murder, a coalition of groups, which came to be called the '14 March coalition' came together unified by their opposition to Syrian involvement in Lebanese political life. Faced with this reaction, Syria agreed to withdraw in April 2005.

Meanwhile, fighting once again escalated between Israel and pro-Palestinian forces, now led by Hizbollah, in southern Lebanon. Between July and October 2006 full-scale fighting saw Israeli forces once again occupying south Lebanon up to the Litani River north-south 'border' and carrying out air strikes against targets in Beirut and other cities. Opinion is deeply divided as to the outcome of the 2006 war, but one definite consequence was that the Lebanese Army was been able, after many years' absence, to operate in the south of the country – something long resisted by Hizbollah.

Intense rivalry exists between the opposition and the 14 March grouping, which Hizbollah dismisses as a 'coalition of treason' existing primarily to defend Sunni interests rather than national ones. The government, in return, seeks to characterize Hizbollah as a puppet of Syrian and Iranian interests, and that its continued military independence is a threat to national security. Hizbollah retorts that given the historical weakness of the regular Lebanese Army, it is actually the safeguard of Lebanese independence in the face of regular Israeli invasion. Hizbollah has increased its demands for a 'national unity government' or for the 'broadening' of the cabinet, which is essentially code for granting Hizbollah access to the confessional one-thirds constitutional blocking vote that would enable it, among other measures, to retain its weaponry (including its remaining long-range missiles) and autonomy. Hizbollah has also demanded that General Michel Aoun and his largely Maronite Free Patriotic Movement be included, apparently in an attempt to present itself as more than a Shia sectarian faction.

That Hizbollah commands a considerable popular power base was proven by the massive 10 December 2006 demonstrations when up to a million people took to the streets. Lebanon has not infrequently experienced governmental change through street protests and the Hizbollah demonstrations have tended to alarm the Sunni community, who staged a number of counter demonstrations, although not on the scale of the Hizbollah protests. Inter-communal rioting in Beirut following the November 2006 assassination of industry minister Pierre Gemayel claimed dozens of lives. The general fragility of the situation was also demonstrated in May 2007 when fighting broke out between the Lebanese army and Palestinian militants in the city of Tripoli, and in May 2008 when Hizbollah occupied much of western Beruit following a government ban on Hizbollah's independent telecommunications network, an action Hizbollah condemned as "an act of war". Fighting subsided after a government climb-down.  With Lebanon increasingly starkly divided along potential religious battle lines, and an ongoing background of assassinations and political factionalism, the prognosis for the future cannot be an encouraging one.

# Middle Eastern Christians

Two thousand years after the time of Christ, Christians in the region of his birth face an uncertain future, with discrimination, low birth rates and outward migration all contributing to falling numbers among some of the oldest Christian communities in the world.

The region today known as the West Bank (part of Palestine) is of particular significance to Christians as the land of Christ's birth and much of his ministry. Christians in the West Bank face a double challenge. For the most part Palestinian Arabs, they suffer from all the restrictions imposed by the Israeli occupation; as a minority within the Arab population, they run the risk of exclusion by their Muslim neighbours. In general, however, relations between the Christian and Muslim Palestinians have been largely peaceful, and in some areas specific accommodation of Christians in the political process has been achieved. Both the mayor and deputy mayor of Bethlehem are required to be Christians, for example. Nevertheless, the poor security situation, coupled with Israeli imposed curfews and labour restrictions, combined with the loss of tourist income to Christian holy sites, has led to emigration by many Palestinian Christians. The Christian Palestinian population generally supports the aspirations of the Palestinian people overall for an end to Israeli occupation and the achievement of full statehood. Christians in Israel proper are similarly a minority within a minority. Around 2% of Israel's population is Christian and most are Israeli Arabs, who constitute approximately 16% of the total population. Although the Israeli state in theory guarantees full freedom of worship, Christians, in common with other Israeli Arabs, suffer from land restrictions and other anti-Arab discrimination. In addition to Arab Christians, there exists in Israel a community of Messianic Jews – Jews who have accepted Christ – and a vocal Christian Zionist movement with links to evangelical US movements. The Christian Zionists, being fanatically pro-Israeli, are largely at odds with their Arab Christian co-religionists.

Lebanon is the only Middle Eastern country where, in modern times, Christians have been politically ascendant and where they continue to be a significant political force. Under Lebanon's 'confessional' constitution *(See 4.04)* the President of Lebanon must be a Christian. Officially, the Christian population stands at around a third. However, this is certainly an over-enumeration, as the last census was conducted in 1932. During Lebanon's civil wars of the mid 1970s various Christian movements, most notably the Phalangists, acted as allies and proxies of Israel. Direct Christian military influence has since declined, although the Lebanese army officer corps continues to be largely drawn from the largest Christian denomination, the 4th century Maronite church, which is in communion with Rome but retains much of its own liturgy. Poor security and civil strife, plus strong cultural links between Lebanese Christians and Europe, America and Australia, have encouraged large-scale emigration, contributing to falling numbers.

Egypt has, proportionately, the second largest Christian population in the region with some 16% of the population being Christian, largely from the ancient Coptic confession, which uses a language descended from that of ancient Egypt. Copts have increasingly found themselves under both informal and official harassment and restrictions as well as suffering from a declining security situation. In December 2007 riots were reported between Coptic and Muslim demonstrators in the south of the country.

Syrian Christians are able to worship freely and openly, but their declining numbers is an issue. Jordan's 4% Christian minority is similarly suffering a gradual decline. Churches must be registered with the government, and proselytizing Muslims is not permitted. Conversions from Islam are not permitted, and Christians who have converted from Islam are subject to official persecution.

> **Christian populations in selected Middle Eastern countries**
>
> **Iran:** 0.6% of population. Mainly Armenian.
>
> **Iraq:** 2.7%. Chaldean-Assyrian.
>
> **Israel:** 2.1%. Greek Orthodox; Catholic. Also Messianic Jews and Christian Zionists.
>
> **Jordan:** 4%. Catholic, Greek Orthodox.
>
> **Egypt:** 16%. Coptic.
>
> **Lebanon:** Officially 34%. Maronite, Greek Orthodox.
>
> **Syria:** 9.4%. Greek Orthodox, Catholic
>
> **West Bank/Gaza:** 2.4%. Greek Orthodox, Catholic.

Christians in Iraq have been subjected to harassment since the 2003 fall of Saddam Hussein, prompting widespread emigration. Christianity has had a foothold in Iraq since the second century and is home to the ancient Chaldean-Assyrian sects. Chaldeans are also to be found in Turkey, where the secular constitution in theory preserves full religious freedom. Christians have, however, been subject to bureaucratic and other petty restrictions in practice.

Iran's tiny Christian minority, largely of the Armenian confession, suffers from informal discrimination, although the religion is recognized in the constitution. In the Gulf states, Christianity, at least among the indigenous population, is almost wholly suppressed and conversion from Islam to Christianity is subject to severe penalties, including floggings and, occasionally, the application of the death penalty. In most Gulf states expatriate workers have, in theory, some freedom of religion, but public expressions of Christianity, any efforts to promote the faith, and religious gatherings, are all subject to very severe restrictions.

# Yemen

**Principal protagonists**

Mainly Sunni Yemeni government.

Zaydi Shia insurgents.

Al Qaeda attacks.

**Nature of conflict**
Intra-Muslim Sunni/Shia conflict

☠ 800.
👣 Up to 100,000 IDPs.

**Population/ethnic composition**
Yemen population: 22.2m. Arab 92.8%, Somali 3.7%. Religious mix: Sunni, 60%; Zaydi (Shia) 40%.

**Territorial extent**
Primarily the northern Sa'dah and surrounding regions, but clashes reported in San'a and elsewhere.
Yemen total: c 528,000 km².

**Timeline**
30 Oct 1918: North Yemen independent of Ottoman Empire as Zaydi Mutawakkilite Kingdom of Yemen.
30 Nov 1968: South Yemen (Aden) independent of Britain. Later forms People's Democratic Republic of Yemen (PDRY).
27 Sep 1962: Monarchy overthrown. Yemen Arab Republic proclaimed.
22 May 1990: North and South Yemen unified as Republic of Yemen.
21 May-7 Jul 1994: Resurgent PDRY in rebellion.
Jun 2004-present: Zaydi insurgency.

**Current status**
Unstable. Insurgency continues.

Yemen, one of the poorest countries in the Arab world, has suffered debilitating internal conflict throughout much of its modern history. From 1918 until 1962, northern Yemen was ruled by the Mutawakkilite dynasty, whose kings, as heads of the Zaydiyyah sect within Shia Islam, exercised both spiritual and temporal power. In 1962 the monarchy was toppled by military officers backed by Egypt, and civil war continued until 1970. Following unification of north and south Yemen in 1990, Marxists in the south sought a resurrection of their People's Democratic Republic of Yemen, plunging the country again into civil war, albeit briefly, in 1994.

In the 21st century, religious divisions have proven a source of renewed conflict. Since mid-2004, Zaydi Shias have been in armed insurrection against the central government, which is largely Sunni. Initially led by Hussein Badreddin al-Houthi, and, subsequent to his death at the hands of government forces, by his son, the rebels claim they are fighting Sunni discrimination. Fighting subsided in 2006, but flared again in 2007 and 2008.

The insurgency is primarily in the extreme north Sa'dah region and the eponymous city, where 18 worshippers were killed in an April 2008 explosion at the Ben Salman mosque (the al-Houthi faction denied responsibility.) A series of further mosque attacks continues during May 2008, and the rebels accused the government of causing widespread civilian casualties during airstrikes against Shia targets.

The Yemeni government, which also faces pressures from Al Qaeda linked Islamist factions and a potential renewal of Marxist insurgency in the south, accuses the Zaydis of seeking a return of the theocratic monarchy deposed in 1962. It has also accused Iran of financing and directing the uprising. While this explanation is perhaps tenable, it is worth noting that the Zaydiyyah sect, which rejects the concept that imans are infallible or that they receive divine guidance, is regarded as heretical by many Shias and diverges sharply from the conservative interpretation of Shia that is the official ideology in Tehran.

# Kurdistan

**Principal protagonists**

Kurds. Various factions. *(See text.)*

Governments of Turkey, Iraq, Iran. (Also Syria.)

*See section on Turkey, 4.02, for details of the Kurdish/Turkish conflict.*

**Nature of conflict**

Long-standing nationalist issue. Ongoing insurgency in Turkey. Civil war in Iraq. Low level conflict in Iran and Syria.

- Widespread human rights abuses allegedly perpetrated by Turkish security forces. Documented war crimes in Iraq. Varying levels of persecution in Iran and Syria.
- Contemporary death toll disputed.
- Up to 2 million, Iraq, 1991-2. 300,000, Turkey, 1980s. Unknown number currently displaced by Iraqi civil war.
- Major oil reserves in Iraqi Kurdistan.

**Population/ethnic composition**

Kurdistan population: 25m-30m (of which 20 million Kurds).

**Territorial extent**

Kurdistan total: c191,000 km².
Kurdistan Autonomous Region (Iraq): 80,000 km².

**Timeline**

1920: Kurdish state proposed under Treaty of Sevres. Never implemented.
1991: Iraqi Kurds rise in revolt at conclusion of first Gulf War. Uprising suppressed; 2 million refugees flee. UN safe haven and Kurdish autonomous region established as consequence.
2003: Kurdish militia forces participate on side of international coalition in second Gulf War, which topples Saddam Hussein.
14 Jun 2005: Kurdistan Autonomous Region established in Iraq.

**Current status**

Iraqi Kurds autonomous. Status of Kurds in other countries unresolved.

**The Kurds, a mountain people descended from Indo-European tribes who settled west of the Caspian Sea around 4,000 years ago, have long maintained a separate cultural identity despite being at the crossroads of larger competing powers. Today, around 10 million Kurds live in south-eastern Turkey, about 5 million in Iran, 4 million in Iraq and smaller populations in Syria, Azerbaijan and Armenia. Although it has never existed as a political entity, the Kurdish inhabited regions are collectively known as 'Kurdistan.'**

The Kurds are one of the largest ethnic groups in the world not to have a state of their own. Straddling several other nations, Kurdish interests have frequently been subordinated to the rivalries of their host nations. While suppressing domestic Kurdish opposition, Turkey, Iraq and Iran have all used Kurdish dissents in neighbouring states to foment trouble. This has contributed to rivalry within the Kurdish population groups, which have rarely achieved unity among themselves – a problem exacerbated by the fact that regional Kurdish dialects are not mutually understandable.

The Kurds of Turkey rose repeatedly in revolt against their Ottoman rulers throughout the 19th century. With the collapse of the Ottoman Empire in the aftermath of the First World War, statehood briefly appeared attainable. The 1920 Treaty of Sevres, which established the French and British mandates in the Middle East, spoke of the creation of a Kurdish state. This aspect of the Treaty was never implemented however, being submerged with the rise of the Turkish Republic under Kemel Ataturk. Further Kurdish revolts, both against the Turks and the Iraqis, continued into the first half of the 20th century. In December 1945, following the Anglo-Soviet occupation of Iran during the Second World War, a Kurdish Republic of Mahabad was created in Iran. After the Soviet withdrawal in 1946, however, this state was crushed by the Iranians.

Kurdish aspirations in Iraq have fared little better. After the Iraqi revolution of 1958 there was a temporary thaw in Iraqi-Kurdish relations, but in 1961-2 the Kurds were subjected to a full scale military onslaught by Iraqi forces, which continued under the Ba'athist regime from 1963 onwards.

Throughout the 1960s and 1970s Iranian hostility towards Baghdad prompted Tehran to arm and support Kurdish insurgents in Iraq. Iraq similarly supported the Kurds of Iran, particularly in the period after the fall of the Shah in 1979.

During the 1980s, Kurds clashed with the security forces of Turkey, Iran and Iraq and were often met with brutal retaliation. In the most notorious incident, Iraq used chemical weapons against the town of Halabja, killing 5,000 and provoking a worldwide outrage but no firm steps by the international community. Incidents such as Halabja inevitably focused attention on what became regularly referred to as 'the plight of the Kurds' but tended to overshadow the equally important Kurdish/Turkish struggle in southeastern Turkey. According to human rights observers, upwards of 3,000 Kurdish villages in Turkey were forcibly cleared during the 1980s, involving the displacement of more than 378,000 people. *(See Turkey, 4.02.)*

Following the end of the first Gulf War in 1991 the Kurds rose in revolt against Baghdad. The degree to which the Kurds were encouraged to rise up by the Americans, and whether they were covertly promised military aid, remains contentious. No aid in fact being forthcoming, the results were horrendous: the uprising was crushed by the Iraqi army and up to two million refugees forced into the mountains under desperate circumstances. Following the 1992 establishment of a safe haven area under UN auspices, Iraqi Kurdistan was established as a distinct region with its own assembly and limited regional powers. (There is also a recognized Kurdistan province in Iran. Turkey and Syria, in contrast, do not acknowledge any part of their Kurdish-inhabited regions as a distinct geographical entity.) Further Kurdish political progress was marred, however, by armed clashes between the two main Iraqi Kurdish parties, the *Partîya Demokrata Kurdistan* (PDK) and the *Yekîtî Nîştimanî Kurdistan* (Patriotic Union of Kurdistan; PUK). Both Iraqi groups also fought the Turkish-based *Partiya Karkerên Kurdistan* (PKK). Part of the reason for the conflict was the double pressure applied by the international economic sanctions against Iraq following the first Gulf War and a blockade by Baghdad. The clear injustice of this position was ameliorated from 1995 onwards when it was agreed that a percentage of Iraqi oil sales (supervised by the UN) could be allocated to the development of Iraqi Kurdistan. This has resulted in relative regional prosperity. The PDK and the PUK agreed a formal ceasefire in 1998.

The Kurdish militia forces, the *peshmerga*, played a role in the overthrow of the Saddam Hussein regime in 2003. In general terms, the Kurds have been seen as supportive of the US-led occupying forces. The Kurds have taken advantage of this relatively favourable position to consolidate their political hold over Iraqi Kurdistan, gaining, in particular, full control over the important oil producing areas around Kirkuk. In June 2005, the Kurdistan Autonomous Region was established with wide powers. Although participating in the central government in Baghdad, Kurdish sentiment continues to broadly favour either outright independence or the creation of a confederal Iraq.

Assuming the overall security situation does not radically deteriorate, continuing Kurdish autonomy in Iraq appears reasonably assured. However, since October 2007 Turkey has openly intervened militarily in Iraqi Kurdistan. Although ostensibly aiming its attacks solely at the PKK, the risk is that the whole Kurdistan region will once again be destabilized. Ankara fears that an effectively independent Kurdish state in Iraq would use its influence to intervene in Turkish Kurdistan, or at the very least, that the emergence of a Kurdish state over the border would further encourage irredentist sentiment in Turkey. In that case, broader geopolitical interests, including those of the United States, the EU and NATO – who, under Turkish pressure, regard the PKK as a terrorist organization – may once again intervene to block Kurdish aspirations.

# Iraq

**Principal protagonists**

Government of Iraq (primarily a coalition of Shia and Kurdish elements). US-led coalition forces.

Elements in Sunni population.

Shia elements; Al Medhi army.

Islamist insurgents; Al Qaeda.

Elements in Kurdish population. (See separate section on Kurdistan, 4.08.)

**Nature of conflict**

Religiously-based civil war exacerbated by presence of foreign forces.

- Human rights abuses by governmental agencies regularly reported.
- Shia/Sunni conflict a core issue.
- Death toll disputed. Up to 670,000.
- 1.6m. Additional 1.5m IDP.
- Very significant oil reserves.

**Population/ethnic composition**

27.5m. Arab 64.4%, Kurdish 23%, Azrei 5.6%. Religious mix: Shia 62%, Sunni 34%, Christian 3.2%.

**Territorial extent**

Iraq: 438,317 km².

**Timeline**

3 Oct 1932: Modern Iraq independent.
16 Jul 1979: Saddam Hussein takes power.
22 Sep 1980-20 Aug 1988: Iran/Iraq war.
1986-88: Al Anfal campaign against Kurds.
2 Aug 1990: Iraq occupies Kuwait, triggering first Gulf War.
28 Feb 1991: Iraqi defeat in first Gulf War.
20 Mar 2003: Start of second Gulf War.
12 Apr 2003: Fall of Baghdad marks effective end of Ba'athist regime. Iraq occupied by US/coalition forces.
15 Oct 2005: New constitution approved by referendum.
15 Dec 2005: First legislative elections under new constitution.
30 Dec 2006: Saddam Hussein executed.

**Current status**

Unresolved and highly unstable.

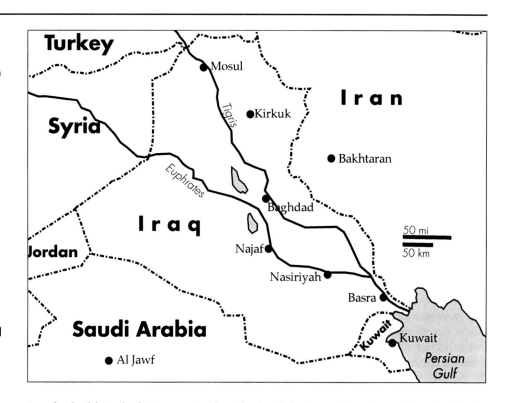

Iraq is the historical Mesopotamia – the land 'between the rivers' (i.e., the Tigris and Euphrates) – that was home to one of the earliest human civilizations, the Sumerians, who emerged as early as 5000 BC. Subsequently under the rule of the Umayyad and Abbasid Caliphates (under whom Baghdad became the largest city of the Middle Ages), the Ottomans and, after the First World War, the British, modern Iraq became independent in 1932. Stability, however, has frequently eluded the country. Its early years were plagued by military coups and in 1941 Britain re-occupied the country, removing a pro-Nazi government. In 1958 a military coup deposed the monarchy and in 1968 a further coup brought in the Sunni-dominated Arab Socialist Ba'ath Party led, from 1979 onwards, by Saddam Hussein.

There are two major ethnic cleavages in modern Iraq. The first is between the Arab population and the Kurds of northern Iraq. The second is between adherents of the Sunni and Shia subdivisions within Islam. Although the Kurds are Sunnis this has not resulted in any significant common ground between Kurds and the Arab Sunnis. During the Al Anfal campaign of 1986-88 over 100,000 Kurds were systematically massacred by primarily Sunni Arab forces in the regular Iraqi army, and in the Halabja massacre of 16 March 1988 at least 5,000 Kurds died as a result of chemical weapons attacks. Other ethnic minorities include the dwindling Christian communities and the 'Marsh Arabs' of southern Iraq, who are mostly Shia and who suffered greatly under the Saddam regime. In August 2007, the small Kurdish Yazidi sect suffered a devastating attack by Islamic extremists when suicide bombers killed over 400 in the largest single attack of its kind.

As a major state in the vital Middle Eastern oil producing region, Iraq has long had a considerable geopolitical significance for Western planners. American strategy in the region has traditionally had two objectives. The first is to ensure that no one local power comes to dominate the whole region and the second, which follows from the first, is to ensure US access to oil supplies. (During the Cold War there was an additional requirement to contain Soviet influence.) US strategy has been greatly aided by the historic enmity between Iraq and Iran, which dates back to the time of Babylon and Persia. Partial Iraqi victory in the Iran/Iraq war of 1980-1988 (in which the US provided tacit aid to Iraq) altered the regional balance in favour of Baghdad, and apparent US acquiescence in this process encouraged Saddam to believe that his subsequent August 1990 annexation of Kuwait would be tolerated. This proved to be a miscalculation: alarm at Iraqi power both in Washington and regional capitals led to a robust international military response to Iraq's occupation of Kuwait, ending in Iraq's expulsion in February 1991.

The 2003 second Gulf War, in the aftermath of the 9/11 terror attacks and the widely supported toppling of the Taliban in Afghanistan, saw the whole of Iraq invaded and occupied by a US-led coalition. The invasion had a number of motives. Simplistically, it was seen as being over control of oil and the completion by George W Bush of the work left unfinished by his father at the end of the first Gulf War. Geopolitically, the US calculated that control of Iraq would enable pressure to be applied to Syria, Iran, and, above all, Saudi Arabia in the event of anti-US fundamentalists gaining the upper hand in Riyadh. Publicly, the aims were the continuation of the 'war on terror', the elimination of 'weapons of mass destruction', and the removal of an unpleasant dictatorship. None of these comfortably bears serious scrutiny. The militarist/socialist regime in Baghdad had little in common with the medieval fundamentalism of Osama Bin Laden and his Al Qaeda movement. It was only after the defeat of Saddam Hussein that Al Qaeda acquired a toe-hold in the country and today it is estimated that there are only 1,600 Al Qaeda fighters in Iraq, whereas the indigenous Shia Medhi Army, to take one example, comprises at least 60,000 men. (A more legitimate source of US concern over external involvement is the arming and training of Shia insurgents by Iran.)

Secondly, although Iraq undoubtedly *did* have weapons of mass destruction – it used chemical weapons against the Kurds (particularly during the notorious Al Anfal Campaign of 1986-8) and the Iranians during the Iran/Iraq war – no subsequent evidence of a systematic weapons of mass destruction programme emerged either during or after the 2003 war.

Whilst removing the dictatorial Saddam Hussein – who was subsequently executed – the US-led invasion did not lead to national stability or reconciliation. Far from allowing the development of civil society, as was intended, the introduction of multiparty democracy simply resulted in the establishment of parties along racial/religious lines, while the need for inter-communal power sharing arrangements led to factional horse-trading and governmental paralysis.

Under the three-way stresses of conflict between Kurds, Sunnis and Shias, as well as insurgencies directed against Coalition forces, Iraq could effectively break up into regions and segregated townships in which religiously based factions vie for effective control of resources, including patronage from Coalition military forces. Inter-religious conflict, including suicide and other terrorist

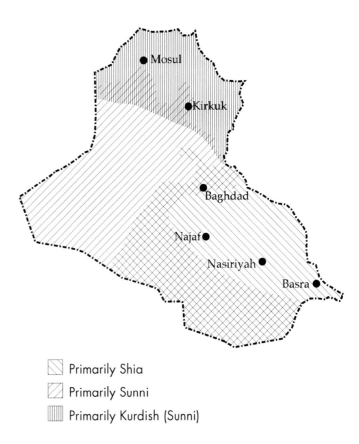

**Generalized ethnic map of Iraq**

◊ Primarily Shia
◊ Primarily Sunni
◊ Primarily Kurdish (Sunni)

bombings, are endemic throughout the country. Arguably, the effective division of Iraq as a whole into three competing entities – for Kurds, Sunnis, and Shias – is already well advanced. The autonomous Kurdish state in northern Iraq is the most developed (and stable) and enjoys at least tacit endorsement from the US. *(See Kurdistan, 4.08.)* Elsewhere in the country, particularly the central region where populations of Sunnis and Shias are intermixed, violence and ethnic cleansing is rife as the religious demarcation lines are fought out. As in Bosnia a decade earlier, it may well be that international recognition of this reality – a Dayton Plan for Iraq? – will occur, but only after horrendous suffering by displaced populations. Stability is only likely to come about if there are specific agreements defining regional power, territory, and responsibilities.

As part of the 'Iraqification' of the country there is an ongoing policy of transferring responsibility for security to US or British trained Iraqi forces. But the problem remains that various sections of the security apparatus have been heavily infiltrated and effectively parcelled out between the competing factions. In many cases, therefore, all the Americans and British are doing is providing arms, uniforms and training to ethnic militias who have proven themselves, for the most part, entirely unwilling to act against their own communities if required to do so.

The December 2006 report of the US Iraq Study Group (better known as the Baker-Hamilton report) was the first substantive appraisal to significantly address four areas that had previously been anathema, at least in public, to US planners. The first was that the conflict in Iraq has all the characteristics of a civil war. The second was that the possibility of wholesale disintegration of central government and Iraq's consequent falling into 'failed state' status is a very real one. The third conclusion, drawing from the first two, was that a high degree of regionalization – partition in all but name – was inevitable in any successful conflict resolution. Finally, Baker-Hamilton recognized that an unstable or collapsed Iraq state would have grave consequences for the region as a whole and that accordingly other regional powers, such as Syria and Iran, both could and should be involved in an overall settlement. Baker-Hamilton also highlighted the failure of the Iraqi government to make significant progress on the creation of functioning national institutions.

Perhaps predictably, the conclusions of Baker-Hamilton were never fully acted upon by the US government, which preferred instead to rely on increased, if ostensibly temporary, US troop deployments (the 'surge'). The equivalent British experience in the southern city of Basra, however, suggested that militants might simply 'ride out' the 'surge', either disappearing into the local community or being absorbed into existing security forces before reclaiming power when the foreign troops are withdrawn. Following an upsurge in violence in Basra in mid-2007, British forces were effectively restricted to their barracks, able to defend themselves but not to extend influence to the rest of the city, which was officially handed back to the Iraqi 'authorities' (i.e., the militias) in December 2007. Significantly, much of the violence in Basra, Baghdad and elsewhere now has less to do with driving out the Americans and their allies and more to do with the control of populations, districts, institutions and resources.

The concept of a federal Iraq was accepted in the new constitution adopted in 2005. This was passed by a 78% majority in a referendum in which two thirds of Iraqis voted. Although supported, therefore, by an overall majority – and by the Kurdish and Shia communities – the constitution was heavily rejected by Sunni Arabs. Subsequent elections, in December 2005, produced a parliament almost wholly comprised of religiously predicated parties.

In October 2006 Iraqi MPs passed a Shia-sponsored Federalism Bill facilitating the division of the country into autonomous regions. The legislation allows existing provinces to group together to form self-ruling regions (as has already happened in Iraqi Kurdistan). This measure may well see the crystallization of Sunni and Shia states in the west and south of the country respectively. The new law was bitterly opposed by Sunni Arabs (who abstained on the vote in a failed attempt to deny it a quorum) but also by anti-government Shia elements, most significantly the Medhi Army, who, for different motives, oppose the break up of Iraq. The Sunnis fear they will be defeated by the Shia majority in any unitary Iraq but, slightly paradoxically, many do not favour partition as this would lead, they believe, to an Iran-dominated Shia state in the south in which Sunnis would be persecuted. Following the general election of 2006, the core of the Iraqi government is an uneasy alliance between Shia and Kurdish parties; in August 2007 the largest Sunni party, the Sunni Accordance Party, walked out of the government.

Supporters of the Medhi Army, led by Shia cleric Muqtaba al Sadr, had previously left the government, further weakening its basis of support. Intra-Shia conflict is a significant element in the civil conflict. An October 2007 ceasefire between the Supreme Council for the Islamic Revolution (which remained within the government) and the Medhi Army, on terms broadly favourably to the former, led to temporary reconciliation within the Shia community, but this accommodation broke down violently in March 2008, necessitating wholesale intervention by US and British forces in an attempt to contain intra-Shia fighting that left hundreds dead. Following a resumption of the truce in May 2008, however, some 10,000 Iraqi police and troops were able to occupy Sadr City, the Medhi Army's main Baghdad stronghold, without resistence.

Iraq stands as a salutary reminder to Western policy makers that the introduction of democratic structures on an open franchise does not of itself create a stable or peaceful society. Unlike intervention in, say, Sierra Leone, where British involvement has gradually guided a failed state back to a semblance of normality, the US-led intervention in Iraq runs the risk of having the opposite effect: the unintended consequence of the removal of the dictatorial Ba'athist regime of Saddam Hussein being the creation of a power vacuum into which local militia and factions can move. Currently, there can be little doubt that the Nouri al-Maliki government would simply collapse were Western military support to be withdrawn, leaving Iraq with no functioning central authority – in other words, as a failed state.

# Sinai

**Principal protagonists**

Government of Egypt.

Marginalized Bedouin Sinai inhabitants, including sympathizers with the Palestinian cause and Islamist fundamentalism.

**Nature of conflict**

Terrorist bombing campaign fuelled by local marginalization and broader Middle Eastern conflict.

☠ c100 civilian deaths in bombing and other incidents.

**Population/ethnic composition**

380,000. Bedouin Arab majority, Palestinian minority, Nile Valley settlers. Relative percentages disputed.

**Territorial extent**

Sinai Peninsula: 61,000 km².

**Timeline**

1260: Sinai comes under Egyptian (later Ottoman) rule.

26 Jul 1956: Egypt nationalizes the Suez Canal leading to British, French and Israeli intervention in Sinai in October.

5-10 Jun 1967: Israel occupies Sinai during the 'Six Day War'.

6-26 Oct 1973: Sinai one of the main theatres of the Yom Kippur war.

17 Sep 1978: Camp David Accords lead to peace treaty between Israel and Egypt. Phased Israeli withdrawal from Sinai begins in 1979

25 Apr 1982: Final Israeli withdrawal from Sinai.

7 Oct 2004: Sporadic terrorist bombings begin.

22 Jan 2008: Palestinians successfully storm and open the restricted Gaza/Sinai border crossing.

Jul-Sep 2007: Major Bedouin demonstrations.

**Current status**

Unresolved. Egyptian government continues to treat terrorist and civil rights campaigns as security issues rather than having a broader social/ethnic dimension.

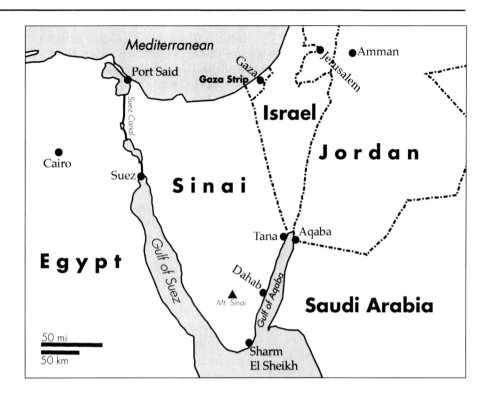

**Geographically and culturally separate from the rest of Egypt, Sinai has long been excluded from the Egyptian mainstream, and much of its population does not identify with the 'Pharaonic' heritage of the rest of Egypt.**

A significant minority of the Sinai population is of Palestinian extraction, which has close political and familial ties to the populations of Gaza and the West Bank. The majority Bedouin have links to tribal groups in Israel/Palestine and Jordan.

Following Egypt's defeat at the hands of the Israelis in 1967, the entire Sinai region was occupied by Israel until the historic peace agreement between Cairo and Tel Aviv in 1979 saw a phased Israeli withdrawal under international supervision. Israel retains rights to maintain a security presence on the Egyptian side of the Sinai/Israeli border.

Since 2004, Sinai has been the scene of a sporadic series of terrorist bombings, which the Egyptian government ascribes to supporters of the Palestinian cause, Al Qaeda, or both. Attacks on hotels and other tourist targets, while involving a relatively low loss of life, have had a hugely negative effect on the local economy, which is heavily dependent on visitors from Israel.

The Egyptian government has made little effort to integrate Sinai into national life. It has, however, promoted the immigration of Nile Valley settlers, further increasing local tensions and alienation. Critics claim the immigration policy is deeply discriminatory, with the settlers being given favourable access to land, grants, and other benefits, in an attempt to create a stable pro-Cairo client population. Significant Bedouin demonstrations calling for basic amenities took place throughout the territory in mid-2007.

The geopolitical status of Sinai as a buffer zone between Israel and Egypt, means it has crucial security implications for both sides, as well as for those who would seek to promote unrest in the region. The storming, by Palestinians, of the heavily restricted Gaza/Sinai border in January 2008 suggests that Sinai may once again become a significant regional flashpoint.

# The Islamic Caliphate

**Principal protagonists**

Islamist (mainly Sunni) supporters of the restoration of the Caliphate; Al Qaeda and other Islamist groups such as Hizb-ut-Tahrir.

**Nature of conflict**

Proponents of the Caliphate see it in terms of the historic struggle by Muslims against Christian/Western domination. Within Muslim majority states it is essentially a power struggle with the relationship between religion and state at its heart.

**Population/ethnic composition**

Theoretically, the population of the Caliphate would be in excess of 1 billion.

**Territorial extent**

Theoretically all states in which there is either a Muslim majority or which were historically under Islamic rule. *(See map opposite.)*

**Timeline**

632 AD: Death of Mohammed. His successor, Abu Bakr, assumes power as Caliph.

7-8th century: Umayyad Caliphate.

8-13th century: Abbasid Caliphate.

15-20th century: Ottoman Caliphate.

3 Mar 1924: Ottoman Caliphate formally abolished.

1990s: Rise of pro-Caliphate Islamist sentiment in aftermath of Soviet defeat in Afghanistan and collapse of USSR.

1996: Taliban regime declares Afghanistan an 'Islamic Emirate.'

11 Sep 2001: Islamist terrorist attacks on continental US targets mark start of 'war on terror'.

Nov 2001: NATO forces overthrow the Taliban in Afghanistan.

**Current status**

Worldwide Islamist terrorism and related conflict remain a key global security issue.

Historically, the 'Caliphate' refers to the Islamic polity that unified all Muslims under a common ruler, the Caliph, who was seen as the political successor to the prophet Mohammed. In ethnological terms, the Caliphate is a classical example of a shared past (and, by implication, shared future) that serves to unite an otherwise racially and culturally disparate group of populations. As a romanticized 'golden age' the Caliphate counterpoints strikingly with the corruption, poverty, political weakness and economic failure that characterizes the day-to-day lives of many Muslims. The Caliphate thus serves as an obvious rallying point for radical, disaffected and marginalized groups within Muslim societies.

The Caliphate, though never as unified as its proponents would seek to suggest, formed a major political entity from the seventh century onwards when it covered much of northern Africa and the Middle East, parts of south-eastern Europe, and the Iberian peninsula. The term was also adopted by the Ottomans and used formally until 1924. Today, calls for a restored Caliphate form part of the agenda of radical Muslim groups of the which the Al Qaeda terrorist organization is the best known. Formal support for the restoration of the Caliphate is more pronounced among Sunni Muslims than from the Shia branch of Islam. Sunnis believe that the Caliph can be elected or chosen by a consensus of the population. Shias take a narrower view, maintaining that only direct descendants of Muhammad are eligible rulers. The Shia government of Iran, although strongly Islamic, has never formally proclaimed or supported the re-creation of the Caliphate. In contrast, the Sunni fundamentalist Taliban regime in Afghanistan, which ruled most of the country from 1996 until 2001, formally proclaimed Afghanistan an 'Islamic Emirate' and thus, at least theoretically, part of a putative restored Caliphate. *(See Afghanistan, 5.22.)*

Proponents of the Caliphate envisage it as a single state under Islamic *sharia* law, which would unite all lands in which Muslims are currently a majority, as well as those formerly ruled by Muslims. The latter would include Spain and Portugal, much of south-eastern Europe, and India, formerly under Moghul rule. The territorial claims of supporters of the restoration of the Caliphate are thus, to put it mildly, far reaching. Furthermore, at least implicitly, many proponents of the Caliphate see the restoration of its historical boundaries as merely the first step to the establishment of *Ummah*, a global Islamic state.

Effectively a dormant issue from 1924 onwards (when Ataturk formally abolished the Ottoman Caliphate) calls for the restoration of the Caliphate have acquired a new urgency in recent years as it is one of the central demands of Islamist extremists such as Al Qaeda and associated groups.

Al Qaeda was established under the leadership of Saudi-born Osama Bin Laden in the aftermath of Soviet withdrawal from Afghanistan. Encouraged by successful Islamic resistance to the Soviet occupation of Afghanistan, the movement sought to continue and extend the Islamic struggle against what it saw as foreign influence or occupation of Muslim states, whether Communist or Western. Following the collapse of the USSR as a world power in the 1990s, the anti-Western emphasis came to dominate Islamist rhetoric and strategy. This intensified further after the Saudi government (after allegedly spurning Bin Laden's offers of assistance) permitted the stationing of US troops in Saudi Arabia during and after the first Gulf War. Al Qaeda and its affiliates were responsible for a series of terrorist attacks against US and other Western targets throughout the late 1990s and early 2000s, culminating in the devastating '9/11' attacks on New York and Washington DC in which hijacked civilian airliners were used as flying bombs against the World Trade Center in New York and the Pentagon in Washington.

Al Qaeda was rapidly identified as the group behind the attacks and its leader, Osama Bin Laden, immediately became a household name. The

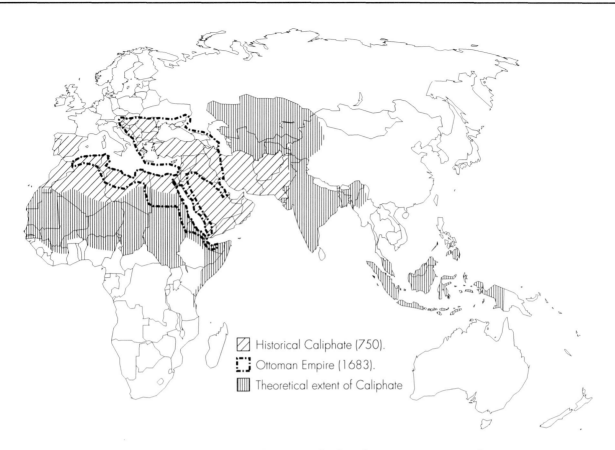

Historical Caliphate (750).
Ottoman Empire (1683).
Theoretical extent of Caliphate

US also identified Taliban-controlled Afghanistan as harbouring the main Al Qaeda training and leadership camps (including hosting Bin Laden himself) and, with support from NATO and anti-Taliban elements in Afghanistan, invaded and toppled the Kabul regime in November 2001, although failing in their objective of capturing or killing Bin Laden. In the subsequent 'war on terror' the United States also led the 2003 invasion of Iraq which removed Saddam Hussein.

Whether Al Qaeda predicted the US-led interventions in Afghanistan and Iraq is a matter of some controversy within defence and intelligence circles. Some contend that Osama Bin Laden saw 9/11 as the prelude to a universal Islamist uprising against current regimes, including those nominally led by Muslims, throughout the Islamic world. Clearly, this uprising did not occur. The weakness in this interpretation is that Al Qaeda and its local surrogates do not appear to have done much to encourage such an uprising in the immediate post-9/11 environment. The alternative hypothesis is that Bin Laden anticipated, and welcomed, US intervention in Afghanistan as a means of drawing it into a protracted 'Vietnam' style conflict (which, by Islamist reading, the US is psychologically unable to undertake). By this reading, the US invasion of Iraq – where the secular/socialist/militarist regime of Saddam Hussein, although predominantly Sunni, was deeply hostile to Al Qaeda's aspirations – was something of a bonus for Bin Laden. The assumption has to be that Bin Laden calculated that the US would invade Afghanistan, but whether the rapid ousting of the Taliban government was considered a likely, or even a desirable, outcome has to be speculative. It should also be noted that, although Al Qaeda doubtless welcomes the sight of the Americans becoming bogged down in an unwinnable war of attrition in Iraq, the likely successor regime in Baghdad should the US be expelled – a Shia government more closely aligned to Iran – is not necessarily one which would be sympathetic to Al Qaeda and its aspirations for the re-creation of the Islamic Caliphate.

Islamist grievances over Israel/Palestine, the US military presence in Saudi Arabia, the general corruption and poverty of governments in much of the Muslim world, and the alleged maltreatment of Muslim minorities elsewhere, continue to provide the raw fuel for recruitment to militant groups. Their broader goal, the creation of an Islamic world government, may appear wholly unrealistic, but it is for that very reason that dialogue, let alone accommodation, with militant Islam is unlikely to be easy to achieve. In the context of the 'war on terror', the Islamist aspiration of re-creating the Caliphate remains a crucial international security concern.

# Israel/Palestine

**Principal protagonists**

State of Israel; Jewish population.

Palestinian population; Palestinian National Authority; Palestine Liberation Organization (various factions); Hamas.

**Nature of conflict**
Long-standing territorial issue.

- Retaliations against civilians by Israeli authorities reported.
- Muslim/Jewish conflict an issue.
- c17,000 since 1948.
- 4.25 million, including Jordan 1.78m; Gaza 0.96m; West Bank 0.68m.

**Population/ethnic composition**
Israel: 6.4m. Jewish 76%. Remainder mostly Arab.
Gaza Strip: 1.4m. Arab and others 99.4%. All Jewish settlers evacuated 2005.
West Bank: 2.5m. Palestinian Arabs and other 83%, Jewish 17%.

**Territorial extent**
Israel, including Golan Heights and East Jerusalem: 22,145 km²; West Bank: 5,860 km²; Gaza Strip: 360 km².

**Timeline**
See opposite.

**Current status**
Unresolved. Ongoing conflict between Israel and Palestinian forces, as well as intra-Palestinian conflicts.

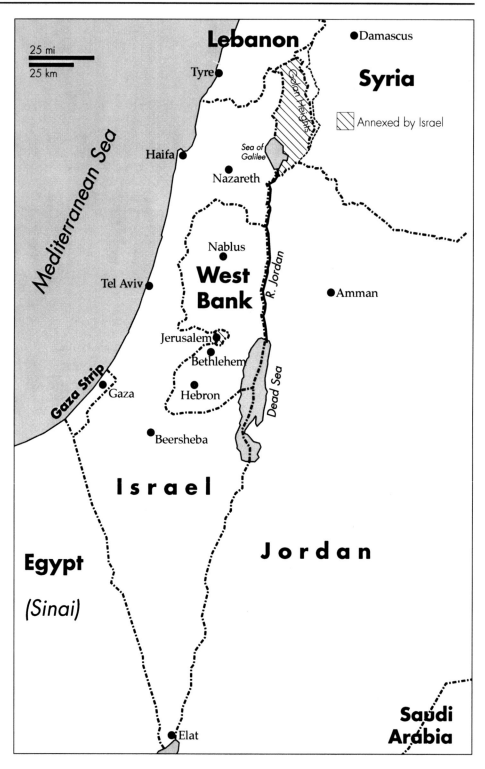

**One of the longest running and geopolitically dangerous of all ethnic conflicts, the Jewish/Palestinian dispute has seen more or less continuous conflict, including several full regional wars, since the creation of the State of Israel in 1948.**

Seemingly intractable, the roots of the conflict go back into antiquity. In 135 AD, the Roman Emperor Hadrian expelled the Jews from Jerusalem and the eventual worldwide emigration of Jews created the Jewish diaspora. Zionism, the movement advocating the creation of a Jewish homeland in Palestine, originated in the early 19th century and saw the first modern establishment of Jewish settlements in Palestine, which at this stage was part of the Ottoman empire. By 1914, around 90,000 Jews lived in Palestine, as compared to around half a million Arabs.

The First World War saw Britain in conflict with the Ottoman Turks, and, in an attempt to court international Jewish support for the war, the British publicly endorsed the concept of a Jewish homeland in Palestine in the 'Balfour Declaration'. In December 1917, a British army marched into Jerusalem (becoming the first Christian army to occupy the city since the Crusades) and in the post-war settlement Palestine, together with Transjordan (modern day Jordan and West Bank) were mandated to the British by the newly created League of Nations.

The League required Britain to press ahead with the Balfour Plan, an action that was seen as a betrayal by the Arabs (and their British supporters, most notably Laurence of Arabia) since the British had also previously promised to support Arab independence. With the rise of Hitler in the 1930s and increased Jewish immigration pressures, the British were placed in the invidious position of being required to establish a Jewish state while simultaneously limiting Jewish settlement.

In 1937, the British advocated the partition of Palestine into separate Jewish and Arab states. This was rejected by the Arabs but accepted, albeit with reservations, by the Jews. Inter-communal violence, and attacks by both sides on British forces were only partially halted by the advent of the Second World War. In 1947 the United Nations again recommended partition. Against a declining security situation, with widespread attacks upon them by Jewish terrorist organizations, the British announced the termination of their mandate on 15 May 1948.

On 14 May 1948 the Jewish National Council proclaimed the State of Israel, which was immediately attacked by Arab forces from the surrounding states. The new Israeli state withstood these attacks, gaining, by the time an armistice was signed in 1949, control over 60% of the territory of Palestine. The widespread displacement of Arabs from the new state formed the basis of a refugee population that continues to the present day.

In 1964, the Palestinian Charter was adopted and the Palestine Liberation Organization was formed. The already poor relations between Israel and the Arab states deteriorated until, in June 1967, Israel staged a pre-emptive strike against her neighbours. Israeli victory in this, the Six Day War, saw Israel occupy the Golan Heights (from Syrian), the Sinai Peninsula (from Egypt), the Gaza Strip, the West Bank, and East Jerusalem. This was to have crucial results for the future trajectory of the conflict, as Jewish settlement, often by hardliners to whom the new regions were an integral part of the Biblical Israel, commenced in areas previously held by Arabs. The 1973 war, involving attacks by Syria and Egypt, failed to reverse Israeli gains and it was not until 1979, following delicate peace talks between Israel and Egypt, that peace was signed between the two and a phased withdrawal of Israeli forces from Sinai commenced. Meanwhile, terrorist attacks by the PLO continued against Israel, which met force with force. In 1980, Israel formally annexed East Jerusalem, declared Jerusalem the capital of Israel, and announced plans for an ambitious programme of Jewish settlement in and around the city.

At its most fundamental level, the conflict is about land, access, and resources. Under Israeli rule, Palestinians (as well as Arabs in Israel proper) are denied equality in land acquisition. Furthermore, under the guise of security measures, Palestinian movements are restricted, cutting them off from grazing and employment opportunities. The most pressing disparity is that over water resources. Upon occupying the West Bank, Israel closely restricted the construction of new boreholes and pipelines while expanding availability both to Israel proper and to the new Jewish settlements. As a consequence, there is a severe imbalance in water usage, with Israelis using an average of 350 litres per day compared to a Palestinian average of only 60 litres.

Repeated efforts at a negotiated solution to the problem have floundered on the fundamental incompatibility of the two sides aims. In 1987, in the first *intifada* ('uprising' – literally 'shaking off'), Palestinians in the occupied territories launched a general uprising against Israeli occupation. In 1988, however, the PLO, under the long-standing leadership of Yasser Arafat, declared Palestin-

### Timeline

135 AD: Romans expel Jews from Jerusalem.

7 Nov 1917: Balfour Declaration of British support for the creation of a Jewish state.

25 Apr 1920: League of Nations created Palestinian Mandate, under British control.

14 May 1948: State of Israel proclaimed.

15 May 1948: Formal end of British mandate.

24 Feb 1949: Armistice between Israel and Arab states consolidates border of State of Israel.

26 Jun 1964: Palestine Liberation Organization (PLO) created.

5-10 Jun 1967: Six Day War leaves Israel in control of greatly expanded territory.

6-26 Oct 1973: 'Yom Kippur' war.

17 Sep 1978: Camp David Accords lead to peace treaty between Israel and Egypt.

8 Dec 1987: Start of first *intifada*.

15 Nov 1988: Palestinian declaration of independence. (PLO recognizes Israel within 1949 borders.)

20 Aug 1993: Oslo Accords lead to formation of Palestinian Authority in 1994.

Sep 2000: Start of second *intifada*.

1 Mar 2002: Start of Israel re-occupation of West Bank.

25 Jan 2006: Election of Hamas parliamentary majority in Gaza.

7-14 Jun 2007: Hamas takes full control of Gaza Strip, expelling Fatah (PLO) elements.

15 Jun 2007: Palestinian President dissolves Hamas-led government.

ian independence whilst recognizing the right of Israel to exist within its 1949 borders – effectively conceding that the Palestinian state would comprise the West Bank (over which Jordan effectively ceded sovereignty in 1974) and the refugee-crowded Gaza Strip.

Under the 1994 Oslo Accords, a Palestinian Authority was created with control over security and civil affairs in urban areas in the West Bank and Gaza (areas classed as 'Area A'), and civil authority in 'Area B' rural areas. 'Area C' areas, including key roads, border areas and Israeli settlements, remained under Israeli control under what was originally envisaged as a five-year transition period.

Yasser Arafat returned to the West Bank in 1994 and was elected President of the Palestinian Authority in 1996. Although the Palestinian Authority was seen by many as a transitional structure, which could lead to full sovereignty, it proved incapable of meeting Israel's security needs nor, in an atmosphere of increasing corruption, of satisfying the domestic aspirations of many Palestinians. In 2000 the 'second *intifada*' commenced and in 2002 Israel re-occupied the West Bank.

The inability of the Palestinian Authority to operate as a functioning regime exacerbated the rivalries within the Palestinian movement, particularly between the pro-Arafat Fatah movement and the more radical Hamas organizations, which was formed in 1987. Within the PLO the Fatah faction has traditionally been dominant, but Arafat's declining health and eventual death in November 2004, contributed to an erosion of its authority within the overall Palestinian cause.

In January 2006, elections took place for the Palestinian Legislative Council, the 'parliament' of the Palestinian Authority. These resulted in the election of a Hamas majority, which precipitated a withdrawal of political and financial support to the Palestinian Authority by Israel, the US and the European Union. In June 2006, Fatah and Hamas announced the creation of a national unity government, but factional fighting continued until, in June 2007, Hamas seized outright control of the Gaza Strip, effectively splitting 'Palestine' into two competing statelets. As a consequence of the Hamas takeover of Gaza, Palestinian President Mahmoud Abbas dismissed the Hamas-led government. Subsequent Israeli air and ground raids left hundreds dead. In June 2008, Israel and Hamas declared a ceasefire for the Gaza region, but this broke down within days when Hamas resumed rocket attacks into southern Israel, and the Israelis once more closed the border. No speedy resolution to the Israel/Palestine conflict can be envisaged.

**Israeli expansion since 1948**

- Jewish territory under 1947 UN partition plan
- Annexed by Israel, 1948-9
- Occupied by Israel, 1967
- Occupied by Israel, 1967. Subsequently annexed
- Occupied by Israel, 1967. Subsequently returned
- Southern Lebanon periodically occupied by Israel

# Section 5: **Central and West Asia**

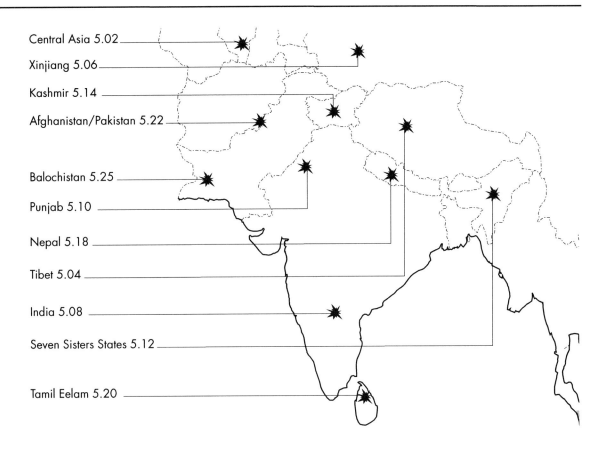

Central Asia 5.02
Xinjiang 5.06
Kashmir 5.14
Afghanistan/Pakistan 5.22

Balochistan 5.25
Punjab 5.10
Nepal 5.18
Tibet 5.04
India 5.08
Seven Sisters States 5.12

Tamil Eelam 5.20

Chagos Islands 5.17

*Minorities in China 5.07*
*Nepal's Bhutanese refugees 5.19*
*NATO and 9/11 5.24*
*Pakistan's political problems 5.26*

v4.0　　　　　　　　　　　　　　　　　　　　　　　　　　　　　　　*Fields of Fire – An Atlas of Ethnic Conflict*　　**5.01**

# Central Asia

**Principal protagonists**

Governments of Kazakhstan, Kyrgyzstan, Tajikistan, Turkmenistan and Uzbekistan.

Ethnic/tribal factions.

Islamist insurgents.

**Nature of conflict**
a) Ethnically-based land use conflicts, Fergana Valley. b) Islamist insurgency, Uzbekistan and generally. c) Ethnically-based factional war, Tajikistan.

🕴 Human rights abuses by governments reported. (In May 2005, Uzbeki security forces shot up to 1,000 demonstrators.)
☠ 60,000 (Tajikistan, 1992-7).
👪 1.2m (Tajikistan, 1992-7).

**Population/ethnic composition**
See table opposite.

**Territorial extent**
Kazakhstan: 2,724,900 km².
Kyrgyzstan: 200,000 km².
Turkmenistan: 488,000 km².
Tajikistan: 143,100 km².
Uzbekistan: 447,400 km².

**Timeline**
18th century: Central Asia absorbed into Russian Empire.
1924-36: Present day Central Asian republics created as Soviet Socialist Republics.
1991: Central Asian republics gain independence after collapse of USSR.
1992-7: Full-scale civil war in Tajikistan.
2005-6: Islamist demonstrations throughout region met with severe governmental repression.

**Current status**
Low-level Islamist insurgency continues. Possibility of ethnic and religious flare-ups exists.

The Central Asian region became part of the Tsarist Empire in, for the most part, the latter half of the 18th century, and for much of its history has been an area of relatively low levels of political awareness. Home to more than 100 ethnic groups, the region's borders were drawn fairly arbitrarily by the Soviet authorities. The Uzbek and Turkmen SSRs were created in 1924. Tajikistan, initially an autonomous region within Uzbekistan, achieved full SSR status in 1929; Kazakhstan and Kirghizia (as it was then known) only became SSRs in 1936. Unlike other parts of the USSR, such as the Baltics and the Caucasus, there was very little agitation for independence prior to the collapse of the Soviet Union. In common with the other SSRs, however, the 'five stans' became independent states in 1991.

Since 1991 the Central Asian republics have followed differing courses while uniting on common issues such as their opposition to Islamist extremism, a cause they share not only with Moscow and the West but with their Chinese neighbours, who have their own reasons for opposing Islamic-based nationalism in Xinjiang (See 5.06). Kazakhstan, the largest of the Central Asian republics (and the one with the largest Russian minority) has generally been the most stable, with significant moves towards a free market economy that have not, for the most part, been marked by political freedom; Kazakhstan politics remaining for the most part authoritarian and personality-driven. Turkmenistan, too, has generally remained peaceful despite – or because of – the authoritarian, and increasingly eccentric personality cult that surrounded Life President Saparmurat Niyazov Türkmenbaçy until his unexpected death, aged 66, in December 2006. Krygyzstan, Tajikistan and Uzbekistan have all wrestled with the problems of Islamist activism and insurgency, with Uzbekistan generally taking the hardest line against *Hizb-ut-Tahrir* and other underground Islamist groups. Ethnic tensions between Russians and indigenous groups have been a feature of the post-independence environment, with some 2 million Russians emigrating from Uzbekistan to Russia.

Tajikistan has seen significant post-independence violence. As the Soviet Union collapsed the generally conservative and hard-line Tajik regime began to adopt a more nationalist position, supporting the 1989 law which gave the Tajik language primacy in the republic and establishing a foundation to preserve Tajik culture. These attempts to build a nationalist power-base were only partially successful, however, as splits developed between the urban political elites and the more culturally and religiously conservative rural regions. Weak civil institutions, religious, regional and tribal animosities, and factional conflicts within the ruling elite, all contributed to a rapid descent into full-scale civil war in Tajikistan. Fighting broke out in May 1992 between the Moscow-backed government, Islamists, and regional groups centred on the Garm and Gorno-Badakhstan districts. With the aid of Russian and Uzbekistan troops, the Tajiki government initially gained the upper hand and in December 1992 a new government was formed under Emomali Rahmonov, who was heavily dependent on militia support from his home Kulyab region. These militias launched an at times ferocious attack on opposition factions, including militants from the Islamic Renaissance Party, the pro-Islamist Garmi people of Qurgonteppa, and the Pamiri, the latter hailing from the Gorno-Badakhstan region. Hundreds of thousands of Pamiri and Garmi were driven into Afghanistan in ethnic cleansing operations. There, elements became aligned with the Islamic Movement of Uzbekistan, while others re-armed with the aid of Islamist militants from groups such as *Jamait-I-Islami*. In fighting in 1996 (which spread as far as the capital) Afghan militants were encountered amongst the combatants.

In 1997 a UN-brokered agreement led to a ceasefire, and peaceful elections were held in 1999.

A regional nexus of ethnic and religious conflict in the Central Asian region is the Fergana Valley, which straddles regions of Uzbekistan, Kyrgyzstan and Tajikistan. As in other regions of the former USSR, the republic borders did not matter too much while the whole region was geared to a single economic activity – cotton production – and it was united by a common political structure. With the collapse of the USSR, however, many communities found themselves on the 'wrong' side of an international border, while transport across the region acquired new difficulties. Regional conflict has led to the frequent closure of borders between Uzbekistan and its neighbours, making communications problematic. To compound the issue, Fergana is the site of a number of exclaves: four Uzbeki, one Tajik, and one Kyrgyz. The exclaves range in population from the Uzbek town of Sokh with a population of more than 42,000, to the tiny Kyrgyz village of Barak, which has a population of 627.

Land use and water resource pressures, together with the threat of Islamist extremism in this religiously conservative area, all play a part in ethnic tensions in the Fergana region. In 1989 and 1990 there were riots between Uzbek and Kyrgyz residents in the town of Uzgen, and in May 2005 Uzbek troops opened fire on Islamist demonstrators in the town of Andijan, killing around 1,000. In a particularly severe clampdown on Islamist activity, since partially rescinded, local officials restricted public prayers, insisted that all restaurants sell alcohol, and banned mosques from broadcasting their traditional calls to prayer. In Osh, as well as in the Kyrgyz capital Bishkek, protesters demanded the removal of Kyrgyz officials (including the Chief Mufti, who was accused of betraying *sharia* law) and challenged the right of Government's State Agency for Religious Affairs to regulate religious activity.

Regionally, the conflict against Islamist insurgents may now be said to be contained at a low level, aided by inter-governmental co-operation (which includes China) on 'counter-terrorist' measures. Although regional governments have legitimate fears over Islamist extremism spilling over from Afghanistan, the danger remains that over-enthusiastic restrictions may produce a result opposite to that which is intended.

**Racial composition of the Central Asian republics (total population in brackets).**

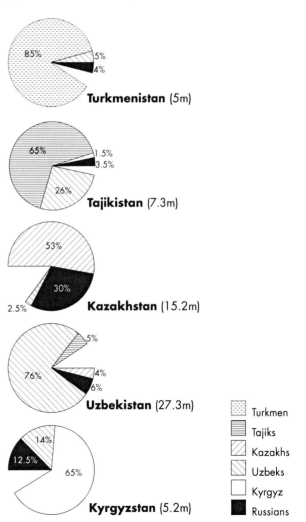

# Tibet

**Principal protagonists**

Tibetan people; Tibetan Government in Exile.

Chinese government; Han Chinese and Hui (Muslim) immigrants.

**Nature of conflict**
Nationalist self-determination issue.

- Routine oppression of political, separatist and religious dissidents by Chinese state.
- Repression of Tibetan Buddhists an issue.
- 87,000 in 1959 uprising.
- 100,000 Tibetan refugees, mostly to India.

**Population/ethnic composition**
Tibetan Autonomous Region: 2.75m. Tibetans 92.8%, Han Chinese 6.1%. (2000 census. Tibetan activists claim official figures dramatically under-represent the scale of Han migration.)

**Territorial extent**
Tibetan Autonomous Region: 1,228,400 km². Qinghai: 721,000 km².

**Timeline**
- c600 AD: Kingdom of Tibet founded.
- 1244: Tibet falls under Mongol rule.
- 1720: Under suzerainty of the Qing (Chinese) Empire.
- 28 Oct 1912: Tibet rejects inclusion in the Republic of China.
- 7 Oct 1950: Invaded and occupied by People's Republic of China.
- 23 May 1951: Formally annexed by China.
- June 1956-1959: Tibetan uprising.
- 31 Mar 1959: Dalai Lama flees into exile.
- 15 Mar 2008: Widespread protests against Chinese hosting of the Olympic games. Over 100 killed.

**Current status**
Unresolved. Chinese occupation of Tibet continues.

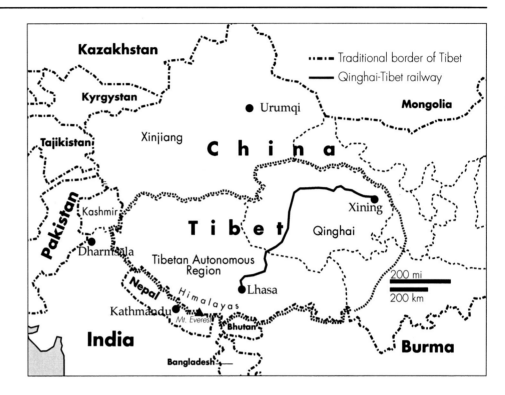

A vast land lying to the north of India, Tibet is home to an ancient and distinctive form of Buddhism of immense cultural significance. An extremely isolated (and isolationist) country, Tibet had little contact with the modern world until the beginning of the 20th century. Cultural links exist with northern India, Nepal and Bhutan, but the Tibetan language bears little relationship to those of India or China. The spiritual and temporal leader of the Tibetan people is the Dalai Lama, who is viewed as a reincarnation of the *Buddha Avalokitesvara* or 'Buddha of Compassion.' The current Dalai Lama is the 14th in a line dating back to the 15th century. Since 1950 Tibet has been under the occupation of the People's Republic of China, which claims the territory as an integral part of China.

Formerly a powerful state in its own right, Tibet was invaded by the Mongols in the 13th century, although a high level of religious autonomy was maintained. In 1705 the Mongols invaded in force, with the support of the Chinese emperor. Tibet's Amdo province and the eastern part of Kham province were placed under direct Chinese rule in 1724 and 1728 respectively. In 1904 a British military expedition forced its way to the capital, Lhasa, intent on opening up the country to British diplomacy and trade. In treaties of 1904 and 1906 (the latter with the Chinese) the British demarcated the Tibetan/Nepalese border and undertook neither to annex Tibet nor to interfere with its governance. In the Anglo-Russian treaty of 1907 and the Conventions of Simla in 1914, Britain recognized Chinese suzerainty, but not sovereignty, over Tibet.

The Republic of China was formed in 1912 and, after a period of imprisonment at the hands of the Tibetans, the Chinese garrison in Lhasa retired to China proper. Lhasa's rule at that time extended over an area roughly continuous with today's Tibetan Autonomous Region, namely the western U-Tsung province and western Kham. The traditional Tibetan eastern regions of Amdo and eastern Kham (approximately modern Qinghai) remained outside its control, however.

Tibet remained independent until 1950. In that year, the People's Liberation Army of the newly created People's Republic of China invaded, citing past claims of sovereignty and the need to 'liberate' the Tibetan people from serfdom. The small and under-equipped Tibetan army was swiftly brushed aside by the invaders. In 1951, the Tibetan Autonomous Region was proclaimed and an agreement concluded (which the Tibetans claim was signed under duress) that recognized Chinese sovereignty.

Rebellion flared in Tibet in 1956 and reached a peak in 1959. In that year, following fierce fighting, the Dalai Lama fled into exile, subsequently establishing a Government in Exile in India. The Chinese authorities have since periodically sought to use the Panchen Lama, the number two in the Tibetan hierarchy, as a figurehead. The Panchen Lama was imprisoned in 1962, but was subsequently released. In 1989, after staging a series of increasingly outspoken attacks on Chinese rule, the Panchen Lama died aged 50 under circumstances which have inevitably attracted some suspicion. Rival reincarnations of the Panchen Lama were subsequently identified by the Dalai Lama and Beijing respectively. (Despite claiming to be an atheistic state, the People's Republic nevertheless cited alleged historical Chinese rights to ratify a new Panchen Lama.) The Dalai Lama's candidate, six-year-old Gedhun Choekyi Nyima promptly disappeared and was claimed by Tibetan supporters to be "the world's youngest political prisoner." To forestall the likelihood of Beijing seeking to impose a client Dalai Lama after his death, the current incumbent has indicated that his next incarnation may be born outside of Tibet.

The March 2008 anniversary of the 1959 uprising saw widespread disturbances in Lhasa that subsequently spread to Tibetan populated districts of Gansu, Qinghai and Sichuan provinces. Ten thousand Chinese troops were deployed in Lhasa – which has a population of only 160,000. The Chinese media claimed that Han and Hui (Muslim) citizens and property were targeted; Tibetan groups claim over a hundred Tibetan civilian casualties. Tibetan groups also protested worldwide against Tibetan exclusion from the 2008 Beijing Olympics.

Chinese rule over Tibet has been one of extreme repression. Destruction of monasteries and the imprisonment of monks and nuns was widespread, particularly during the periods of the 'Great Leap Forward' and the 'Cultural Revolution' in the late 1950s and 1970s. During this period over 6,500 monasteries were destroyed and most of the remainder damaged or forcibly closed. Hundreds of thousands of monks and nuns were forced to abandon their religious duties to be 're-educated' for secular roles. Although it is now officially accepted by the Chinese regime that 'mistakes' were made, it is clear that much of Tibet's religious and cultural infrastructure has been destroyed despite attempts since the 1980s to re-open a number of monasteries. Tibetans continue to flee into exile in India, often undergoing great personal hardship to achieve this. China claims that its policies in Tibet are entirely progressive. Chinese macro-economic policy envisages the westward spread of prosperity from the wealthy eastern Chinese seaboard to outlying provinces such as Tibet. Critics claim that the policy is essentially one of internal colonialism, with primary resources being shipped from west to east to fuel eastern economic progress. Under this interpretation, the China Western Development programme and infrastructural developments such as the Qinghai-Tibet railway, have essentially political, military and exploitative purposes. A related issue of contention is the immigration of Han Chinese into Tibet. Although the census shows a relatively modest percentage of Han, it is claimed that the numbers are under-enumerated and that, moreover, the Han enjoy preferential access to education and governmental jobs.

The Chinese position remains that China has historically enjoyed sovereignty over Tibet and that attempts by the Dalai Lama and Tibet activists are aimed at splitting the country. Pro-Dalai Lama sentiment, including the display of his portrait, is severely repressed within Tibet itself. The Dalai Lama is on record as seeking a dialogue with Beijing aimed at a new political dispensation for Tibet, which might fall short of full independence, but even this compromise is rejected by Beijing. Following the 2008 disturbances, however, Beijing – while continuing to heap media opprobrium on the Dalai Lama – announced a willingness to meet his representatives, and low-key talks started in May 2008.Most Tibetans would maintain that, whatever China's historical claims to sovereignty, these cannot be allowed to stand in the way of Tibetan self-determination – and cite the UN declarations on decolonization in support of this position. Although the Tibetan cause has attracted a wide degree of international support and sympathy, the chances of real progress, at least while the Beijing Communist regime remains firmly in charge of China's political and economic life, remain slight.

# Xinjiang

**Principal protagonists**

Chinese government; Han (Chinese) immigrants.

Indigenous Muslim groups and separatists.

**Nature of conflict**

Religious and racial differences exacerbated by immigration and land resource exploitation. Regular uprisings up until 1949, sporadic riots since.

- Routine oppression of political, separatist and religious dissidents by Chinese state.
- Repression of Muslims an issue.
- Up to 100 politically motivated executions reported per annum.
- Up to 100,000 to Soviet Union, 1951-62
- Potentially very significant unexploited reserves of oil discovered in 1953.

**Population/ethnic composition**

9.6m. Uyghur 45%, Han Chinese 41% (rising), Kazakh 6.75%, Hui 4.5%.

**Territorial extent**

Xinjiang Uyghur Autonomous Region: 1,660,000 km².

**Timeline**

840 AD: Uyghur kingdoms established.
1884: Region annexed to Manchu (Chinese) Empire. Frequent uprisings.
1933-44: Two short-lived independent 'Republics of Eastern Turkestan' established under Soviet influence.
1949: China occupies region. Immigration of Han (Chinese) commences.
1951-62: Large-scale expulsion of Muslim dissidents.
1 Oct 1955: Xinjiang Uyghur Autonomous Region created.
2008: Increased repression reported in lead-in to Beijing Olympics.

**Current status**

Widespread discrimination against indigenous communities and religious minorities continue.

**Although less well known than the situation in Tibet (*See 5.04*) ethnic stresses in Xinjiang follow a similar pattern: historical claims to independence compounded by mass immigration, resource exploitation and the suppression of religious and cultural rights. Xinjiang, the largest political sub-division of China, covers about one-sixth of the country, and is remote and sparsely populated. The Dzoosotoyn Elisen Desert is the place on the Earth's land surface furthest from the nearest ocean.**

Xinjiang is home to a number of Muslim Turkic groups, principally the Uyghurs and the Kazakhs. These peoples are historically and culturally linked to other Turkic peoples, particularly the Uzbeks, in Central Asia and Turkey itself. As in Tibet, large-scale immigration of Chinese Han has destabilized the demographic balance and caused great resentment, as has the emphasis on the use of the Chinese language in government, commerce and education. From 6% in 1949, the Han population has risen to 41% and they are a majority in the capital, Urumqi. Much of the Han immigration is under the auspices of a semi-military parastatal organization, the Xinjiang Production & Construction Corps, which is responsible for the establishment of semi-colonial farms and businesses throughout the region. Land and water pressures between the Han settlers and the indigenous population are a significant source of tension. A major oil pipeline from Xinjiang to Shanghai is under development. The official figures for Han immigration do not include the large numbers of military personnel and their families purportedly based in the region.

The history of the region is a complex tangle of invasion and counter-invasion between competing regional powers. China first asserted control in around 121 BC when it garrisoned the region and used it both as a bridge to the Silk Route across Central Asia and to establish diplomatic and trading relations with other powers, most notably Persia. Chinese control of Xinjiang has long served the dual role of facilitating trade and protecting the Chinese hinterland from foreign invasion. 'Xinjiang', a term first used in 1768, means 'New Frontier' in Chinese and the name is significant as emphasizing both that Xinjiang is not a core Chinese territory and its status as a buffer state between China and its neighbours. It is not the name used by the indigenous population for the territories; East Turkestan (implicitly linking the region culturally to fellow Turkic peoples to the west) or Uyghurstan being preferred.

Chinese control waxed and waned over the centuries, depending on the relative strengths of the Chinese state and its neighbours. In 751 AD, Chinese power in the Central Asian region was decisively truncated following their defeat at the hands of the Arabs at the Battle of Talas, northeast of Tashkent. In 840, the Uyghurs, having been driven out their ancestral homes by the Mongols, established kingdoms in what is now Xinjiang, and gradually adopted Islam. In 1884, Turkestan (as it then was) was incorporated into the Manchu Empire. Between 1884 and 1949, over forty armed uprisings took place against the Chinese governors. Two short-lived independent republics were established, under Soviet influence, in 1933 and 1944. Only after the creation of the People's Republic of China in 1949 and the subsequent occupation of the region was it brought definitively under Chinese control. In subsequent purges, up to 40,000 'pro-Soviet' Muslims were forced to flee the country. The Xinjiang Uyghur Autonomous Region was created in 1955. In 1957, in a further move aimed at reducing Russian/Soviet influence, the Chinese authorities banned the use of Cyrillic script for the Turkic languages of Xinjiang. A second mass exodus of Muslims to the Soviet Union took place in 1962. Ethnic riots broke out in 1980 and again in 1982 in the towns of Kashgar and Aksu. In 1997, riots broke out in Yining after the police broke up a peaceful demonstration, and in 1998, Chinese President Jiang Zemin visited the region and called for a "people's war" against "separatist elements."

Even prior to the 9/11 attacks on the US, the Chinese government had consistently raised the spectre of Islamic terrorism as its justification of the suppression of Muslim dissent. In 1998, it announced the destruction of 20 Xinjiang terrorist cells 'linked to Pakistan and Afghanistan'. Immediately after 11 September 2001, the Chinese authorities alleged that Uyghur groups had links to the Taliban in Afghanistan, but failed to furnish any evidence. In the same year, the local authorities announced that the 'Strike Hard' 'anti crime' initiative would have the key aim of striking "strongly against separatist terrorist forces." In March 2008, Beijing announced that it had "smashed" an Islamist terrorist cell and prevented the hijacking of an internal flight to Urumqi. In April the detention of 70 activists was reported.

Beijing has also applied pressure on Central Asian governments to suppress any possibility of Uyghur separatist groups taking root in neighbouring countries. Central Asian governments, beset with their own fears of Islamic terrorism, have generally required little urging to suppress Uyghur and other dissent in their own territories. In 2001, the Shanghai Co-operation Organization (an international body linking China with the Central Asian republics and Russia) agreed to the establishment of an 'anti-terrorist centre' in Bishkek with a primary aim of preventing cross-border terrorism. Today, although Uyghur human rights and separatist movements exist in Turkey and the West, they are unable to operate effectively in Central Asia – and certainly not in Xinjiang itself, where restrictions on basic freedoms of movement and association make the public emergence of a dissident movement all but impossible. According to Amnesty International, up to 100 executions of political prisoners take place in Xinjiang each year. The various Xinjiang groups are themselves divided, being organized along ethnic lines. There is little co-operation between groups representing Kazakhs, Uyghurs, Tajikis, etc, in the Xinjiang Muslim diaspora.

With the disputed exception of a 1997 series of bombings in Urumqi and the alleged March 2008 hijacking attempt Uyghur nationalists have no history of directing terrorist violence against civilian targets. Depending on its commercial and political needs, the Chinese government alternatively presents Xinjiang as a stable area for investment, or as a hotbed of Islamic fundamentalism. Harsh repression of ethnic and general political rights is a consistent hallmark of Chinese Communist rule in Xinjiang, and the general culture of oppression shows no signs of lifting.

**Minorities in China**

Although the Han, China's largest ethnic group, comprise over 90% of the Chinese population, China is home to over 50 ethnic minority groups – many themselves numbering several million individuals. The Chinese government's position on minorities owes much to the traditional 'Great Han' school of thought that holds that all the inhabitants of China belong to one (Han) family and that 'incidental' differences of culture, language and religion should be suppressed. In particular, Beijing routinely claims to be confronted with 'extremist religious forces.' Violations of freedom of religion have increased markedly in recent years. The 2001 'Strike Hard' campaign, purportedly aimed against law breakers, has been widely reported as having a secondary agenda of suppressing ethnic and religious dissent. Courts were 'rewarded' for a high number and speed of convictions, and 'mass sentencing' rallies have been reported. In few cases were the accused allowed a defence.

Faced with an explosive expansion of religious observance, particularly amongst the severely restricted Christian population – purportedly 100 million strong – and the Falun Gong Buddhist movement, which claims 70 million practitioners, the Chinese government response has been one of increased repression. Since 1998, religious leaders and civic groups are required to register with the government, and a condition of registration is unambiguous support for the territorial integrity of the Chinese state and support for the Communist government. Even after registration, groups may be subject to 'rectification drives' if they are deemed to be straying from the government line. Observers report the routine arrest, torture and imprisonment of religious and other dissidents, as well as documented cases of the use of organs from executed prisoners in transplant surgery. It is clear that, regardless of Beijing's moves towards economic liberalism, it remains a highly oppressive regime that is currently incapable of accommodating minority views.

# India

**Principal protagonists**

Government of India.

Minority religious groups; regional secessionists; tribal groups.

**Nature of conflict**
*See text and following sections on Punjab, Seven Sisters States, and Kashmir.*

- Infringements of civil liberties by Indian authorities regularly reported.
- Hindu/Muslim conflict a key issue.
- 1 million during the 1947 partition of India. 8,000 in inter-communal rioting in past 20 years.
- Massive population exchange – up to 10 million – at time of partition of India, 1947.

**Population/ethnic composition**
1 billion. Indo-Aryan 72%, Dravidian 25%, Mongoloid and other 3%. Religious mix: Hindu 73%, Muslim 12%, Christian 6%, Sikh 2.2%, traditional beliefs 3.4%, Buddhist 0.7%, Jainist 0.4%.

**Territorial extent**
India (including Jammu & Kashmir): 3,166,414 km².

**Timeline**

3300 BC: First Indus Valley civilization established.

27 May 1526: Formal establishment of Moghul empire.

29 Mar 1858: Last Moghul ruler deposed.

2 Aug 1858: India formally comes under British rule.

1906: Muslims successfully seek representation on separate electoral role; Muslim League splits from Indian National Congress.

15 Aug 1947: India independent from Britain. Partition of India/Pakistan. 'Untouchability' officially abolished.

2002: Renewed Islamic/Hindu rioting in Gujarat leaves 2,000 dead.

**Current status**
Religious conflict and regional secessionist/tribal issues largely unresolved. *(See text and following sections for details.)*

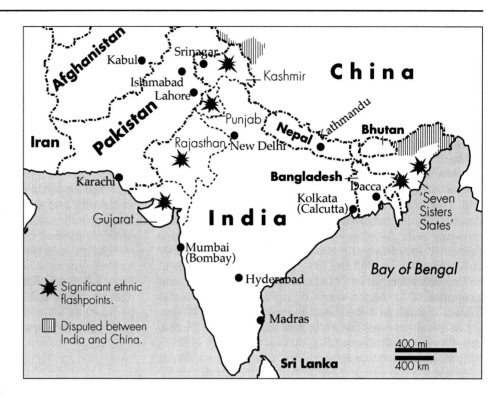

**India is the second most populous country in the world, one of its fastest growing economies, and the world's largest democracy. It nevertheless has to resolve some fundamental and deep-rooted issues. In addition to the political and economic problems confronting any large complex state, the country faces a number of racial, cultural and religious conflicts.**

India is the birthplace of Buddhism, Jainism, Sikhism and Hinduism, and is home to a multiplicity of ethnic groups, who between them speak a total of 1,652 languages. Given its diversity, it has been inevitable that post-independence Indian governments have sought to identify unifying features in an attempt to build a cohesive Indian nation. Its advocates regard Hinduism as one such unifying force, but the consequences of this approach have frequently been divisive.

The Indian constitution is officially secular, providing equal rights for all citizens regardless of their religion. In practice, citizens of Muslim, Christian, Sikh and other faiths are often considered second-class citizens and allowed only limited economic, social and cultural rights, as is the 'Dalit' or 'untouchable' grouping within Hinduism. The growth in Hindu chauvinism, represented politically in the rise of the Bharatiya Janata Party (which headed the coalition government of 1998-2004), demonstrates the underlying weakness in Indian secular unity.

Furthermore, the Indian state has frequently had recourse to draconian national security legislation that significantly affects civil liberties. Particularly restrictive regulations have been applied in areas of ethnic unrest, including Kashmir, the 'Seven Sisters States', and Punjab (as well as Andhra Pradesh where unrest is primarily Maoist in origin).

In the early 1950s, linguistic conflict was a significant issue as the government attempted to declare Hindi the national language of India. In 1956, however, the government ostensibly reversed direction, with the promulgation of the controversial States Reorganization Act. This recognized the principle of linguistically homogeneous states. Critics saw in these efforts by the central government in Delhi a crude attempt to divide-and-rule. Certainly, the practical result has been the creation in India of a plethora or small and linguistically partisan smaller states, several of which have turned to separatism as a perceived palliative for their weakened relationship with New Delhi.

India also suffers from an ongoing Maoist insurgency, which is said to affect half of the country's states, mainly those in the forested central and eastern regions. The Maoists, known as Naxalites, claim to be fighting on behalf of the rural poor, but in many areas it is has been tribal peoples who have been the most affected. In Chattisgarh, one of the worst affected areas, a reported 46,000 tribal people have been moved to ill-equipped government camps.

In 1975, India faced a direct threat to its democratic institutions. On 17 June of that year, India's High Court dismissed the Prime Minister, Indira Ghandi, for alleged corruption. Mrs Ghandi refused to accept the ruling, forced the President to sign a Proclamation of Emergency, suspended the constitution and arrested upwards of 100,000 opponents. Although Mrs Ghandi's defeat in the 1977 election effectively brought an end to the Emergency, the shock to India's political institutions was profound. Following a period of intense faction-fighting, Mrs Ghandi was re-elected in January 1980.

The continued persistence of the caste system presents its own set of problems. The traditional caste system within Hinduism recognizes a hierarchy headed by the Brahmins (scholars and priests), followed by the Kashatriyas (landowners, and warriors), the Vaishyas (traders and artisans), and lastly the Shudras (farmers and labourers). Outside the caste system and assigned the lowest positions in society were the 'untouchables' or Dalits, who constitute around a quarter of the Indian population. (Mahatma Ghandi called the untouchables 'Haridjans' – children of god – in an attempt to limit the prejudice against them.) Officially, untouchability was eliminated at independence, but in practice discrimination and caste violence continue. Dalits continue to be largely confined to their traditional, low-caste occupations of waste disposal, removing dead animals, leather working, cobbling and street cleaning. One response from the Dalit community to their continued alienation from mainstream Hindu society has been their mass conversion to Buddhism, on the basis that defection from Hindu society to another religion will at least make them 'separate but equal'. In October 2006, an estimated 200,000 Dalits underwent a mass conversion in Hyderabad and elsewhere in the country. Some Dalits have also converted to Sikhism or Islam.

Inter-communal violence continues to plague Indian life. In May 2008 over 40 were killed and rioting spread to Delhi as members of the Gujjar ethnic group (who are significant in northern and western India) protested against their exclusion from an official list of disadvantaged groups that would otherwise have enabled them to access preferential government employment and educational opportunities. Christians are subject to various semi-official restrictions as well as attacks by militants, particularly in the eastern Orissa province, where violence flared between Hindu extremists and Christians at the end of 2007. Converts from Islam are routinely subjected to harassment from Islamists, as are followers of other faiths. The main religious flashpoint, however, has been the deep historical animosity between Hindus and Muslims, which has resulted since 1947 in massive population movements and tens of thousands of casualties.

Around 12% of the population – over 130 million individuals – profess Islam, making it the second largest Islamic population in the world, after Indonesia. Islamic influence in India, particularly in its Sufist variant, predates the wholesale Islamic invasions of the sub-continent that took place under the Moghuls in the 16th century. (The mystic elements of Sufism – regarded as heretical by orthodox Muslims – made it easier for potential Hindu converts to accommodate their new faith.) The earliest mosque in India was in fact built within the lifetime of the Prophet Mohammed, in 629 AD. Nevertheless, Islam is still regarded by many Hindu Indians as an alien import, and one moreover which was imposed on India by force. Hindu antithesis to Islam runs deep into the politics of communalization in India and lingering resentment over the partition of India in 1947.

The irreversible national schism between Hindus and Muslims can perhaps be most directly traced to the request by Muslims, in 1906, to be granted representation on a separate electoral role to Hindus. In the same year, the formation of the Muslim League led to there being two parties working for independence, the Muslim League and the largely Hindu Indian National Congress. Ultimately, the impossibility of accommodation between these two groups led to the partition of India into Hindu-majority India and Muslim-majority Pakistan.

The immediate focus for Muslim/Hindu violence in recent years has been the semi-official policy of closing, and in some cases destroying, mosques where their siting is alleged to be in conflict with Hinduism. One particularly notorious incident saw the destruction of the 464-year old Babri Mosque in Ayodhya in 1992, which it was claimed was constructed on the birthplace of the Hindu god Ram. The following year was marked by a series of bombings in Mumbai (Bombay) by Muslim radicals.

In 2002, major rioting between Muslims and Hindus erupted in Gujarat. This quickly developed into a series of tit-for-tat inter-communal attacks, which saw 2,000 people (mostly Muslims) killed in some of the worst ethnic violence since partition. Incidents included the murder of some 50 Hindus burnt alive on a train in retaliation for the Babri Mosque attack. More recently, in Rajasthan, an attempt by the state government to ban Hindus carrying their traditional trident religious icon has increased tensions in that state.

A number of Islamist groups operate in India and/or Kashmir. These include the Students Islamic Movement of India (SIMI), *Lashkar-e-Tolba,* and *Jaish-e-Mohammed* – the latter two groups being allegedly responsible for the July 2006 Mumbai train bombings, which killed nearly 200 people.

# Punjab

**Principal protagonists**

Government of India.

Sikh community; putative Sikh state of Khalistan. (Minority support for independence.)

**Nature of conflict**

Self-determination issue and inter-communal violence. Insurgency, 1986-92.

- Infringements of civil liberties by Indian authorities regularly reported.
- Hindu/Sikh conflict a key issue.
- 10,000 in 1984 disturbances. 20,000 1986-92
- Massive population exchange – up to 10 million – at time of partition of Punjab between Pakistan and India, 1947.

**Population/ethnic composition**

Indian Punjab: 24.3m. 60% Sikh. (Sikhs comprise c2% of total Indian population.)

**Territorial extent**

Punjab (Indian province): 50,362 km².
Himachal Pradesh: 55,673 km².
Haryana: 44,212 km².
Punjab (Pakistani province): 205,344 km².

**Timeline**

14-15 Aug 1947: Pakistan and India independent from Britain. Punjab partitioned.

1 Nov 1966: Haryana and Himachal Pradesh states created.

15 Dec 1983: Occupation of Golden Temple by Sikh separatists.

3 Jun 1984: Storming of Golden Temple by Indian forces.

31 Oct 1984: Indira Ghandi assassinated.

29 Apr 1986: Renewed declaration of an independent Khalistan prompts violent insurgency, which lasted until 1992.

**Current status**

Security situation largely stabilized although many underlying issues remain unresolved.

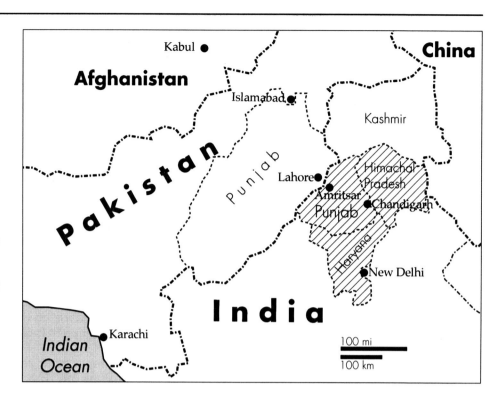

**Sikhism, the world's fifth largest organized religion, emerged as a distinct faith towards the end of the 15th century. Unlike Hinduism and Buddhism, Sikhism is strictly monotheistic and rejects also the worship of idols, features that have on occasion brought them into conflict with their neighbours. A proud and largely disciplined people, the Sikhs are renowned for their martial prowess, providing a disproportionately high number of recruits to the (British) Indian Army, as well as to the ranks of those militantly opposing colonial rule.**

Although Sikhism claims adherents worldwide, a majority of the religion's 23 million followers live in the Punjabi region of north-west India. In recent years, calls for an independent Punjab have largely become aligned with the cause of Sikh religious nationalism.

As India moved towards independence from Britain in the late 1940s, plans were advanced for the partition of the country into the largely Hindu Indian state, and the largely Muslim Pakistan. The creation of India and Pakistan made no allowance for Sikh aspirations, and prompted some Sikhs to call for their own 'Khalistan' ('land of the pure'), independent of both India and Pakistan. These demands were ignored, and instead the former province of Punjab was divided roughly evenly between the two new states.

The partition of Punjab prompted a colossal refugee crisis, with up to ten million people leaving their homes under varying degrees of duress. Both sides committed excesses; Sikhs (and Hindus) were expelled from their homes in west Punjab, while Sikhs in the east started expelling non-Sikhs in anticipation of a massive influx of their co-religionists from Pakistan. Barely a month after Indian independence, vicious inter-communal rioting erupted in Delhi and other centres, sparked in large part by anger over the plight of Punjabi refugees from the western (i.e., Pakistani) part of the region.

Throughout the 1950s and 1960s, Sikh dissatisfaction with their position in the new Indian state continued. From the Sikh point of view, the situation was to decline with the subsequent further dismemberment of the Punjab under the States Reorganization Act of 1956. This sought to divide Indian states along largely linguistic lines. Although under the original terms of the States Reorganization Act Punjab (and Bombay) were excluded on the grounds that they were bilingual, in

November 1966 the new states of Haryana and Himachal Pradesh were created. This left Punjab effectively a rump state, albeit one in which Sikhs were, for the first time, in a majority.

With Punjabi, and therefore, by extension, Sikh influence in India now seen by many as being deliberately marginalized, many Sikhs began to question their future place in the Indian union. This in turn led to a rise of religious bellicosity on the part of some Sikhs, with the main Sikh party, the Akali Dal, adopting, albeit comparatively briefly, a more stridently religiously partisan position. Electorally, the playing of the Sikh religious card by the Akali Dal was an error, the party losing control of the provincial government in 1972.

In a separate conflict, clashes broke out in the 1970s between Sikhs and the Nirankari sect, mainly over access to religious sites.

By the early 1980s inter-communal tensions were steadily rising. Matters were not helped by what were seen as increasingly one-sided and draconian measures by the Indian state, which included, for example, the Armed Forces (Punjab and Chandigarh) Special Powers Act of 1983 empowering any military officer (however lowly his rank) to occupy and destroy any property *on suspicion* of its being used for terrorist activities.

During the latter half of 1983, protests focused on Article 25 of the Indian Constitution (which defines Sikhs, Jainists and Buddhists as being part of the broader Hindu community). This prompted Sikh demonstrators to publicly burn copies of the Indian Constitution, which action was interpreted in some circles as a challenge to the unity of the Indian state as whole.

On 15 December 1983, in an increasingly tense atmosphere, Sikh leader Jarnail Singh Bhindranwale and around 250 of his supporters occupied the Golden Temple (Hanmandir Sahib) in Amritsar, Sikhism's holiest shrine, from where they advocated the formation of a Sikh state and issued a serious of inflammatory anti-Hindu proclamations.

Fearing a wholesale breakdown of state control in the Punjab, the Indian authorities opted for a military solution, one that was to have devastating consequences not just for the Punjab but also for the country as a whole. On 3 June 1984 a curfew was declared. This had the perhaps unintended effect of trapping many pilgrims within the Golden Temple as it coincided with the anniversary of the martyrdom of the original builder of the Hanmandir Sahib. Initial attempts by the Indian army to storm the temple were repulsed, and the fighting quickly escalated into a full-scale battle. Eventually, 6,000 troops, backed up by tanks and artillery, successfully stormed the Golden Temple. In the ensuing carnage, both during the assault and in subsequent nationwide anti-Sikh rioting, some 5,000 died (including Bhindranwale) before an uneasy peace was imposed. Five months later, on 31 October 1984, Indian Premier Indira Ghandi was assassinated by two Sikh bodyguards, in what was widely interpreted as a revenge attack for the storming of the Golden Temple (although in fact the motives of the assassins have never been conclusively identified). Delhi erupted into rioting, in which a further 5,000 people, mostly Sikhs, perished.

On 26 January 1986 the proclamation of an independent state of Khalistan, at a rally attended by thousands of Sikhs at the Golden Temple complex, triggered another round of violence in which Hindus and Nirankaris were targeted. The proposed Khalistan, according to its self-declared President Jagjit Singh Chauhan, was to encompass the Indian states of Punjab, Haryana and Himachal Pradesh as well as Pakistani Punjab.

Throughout the 1980s and 1990s, a high level of violence continued, with notorious incidents such as the Lairu massacre, in which 32 Hindus were dragged out of a bus and shot. Although the militants initially enjoyed a level of support, the violence, and the economic damage to Punjab arising from the conflict, turned the majority of Sikhs against the separatist movement. This, in combination with more effective actions by the security forces, brought the insurgency to an effective end in the early 1990s.

Since the early 1990s the Khalistan Zindabad Force (KZF) has been intermittently active, launching terrorist attacks in Punjab, Kashmir and Delhi. The Indian authorities claim the KZF is the instrument of the Pakistani security services, a contention given some weight by the fact that the KZF does not, apparently, include the Pakistani Punjab state in the borders of its proposed Khalistan. Arrested KZF operatives have also confessed to receiving explosives and training from Pakistan.

In 2001 Jagjit Singh Chauhan returned from exile. Claiming now to advocate peaceful evolution of 'the idea of Khalistan', Chauhan was not detained, an apparent indication that the Indian authorities no longer saw him as a credible threat. His death in April 2007 was seen as drawing a line under the period of militant separatism, which has largely failed to secure a support base among the younger generation of Punjabi Sikhs.

The present security situation within Punjab appears contained, with the militant pro-independence movement unable to command much indigenous backing, while still enjoying some support especially among the Sikh diaspora. In May 2004 a Sikh, Manmohan Singh, was appointed Prime Minister of India, and this may have contributed to calming Sikh concerns about their overall status in Indian political life.

# Seven Sisters States

**Principal protagonists**

Government of India.

Separatist movements in Seven Sisters States. (Flags shown are those of Manipur and Tripura when they were Princely States. These no longer have official status.)

**Nature of conflict**

Self-determination and inter-ethnic conflicts.

🕴 Infringements of civil liberties by Indian authorities regularly reported.
☠ At least 1,000.

**Population/ethnic composition**

Regional total c37m, around 4% of Indian total. (See panel opposite for state details.)

**Territorial extent**

See panel opposite.

**Timeline**

35 AD: Manipur state founded.
c100 AD: Tripura state founded.
1824: Manipur becomes British protectorate.
1826: Assam annexed by Britain; becomes part of British India.
1871: Tripura becomes British protectorate.
15 Aug 1947: India independent from Britain. Tripura annexed.
15 Oct 1949: Manipur accedes to Indian rule.
10 Oct 1962: Sino-Indian war. Chinese occupy most of Arunachal Pradesh but withdraw in November 1962.
1 Dec 1963: Nagaland state created.
25 Jan 1971: Meghalaya state created.
20 Feb 1987: Arunachal Pradesh and Mizoram states created.

**Current status**

Regional insurgencies and inter-ethnic conflicts continue.

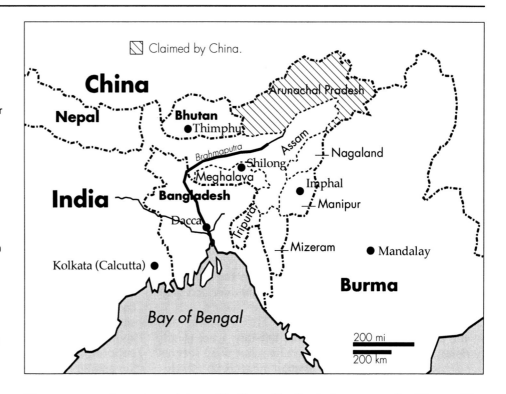

The seven north-eastern states of India, collectively known as the "Seven Sisters States" are geographically and culturally isolated from the rest of India. Almost wholly cut off by Bangladeshi territory, only a narrow corridor of land, the "Chicken's Neck", connects them to the 'mainland'. The numerous peoples of the Seven Sisters are largely of Burmese, Tibetan and Thai stock, while the high percentage of Christians – Meghalaya, Mizoram and Nagaland are the only Indian states with a Christian majority – further distinguishes the region, as does the fact that the 'tribal' peoples are considered to be outwith India's caste system.

Separatist sentiment and inter-ethnic conflict are both widespread throughout the region. In general, the situation in the Seven Sisters remains dangerous and confused, although there are considerable local variations in the intensity of the various conflicts. Insurgency is at its highest in Manipur and Tripura; in contrast, Maghalaya (a state with a Christian majority) does not have a history of sustained armed ethnic conflict.

Assam became a British province in 1826, after the territory was ceded by the Burmese. The ancient states of Tripura and Manipur, both of which had existed since the first century AD, also came under British control in the 19th century. Manipur became a British protectorate in 1824, having been occupied by Burma in 1819; Tripura did not become British until 1871.

The British ruled in India through provinces, which were administered centrally and which comprised 'British India', and through 'princely states.' These states, under local rulers, retained nominal independence, although the British were responsible for foreign affairs and overall defence. More than 500 princely states, several of them significant geographical territories, existed at the time of India's independence, and some of these resisted incorporation into the Indian state.

At the time of Indian independence, the North East region comprised two princely states, Manipur and Tripura, and one province, Assam. Tripura acceded to Indian rule immediately upon Indian independence in 1947, but Manipur held out until 15 October 1949 when the Manipur Merger Agreement came into effect. The legitimacy of this agreement is still contested by local nationalists, and in 1979 the Revolutionary People's Front (RPF) emerged to fight for Manipur independence. Although Manipur achieved statehood in 1972, fighting continues, with 15 Indian soldiers being reported killed in clashes in 2007 and 7 Hindu settlers in 2008. The RPF claims to represent the entire population, but in addition to fighting between the rebels and the Indian government, the situation is complicated by inter-ethnic fighting between the settled Meiteis, who constitute the majority population and the members of the 'Hill Tribes', of whom the Nagas and the Kuki-Chins are the largest. Fighting between these two groups peaked in 1993 with the destruction of several villages. Manipur remains a conflict area, with a curfew in force and outside visitors firmly discouraged. In April 2008, the murder by rebels of 14 Hindi-speaking migrant workers was reported.

Indian rule was also resisted in Nagaland, which was at the time part of Assam. From 1947 onwards the Naga National Council (NNC) waged a guerrilla war against India and in favour of Naga independence. In 1963, a separate Nagaland state was created. In 1974, a more moderate faction, the United Democratic Front, successfully won the election for the state government and a peace treaty was agreed with New Delhi. The NNC continued with the armed struggle, splitting in 1980, with the National Socialist Council of Nagaland (NSCN) breaking away. This movement has since itself split, with some factions entering into ceasefire agreements. Armed elements of the NSCN continue to operate. The Naga were originally a Tibetan people, who later migrated into parts of Burma, Malaysia and Indonesia as well as India.

The original Tripuri are of Tibeto-Burmese stock who originally migrated from western China, establishing Tripura as early as 35 AD. Since 1949, when the Tripuri constituted 85% of the population, they have been displaced by influxes of Bengalis from Bangladesh and other immigrants. Today the Tripuri population is around 25% of the Tripura total. Tripura's existence as an independent state prior to colonization and Indian annexation, together with cultural and land use conflicts with the immigrant groups, has provided a powerful motivator for Tripuri resistance. A number of older groups merged to form the National Liberation Front of Tripura (NLFT) in 1989. The main demand of the NLFT is an end to the political and cultural displacement of tribal peoples at the hands of immigrant groups such as the Bengalis, arguing that the Tripura face imminent extinction as a people. A low intensity insurgency continues in the area.

The present state of Assam, which is much smaller than the historical territory, has the most complex ethnic mix in the Seven Sisters region. The numerically and politically dominant Assamese, a Hindu people, are in conflict with the Bengalis, many of whom are Muslim, and the tribal peoples such as the Bobo, the Karbis, and the Mishings. The Bobo are in turn in opposition to other tribal groups, with Bobo expansionism being the main issue. In April 1979 the United Liberation Front of Asom was formed to press for independence for Assam. The overall security situation in Assam remains poor, with banditry as well as ethnically motivated attacks being regularly reported.

In Mizoram, alleged indifference and inefficiency on the part of New Delhi towards periodic droughts has been the root cause of the development of political militancy in the region. In 1959 an organization was formed called the Mizo Famine Front with the initial objective of combating drought related problems. This group developed into the armed Mizo National Front (MNF) with the political objective of an independent Mizoram. In 1967, in a heavy-handed government clampdown on militants, thousands of Mizo were interned in protected villages.

The MNF was backed by Pakistan, and support declined after Bangladeshi independence. Statehood was granted in 1986 in return for a cessation of armed insurgency. The MNF has operated through the political process since that date, although sporadic attacks by individual groups of militants have occurred since. More recently, unrest has broken out between the Mizos and another tribal group, the Reang, with up to 15,000 Reang being reported as having been driven from their homes in western Mizoram. The Mizoram government alleges that the violence has been provoked by a Reang 'Bru Revolutionary Army' in pursuit of their aim of an autonomous Reang district.

In Arunachal Pradesh the majority of the people are either of Tibetan or Burmese origin. Here, the main issue has been conflict between China and India. In 1962, during the Sino-Indian war, the Chinese occupied most of the region, but withdrew at the end of the conflict. Although China still refuses to recognize Indian sovereignty over the area, which it claims is part of Tibet, a resumption of conflict currently appears unlikely.

**Key data for 'Seven Sisters States'**

| State | Population/ethnic composition | Area |
|---|---|---|
| Arunachal Pradesh | 1m. Tibetan/Thai-Burmese, 65% | 83,743 km$^2$ |
| Assam | 26.6m. Assamese majority, Bengali minority; numerous other tribal groups. | 78,438 km$^2$ |
| Meghalaya | 2.3m. "Hill Tribes" (Khasis, Garos and Jaintias are largest groups), 85%. Christian majority. | 22,429 km$^2$ |
| Manipur | 2.4m. Meiteis, 70%; "Hill Tribes" (Nagas and Kuki-Chins are largest). | 22,327 km$^2$ |
| Mizoram | 888,000. Mizo, c75%. Christian majority. | 21,081 km$^2$ |
| Nagaland | 2m. Various Naga tribes; Kukis. Christian majority. | 16,579 km$^2$ |
| Tripura | 3.2m. Bengalis, 70%; Tripuri, 30%. | 10,492 km$^2$ |

# Kashmir

**Principal protagonists**

Indian government; Jammu & Kashmir

Pakistani government; elements within the Muslim population of Kashmir; Azad Kashmir.

Kashmiri nationalists.

**Nature of conflict**

Territorial and self-determination dispute. Full-scale war between India and Pakistan, 1947, 1965, 1999. Sino-Indian war, 1962. Major uprising in 1989. Further clashes between India and Pakistan to present.

- Widespread abuses, including the shooting of unarmed demonstrators, claimed against Indian authorities.
- Hindu/Muslim rivalry a key issue. Danger exists of issue being hijacked by Islamists.
- 45,000-100,000.
- Up to 350,000.

**Population/ethnic composition**

Population around 10 million in Indian administered areas; 3 million on Pakistani side. 70% of the population in the Indian administered region is Muslim.

**Territorial extent**

Kashmir; territory divided between Indian, Pakistani and Chinese territorial claims. *(See text for details.)*

**Timeline**

*See opposite.*

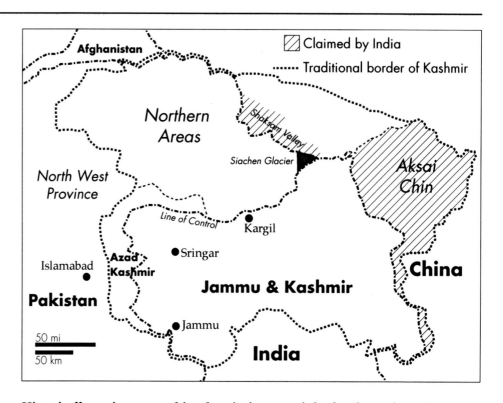

**Historically an important kingdom in its own right, by the early 19th century Kashmir had largely passed into the control of conquering Sikh armies. Following the Anglo-Sikh War of 1846 the British sold Kashmir to Maharajah Gulab Singh as part of the Treaty of Amritsar. Later in the century Kashmir came to be ruled by the Dogras, a predominantly Hindu people.**

In 1947, as India moved towards full independence from Britain, there were some 560 nominally independent princely states in the sub-continent, including Kashmir. Under arrangements for the independence of India and its partition into two states, Hindu India and Muslim Pakistan, the princely rulers were obliged to decide which of the two states they wished to join. Originally set for June 1948, the date for Indian independence was later brought forward to 15 August 1947, allowing little time for the decision.

In Kashmir, which had a Hindu ruler but a largely Muslim population, the Maharajah favoured continued independence, but this was not presented as a option. Faced with a Pakistani-backed invasion, the Maharajah appealed for Indian assistance in October 1947, which it was made clear would not be forthcoming unless Kashmir accepted incorporation into India. The legality of the Maharajah's resultant accession to Indian rule continues to be hotly disputed by Pakistan and by Kashmiri nationalists. Certainly, the Maharajah acted under duress, although possibly favouring Indian rule as the lesser of two evils.

Fighting between India and Pakistan continued until a UN brokered ceasefire at the end of 1947 partitioned the territory along an armistice line, the Line of Control, which remains the *de facto* border between India and Pakistan.

This left India in control of roughly 45% of the disputed territory, organized into the state of Jammu & Kashmir of some 101,387 km², which India claims is an integral part of Indian territory. Some 70% of the population of Jammu & Kashmir is Muslim. The Pakistani portion of Kashmir is divided into two zones, the Northern Areas (72,496 km²) and Azad Kashmir ('Free Kashmir') of 13,350 km².

In addition, there are rival claims between China and India over the Shaksam Valley (in fact ceded to China by Pakistan) and the much larger Aksai Chin region, and also with Pakistan over the Indian-held Siachen Glacier, which is said to be the highest battlefield in the world. The Chinese and Indians clashed in 1962, and over a month of full-scale fighting took place between India and Pakistan in 1965.

Ongoing discontent at Indian rule erupted into violence throughout Kashmir in 1989, with some protesters seeking independence for Kashmir, while others sought integration with Pakistan. India accused Pakistan of fuelling the violence, and increased its already heavy security presence. Initially focused on secular and nationalist demands, the emphasis among Kashmiri militants has, from the early 1990s (and particularly since the US-led overthrow of the Taliban in Afghanistan) switched to a more overtly Islamist agenda.

In 1999 direct warfare again broke out between Pakistan and India when India launched a full offensive, including air strikes, against Pakistani-supported insurgents in Kargil. Tensions between the two nations continued to escalate, particularly after December 2001, when gunmen, allegedly pro-Pakistani Kashmiri militants, attacked the Indian parliament. Following troop build ups by both sides, over a million soldiers, potentially backed up by nuclear weapons, confronted each other over the Line of Control by the end of 2001. Within Kashmir itself, India initiated a heavy-handed security clampdown. Militants, in turn, carried out bombings of government targets and suspected Indian sympathizers. Although both sides stepped back from the brink of war, tensions between the two regional rivals were only marginally diminished.

Kashmir was hit by a massive earthquake in 2005, which prompted both Pakistan and India to put aside their differences, at least to a limited extent, in favour of joint humanitarian efforts. Since then, however, conflict has once again increased, although not to the levels of 2001. Ongoing talks were suspended in June 2006 after a series of bombings on Mumbai (Bombay) commuter trains killed 180; India accusing Pakistan-based militants of being behind the attacks. Cross-border incursions by Pakistani-based insurgents continue to be a feature of the Kashmiri political and military landscape.

Essentially, neither side will agree to the other ruling Kashmir. An obvious third option, independence, is rejected by both India and Pakistan, although it does command some support amongst Kashmiris themselves. Although it might emerge as a compromise position, clearly an independent Kashmir would require significant international underpinning if it were not to fall victim either to irredentist forces from Pakistan or India, or to Islamist extremism. High-sounding proposals (usually by academics) for joint sovereignty over all or part of the disputed territory appear even less probable. Many in India favour formalizing the current partition by making the Line of Control the official international border, but this is opposed by Pakistan. The territorial disputes in the region between China and India further complicate matters. Realistically, there is little hope of a solution to the dispute in the short term.

A nationalist group, the Jammu-Kashmir Liberation Front was active in the 1989 uprising. It declared a ceasefire in 1994 and is now working through political means for Kashmiri independence. Numerous factions, exist, including pro-Pakistani, pro-independence, or broadly pro-Indian elements. A separatist political alliance in Indian-controlled Kashmir, the All Parties Hurriyat Conference, is itself split between those who support negotiations with the Indian government and more hard-line elements. In general, however the lead role in Kashmiri insurgency has been taken over since the 1990s by Islamist militant groups operating from rear bases in Pakistani-held territory. These organizations want the entire territory to be allocated to Pakistan. The attitude of the Pakistani government towards these groups is ambivalent. Essentially, the Pakistani government finds itself under two competing pressures: that of secular elements within the military, and that from domestic Islamist groups. Under US pressure since 2001, Pakistani policy emphasis, at least in public, has been directed towards the former, but the Pakistani authorities are astute enough to realise that taking a hard line with India over Kashmir represents a 'safety valve' for potential domestic discontent both in the military and the Islamist community. The dangers, however, in provoking the much greater conventional power (let alone nuclear) of India are self-evident. For this reason, pragmatic Pakistani policy favours the continuation, but hopefully containment, of the conflict, while enhancing its 'war on terror' credentials with the Americans through the banning of the more extreme Islamist groups, such as *Lashkar-e-Taiba,* the group implicated in the 2001 assault on the Indian parliament, which was outlawed by Pakistan a year later. India, for its part, will continue to highlight (with

**Timeline**

Early 19th century: Kashmir becomes part of the Sikh kingdom. Later in the century the territory becomes a princely state under the British.

15 Aug 1947: India and Pakistan become independent. Kashmir declines to join either state.

Aug-Oct 1947: Pakistani-backed invasion. Maharajah accepts Indian sovereignty in return for military support. UN ceasefire creates current Line of Control.

Aug-Oct 1962: Sino-Indian war. Chinese unilaterally declare ceasefire, after defeating Indian forces.

Apr-Sep 1965: Second Kashmir War, between India and Pakistan.

May-Jul 1999: Kargili war between India and Pakistan.

2001: Clashes and high levels of tension between India and Pakistan, both of which nuclear-armed.

**Current status**

Unresolved and highly unstable. Armed clashes between Indian forces and Pakistani-based insurgents continue.

some justification) the Islamist nature of the cross-border threat. Whether India will feel the need in the foreseeable future to come to terms with moderate and/or separatist elements in Kashmir itself remains debatable.

As one of the potential fulcrums of the 'war on terror' as well as being the only ethnic conflict that has a realistic chance of developing into a nuclear holocaust, Kashmir should be of far greater concern to the wider world than has thus far been the case. Unless concerted pressure towards an equitable settlement, or at the very least towards restraint, is placed upon both parties, Kashmir is likely to remain a critical geopolitical flashpoint not merely for the region but for the wider world.

# Chagos Islands

### Principal protagonists

British government (British Indian Ocean Territory); US government.

Chagos islanders.

### Nature of conflict

Illegal deportation of islanders; long-running legal battle in British courts.

⚑ c2,000 islanders deported, 1968-73.
♛ Strategic location seen as essential resource by US/UK.

### Population/ethnic composition

c4,000 Chagossians (Ilois), mostly on Mauritius. The islands have a transient population of c3,000, mostly US and UK military personnel and civilian contractors.

### Territorial extent

Chagos archipelago (British Indian Ocean Territory): 60 km². Diego Garcia: 30 km².

### Timeline

17 May 1810: Annexed by UK (from France).
8 Nov 1965: British Indian Ocean Territory established.
17 Jul 1966: Deportation of islanders begins (completed by 1973).
30 Dec 1966: Diego Garcia leased to US.
3 Apr 1967: Britain buys all the plantations on the islands.
2 Nov 2000: British High Court overturns 1971 immigration ban.
9 Oct 2003: High Court rules islanders have no right to compensation.
11 June 2004: BIOT law overturns 2000 court ruling
3 Apr 2006: Islanders granted limited rights to visit Diego Garcia.
11 May 2006: 2004 BIOT law overturned.
23 May 2007: High Court confirms deportations illegal and that islanders have right to return.

### Current status

2007 ruling allowing islanders to return continues to be resisted by US/UK governments

**A conflict that has been fought in the courtrooms rather than on the battlefield, the case of the Chagos islanders demonstrates the cavalier approach which can be taken by major powers towards marginalized communities when strategic interests are seen to be at stake.**

The Chagos islands, which are a British colony, the British Indian Ocean Island Territory (BIOT), were home to the Ilois or Chagossians, who started arriving, some as French-owned slaves, others as fishermen and coconut plantation workers, from the late 18th century. They are a French Creole speaking community with roots in Mozambique and other parts of mainland Africa as well as links to Mauritius and the Seychelles.

BIOT was created in 1965 and a new constitution promulgated (without any local consultation) that included no democratic accountability at all and prohibited residence on the islands without a permit. In 1968, the entire population was deported to make way for a US-leased air and naval installation on Diego Garcia, the main island in the group. During the Cold War, Diego Garcia was an important strategic base for controlling the Indian Ocean sealanes as well as potentially threatening the southern USSR with attacks by long-range strategic bombers. This strategic role has continued since the end of the Cold War, with the base being used operationally in both Gulf wars and for airstrikes against Afghanistan. Diego Garcia is also an important tracking station, an emergency landing site for the Space Shuttle, and is one of the three ground stations for the Global Positioning System (GPS) network, which has a worldwide civilian as well as a military application.

Widely regarded as a disgraceful episode, the legality of the deportation of the islanders has repeatedly been successfully challenged in the British courts, which have demonstrated continued independence in the face of huge pressure by Washington and London. Using unusually strong language for a British court, the High

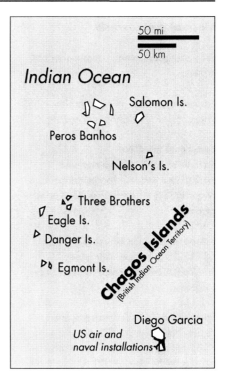

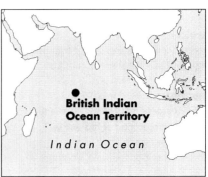

Court in 2006 described the deportations as "outrageous, unlawful, and in breach of accepted moral standards." The islanders have accepted that they will not be allowed to return to Diego Garcia, but US-led demands that they be denied access to other islands in the 65-atoll group were thrown out by the British Appeal Court in May 2007. In November 2007 the British Government launched yet another legal appeal against the decision. Chagossian supporters see this as an attempt to stall the return of the increasingly aging islanders to their homes until they have all died out.

# Nepal

**Principal protagonists**

Nepalese government; Communist Party of Nepal.

Madhesi and other ethnic minority groups. Several factions *(see text)*.

**Nature of conflict**
a) Ethnic minority grievances over political and cultural discrimination. b) Long-standing refugee crisis. *(See panel opposite)*.

☠ Around 30 since November 2006. (13,000 in Maoist insurgency).
👥 106,000 refugees from Bhutan since 1990.

**Population/ethnic composition**
28.3m. Nepalese 55.8%, Maithili 10.8%, Bhojpuri 7.9%, Tharu 4.4%, Tamang 3.6%, Newar 3%, Magar 2.5%, Awadhi 2.7%, Gurkha 1.7%.

**Territorial extent**
Primarily the southern Terai (Madhesi) region. Total Nepal area: 147,181 km².

**Timeline**
1950: Nepal/Indian treaty facilitates greater migration of Indians to Madhesi region.
1965: Hindi banned as a language of instruction.
Sep 1990: Ethnic Nepalese refugees expelled from Bhutan.
1996: Communist Party of Nepal (CPN) Maoist insurgency begins.
6 Nov 2006: Peace agreement signed between government and CPN.
Dec 2006: Clashes break out between Madhesis and security forces.
15 Jan 2007: New constitution proclaimed.
28 Dec 2007: Parliament votes for abolition of the monarchy,

**Current status**
Unstable. Elections (originally scheduled for 2007) postponed until mid 2008.

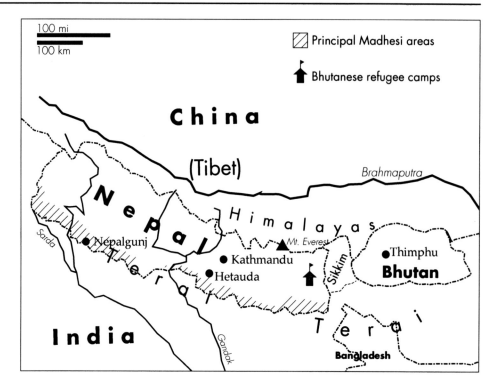

With the signing of a comprehensive peace agreement in November 2006 it appeared that the kingdom of Nepal was entering a new era. The Maoist Communist Party of Nepal (CPN) – who had been fighting a guerrilla insurgency throughout the country since 1996 – had been co-opted into government, the power of the monarchy had been significantly curtailed, a United Nations team was in the country, and a new constitution designed. Yet within weeks Nepal was once again wracked with violence, when protests by the Madhesi ethnic minority descended into rioting and widespread inter-communal clashes. Amid the self-congratulation among politicians the architects of 'the new Nepal' had overlooked the ethnic dimension to communal conflict.

Nepal is home to over 100 ethnic minorities, many of whom are in turn deeply divided along caste and political lines. The signing of the 2006 agreement, after years of war and discontent, largely ignored the long-standing demands of ethnic minorities for greater cultural and political autonomy. Furthermore, the success of the CPN in fighting its way to a share of power sent the very clear message that the only language Kathmandu, and the political elites (now including the Maoists themselves), would understand was a violent one.

Geographically, Nepal is conventionally divided into three regions, the Himalayan mountainous regions, the Hills region (the Mahabarat and Shivalik ranges) and the low-lying swampy Terai, or Madhesi, which blends into similar territory over the southern border in India and which is the main agricultural region of Nepal. The people of the Terai are generally known collectively as 'Madhesi' or 'people of the plains' (in contrast to the Pedhasi, the 'people of the hills'). For the most part, the Madhesi are Hindi-speaking Hindus, with links to their co-linguists in India. Most of Nepal's Muslim community is also Madhesi.

Some controversy exists as to what constitutes a Madhesi. A number of ethnic groups, the Maithili, Bhokpuri and Abadhi in the east, central and west of the region respectively, are generally regarded as Madhesi, as are the Tharu people, who live throughout the region. Furthermore, as Hindus, the Madhesi operate a complex hierarchical caste system. Untouchability (as in India, the Untouchables are called Dalits) is still widely practised within Madhesi society. Attempts at political unity have been limited by intense factionalism within the various Madhesi movements.

The clashes, which started in December 2006 in the city of Nepalgunj, arise from long-standing grievances. The Madhesi (and other ethnic minority groups) have long called for the re-constitution of Nepal along ethnically-based federal lines. One of the earliest Madhesi political parties, the Nepal Sadhanava Party was formed in 1983 and contested elections until 1999. The Maoist insurgency also played to ethnic sentiments, officially supporting ethnic autonomy (a policy condemned by some Maoist activists as being contrary to the Communist class-based ideology theoretically endorsed by the movement). In June 2006, the Madhesi inaugurated a campaign calling for the inclusion of ethnic needs on the agenda for re-constructing Nepal, but now feel that this demand has been ignored.

Madhesi complaints include land rights issues – only a minority own their own land, and land dispossession by Pahade migrants is an additional factor – exclusion from employment in the Army and police, and restrictions on the use of Hindi, which was banned as a medium of instruction in 1965. Political under-representation is significant grievance; the lowland areas have much higher population density than the hills and mountainous regions, but this is not reflected in parliamentary representation. Hill constituencies with only a few thousand electors are contrasted with Terai constituencies where up to 80,000 voters elect only one parliamentarian. Denial of citizenship, with the Nepal government seeking to classify the Madhesi as Indians, is a further issue.

Attempts have been made to portray the Madhesi as the vehicle of monarchists, Hindu extremists, or of the Indian government. Madhesi activists are hostile both to the mainstream government parties and to the CPN. Clashes have taken place between the Madhesis and Maoists. This in part may have a factional origin: one of the Madesi groups, the *Janatantrik Terai Mukti Morcha* originally split from the Maoists and so they are long standing rivals.

Although attention has focused on Madhesi violence, other ethnic groups, such as the Limbuwan Federal Republic and the *Newa Mukti Morcha*, are known to be active. All broadly share the Madhesi agency of a federal Nepal subdivided on ethnic lines, as does the broadly-based Nepal Federation of Indigenous Nationalities, which includes members of the hill tribes.

Throughout 2007 political progress remained largely stalled, and elections planned for June 2007 were postponed until April 2008. In December 2007, parliament voted to abolish the 240-year old Nepalese monarchy and create a "federal democratic republican state". The decision was primarily aimed at bringing the Maoists back into government, although the demand for a federal state is also a key Madhesi demand. Madhesi views on the monarchy have been ambiguous; some militants support its abolition, others argue that, in a multi-ethnic society, a monarch is a useful unifying institution. In December 2007 three Madhesi deputies resigned from parliament over the lack of progress on Madhesi demands.

The re-emergence of political violence in Nepal is a reminder that deals cut between political elites do not always match the aspirations of the people themselves. The resolution of this issue relies on how Nepal's leaders respond to the challenge of incorporating ethno-political issues into the new political dispensation. Should they fail in this task Nepal may face a future of further violence.

### Nepal's Bhutanese refugees

Since 1990, eastern Nepal has been host to 106,000 refugees from Bhutan, whose future remains uncertain. The refugees are Nepalese-speaking Hindus who originally moved to Bhutan in search of work.

The broader background is extreme cultural sensitivity amongst the Bhutanese, who feel that their Buddhist/Tibetan culture is under threat. Bhutan has attempted to impose national cultural values on minority groups, including dress and use of the Drukpa language. Buddhism has also been actively promoted. The Bhutanese themselves migrated to the region from Tibet and regard more recent arrivals – such as the Nepalese – as a threat to their predominance in the country. In 1998, the Government instituted a 'one nation, one people' campaign that stated that anyone who could not prove residency back to 1958 was no longer a citizen.

In response to these restrictions, the Nepalese staged an anti-government uprising in September 1990 and were deported *en masse* as a consequence. The refugees have been demanding the right to return to Bhutan. Bhutan has refused this, claiming the refugees are not Bhutanese.

In 2000 a joint team was established to establish the nationality of individual refugees, but no concrete progress was made on the issue. Despite repeated talks, not a single refugee has been re-admitted to Bhutan. Limited offers of resettlement in other countries have been made, but this has divided opinion among the refugees, with some arguing that it legitimizes their deportation from Bhutan.

The protracted crisis has been punctuated by organized protests on the part of the refugees themselves. In 1996 they attempted unsuccessfully to stage a protest march to Bhutan to appeal directly to the Bhutanese king, Jigme Wangchuk, and in 2003 they organized a hunger strike. Officially forbidden to work and confined to eight damp and malarifious camps where they are dependent on the UN for food and essential services, the refugees have been largely abandoned by the wider world.

# Tamil Eelam

**Principal protagonists**

Sinhalese community; Government of Sri Lanka.

Tamil community; Liberation Tigers of Tamil Eelam (Tamil Tigers, LTTE).

Indian Peace Keeping Force (IPKF) 1987-90.

**Nature of conflict**

Long-standing secessionist war. Linguistic and other Tamil civil rights are the underpinning issues.

⚐ Widespread human rights abuses by both sides reported.
☠ 68,000.
⚭ 1 million IDPs.

**Population/ethnic composition**

Sri Lanka total: 20.2m. Sinhalese 73.8%, Sri Lankan Moors 7.2%, Indian Tamil 4.6%, Sri Lankan Tamil 3.9%. Tamil Eelam population: 3.1m.

**Territorial extent**

Sri Lanka total: 65,610 km². Tamil Eelam: 19,509 km², of which 40-50% actually controlled by LTTE.

**Timeline**

16 Feb 1796: Ceylon (Sri Lanka) comes under the control of the British East India Company.
4 Feb 1948: Sri Lanka independent from Britain.
1972: Tamil New Tigers founded.
1976: Independent Tamil Eelam proposed by Tamil political groups.
5 May 1976: TNT renamed Liberation Tigers of Tamil Eelam.
23 Jul 1983: 'Black July'. Outbreak of full-scale war.

**Current status**

Unresolved. Fighting continues.

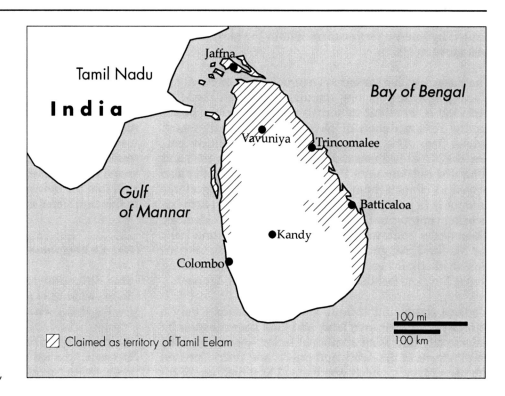

Ceylon – modern day Sri Lanka – has been the scene of conflict between the majority Sinhalese population (who are mostly Buddhist) and the mainly Hindu or Catholic Tamil minority since at least the 1920s. In the past two decades, the island has been witness to a vicious secessionist war that shows little signs of abating. Since the 1980s, the Tamils have been fighting for an independent homeland, Tamil Eelam, in the north and north-east of the island.

Both the Sinhalese and Tamil communities claim to have been the original settlers of the island. The basis of Tamil nationalist claims is the assertion that the British colonial authorities recognized the existence of more than one state on the island when they assumed control at the end of the 18th century. Since independence from Britain in 1948, Tamils have complained of discrimination in language use, educational opportunities and access to land. The Sinhalese-dominated government counters by arguing that it is redressing the alleged favouritism shown towards the Tamils by the British colonial government.

Although there is no state religion, the law in practice accords Buddhism a favoured position. It is, however, in the promotion of Sinhala as an official language that the main genesis of Tamil discontent is to be found. The tipping point in the decline in the post-independence relationship between the Tamils and the Sinhalese was the passing of the 1956 Sinhala Only Act. This replaced English as the country's official language with Sinhala. This had the effect not only of excluding many Tamil speakers from official positions, but also limited their educational opportunities, since many Tamils – having English as a second language – had benefited from English-language higher education. In 1970, the government banned the importation of Tamil language media and placed further practical restrictions on Tamils seeking education in India and Britain. In the same year, the official name of the country was changed from Ceylon to Sri Lanka – a Singhalese name.

Sri Lankan Tamils have ethnic and kinship ties to Tamils on mainland India, notably in the Tamil Nadu region. In addition to Sri Lankan Tamils, there is a sizeable community of Tamils of Indian origin, the so-called Hill or Tea Tamils, who migrated to the island in the 19th century in order to work the plantations. In 1949, these 'Indian' Tamils were stripped of their Ceylonese citizenship, significantly reducing the electoral strength of the overall Tamil population. In 1962, with the agreement of India, the mass expulsion of some 600,000 of the Indian Tamil community was proposed. Around half this number were in the event deported, but the balance continued to be denied Sri Lankan citizenship until 2003. The explusions of the Indian Tamil community, together with immigration by Sinhalese, meant that Tamils become a minority in many areas they considered part of their traditional homeland.

Tamil opposition initially focused on political means, the concept of an independent Tamil Eelam being first proposed by the Tamil United Liberation Front (TULF), a coalition of Tamil political parties, in 1976. Tamil nationalism developed a militant edge with the formation of Tamil New Tigers by Velupillai Prabhakaran in 1972; in 1976 his group was renamed the Liberation Tigers of Tamil Eelam (LTTE, or Tamil Tigers).

From 31 May to 2 June 1981 anti-Tamil rioting in Jaffna saw the destruction of many Tamil properties as well as 95,000 mostly Tamil language volumes in the Jaffna Public Library. From this point onwards, the descent into sustained conflict was seen by many as inevitable. In July 1983 the LTTE launched its first major attack in the north of the country, killing 13 soldiers and triggering severe rioting in Colombo. Now called 'Black July' this month is generally regarded as marking the start of full-scale war. In a tactic that was to become their hallmark, the LTTE also launched their first suicide attack, killing 40 soldiers – the LTTE has, in fact launched more suicide attacks than any other insurgent group worldwide. Fighting rapidly spread to other parts of the country.

At their peak, the Tigers had effective control of up to half of the claimed territory of Tamil Eelam, mostly in the north, and including, for many years, the city of Jaffna. In the areas they control the LTTE have established a number of civil structures, including police and courts, none of which are recognized by the Colombo government – which continues to pay civil servants' salaries even in the LTTE controlled regions.

Tamil politics have long been subject to splits and internecine conflict between the LTTE and other groups. In 2004 the LTTE suffered a major blow when the Tigers in the east of the island broke away under the leadership of Karuna Amman. The LTTE has since accused the Karuna faction of fighting with the government, while there are human rights accusations that Columbo has turned a blind eye to Karuna faction abuses, including the recruitment of child soldiers.

The LTTE itself has been accused of numerous excesses, including use of forced and child labour, use of antipersonal mines, kidnappings and hijackings, and the expropriate of food resources. Similarly well founded accusations of brutality have been made against government forces.

India became increasingly involved in the conflict in the late 1980s, although its partiality (with an eye on potential Tamil discontent in India itself) was ambiguous. On 29 July 1987, under Indian auspices, a peace agreement was signed between the LTTE (and other groups) and the Sri Lankan government. The deal included provision for the merger of mainly Tamil provinces into a single administration and for the deployment of an Indian Peacekeeping Force (IPKF). The initial results were encouraging: a withdrawal of Sri Lankan troops from Tamil areas took place and some militant groups, although not the LTTE, disarmed. Part of the motivation, from Colombo's point of view, was the need for troops to put down the unrelated uprising by the *Janatha Vimukthi Peramuna* group in the south of the country. Clashes, however, soon broke out between the LTTE and the IPKF, whose withdrawal on 24 March 1990 marked the end of the peace process, with the LTTE largely occupying those districts of the country vacated by the departing Indian troops. Indian opposition to the LTTE further hardened after a female LTTE suicide bomber assassinated former Indian Prime Minister Rajiv Ghandi in 1991. Fighting continued throughout 1992 and 1993, in which year another suicide bomber killed Sri Lankan President Ranasinghe Premadasa. Not until 1995 was the government able to retake the initiative, re-capturing Jaffna (after ten years of LTTE control) on 5 December 1995. Government offensives and LTTE counter-offences continued throughout the remainder of the 1990s. Towards the end of 2001, with both sides largely exhausted, substantive peace talks resumed (under Norwegian auspices) and a 'Permanent Ceasefire Agreement' was signed on 22 February 2002. This, however, has proven to be neither a ceasefire nor permanent, and full-scale hostilities resumed in 2005. Intense fighting took place in the eastern Batticaloa region and the northern Vavuniya district in November 2006. A focus of the fighting was the town of Vaharai near Trincomalee, a key LTTE base since 1995, which fell in January 2007. In a further major offensive, government forces moved into LTTE controlled areas of north-west Sri Lanka. Subsequent fighting has generally been characterized by government advances, although LTTE naval and airborne attacks, as well as fierce land fighting continues.

The conflict continues to have a disastrous impact on Sri Lanka's attempts at economic development, particularly in the aftermath of the 2004 South East Asian tsunami. Currently, the government is prepared to offer autonomy, but not the full independence demanded by the LTTE. It is clear that neither side envisages a political settlement in the foreseeable future.

# Afghanistan/Pakistan

**Principal protagonists**

Government of Afghanistan; NATO forces actively engaged.

Taliban, Al Qaeda, and other Islamist militants.

Pakistan Government (officially allied to US/NATO. Elements of government and security forces ambivalent).

**Nature of conflict**
Full-scale conflict between Islamists and Afghan government/NATO forces; Cross-border insurgency between Afghan and Pakistani borders; Clashes between pro- and anti-Taliban groups in FATA..

- Pakistan: Muslim/Christian. Routine harassment of Christians by the authorities and attacks, including murders, by Islamic militants.
- Uncertain. 5,000-8,000 civilian casualties estimated.
- 2.4m Afghan refugees in Pakistan.
- Afghanistan: Significant narcotics (opium poppy) production.

**Population/ethnic composition**
Afghanistan: 31m. Pashtun 42%, Tajik 27%, Hazara 9%, Uzbek 9%. Religious mix: Sunni Muslim 80%, Shia Muslim 19%.
Pakistan: 165.8m (of which 3.3m in Federally Administered Tribal Areas). Punjabi 52.6%, Pashtun (Pathan) 13.2%, Sindhi 11.7%, Muhajir 7.5%, Balochi 4.3%.

**Territorial extent**
Afghanistan: 652,090 km².
Pakistan: Federally Administered Tribal Areas (including the 'Islamic Emirate of Waziristan'): 27,220 km².

**Timeline**
*See opposite.*

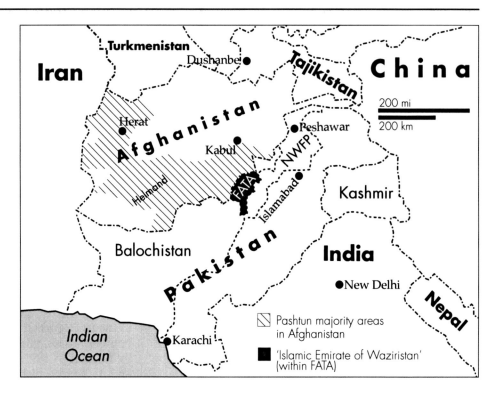

**Afghanistan has long been a country that is notoriously difficult to rule – either by foreigners or by the Afghans themselves. Since 1979 the country has experienced virtually continual civil strife and foreign intervention. Following the implication of the ruling Taliban of involvement in the 11 September 2001 terrorist attacks on the United States, Afghanistan's troubled history entered a new phase, with the overthrow of the Kabul government by US-led forces. Efforts at creating a genuinely national government continue to flounder on the rocks of tribal and ideological animosities and the contradictory ambitions of international players.**

Central to an understanding of the current conflict is an appreciation of the cross-border nature of ethnic politics in the region. Pashtuns, who form the largest single ethnic group in Afghanistan and comprise the majority in the Pakistani border areas, have provided the ethnic bedrock of Taliban support, despite the movement's claims regarding the universality of its creed. Despite denials by Islamabad, there is ample evidence that elements within the Pakistani security apparatus are continuing to provide critical assistance to the Taliban, the movement they were instrumental in creating in the 1990s.

A strict Sunni Muslim movement, the Taliban was formed in 1993 at the instigation of the Pakistani military and intelligence services, probably with covert support from the Americans, as a vehicle for exerting pressure on the then Afghan government. Many of its early recruits were Afghan Pashtun refugees then living in Pakistan who were radicalized in *madrassa*, or Islamic schools – hence the name 'Taliban', which means 'students'. From the US point of view at least, this programme backfired disastrously. By 1996 the Taliban, which drew its support overwhelmingly from the Pashtun population both in Afghanistan and Pakistan, was in control of 80% of Afghanistan and out of control as far as its original mentors were concerned. In 1997, the Taliban proclaimed the establishment of the Islamic Emirate of Afghanistan, under its leader Mullah Mohammed Omar. This state achieved recognition only from the UAE, Saudi Arabia, and – significantly – Pakistan. The Taliban instigated a draconian rule in those parts of Afghanistan under its control. Dancing and music were banned, women were forced out of paid employment and girls were banned from schools and universities. Minor infringements of Islamic dress codes by women were summarily punished by public flogging. The Taliban further gained international opprobrium by the destruction in March 2001 of the historic Bamiyan Buddha statues on the grounds that they were graven images.

Osama Bin Laden moved to Afghanistan following his expulsion from Sudan in 1996, and rapidly forged a close alliance between his own Al Qaeda organization and the Taliban. Following the 11 September 2001 attacks on the World Trade Center and other targets in the US, the Taliban continued to shelter Bin Laden. On 7 October 2001, the United States, supported by NATO allies, launched air attacks against Taliban/Al Qaeda targets in Afghanistan and commenced direct land support to the Northern Alliance, the coalition of anti-Taliban forces that had continued to resist Taliban rule. Although both Bin Laden and Mullah Omar escaped capture, the Taliban regime was effectively overthrown by December 2001.

Following the defeat of the Taliban, attention turned to the creation of effective central government institutions for Afghanistan. A national *Loya Jirga* (council of elders) was convened in 2002. This established Hamid Karzai as Interim President of Afghanistan and was followed in 2003 by the ratification of a new constitution. In October 2004 Karzai was elected President in a nationwide election, and legislative elections were held in September 2005. However, the reality on the ground remained discouraging and 2006 was, in fact, marked by an upsurge in rebel activities, particularly in the southern Helmand province, where NATO forces, particularly the British, continue engage Taliban forces.

Critical to gaining control in Afghanistan is suppressing the cross-border insurgency from Pakistan. But, for any government, effective control of the frontier district between Pakistan and Afghanistan has historically proven all but impossible. The Durant Line – the border arbitrarily demarcated by the British in 1893 – has been a bone of contention between the two countries since its creation and one that has, moreover, been largely ignored by the semi-nomadic Pashtun and other communities on both sides of the line. For many years, Afghanistan pressed an irredentist claim over the Pakistani regions of the Federally Administered Tribal Areas and the North West Frontier Province. Pakistan, in turn, has supported Islamist Pashtun movements in Afghanistan both to counterweight Pashtun agitation within its own borders and to exert influence over its neighbour. The creation of the Taliban was thus part of long-standing political tradition on the part of Islamabad.

Until 2006, authority in the borderland Federally Administered Tribal Areas derived from the colonial era Frontier Crimes Regulation introduced in 1901 and carried over into independence, with Islamabad agreeing not to station troops in the tribal border areas. The FCR combined traditional patterns of governance and crime prevention with the central state reserving interventionist powers that bypassed the legislative processes applicable in other parts of the country. The FCR vested practical authority in the hands of a Political Agent who headed the local administration of each FATA agency. The Political Agent in turn worked through local proxies, granting tribal elders the status of *malik* and a financial stipend in return for suppressing crime and generally supporting the government. While this structure was suitable for a colonial system of indirect government, it was open to widespread corruption and poor governance and proved inadequate for dealing with modern security needs. In 2004 Pakistani troops, for the first time, moved into the FATA region (prompting clashes with local tribal militias) and in April 2006 President Musharraf announced plans to end the FATA system.

In September 2006, following two years of conflict, the Pakistani government agreed a truce with militants of the self-styled 'Islamic Emirate of Waziristan' in the Waziristani districts of the Federally Administered Tribal Areas. A key element of the agreement was a prohibition on the use of the territory for cross-border operations into Afghanistan and some commentators argued that this would facilitate the interception of Taliban insurgents crossing the border from Pakistan. Speculation continues that Osama Bin Laden and Mullah Omar have found sanctuary in these regions, possibly under the protection of elements of the Pakistani security forces, and mounting evidence that the Pakistani authorities are turning a blind eye to an increas-

**Timeline**
1893: British demarcation of Afghan/ Pakistani border – the 'Durant Line.'
1901: British establish Frontier Crimes Regulation as mechanism for indirect governance of the then North West Frontier Province. Still applied by Pakistani government to Federally Administered Tribal Areas.
8 Aug 1919: Modern Afghan state proclaimed. (Recognized by Britain 22 Nov 1921.)
14 Aug 1947: Pakistan achieves independence from Britain.
25 Dec 1979-15 Feb 1989: Afghanistan occupied by the Soviet Union.
c1993: Taliban created at instigation of Pakistani security forces.
26 Oct 1997: Taliban-led Islamic Emirate of Afghanistan proclaimed. Resistance by Northern Alliance continues.
11 Sep 2001: Terrorist attack on World Trade Center, New York, claims over 3,000 casualties. Taliban implicated.
7 Oct 2001-Dec 2001: US-led forces in conjunction with the Northern Alliance overthrow Taliban rule.
2004: Pakistani troops occupy FATA. Local fighting ensues.
5 Sep 2006: Pakistan signs truce with 'Islamic Emirate of Waziristan'.
18 Feb 2008: Pakistan Peoples' Party leads new government in Pakistan.

**Current status**
Widespread fighting continues.

ing number of cross-border incursions and movements of weapons led to increasing American disquiet. The US continued strikes on specific targets in Pakistan, usually under the pretence of 'joint action' with Pakistani forces. In one particularly well-publicized incident in October 2006 US forces attacked a madrassa in the extreme north of the FATA region, allegedly targeting high-ranking Al Qaeda officials, but resulting in significant civilian casualties. In January 2008, two forts in Waziristan were reported as having been taken over by the Taliban, having been abandoned by their Pakistan army defenders.

Following its election in February 2008 *(See Pakistan's political problems, 5.26)* the new Pakistani government has adopted a more aggressive approach to militants in the FATA region, moving some 30,000 troops into South Waziristan, whilst simultaneously encouraging dialogue with tribal leaders. Clashes between Pakistani regular forces and the Taliban have become more marked, such as the fierce fighting, including the use for the first time of artillery by government forces, around Peshawar in June 2008.

The policy of co-opting tribal leaders builds upon the indications that Pashtun groups are tiring of the association between their communities and the Islamist cause. In November 2006, a unique jirga of Pashtun groups in Peshawar complained that authentic Pashtun voices were in danger of being drowned out by the violence of the insurgency. The legitimacy of Taliban claims to speak for the Pashtun people was called into question, with leaders arguing that the Taliban is the creation not of the Pashtun people but of the Pakistani military. Fears were also expressed about the creeping 'Talibanization' of Pashtun governmental and civil society. This trend is also manifest in Taliban attacks against tribal leaders, such as the kidnap and murder of 22 members of the Bhittani tribe in the South Waziristan town of Jandola in June 2008 by pro-Taliban Mehsud tribesmen. (The Mehsud, led by Baitullah Mehsud, is the dominant tribe in South Waziristan.) Traditional Pashtun society revolves around the *masjid* (mosque) and the *bujra* (the seat of the tribal chief) and this separation of powers between the religious and political spheres is anathema to the Taliban. The notoriously independently minded Pashtun may reassert their resentment of any kind of central authority, whether imposed by the Taliban or Islamabad.

*See 5.26 for summary of the overall political situation in Pakistan.*

## NATO and 9/11

The North Atlantic Treaty Organization was created in 1949 as a defensive alliance against the possibility of a Soviet attack on Western Europe. Central to the Alliance's doctrine is the concept of collective security, enshrined in Article 5 of the NATO Charter, which decreed that an attack on one member of the Alliance was to be deemed an attack on all. This was principally to assure European members (and the Soviet Union) that the United States would intervene immediately in any emergency in Europe.

At the end of the Cold War NATO's original *raison d'etre* became largely redundant. In 1999, three of NATO's former potential adversaries, Hungary, the Czech Republic and Poland, became the first former Communist bloc states to join the Alliance.

It is one of the ironies of history (but also arguably a testament to the success of NATO as a peacekeeping alliance) that Article 5 has only been invoked once by a member state – and that member was the United States. The US invoked Article 5 within hours of the 11 September 2001 terrorist attacks against US cities. On 4 October 2001 NATO confirmed that the 9/11 attacks were a legitimate *casus belli* that did indeed fall within the terms of the North Atlantic Charter. The first (and so far only) NATO military exercises to be conducted under the terms of Article 5 – Operation Eagle Assist and Active Endeavor – were air surveillance operations carried out over the continental USA by NATO aircraft. Crews from 13 NATO countries participated.

The military attack on the Taliban in Afghanistan (Operation Enduring Freedom) was technically not a NATO operation, although many of the Alliance's members contributed. (The designation operation Enduring Freedom also covered counter insurgency actions against Al Qaeda targets in the Philippines and in the Horn of Africa.)

On 11 August 2003, NATO took over formal command of the International Security Assistance Force (ISAF) in Afghanistan, the first time NATO forces were actively deployed outside the European theatre. NATO operations in Afghanistan continue.

# Balochistan

## Principal protagonists

Pakistan government and military; government of Balochistan province; Pashtun and Islamist elements. Also government of Iran.

Baloch people; Baloch National Party; Baloch Liberation Army and other organizations.

## Nature of conflict

Nationalist/self-determination conflict.

⚡ Routine excesses by authorities reported.
☠ c10,000.
👥 Up to 200,000 IDP at peak; 2m Afghan refugees.

## Population/ethnic composition

Balochistan (Pakistan): 9.9m. 50% Baloch, 50% Pashtun and others. Balochs comprise around 2% of the Iranian population.

## Territorial extent

Balochistan Province (Pakistan): 347,190 km². Area of Baloch inhabitation in Iran c120,000 km².

## Timeline

1638: Khanate of Kalat founded.
1876: Kalat signs treaty of friendship with Britain.
1 Oct 1887: Balochistan occupied by British.
1928: Western Balochistan occupied by Iran.
31 Mar 1948: Kalat accedes to Pakistan.
16 May 1948: Start of first Baloch uprising against Pakistan.
1 Jul 1970: Balochistan Province formed.
2004: Start of current uprising against Pakistan.
15 May 2006: Iranian military offensive against Baloch separatists.

## Current status

Continuing violence. Issues in both Pakistan and Iran remain unresolved.

The Baloch are a tribally based, largely mountainous people numbering some 15 million who live in Pakistan, southern Afghanistan, eastern Iran and in communities throughout the Middle East and beyond. In the latter half of the 19th century the region came under increasing British influence. In 1876 the Khanate of Kalat (in the east of modern Balochistan) signed a treaty with the British (becoming one of the princely states of British India) and by 1887 the whole area had been incorporated, at least nominally, into the British Empire. In 1893 the establishment of the 'Durant Line' sought to demarcate the borders between the British Empire, Persia and Afghanistan. These borders continue to be disputed by the various parties, not least the Baloch, who found their historical territory now divided between three powers.

The eastern portion of Balochistan remained British until the partition of India and the creation of Pakistan in 1947. In 1948 the Khanate of Kalat acceded to Pakistan, despite claims by Baloch nationalists that the original 1876 treaty preserved Kalat independence. This first of a series of nationalist revolts – which have continued intermittently to the present day – erupted in mid 1948.

The modern Pakistani province of Balochistan is the largest of the four federal states in Pakistan. However, Baloch inhabitation is not co-terminous with the Balochistan province; in the northern half of the region other ethnic groups, primarily the Pashtuns, form a majority. Baloch grievances are fuelled not just by the division of their territory across international borders, but the lack of a distinctively Baloch province within Pakistan. Furthermore, Balochistan remains the poorest and least developed of the provinces of Pakistan, which local nationalists ascribe to deliberate government neglect. Significant oil and gas reserves are believed to exist in the region, but these have not been fully exploited, and Balochs fear that development, should it take place, will not benefit the local community.

The historical conflict in Balochistan has been hugely exacerbated by the current war in Afghanistan, which has a significant cross-border dimension (See Afghanistan/Pakistan, 5.22). The Taliban Islamists in Afghanistan are largely Pashtun in origin and have close links with their fellow Pashtuns in Pakistan. Furthermore, there are close connections between elements of the Pakistani security forces and Pashtun/Taliban militants. These connections have also penetrated the political sphere. The Islamist/Pashtun *Jamiat Ulema-e-Islam* (JUI-F) party is the leading player in the broader Islamist alliance, the *Muttahida Majlis-e-Amal* (MMA) that in turn is the dominant coalition partner, with President Musharraf's Pakistan Muslim League, in the provincial government. In October 2007 the JUI-F/MMA withdrew from the coalition, however, and entered into an unlikely opposition alliance with the Baloch National Party and other Baloch parties.

Although Baloch society is largely Sunni and often deeply conservative, Balochs find themselves at odds both with Islamists and with the Pakistani authorities. Traditional values and customary laws ('*rawaj*') have always been given primacy in Baloch society over religious orthodoxy. While maintaining links and alliances with Islamist elements, the military have consistently clamped down on demonstrations of Baloch separatism. The transfer of law and order away from traditional Balochistani levies to the regular (Punjabi-dominated) police, the creation of military cantonments, arbitrary and extra-judicial arrests and imprisonment of Baloch activists are routinely reported, as is the 'disappearance' of individuals suspected of links to Baloch militants. Baloch activists have asked, not without justification, why US military and political support to the Pakistani state is being diverted for use against a largely moderate community, while at the same time the Pakistani security and political apparatus actively and openly engages in alliances with pro-Taliban elements.

Despite divide-and-rule tactics by the Pakistani authorities, Baloch nationalists have found some common ground with non-Islamist Pashtuns separatists, who have their own quarrels with the Taliban. However, the ethnic division of Balochistan itself presents a further area of dispute. Some Pashtun activists favour the separation of Balochistan into a 'Pashtunistan' north, potentially merged with the North West Frontier Province, and a purely Baloch south. This is rejected, for the most part, by Baloch nationalists, whose goal remains, if not an independent Balochistan, then as a minimum better representation at the existing state level. This in turn can only be achieved if free and fair elections (such as have been consistently denied) enable a greater and more genuinely representative Baloch voice to be heard at the provincial level. The necessary political and military adjustments to achieve this are only likely to occur in the context of general democratization of the Pakistani state.

Western Balochistan was only annexed to Iran in 1928. Although related to the Iranians, the Baloch have been distrusted by Tehran because of their ethnic divergence from the 'Persian' national norm, and, particularly since the fall of the Shah, for their adherence to Sunni Islam (the regime being firmly Shia in doctrine). The Baloch language is forbidden in Iran and economic neglect and claimed employment discrimination has further alienated the Baloch. Ongoing tensions and clashes between the Iranian authorities and the Balochs erupted into general fighting in 2006 and local incidents continue to be regularly reported. The cultural marginalization of Baloch history, language and religion in south eastern Iran continues.

**Pakistan's political problems**

The future trajectory of ethnic conflicts in Pakistan and its neighbours is inevitably closely bound up with the political future of the country as a whole.

The military coup of 12 October 1999 saw General Pervez Musharraf installed as President. The military take-over initially led to Pakistan being ostracized (it was, for example, suspended from the Commonwealth) but the 9/11 attacks on the US saw Pakistan emerge as a key ally of the United States in the 'war on terror'. Ostensibly anti-Islamist, in practice the Pakistani government, and, more importantly, elements of the security forces, have been deeply ambivalent in their treatment of Islamist militancy as they steer a careful line between the valuable US alliance and populist domestic sentiment. Domestic sensitivity can be gauged by the widespread rioting which followed the storming by government forces of the Lal Masjid mosque in Islamabad on 11 July 2007, an action that was seen as representing a significant clampdown on Islamic extremists.

US pressure for domestic reform rose as the inability of the Pakistani state to reign in Islamist extremists became more apparent. Nevertheless, in October 2007, Musharraf was elected President by the Pakistani legislature, in a move that was fiercely contested legally by the Pakistani courts.

As part of the process aimed at holding a general election in January 2008, political exiles were allowed to return to the country, most notably Benazir Bhutto. Her return to Pakistan was marred by bombings aimed at her motorcade that killed 130 of her supporters. Emergency rule was declared on 3 November and Musharraf was sworn in as civilian President on 29 November, having officially stepped down from his military position. Emergency rule was lifted on 17 December, but Bhutto's assassination on 27 December threw the country into further political turmoil and violence, resulting in the postponing of the planned 8 January 2008 elections. Following the poll, which took place on 18 February, a coalition government was formed with Yousef Raza Gilari (of the late Bhutto's Pakistan Peoples' Party) as Prime Minister. Bombings and other political violence continue throughout the country.

# Section 6: **South East Asia and Oceania**

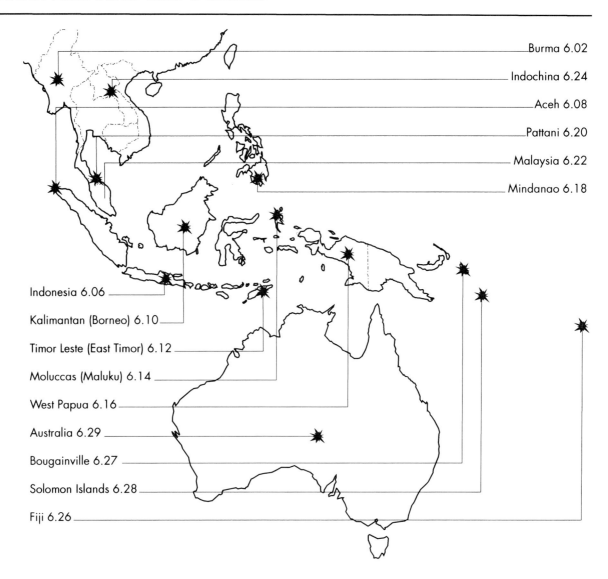

Burma 6.02
Indochina 6.24
Aceh 6.08
Pattani 6.20
Malaysia 6.22
Mindanao 6.18
Indonesia 6.06
Kalimantan (Borneo) 6.10
Timor Leste (East Timor) 6.12
Moluccas (Maluku) 6.14
West Papua 6.16
Australia 6.29
Bougainville 6.27
Solomon Islands 6.28
Fiji 6.26

*Ethnic conflict in Luzon 6.19*
*Ethnic resistance to the Burmese state 6.03*
*Indonesia's transmigration policy 6.11*
*Nuclear conflict in the Pacific 6.30*
*The* dwifungsi *policy 6.13*

Fields of Fire – An Atlas of Ethnic Conflict

# Burma (Myanmar)

**Principal protagonists**

Government of Myanmar: the State Peace and Development Council.

Numerous ethnically-based insurgencies. (See panel opposite and text for details.)

**Nature of conflict**

Long-standing human and minorities rights issues. Ongoing insurgencies against central government.

☧ Widespread and systematic human rights abuses by government and armed forces.

☪ Muslim/Buddhist conflict an issue in case of Rohingya. Christian/Buddhist tensions an issue in some communities.

☠ Not accurately reported. Certainly in excess of 10,000.

☖ 250,000 Rohingya refugees in Bangladesh, 1991-2. Tens of thousands of refugees, especially Karen, in camps in Thailand. Up to 1 million IDPs in Burma itself.

**Population/ethnic composition**

Population figures issued by the regime disputed; believed to be up to 55m. Burmese 56%, Karen 9.5%, Shan 8.5%, Rakhine 4%, Yangbye 2%, Kachin 2%, Rohingya 2%, Mon 1.5%, Han Chinese 1%, Wa 1%. Many others.

**Territorial extent**

Burma (Myanmar): 678,000 km².

**Timeline**

849 AD: First Burmese kingdom established, in Pagan region.
1824-1885: Anglo-Burmese wars.
1 Apr 1937: Burma becomes a separately administered territory.
4 Jan 1948: Burma achieves independence from Britain.
1948 onwards: Multiple ethnically-based uprisings against Burmese rule begin.
1962: Military coup ends democratic rule.
8 Aug 1988: Second military coup
1989: The country's name is officially changed from 'Burma' to 'Myanmar'.

**Current status**

Widespread violence and human rights abuses continue.

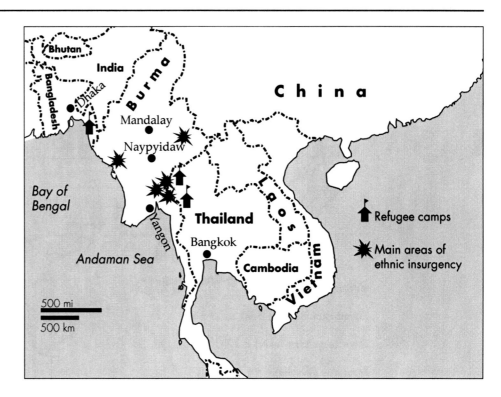

**Burma – or 'Myanmar' as the ruling junta prefers to call it – is one of the most repressive states in the world. Ruled since 1988 by the military-run State Peace and Development Council (known until 1997 as the State Law and Order Restoration Committee), persecution of opposition groups, including those calling for self-determination for ethnic minorities, is routine, brutal, and systematic. In 1990 the opposition party of Nobel Peace Prize winner Aung San Suu Kyi won a general election. This result was promptly annulled by the military regime, and she remains under house arrest.**

Burma is officially divided into seven purely Burmese divisions and seven states with non-Burmese populations. (See map, 6.04.) The majority Burmese are a Sino-Tibetan people and comprise around 56% of the population (excluding the Rohingyas [see below] who are racially similar but whose Islam sets them apart from the Buddhist population).

The Burmese began moving into the region from Tibet in the seventh century AD and by the eleventh century their influence had expanded to cover much of the present-day territory of Burma. Expanding Burmese and British influence brought the two countries into collision in the 19th century, and Anglo-Burmese wars took place in 1824, 1851 and 1885. The final war left the British in overall control and on 1 January 1886 Burma was given to Queen Victoria as a New Year's Day present. Burma regained independence in January 1948.

Today, 135 distinct ethnic groups are officially recognized. The borders of Burma do not correspond to ethnic divisions; populations from the ethnic minority groups exist in Thailand, China, Bangladesh, Laos and elsewhere in the region. The Karen, for example, are the largest hill tribe in Thailand, where they number some 400,000.

The 1982 Citizenship Law sought to draw a distinction between 'genuine' Burmese, whose settlement purportedly pre-dates the first British occupation in 1824, and more recent arrivals who have no citizenship, and extremely curtailed civil rights. In practice, the process is arbitrary and politically partisan; pro-government groups and militias have been accorded 'Burmese' status, while opponents of the regime have not. This, combined with direct military muscle (particularly since 1988) has proven to be an effective coercive bargaining tool in dealing with minority groups,

**Ethnic resistance to the Burmese state**

| Ethnic group/homeland | Main opposition movement | Number of fighters | Total population* | Burmese region |
|---|---|---|---|---|
| Arakan people | National United Front of Arakan | 200 | 4 million. | Rakhine (Arakan) State |
| Chin people | Chin National Front | n/a | 1.5 million | Chin State |
| Kachin people; Kachinland | Kachin Independence Organization | 5,000 | 2 million | Kachin State |
| Republic of Kawthulei | Karen National Union | c3,500 | 7 million | Kayin (Karen) State |
| Karenni people | Karenni National Progressive Party | 200 | 300,000 | Kayah State |
| Lahu people | Lahu National Organization | 150 | 200,000 | Northern Burma |
| Mon people | New Mon State Party | 3,000 | 8 million | Mon State |
| Palaung people | Palaung State Liberation Party | 500 | 1 million | Northern Burma |
| Pa-O people | Pa-O National Organization | 300 | 1.6 million | North-eastern Burma |
| Rohingya people | Arakan Rohingya Islamic Front | n/a | 1.4 million | Western Burma |
| Shan people | Shan State Army South | n/a | 4.7 million | Shan State |

The flags shown are unofficial and may be disputed. Additional factions also exist within many of the ethnic groups. The case of the United Wa State Army, which collaborates with the Burmese state, is covered in the text.

* Includes contiguous populations in regions bordering Burma as well as those in Burma itself.

elements of which have been drawn into 'ceasefires' with the government.

Burma can lay claim to the dubious title of having the most ethnic insurgencies aimed against central government rule of any state. Several of these have been in progress during the whole period of Burmese independence. The 7 million strong Karen claim their insurgency, which started in 1947 in support of an independent homeland to be called Kawthulei, is the longest running ethnic conflict in the world (although the century-old conflict in Aceh *[See 6.08]* may have a stronger claim). The Mon, who, despite having been among the first peoples to occupy the region, fall outside the 1982 Act, have similarly been attempting to establish a 'Mon Federated State' since the late 1940s. (The Mon people speak a Khmer language that has no similarities to Burmese. Numbering around 8 million, they were established in the region by 900 AD, with the last Mon kingdom being suppressed by the Burmese in 1757.) The Karenni (not to be confused with the Karen) have staged active resistance in Kayah State since 1957, apart from a brief ceasefire *(see below)* in 1995. An ongoing uprising by the Shan and Lahu people in what is now Shan State started in 1958. The Kachin have been in armed revolt since 1976 (with some support from China).

Oppression of ethnic minority groups includes forced re-settlement, rape and sexual enslavement, forced porterage and other forced labour, and direct military action. In all cases ethnic resistance has been met with human rights abuses, destruction of infrastructure, and internal displacement of populations by the *Tatmadaw* (the Burmese military) which has grown considerably since 1988 and now numbers half a million. Burma has an estimated 100,000 child soldiers, in breach of international conventions. Some observers believe the *Tatmadaw* favours the continuation of regional insurgencies, albeit at a tokenistic level, as a means of justifying high military and security expenditure.

It should be noted that there is little unity between the ethnic minority groups, despite their shared experience of oppression. Differences in religion, political goals, and ideology have resulted in widespread factionalism, both within and between ethnic minority groups. Factionalism within the ethnic populations has on occasion resulted in internecine violence, as have clashes between groups over resources, for example fighting between the Mon and the Karen over access to Thai border crossings. Rivalry within the ethnic groups has been successfully exploited by the authorities.

Typically, military action against the insurgents is coupled with extreme brutality towards the civilian population and the forced resettlement of villagers into government controlled areas. To take just one illustrative example, the government, in an attempt to choke off support for Shan rebel groups, began the forcible re-location of over 100,000 Shan to 45 militarized 'relocation sites' in 1996. Their villages were thereafter declared 'free fire' areas.

**Burma administrative divisions**

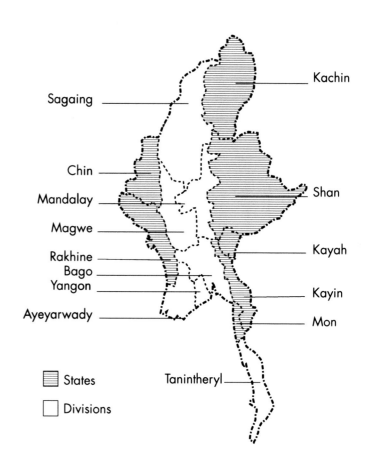

The position of the United Wa State Army (UWSA) in southern Shan state is anomalous in any consideration of ethnic unrest in Burma. With some 20,000 soldiers and up to 40,000 civilian recruits, it is the largest of the non-governmental armies operating in Burma. However, its contemporary role appears to owe more to warlordism and control of local resources than to any genuine support for the self-determination of the Wa people. The UWSA and its leader, Bao Yuxiang, collaborates with the Burmese military in maintaining control over the 'Golden Triangle' region and its potentially lucrative opium poppy industry. The UWSA participated, alongside the Burmese military, in the government's forceable re-settlement programmes. The United States regards Bao Yuxiang as a terrorist on a par with Osama Bin Laden and the late Saddam Hussein and has placed a $3m bounty on his head.

The position of the Rohingyas, the Muslim people of the southern Rakhine (Arakanese) is also somewhat different to that of other ethnic groups, in that the main basis of the dispute is a religious one rather than racial/cultural. Despite racial similarities to the majority Burmese population, the Rohingyas, who number 1.4 million, are not deemed to be Burmese and consequently are denied basic civil access, including to higher education, and even require permission to marry. Ethnic riots broke out between the Muslim

Rohingyas and the Buddhist Rakhine population throughout the 1940s. Upon Burmese independence in 1948, and again in 1954, failed armed uprisings by the Rohingyas prompted a backlash which saw their removal from civic posts and confiscation of property. In 1977 and 1991-2 government persecution, including forced labour, caused an estimated 250,000 to flee, mostly into Bangladesh, which was ill-equipped to receive them. A further exodus took place in 1997. Although the majority of Rohingyas were eventually repatriated by the UN, frequently under duress, a number – possibly as many as 21,000 – remain in the Kutapalong and Nayapara camps in Bangladesh.

Since 1995, the Burmese government has offered ceasefires to rebel groups, while at the same time continuing with widespread military action in a classic carrot-and-stick approach. The New Mon State Party, under pressure from its former Thai sponsors, entered into a ceasefire with the government in mid-1995, but clashes resumed in 2004. Other groups, such as the Shan State Army (North) and the Lahu Democratic Front, have also agreed ceasefires.

In March 1995 the Karenni National Progressive Party similarly entered into an agreement with the government, but this collapsed after three months. More successful (from the government's perspective) has been the formation of the Democratic Buddhist Karen Army (DBKA) as a rival to the Karen National Union (KNU). The DBKA – which claims persecution by Christians in the KNU against Buddhists – was instrumental in facilitating the fall of Manerplaw, the main Karen base, in 1994. The Karen opposition, although severely weakened, continues.

Since 2001, the Burmese government has attempted to climb on board the 'war on terror' bandwagon, with ethnic and religious opposition movements being routinely depicted as 'terrorists' by the Burmese regime. In fact, actions generally associated with 'terrorism' (including the targeting of civilians) are comparatively rare amongst Burmese resistance groups – although a Karen rebel group can lay claim to one of the earliest air hijackings, when they seized an airliner on a domestic flight in 1954.

Both politically and ethnically, Burma remains a profoundly divided society. While the regime retains its military might, and in the current absence of international pressure or intervention, insurgencies by ethnic minority or other opposition groups are unlikely to succeed or even to become a significant threat. Widespread domestic demonstrations led by Buddhist monks in September 2007 failed to seriously damage the regime's grip on power, although the violent suppression of the protests did little for its international reputation. Until and unless the Burmese regime falls, the current position, of ethnic insurgencies countered by massive human rights abuses, is certain to continue. The Burmese government will also continue to seek 'ceasefires' with local client groups and encourage factional divisions within the ranks of its opponents.

# Indonesia

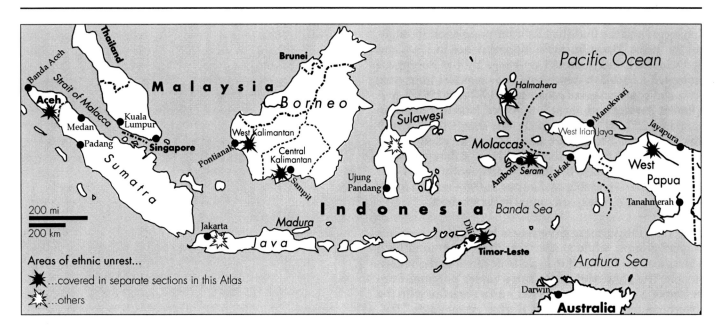

**Key details**

Republic of Indonesia.

**Population and ethnic composition**

223m. Javanese 36.4%, Sundanese 13.7%, Malay 9.4%, Madurese 7.2%, Chinese 4%. Religious mix: Muslim 76.5%, Christian 13.1%, Hindu 3.4%, traditional beliefs 2.5%.

**Territorial extent**

Indonesia: 1.9m km².

**Timeline**

1798: Dutch East Indies established.
1942-5: Under Japanese occupation.
17 Aug 1945: Independence declared. Guerrilla war against Netherlands commences.
27 Dec 1949: Indonesian independence recognized.
12 Mar 1967: Gen. Muhammad Suharto becomes President.
1997 Asian economic crisis precipitates fall of Suharto regime (1998) and general military, political and economic instability.

**Current status**

Significant and ongoing human rights, religious and separatist issues compounded by potential economic and political instability.

**Comprising 17,500 islands, over 300 ethnic groups, more than 700 languages, numerous religious sub-divisions, subject to massive state-planned internal population movements, and having a government that officially denies the significance of ethnicity in its ideology, Indonesia has long been a disaster waiting to happen.**

Dutch influence, which became dominant during the eighteenth century, saw the formal establishment of the Dutch East Indies in the area today comprising Indonesia in 1798. Dutch rule was effectively terminated by the Japanese invasion in 1942, and on 17 August 1945 the nationalist leader Sukarno (who had collaborated with the Japanese during the war) unilaterally declared Indonesia independent. Attempts by the Netherlands to regain control failed, and Indonesia was officially recognized as an independent state in 1949.

Politically, Indonesia is thus a nation born out of the militant rejection of colonialism. Ironically, the Indonesian state is simultaneously committed to the preservation of the same borders that were arbitrarily established by the colonial power. Because it has no other historical *raison d'etre*, elements of the Indonesian state will seek to dogmatically defend its territorial integrity even in areas, such as West Papua, where its basis for doing so is dubious, even within its own terms of reference.

Officially, the Indonesian state is 'colour blind' on the subject of race. Yet at the same time it declares certain racial groups, primarily those of Javanese extraction, to be *Prubumi*, or true Indonesians. Other groups, such as the Melanesians, the Dayaks of Kalimantan and the commercially influential Chinese, are, in varying degree, not considered wholly Indonesian, at least by implication. Intentional or not, this policy has fuelled racial tensions, which have erupted in a number of guises, including violent riots against Chinese commercial interests (and individuals) in the capital, Jakarta, conflict between Javanese and Madurese, and ongoing violence in central Sulawesi. Furthermore, the government-sponsored policy of transmigration *(See panel, 6.11)*, the movement mostly of Javanese populations to more sparsely populated regions of Indonesia, has hugely increased local racial and other tensions in regions such as Kalimantan *(See 6.10)*.

At a simplified level, Indonesian ethnic issues can be summarized as being between the core western Malay/Javanese populations and those of outlying regions who are generally characterized as 'Melanesian' – although this group is itself by no means homogeneous. A further dimension, and one which may well become more balefully influential in future years, is that of religion. Indonesia is the world's most populous Muslim country, with 85% of the population professing Islam. As with race, the official state line on religion is neutral. But the fact that most Javanese are Muslim, whereas many Melanesians and others are Christian or Hindu creates an obvious fault-line in many islands and regions of the country. As the Indonesian state continues to disintegrate, or at best faces ongoing secessionist pressures from non-Muslims, the possibilities of extremist Islamic groups extending their existing foothold appear increasingly likely. Something of the sort has already been seen in the Muslim militia and *'jihadist'* groups responsible for the scorched earth policy in the dying days of Indonesian control over East Timor *(See 6.12)* and in the units formed to 'protect' Muslims in Kalimantan and the Moluccas. The probability, by extension, exists of these groups being co-opted into the broader international Islamist movement. Osama Bin Laden declared a *fatwa* on Australia because of that country's military participation in the UN process that led to East Timorese independence. At least two major terrorist attacks, the 'Bali Bombing' at Kuta on 12 October 2002, which claimed 202 lives, and a second bombing, also at Kuta in 2005, have been linked to Al Qaeda operations. In August 2007, between 60,000-100,000 supporters of the *Hizb ut-Tahrir* movement gathered at a rally in Jakarta to call for the establishment of a global Islamic state.

At its most benign, the state policy of ignoring religious and racial realities has meant that the Indonesian authorities have lacked the insight to appreciate when ethnic tensions are reaching boiling point. The failure of the Indonesian authorities to deal effectively with, for example, inter-ethnic clashes in the Molaccas, probably owes more to incompetence and general demoralization than it does to partisanship. That being said, reported instances abound of the police and army standing by whilst Muslim militias in particular have ethnically cleansed Christian communities.

Although nominally civilian, for most of its history Indonesia has been a 'praetorian' state with the military overtly calling many of the shots. Furthermore, the military is heavily intertwined with the economic life of the country: some 75% of the military budget is generated by military-owned businesses, including legal (or semi-legal) operations in mining and timber, and illegal activities such as prostitution, people trafficking and the export of protected animal and plant species. Thus when economic collapse hit Indonesia in 1997, the military was directly, and adversely, affected financially, quite apart from any political consequences. Unable to adjust sufficiently rapidly to the situation, the long-standing 'New Order' of the authoritarian Suharto regime, already beset with security and corruption difficulties, collapsed in May 1998.

The key military consequence of the 1997 economic crash was that the Indonesian military's capacity for outreach was severely degraded and it was obliged to fall back to its crucial Javan core territories. The most dramatic consequence of this policy was the diplomatic breakthrough in the long-running dispute over East Timor. Although the final path to independence was a bloody one, East Timor gained internationally recognized independence in 2002.

The Indonesian government continues to claim East Timor was a special case, on the basis that the territory was never part of the Dutch East Indies. Nevertheless, the parallel with other outlying territories, particularly West Papua, is all too clear, not least to insurgent movements.

The Abdurrahman Wahid government of 1999-2001 increasingly came to be seen within Indonesia as weak, faction-ridden, and out of its depth both economically and militarily. Clashes, many economically motivated rather than having ethnic content, became a regular feature of Indonesian life. The government's relatively conciliatory attitude towards ethnic conflicts such as East Timor was viewed as treasonous both by the army and by hard-line elements in the government and opposition. Furthermore, its policy of weakening the army (by, for example, splitting army and police control) not only created factionalism within the security forces, but compounded already serious deficiencies in training, *materiel* and discipline. The brutality of the Indonesian state also resulted in international arms embargoes, albeit imposed half-heartedly, by Indonesia's Western suppliers. As in other regions, the benefits of propping up an authoritarian anti-Communist regime appeared, in the post-Cold War environment, to be increasingly marginal. The overall consequences were that the army became less technically able to defend the Indonesian state while simultaneously increasing its antipathy towards the Wahid regime. Abdurrahman Wahid's government fell in July 2001, to be replaced by the harder-line regime of his Vice President (and rival) Megawati Sukarnoputri. The Megawati regime sought to reverse much of the limited liberalism towards ethnic and national minorities shown by Wahid – a series of military-led clampdowns in Aceh was one consequence – but the nationalist cat appears to be very much out of the bag in many parts of Indonesia.

The commercial, political and strategic significance of Indonesia to the broader world means that it is unlikely to be allowed to join the ranks of the world's failed states, even if further military and economic reverses occur. However, the likelihood of international pressure on Jakarta to withdraw from outlying outposts of the Indonesian empire remains a possibility, if only because this may be the only policy perceived by international sponsors as offering hope for the stability of the Indonesian core regions. Indonesia's potential disintegration poses particular problems for Australia, which increasingly sees itself as a potential regional power with an enhanced security role throughout South-East Asia. Australia was, of course, instrumental both in propping up Indonesian rule in East Timor and, when that policy became untenable, in facilitating Timorese moves towards independence. A similar diplomatic and peacekeeping role for Australia in other regions of Indonesia is possible, if only to prevent potentially destabilizing refugee migration to Australia itself.

# Aceh

**Principal protagonists**

Government of Indonesia.

Sultanate of Aceh; *Gerakan Aceh Merdeka* (GAM); *Sentral Informasi Referendum Aceh* (SIRA).

**Nature of conflict**

Long-standing nationalist issue. Ongoing violence between separatists and Indonesian forces. Previous history of warfare between Acehnese and Dutch.

- Indiscriminate retaliations against civilians by Indonesian military regularly reported.
- 15,000 since 1950. Up to 100,000 in conflicts with Dutch.
- Potentially very significant unexploited reserves of natural gas.

**Population/ethnic composition**

4m. Majority Acehnese (a Malay people). Majority Shia Muslim.

**Territorial extent**

Sultanate of Aceh: 57,366 km².

**Timeline**

c850: Muslim Kingdom of Peureulak established.
26 Mar 1873: Dutch attack Aceh. Fighting continues until 1910.
27 Dec 1949: Indonesia achieves independence from Netherlands.
1959: Aceh declared a 'special territory' within Indonesia.
4 Dec 1976: Renewed independence declared by Aceh.
May 1989: Aceh declared an 'Area of Military Operations'.
Feb 1999: SIRA formed.
2003: Sharia law introduced.
26 Dec 2004: South East Asian *tsunami* hits Aceh.
15 Aug 2005: Peace agreement between Indonesia and Aceh.

**Current status**

2005 peace agreement generally holding. Long-term re-construction in aftermath of 2004 *tsunami* is main priority.

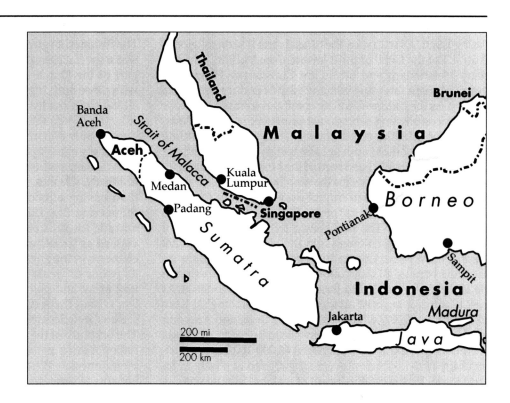

**On 26 December 2004 the South East Asian *tsunami* slammed at full force into the historic seaport of Banda Aceh, capital of the autonomous Sultanate of Aceh within Indonesia, killing over 250,000 people and rendering a further 500,000 homeless, out of a local population of 4 million.**

One silver lining to this particular cloud was that it focused the minds both of local separatists and the Indonesian government. On 15 August 2005 a peace treaty, mediated by former Finnish president and UN negotiator Martti Ahtisaari, brought an end to over a century of conflict between the fiercely independent Acehnese and their Dutch and Indonesian rulers.

Aceh is historically important as it was the route through which Islam entered the South East Asian region. By 850 a successful Islamic kingdom was established and independence was maintained until the end of the 19th century, by which time Aceh was a locally influential power. By the 1870s Aceh was to all practical purposes a modern state, with an efficient army, diplomatic relations with Western powers (including the United States) and strategic control of the Malacca Strait between Sumatra and Malaya. In the later 19th century, Aceh was the producer of more than half the world's supply of black pepper.

Alarmed by Aceh's increasing diplomatic ties, strategic location, and dominance of regional trade, the Dutch attacked Aceh in March 1873. Over three decades of bloody fighting followed before the region was more-or-less pacified in 1904, although Dutch control over areas of the hinterland remained marginal.

In common with the rest of the Dutch East Indies, Sumatra was occupied by the Japanese during the Second World War, but after the war the Dutch made no attempt to re-occupy Aceh. Aceh was thus *de facto* independent when Indonesia achieved independence from the Netherlands in 1949. Initially amalgamated with the Indonesian province of North Sumatra, the Indonesians were soon forced to concede 'special territory' (*'daerah istimewa'*) status to Aceh, which they did in 1959. Although this granted legal and other forms of autonomy to the deeply conservative Muslim state, resentment continued and violence between Indonesian forces and *Gerakan Aceh Merdeka* (GAM) nationalists continued periodically up until the time of the *tsunami*. On 4 December 1976, Aceh made a renewed proclamation of independence, hoisting for the occasion the thousand-year old Aceh flag. (The suspicion may be entertained that one reason for Jakarta's resentment of Aceh is the depth of its cultural history compared to Indonesia proper.)

In 1989 GAM mounted a series of attacks on military and police targets. The Indonesian military responded by declaring Aceh an 'Area of Military Operations' (*daerah operasi militer, DOM*) and over the next decade staged a series of massive counter-insurgency sweeps. These failed to achieve their aim: not only were the Aceh nationalists not crushed, but heavy-handed military operations (frequently entire regions were targeted indiscriminately for attack) further alienated the civilian population. So ill-conceived was the military programme that General Wiranto, commander of Indonesia's military, lifted the DOM in August 1998 and actually apologised to the people of Aceh for their mistreatment. GAM retaliated with further attacks on Army targets.

During 1999 the situation, from Jakarta's viewpoint, markedly deteriorated. At the end of January, Indonesian President Rudy Habibie conceded that East Timor would be allowed a referendum on independence from Indonesia. As in other outlying regions of Indonesia, this inevitably stimulated nationalist demands and confidence. Within weeks a new organization, the *Sentral Informasi Referendum Aceh* (SIRA) had come into being to demand a poll on independence or greater autonomy for Aceh. In November 1999 SIRA staged a demonstration in Banda Aceh that attracted 500,000 people – one in eight of the population. Habibie visited Banda Aceh and repeated Wiranto's apology, although without proposing any reparations. (An 'independent' committee of investigation, headed by an Acehnese woman who turned out to have business links to the military, produced a 500-page report that was widely dismissed as a whitewash.) GAM, meanwhile, consolidated its grip on the countryside by taking over (under duress or otherwise) the local District administrations, successfully running civil bodies and levying 'war taxes' from local businesses.

In March 2001 the Indonesia military announced yet another country-insurgency campaign, and the government officially declared GAM an illegal separatist group, giving the security forces greater leeway to intervene in the region. Violence continued between separatists, the military and the civil population right up to the date of the *tsunami* disaster on 26 December 2004; only after the scale of the humanitarian disaster became apparent did serious negotiations become possible. On 15 August 2005 an agreement was negotiated under international auspices by which both sides would disarm and the region be granted 'special autonomy' including the right to form local political parties. Gubernatorial elections in December 2006 saw the election of former separatist leader Irwandi Yusuf, drawing on a power base among former GAM members.

# Kalimantan (Borneo)

**Principal protagonists**

Flags shown are those of Central Kalimantan (Kalimantan Tengah) and West Kalimantan (Kalimantan Barat) provinces.

Madurese immigrant community.

Indigenous Dayak community.

**Nature of conflict**

Inter-communal violence resulting from immigration and land pressures issues.

☠ At least 1,500.
🚶 Up to 50,000 Madurese refugees.

**Population/ethnic composition**

W. Kalimantan: 3.7m; C. Kalimantan: 1.8m (2002). Dayaks, Malays and Madurese. Relative proportions uncertain following ethnic conflict.

**Territorial extent**

Indonesian provinces of West and Central Kalimantan (Indonesian part of Borneo). Area (combined): 301,000 km$^2$.

**Timeline**

1960s onwards: Inward migration by Madurese under Indonesia's transmigration policy.
1996-7: Dayak wage 'ritual war' against Madurese in W. Kalimantan.
1999: Further violence in W. Kalimantan.
Dec 2000: Fighting breaks out in C. Kalimantan culminating in 'Sampit Massacre' of Madurese, 18 Feb-4 Mar 2001.
By 2003: Majority of Madurese fled or expelled.

**Current status**

Currently largely peaceful, essentially due to completion of ethnic cleansing of Madurese.

*See page 6.06 for map of Kalimantan.*

**Indonesia has always experienced grave regional imbalances in population. In a policy inherited from the Dutch, the Indonesian government has encouraged, through a formally sponsored 'transmigration programme' (See 6.11) the movement of peoples from the overcrowded Javanese and western provinces to other, mostly eastern, areas of the Indonesian archipelago. The island of Madura lies to the north of Java and its poor fertility and general poverty have traditionally led to emigration, such that a majority of Madurese now live elsewhere. The Madurese have therefore been one of the main beneficiaries of the transmigration programme, but their presence has often been greatly resented by host communities in other parts of Indonesia.**

Officially blind to ethnicity, the degree to which Jakarta has deliberately used the transmigration policy to implant sympathetic client groups into troublesome outlying areas, or whether they genuinely failed to appreciate communal pressures resulting from mass immigration, is not clear. The result has been, however, that 'transmigrants' have frequently clashed with local groups, with serious disturbances between Madurese and Javan communities and on-going tensions between Javanese and Melanesians in the Molaccas. In the case of the Madurese influx into Kalimantan (the Indonesian portion of Borneo), the results were particularly disastrous. From 1999 to 2001 a series of relatively minor ethnic clashes escalated into full-scale massacres of Madurese by the indigenous Dayak population of Kalimantan.

It should be noted at the outset that 'Dayak' is not a term which relates to a single ethnic group, nor, indeed, is the name by which the Borneo people refer to themselves. It is, rather, a Indonesian term (a contraction of *"orang Dayak"*) which broadly means 'native' that, like its English equivalent, has acquired largely pejorative undertones.

It has to be granted that the Dayak, as the original Borneo headhunters, have on occasion matched up to the image of the 'savage' popularized in colonial fiction. Vendetta, decapitation of enemies, and consumption of body parts all play a part in traditional Dayak culture. Several of these practices re-surfaced during the conflict with the Madurese, to good effect in encouraging the latter to flee their homes and businesses.

Contemporary violence flared in West Kalimantan in 1996-7 when Dayak tribesmen waged a 'ritual war' against Madurese communities following a fight between youths in which two Dayaks were stabbed. Approximately 500 Madurese were killed and over 20,000 fled. In addition to decapitating the bodies of many of their victims, the Dayaks are also reported to have indulged in the cannibalistic eating of their livers. Throughout 1999-2000 further incidents took place throughout West Kalimantan, with the refugee total rising above 50,000. In February-March 2001, the violence spread to Central Kalimantan, including the city of Sampit, where more than 400 Madurese were murdered, many of the bodies again being decapitated and their heads being paraded by the victorious Dayak around the city.

Ruthlessly efficient at suppressing separatist or political dissent, the Indonesian police and security forces have frequently proven remarkably inept at dealing with communal violence. Whether this is because of indifference to 'domestic' disputes when no broader national security or political interest is at stake, or simple ineptitude, is not entirely clear, although in the case of Kalimantan the latter would appear the more likely. Although full-scale evacuation measures were put in place by March 2001, often their implementation was half-hearted or ineffectual. In one incident, the local police offered refugees who had been hiding in the forests safe passage out of the region. *En route* to the harbour, the party was attacked and the police fled, leading to the deaths of over 100 Madurese.

Violence continued sporadically until 2003. In mid-2003 the Indonesian government suspended the policy of transmigration as it applied to Kalimantan – somewhat unnecessarily since the chance of anyone voluntarily migrating to Kalimantan was by then minimal.

No effective sanction has been taken against the perpetrators of the violence, who are regarded in many cases as heroes within their local Dayak communities. Kalimantan is relatively peaceful today by virtue of the large-scale expulsion of the Madurese settler community. For the Dayaks of Kalimantan, ethnic cleansing – extreme violence coupled with gruesome terror – has proven to be a highly effective policy.

## Indonesia's transmigration policy

Faced with major population imbalances and land pressures – Java, with 130 million inhabitants, is the world's most populous island – Indonesia's rulers have long since used governmental initiatives to redistribute people to more sparsely inhabited parts of the Indonesian archipelago.

At independence, the Indonesian government inherited a transmigration programme initiated by the Dutch colonial government in 1905. Under the Suharto government, the programme – 'transmigrasi' in Indonesian – was continued and expanded, with the intention of addressing food shortages and providing opportunities to landless peoples. At its peak between 1979 and 1985 some 2.5 million people, mostly from Java, Madura and Bali, moved to less heavily populated areas such as Papua, Kalimantan, Sumatra and Sulawesi. In some cases the demographic results were considerable; some 60% of the population of southern Sumatra being migrants, for example.

The consequence was that large communities, predominantly Malay/Javanese, were brought into close and often competitive contact with host populations of different religious and racial characteristics. Tensions and violent conflict between transmigrants and host communities accelerated in the 1990s, particularly in the aftermath of the East Asian economic crisis. In August 2000 the Indonesian government significantly curtailed the programme, although it claimed economic motives for so doing, rather than, for example, the ethnic cleansing of the Madurese in Kalimantan.

The degree to which the transmigration policy had a conscious political agenda – by implanting loyalist client communities in outlying regions of Indonesia – is hotly contested. The negative consequences have, however, been undeniable not only in terms of its cost in ethnic conflict but through overgrazing and unsupervised deforestation in the recipient regions. In some cases, too, the migrants themselves have been implanted in newly created 'transmigration villages' in areas of poor soil and sustainability. Officially, the transmigration programme continues to operate, albeit at a reduced level.

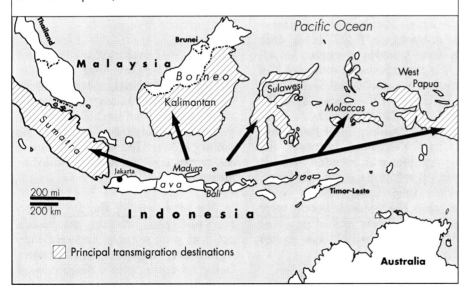

# Timor Leste (East Timor)

**Principal protagonists**

Government of Indonesia. (Until 2002.)

People of East Timor; *Frente Revolutionária de Timor-Leste Independente* (FRETILIN).

**Nature of conflict**

Nationalist/self-determination war, 1975-99

☦ Significant violence by pro-Indonesian militias, 1999-2002.
☠ 200,000-300,000.

**Population/ethnic composition**

947,000. East Timorese 80%. Religious mix: Roman Catholic 87%, Protestant 5%, Muslim 3%.

**Territorial extent**

Timor Leste (including the enclave of Oecussi-Ambeno): 14,609 km².

**Timeline**

1596: Portuguese occupy island of Timor.
1640: Dutch settlement in west of island.
28 Nov 1974: East Timorese independence declared in aftermath of Portuguese withdrawal.
7 Dec 1974: East Timor occupied by Indonesia.
1975-99: Ongoing guerrilla resistance to Indonesia occupation.
1999: Indonesia agrees to international mediation to resolve issue.
30 Aug 1999: UN-sponsored referendum votes for independence.
Aug 1999-2002: Widespread violence by Indonesian militia groups.
20 May 2002: Timorese independence officially recognized by Portugal.
27 Sep 2002: Timor Leste admitted to United Nations.

**Current status**

Resolved. Timor Leste achieved recognized independence in 2002. Subsequent political violence.

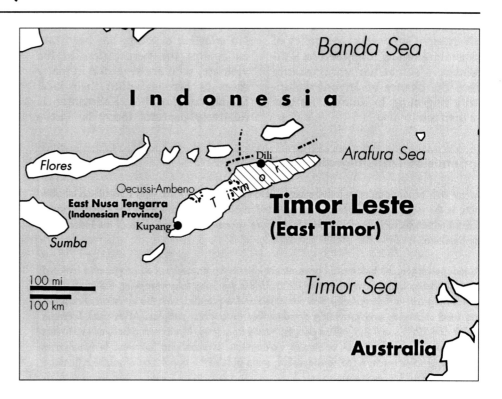

**By the mid-1970s, Europe's last colonial empire was in terminal decline. Portugal, whose discoveries and conquests since the 15th century had done much to usher in the modern world, was assailed by violent nationalist unrest in all her overseas territories.**

Following the 'Carnation Revolution' of 25 April 1974 – a coup brought about largely through military unrest at the continuing cost of Portugal's various colonial wars – the new Lisbon government moved swiftly to negotiate the transfer of power to the various nationalist movements within the Portuguese empire. In the case of Portuguese East Timor, the struggle against the Portuguese had been led by the *Frente Revolutionária de Timor-Leste Independente* (FRETILIN), and, with more pressing concerns in Africa, the Portuguese government had more-or-less surrendered East Timor to FRETILIN within months of the Lisbon coup. On 28 November 1974, East Timor declared itself independent. On 7 December, however, the fledgling state was invaded and occupied by Indonesia. Just at the point, therefore, when independence lay in their grasp, the Timorese people were plunged into a new and even worse nightmare – one which was to last nearly thirty years.

As in the related issue of West Papua *(See 6.16)* the attitude of the Western powers, and in particular the USA – a nation that prides itself on its anti-colonial history – was hardly creditable. From the outset of the Indonesian occupation, the US and Australia made it clear to Jakarta that they would not raise the issue in international forums. In theory, East Timor remained, as far as the United Nations was concerned "a non-self governing territory under Portuguese administration." In reality, it became Indonesia's 27th province.

However, the David and Goliath contest between the Timorese, their oppressors and Western financial interests, was far from over. Armed resistance, and resultant repression from the Indonesian authorities, continued. By the turn of the century, between 200,000-300,000 Timorese, mostly civilians, had been killed in the conflict.

In the aftermath of the 1997 Asian economic crisis, however, Indonesia's political and military capacity was significantly impaired. Furthermore, facing mounting public disquiet over the collaboration of their governments with the Indonesian regime (this was particularly true of Australian public opinion), Western governments were obliged to withdraw much of its previous support for Jakarta on the issue.

Following negotiations between the Portuguese, the Indonesians and the US, an internationally supervised referendum was held on 30 August 1999 that voted (by just under 80%) for full independence from Indonesia.

An Australian-led UN military force, INTERFET (International Force East Timor), arrived on the island in September 1999 and immediately became embroiled in fighting with Indonesian sponsored militias, who were acting as much in fulfilment of a scorched earth policy as in any real hope of preventing Timorese independence. (One consequence of Canberra's involvement was that Osama Bin Laden declared a *fatwa* against Australia.) INTERFET was in turn superseded by the UN Transitional Administration in East Timor in February 2000.

Despite massive last-minute violence from the Indonesian militias and their sympathisers, East Timor progressed to full independence, becoming the United Nations' 191st member state on 27 September 2002 – the first 'new' nation of the 21st century.

East Timor has experienced considerable political unrest since independence, although this does not appear to have a direct ethnic component. In 2006, soldiers mutinied in protest against non-payment of wages and poor conditions. Elections in June 2007 passed off peacefully, but President Ramos-Horta narrowly survived an assassination attempt in February 2008 and a state of emergency continues. Part of the underlying problem is the slow progress made towards the re-integration into society of refugees from the fighting that preceded independence.

**The Indonesian military – the *dwifungsi* doctrine**

Historically, the Indonesian military (*Tentara Nasional Indonesia*, TNI) has operated under a self-imposed doctrine called *dwifungsi* or "dual function" which holds that the task of the military is twofold: to defend absolutely the territorial integrity of the Indonesian state, and to ensure that the government follows an acceptable path of socio-economic development. The TNI therefore has a self-defined mandate going far beyond that normally expected of the military in constitutional states. In 1965, the TNI (by its lights) answered the popular call for intervention by installing General Suharto to replace the weakened founder-president of Indonesia, Sukarno. Until the end of Suharto's 'New Order' the presidency and the military enjoyed a mutually supportive relationship. Not only was the President himself a military man, but military personnel, both active and retired, enjoyed seniority in the civil service and occupied a large number of seats in Parliament.

The contradiction at the heart of the *dwifungsi* policy is that while the Indonesian state is one born out of the militant rejection of colonialism, it is simultaneously committed to the preservation of the self-same borders that were arbitrarily established by the colonial power.

To the military, the loss of East Timor can perhaps be explained away on the grounds that the territory, having being Portuguese, was never part of the Dutch East Indies that Indonesia claims as its heartland. But the reality is that the loss of East Timor was, for the TNI, an ideological disaster and a military humiliation. Furthermore, the success of the struggle in East Timor inevitably gave encouragement to nationalists in other provinces, most significantly West Papua, which has a similarly disputed history.

The current Indonesia government is officially committed to the removal of the army from political life. Whether the TNI can become a constructive force in supporting the emergence of a genuinely constitutional state in Indonesia, or whether it will it revert to a dogmatic pursuit of the *dwifungsi* remains a key question for the future policy. It is certainly true that the Indonesian military is, in the future, unlikely to enjoy the uncritical domestic and international endorsement of its actions to which its previous leaders had become accustomed.

# The Moluccas (Maluku)

**Principal protagonists**

Christian/Melanesian community.

Muslim community.

Government of Indonesia.

Moluccan separatists.

**Nature of conflict**

Inter-communal disputes between Muslim and Christian population, 1999-2002. Sporadic violence by Moluccan separatists including (1970s) international acts of terrorism.

☪ Muslim/Christian. (Relative percentages disputed.)
☠ Over 5,000.
👥 500,000 internally displaced 1999-2002.

**Population/ethnic composition**

2.2m. Composition disputed.

**Territorial extent**

Indonesian provinces of Maluku and North Maluku.

**Timeline**

27 Dec 1949: Indonesia achieves independence from Netherlands.
25 Apr 1950: Independent South Moluccan Republic proclaimed.
Nov 1950: South Moluccan Republic suppressed by Indonesia.
1960s: Large scale immigration by Javanese/Muslims commences.
1970s: International terrorist attacks by Moluccan separatists.
Jan 1999-2002: Widespread inter-communal violence between Muslims and Christians.
1999: Separate North Moluccan province established.
2004: Further inter-communal violence.

**Current status**

Tense, but largely peaceful. However, further violence remains possible.

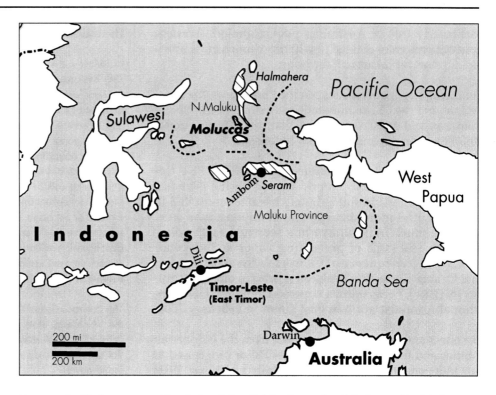

**Romantically known as 'the Spice Islands' during colonial times, the Moluccan Islands – more properly known as the Malukus or simply Maluku – have been a cockpit for violence since the 1950s. The nature of the unrest has, however, largely changed complexion – from separatist violence in the 1950s-1970s to inter-religious conflict today. As a salutary reminder of the potential fragility of the inter-communal relations that exist in many societies worldwide, the violence which flared in 1999 appears to have started as a result of a trivial argument between a Muslim bus driver and a Christian passenger.**

Traditionally inhabited by largely Christian/Melanesian groups, attempts were made by elements of the Dutch colonial army, settlers, and local nationalists to establish a breakaway South Moluccan state during the dying days of Dutch rule. The *Republik Maluku Selatan* (RMS) was proclaimed in April 1950. Although independence was fairly short-lived, being suppressed by Indonesia in November, localized fighting continued for some years afterwards and, although it is improbable that a majority of South Moluccans today support independence, the RMS remains symbolic for all parties to the recent conflict. A South Moluccan government in exile continues to exist, and throughout the 1970s the Moluccan issue made international headlines through terrorist activities, mostly aimed against Dutch targets, by Moluccan militants. Moluccan nationalism thus continues to be a political force, but more amongst the Moluccan diaspora than within the territory itself.

The current cycle of violence, however, is more firmly routed in religious divisions than in nationalist sentiment. As with other eastern regions of Indonesia, the Moluccas have been the destination for thousands of immigrants, mostly Javanese and Muslim, who have arrived under Indonesia's transmigration policy *(See 6.11)*. Although there does not appear to have been any conscious intent on the part of Jakarta to use this policy to destabilize the Moluccas, the result has been an exacerbation of previously underlying racial and religious tensions. By the 1990s Christians/Melanesians found themselves increasingly in the minority in areas which previously had a majority Christian population. It is significant that, initially at least, Christian violence in 1999 was directed mainly against immigrant Muslim communities rather than indigenous Muslim Moluccans. As the violence has escalated, however, hard-line Muslim factions in other parts of Indonesia have become engaged.

Inter-religious violence erupted in Ambon, capital of Maluku Province, on 19 January 1999 and quickly spread to other islands in the group. Fighting also spread to the North Maluku Province (which was split off from Maluku during 1999). Although initially some at least of the fighting in North Molucca appears to have had local, non-sectarian motives, it quickly spread to other sections of the community.

The following three years were characterized by periodic violence between the Christian and Muslim communities, with upwards of half a million people being displaced in the process, largely through targeted ethnic cleansing. In June 2000, President Wahid declared a state of civil emergency and deployed some 14,000 Indonesian troops, whose presence, if anything, added to local tensions.

In January 2000, Muslims staged a 100,000 strong demonstration in Jakarta to claim non-Muslim Moluccan groups had independence as their aim, an assertion fuelled by the rallying of some Moluccan groups (both in Indonesia and internationally) to the RMS flag. One sinister result was the deployment in Maluku of a *'jihadist'* militia, *Laskar Jihad*, committed to the wholesale ethnic cleansing of Christians from the Moluccas. *Laskar Jihad* appears to have been responsible for the bulk of the subsequent disturbances, including clashes with the police and army.

Although in its early days the death toll was roughly fifty-fifty, from 2001 onwards Christians have been the main victims of the violence, with widespread reports of ethnic cleansing and forced conversions to Islam. The Indonesian security forces have responded heavy-handedly, but often ineffectually, against both communities. Reports that elements of the military have been selling arms to both sides probably indicate a lack of discipline in the Indonesian forces rather than any deeper sectarian motivation. Indeed, throughout the conflict, the inability or unwillingness of the security forces to become effectively involved has become a hallmark of the crisis, as has factionalism within the security forces – particularly between the local police and elements of the army brought in from other parts of Indonesia.

Following a series of local peace accords from February-May 2002, there were some signs of a cooling of tensions between the Christian and Muslim communities. However, on the 25 April 2004 anniversary of South Moluccan independence, violence erupted once again, leaving dozens killed and hundreds of properties destroyed in Ambon. The situation remains potentially unstable, with the current peace being largely as the result of the physical separation of the two communities which has been a consequence of the fighting.

# West Papua

**Principal protagonists**

Government of Indonesia; non-Papuan immigrant groups and militias.

West Papuan (Melanesian) nationalists.

**Nature of conflict**

Self-determination and human rights issues. Population pressure a factor.

- Widespread violence by Indonesian military.
- Muslim/Christian conflict an issue.
- Up to 100,000.
- Refugees in Papua New Guinea (8,000+) and Australia.
- Western (esp. US and Australian) mining interests. Also logging and fishing.

**Population/ethnic composition**

2.5m. Majority Melanesian. Religious mix: Muslim, 21%; Christian, 78%. Animism also widely practised, but not recorded in census.

**Territorial extent**

Indonesian provinces of Papua and West Irian Jaya.

**Timeline**

18 Dec 1961: Indonesia invades Dutch New Guinea.
1 May 1963: UN transfers control to Indonesia.
May 1969: Disputed 'Act of Free Choice' confirms Indonesian sovereignty.
1 Jul 1971: West Papua unilaterally declares independence.
1990s: Indonesia initiates mass immigration policy.
23 Oct 2001: Semi-autonomous Province of Papua created.
Feb 2003: Province of West Irian Jaya created. Legality disputed.

**Current status**

Widespread human rights abuses by Indonesian authorities and their allies likely to continue.

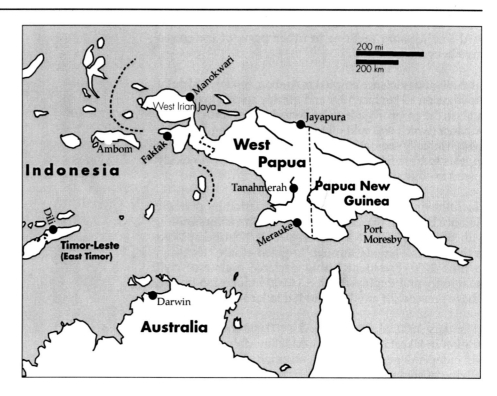

Following elections in 1959 and the agreement, under a 'Revolutionary Provisional Government of West Papua' of a constitution, coat of arms, and national flag, the Dutch colony of New Guinea appeared to be moving smoothly towards independence. On 18 December 1961, however, Indonesian troops invaded the colony, clashing with Dutch forces. The United States secretly pressurized the Netherlands into accepting the principle of Indonesian sovereignty over the colony. A UN temporary administration was established in October 1962 that, in May 1963, transferred governance of the territory to Indonesia.

In 1969, in a blatantly rigged 'Act of Free Choice', 1,205 Papuan men selected by Indonesia to represent the views of the population obligingly voted unanimously for the incorporation of the erstwhile colony into Indonesia. Western governments, with an eye on Indonesia's anti-Communism and, more pertinently, commercial opportunities in the territory (West Papua has large scale reserves of nickel, gold and copper) endorsed the Indonesian position.

The new Indonesian province was called (from 1973) 'Irian Jaya', which means 'Victorious Irian' – the name being taken from an Indonesian nationalist slogan, *'Ikut Republik Indonesia, Anti Nederlands'* ('Join the Republic of Indonesia against the Netherlands'). Agitation for independence from the less than victorious local population has continued ever since, in the face of brutal oppression by Indonesia. On 1 July 1971 the Revolutionary Provisional Government of West Papua declared West Papua independent and the struggle between nationalists and the Indonesian state began in earnest.

The people of West Papua are mostly Melanesian having more in common with their neighbours in Papua New Guinea and with Melanesian populations in East Timor, the Moluccas, and elsewhere in Australasia than they do with the largely Javanese and Sumatran populations of Indonesia proper. In February 2000, the Papua Presidium Council *(Majelus Rakyat Papua)* was established. Representing 245 tribal groups, the Presidium convened the first Papuan National Congress in June 2000, and called on the Indonesian government to recognize West Papuan independence, triggering a further round of repression from the authorities.

In October the following year, however, in a weakening of Jakarta's grip on its unruly outlying provinces, the

Indonesian parliament ratified legislation allowing for the autonomy of four 'special territories' – one of them a new 'Province of Papua'. In a unique dispensation, the Papua Presidium Council was formally recognized as a representative arm of the Papuan government. In practice, widespread repression continued and, in November, Theys Eluay, Chairman of the main Papuan nationalist organization, the *Operasi Papua Merdeka*, was arrested, tortured, and murdered by Indonesian paramilitaries.

Meanwhile, after over twenty years' of often bloody fighting, Indonesia was obliged to withdraw the former Portuguese colony of East Timor, which in 2002 achieved independence as Timor Leste *(See 6.12)*. The East Timor example – independence following an internationally supervised referendum – was naturally seized upon by nationalists in the far larger territory of West Papua as suggesting the template for their own progress towards sovereignty. That this has not, so far, happened confirms that there has been a retrenchment in the Indonesian state's policy toward regional autonomy. The 1999-2001 government of Abdurrahman Wahid, albeit acting under economic, political and military strains, took a more conciliatory position towards the separatist movements. But the more hard-line government of Wahid's successor, Megawati Sukarnoputri (who is quoted as having stated that "without Irian Jaya, Indonesia is not complete") sought to roll back many of the limited gains achieved and 2002, in fact, saw a marked upturn in state violence in West Papua. This process has been manifest in attempts to wrestle back control of chunks of West Papua from the Province of Papua. In February 2003, a new province of 'West Irian Jaya' was created out of the region known (from its shape) as the 'Bird's Head Peninsula' *(Jazirah Doberai)*. The illegality of this decision was acknowledged even by the Indonesian courts – hardly as a rule the impartial arbiters of such matters – who nevertheless ruled that as West Irian Jaya was already in existence, it should be allowed to remain. An attempt to dismember the Province of Papua completely by creating a 'Central Irian Jaya' province did not get off the ground, however, being struck down by the courts (against a backdrop of local rioting) in November 2004. The long-term status of 'West Irian Jaya' remains in dispute, with both sections of West Papua remaining under *de facto* common governance at present.

Although the long-term sustainability of the Indonesian occupation is questionable, in the immediate future there appears no likelihood of a peaceful resolution of this issue, particularly in the absence of significant international pressure. (The United States and Australian governments have consistently put commercial interests above the rights of self-determination for Indonesian minorities, although rising public revulsion at this policy may force its modification.) In an echo of similar tactics in East Timor prior to independence, the Indonesian military has been reported as arming and training pro-Jakarta militias in the province. These militias will draw elements of support from the many migrant workers who have moved to West Papua in search of work in the mining industry. These immigrants, drawn from largely Muslim non-Melanesian ethnic groups, tend to be hostile towards the separatists. (In October 2000, for example, 30 people were killed in clashes between migrants, police, and locals over the display of West Papua's 'Morning Star' flag.) Inter-ethnic and inter-communal conflict is thus likely to continue, and potentially escalate, particularly if further economic and political dislocations occur in the Indonesian state as a whole.

# Mindanao

**Principal protagonists**

Government of the Philippines.

Islamic separatists on Mindanao and outlying islands.

**Nature of conflict**

Long-standing nationalist issue. Sporadic violence between authorities and Islamist groups reported.

- Christian/Muslim clashes an issue.
- Over 100,000 killed in fighting from 1972 onwards.
- 250,000 IDP at peak of violence in 1970s.

**Population/ethnic composition**

2.8m. Moro, 5% of Philippino population overall.

**Territorial extent**

Principally the Autonomous Region in Muslim Mindanao: 12,695 km². (Mindanao island area: 94,630 km².)

**Timeline**

- 1380: Arab missionaries arrive in region. Sulu sultanate established in 1457.
- 1565: Spanish colonization of Philippines begins. Spanish rule not recognized by Sulu until late 19th century.
- 1898: Philippines comes under US rule following American-Spanish war.
- 4 Jul 1946: Philippines independent from USA.
- Early 1970s: Full-scale war in region.
- 1976-89: Negotiations over autonomy eventually lead to establishment of Autonomous Region in Muslim Mindanao on 1 August 1989.
- 1996: Peace agreement between MNLF and Philippines government.

**Current status**

Peace agreements between MNLF and government generally holding, with MNLF involvement in regional government. Continued dispute with MILF and Islamist influence over radical movements.

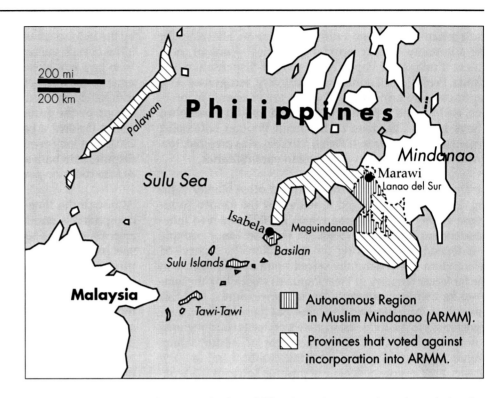

When the Spanish 'discovered' the Philippines in 1521 they found, in the southern island of Mindanao, a number of Islamic sultanates already in existence. The Spanish named the Islamic population 'Moro' (Moors) to distinguish them from the non-Islamic 'Indian' population, sections of which were subsequently Christianized.

Never fully suppressed by the Spanish, the Moro population has consistently resisted incorporation into the Philippines, whether under Spanish, American, Japanese or Philippino rule. Resistance to the Americans, following US victory over Spain in the 1898, was protracted and violent. (The expression 'running amok' apparently stems from the suicidal ferocity of Moro attacks.) In 1903 all Moro land was confiscated and tracts were made available on favourable terms for Christian immigrant settlement.

The Muslims were never, in fact, the majority throughout the whole island, the ancient Sulu and Maguindanao sultanates being centred on the west of Mindanao and its outlying islands. The progressive migration of Christians into the area, together with evangelization, has, however, inflamed religious tensions.

The Philippines became independent of the United States in the aftermath of the Second World War, but Moro resistance has continued, in varying degrees, to the present day. In March 1968, at least 28 Moro army recruits were murdered on Corregidor Island in an incident which became known as the Jabidah Massacre. This triggered widespread Muslim protests and unrest, not just at the murders themselves but over land alienation and other issues in Mindanao. In July 1971, Moro leaders published a manifesto demanding government action to halt attacks on Muslims. This appeal was dismissed by the Philippines government. Instead, in September 1972, the Marcos regime declared martial law over the area, re-igniting full-scale war and precipitating the formation of the Moro National Libertion Front, which called for the creation of an independent Moro state to be called Bangsamoro.

By 1974 the military situation was out of control and the MNLF had gained a degree of international recognition from the Muslim world, being admitted, with observer status, to the Organization of Islamic Conferences. A stalemate in the conflict set in during 1975, and in 1976 the first negotiations between the MNLF and the Philippines government took place. These made slow but steady progress, with the signing of the December 1976 Tripoli Agreement providing for regional autonomy, and in April 1977 a general ceasefire was agreed. The main issue of contention continued to be which provinces were to be incorporated into any putative Muslim state. In view of the fact that Muslims were only the majority in some of the disputed territories, the Philippines government insisted on referendums being held in each province prior to incorporation.

Negotiations, interrupted by periodic renewal of the fighting, continued throughout the 1980s, until, in August 1989, an Autonomous Region of Muslim Mindanao (ARMM) was created. In 1996 a comprehensive peace agreement between the government and the MNLF saw former MNLF leader Nur Nisuari being given the post of Chief Executive. After referendums in 2001 Basilan province and Marawi City opted to join the Region, bringing to five the number of provinces so incorporated.

The relatively conciliatory position of the MNLF has led to the formation of more militant groups, including factions potentially linked to Al Qaeda. In 1981 the Moro Islamic Liberation Front broke away after the MNLF refused to renew the armed struggle in preference to continuing negotiations with the government on the question of autonomy. In 2002 the US committed over 1000 troops to helping the Philippines government combat the activities of the radical *Abu Sayyaf* group. (Significantly, an ongoing Communist insurgency by the New People's Army has received virtually no such attention.) The situation in Mindanao remains unstable, with the potential for Islamist-inspired future unrest. Islamist groups such as *Abu Sayyaf* and *Jemaah Islamiyah* allegedly continue to be active both in Mindanao and more generally throughout the Philippines.

With the MNLF now essentially integrated into the political process, security concerns have focused on the activities of the MILF. In 2003 a tentative ceasefire was agreed between the MILF and the government, but a series of bombings in 2006 were ascribed to MILF militants. Renewed fighting in July 2007 between Government troops and insurgents left 50 dead. As on previous occasions, the issue is over which additional areas will be incorporated into the Autonomous Region. The MILF has called for an additional 1,000 villages to be added to the territory, without a referendum. The government is insisting on a poll. Many of the villages concerned, while having Muslim majorities, are not contiguous with the current borders of the ARMM and are surrounded by Christian territory.

**Ethnic violence in Luzon**

Sporadic outbreaks of ethnic violence have been reported from Luzon, the northernmost of the major Philippine islands, and the one which includes the capital, Manila.

Tribal disputes have on occasion resulted in deaths, although *kayaw* (hunts) against rival tribes are supposedly ritualistic rather than violent in nature. Some tribes, such as the Iocanos, are said to continue the tradition of headhunting. Ethnic tensions may be heightened by the inwards migration of non-tribal peoples.

In 2004 two Kalinga youths were murdered and beheaded in what superficially appeared to be a ritual act. However, local tribal leaders and human tights activists have voiced the suspicion that these and other killings may be the actions of the security forces, using 'ethnic' killings as a cover for their activities. In 2006, a local opposition leader was murdered under similarly unclear circumstances; the police announcing that their swift response had prevented an outbreak of more serious tribal violence.

# Pattani

**Principal protagonists**

Thai government

Muslim insurgent groups (See text).

**Nature of conflict**

Separatist Muslim insurgency and terrorist violence. Language use and economic under-development important factors.

- Human rights abuses by the Thai military reported.
- Muslim/Buddhist conflict a factor.
- Over 2,000.
- Some refugee movement to Malaysia.

**Population/ethnic composition**

596,000 in affected areas.
Malay Muslim 88%.

**Territorial extent**

Thai provinces of Pattani, Yala and Narathiwat. (Pattani area 1,377 km².)

**Timeline**

1902: Kingdom of Pattani annexed by Thailand.
1960s: Ongoing violence by separatists.
Jan 2004: Full-scale violence resumes.
Mar 2005: National Reconciliation Commission established.
20 Jul 2005: State of emergency declared.
19 Sep 2006: Royal Thai Army stages a military coup in Bangkok.

**Current status**

Unresolved. Terrorist and other violence continues.

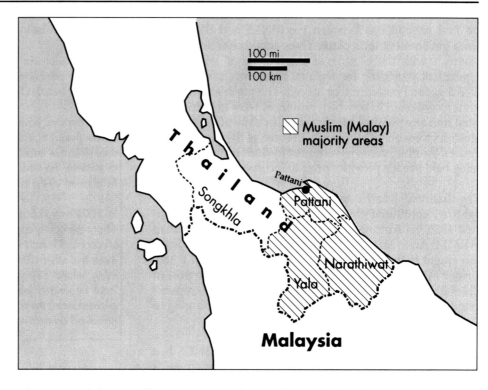

The roots of the Muslim insurgency in southern Thailand go back to the annexation of the Kingdom of Pattani in 1902. This was centred on the current Thai provinces of Pattani, Yala and Narathiwat. In contrast to the rest of Thailand, the majority of whose people are Buddhists, this region was populated by Muslims more closely related to the Malay peoples to the south, although they spoke their own language, Yawi. The imposition of Thai language and culture has long been a source of resentment in the region, as has its relative impoverishment compared to the rest of Thailand.

The 1960s were marked by serious disturbances by separatists. Long-standing economic grievances were re-kindled in the aftermath of the 1997 Asian economic crisis and low-level violence re-commenced in 2001. In 2004, in a major escalation, full-scale fighting resumed with attacks upon police and government buildings, as well as on civilian targets. Attacks included alleged suicide bombings, drive-by shootings, arson attacks, and the murder of officials and Buddhist monks. Over 500 people were killed in 2004, including at least 9 civilians beheaded by Islamic militants.

The Bangkok government of Prime Minister Thaksin Shinawatra initially dismissed the conflict as the actions of bandits. When this position became untenable, the government reversed tactics and responded with a massive military build up. At peak, 40,000 regular troops were deployed in the region. The military, poorly trained in counter-insurgency, proved incapable of permanently quelling the unrest, and may have actually exacerbated the situation.

Hostility has been fuelled by the often heavy-handed response of the security forces to the insurgency. In the most heavily publicised incident, security forces stormed the Krue Sae Mosque, the holiest site in Pattani, killing 32 insurgents who had been sheltering there, and inflaming local opinion. In October 2004, in the so-called Tak Bai incident, 1,300 Muslim protesters where bundled into army trucks for transportation to detention centres. Seventy-nine protesters suffocated.

In February 2005, Thaksin Shinawatra was re-elected Prime Minister in a poll generally regarded as free and fair. No secessionist candidates contested the election in the south of the country, which suggests an unwillingness to put the issue of separatism to a popular vote. In March the government formed the National Reconciliation Commission to look at ways of ending the conflict. Although this apparently promised a political resolution of the dispute, the Thai government declared a state of emergency over the region in July, and Thaksin assumed wide ranging personal powers to deal with the crisis.

The National Reconciliation Commission announced its conclusions in June 2006 with a wide-ranging package of measures, including the admissibility of Islamic *sharia* law in the Pattani region, making Yawi a working language, and establishing peacekeeping forces. Terrorist and other attacks continued, however. On 15 June 2006 over 40 official buildings were bombed in a co-ordinated response to the 60th anniversary of the accession of the King to the Thai throne, and on 1 September 22 commercial banks were simultaneously attacked.

On 19 September 2006 the Royal Thai Army staged a military coup against the Thaksin Shinawatra government. The new Prime Minister, Surayud Chulamont, visited the Pattani region several times in November and apologized for the 'mistakes' made by the previous government. Surayud stated that he was committed to resolving the conflict through talks.

Ironically, Surayud's more conciliatory stance triggered an upsurge in violence, with separatists attempting to undermine any potential reconciliation between the Buddhist and Muslim populations with terrorist attacks on civilian targets. Since the surge of violence in 2006, 90% of the casualties have been civilians. After a brief lull in the fighting immediately after the coup, violence increased in the third week of September, and November 2006 saw the resumption of the bombing campaign. A characteristic of the terror campaign is the anonymity of the perpetrators: no group has claimed responsibility for the attacks.

The largest of the rebel groups, the National Revolutionary Front-Coordinate (BRN-C) dates back to the 1960s. Other groups include the National Revolutionary Front-Congress (regarded by some observers as the most active faction), *Pemuda* (a youth group with links to the BRN-C), the Pattani Islamic Mujahidin Group, which was established by Afghan war veterans in 1995, and the Pattani United Liberation Organization (PULO).

Splits within the rebel movement and lack of overall leadership, combined with what appears to be a deliberate vagueness about aims and demands, has historically hamstrung attempts to negotiate with the insurgents. In May 2004 a 'co-ordinating' group called *Bersatu* emerged, with which the Bangkok government opened negotiations. However, it quickly became apparent that the leaders of *Bersatu* had no influence on the armed militants, and talks were discontinued. It is currently far from clear with whom the government can conduct effective negotiations. Violence throughout the region continued into 2007, with over 70 bombings being reported in February alone. Despite apparent willingness by the Thai government to enter into talks, the prospects for the resolution of the conflict seem low.

# Malaysia

**Principal protagonists**

Malaysian constitution, laws and initiatives that discriminate in favour of Malay/Muslim majority.

Chinese community.

Non-Muslim religious minorities, including Taoists and Christians, particularly Christian converts from Islam.

**Nature of conflict**

Inter-communal racial and religious tensions.

- Legal and social discrimination in favour of Islam an issue.
- c600 in 1963 anti-Chinese riots, sporadic outbreaks of fatal violence since.

**Population/ethnic composition**

24.3m. Malay 50.4%, Chinese 23.7%, Indigenous 11%, Indian 7.1%. Religious mix: Muslim (officially) 60.4%, Buddhist 19.2%, Christian 9.1%, Hindu 6.3%.

**Territorial extent**

Federation of Malaysia: 329,847 km².

**Timeline**

31 Aug 1957: Independence (as Malaya) from Britain.
16 Sep 1963: Accession of Sabah, Sarawak, and Singapore to create Malaysia.
9 Aug 1965: Singapore withdraws from Malaysian federation.
13 May 1969: Race riots aimed against Chinese.
1971: 'New Economic Policy' launched.
30 May 2007: Highest Malaysian court rules conversions from Islam illegal.

**Current status**

Open violence generally at low level, but institutional discrimination against non-Malay/Muslim minorities continues.

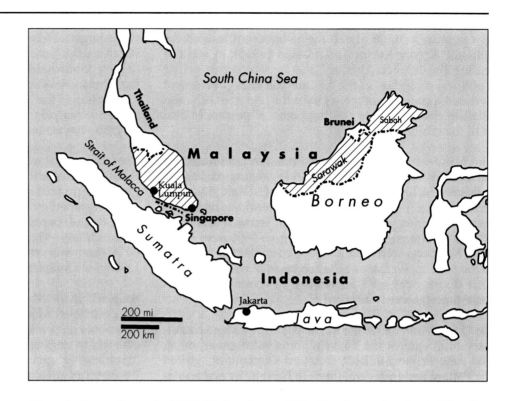

**Since independence in 1957, Malaysian politics has been dominated by the perceived need to bolster the economic and social standing of the Malay majority vis-à-vis that of the more commercially successful Chinese and other groups. Politics is highly stratified along racial grounds, with all major parties being racially exclusive.**

The major population groups in Malaysia are the majority Malay, who by constitutional definition are Muslim, the Chinese community and smaller percentages of Indians and non-Malay indigenous groups, collectively known as the *Orang Asli*, who represent the majority on Sarawak and Sabah.

In 1963, the core Malay region of the state was augmented with the addition of the former British colonial possessions of Sarawak, Sabah and Singapore, to form modern Malaysia. (Brunei declined to join.) Providing a more equitable racial mix was one motive for the incorporation of these territories, but perceived discrimination against Chinese ethnic interests was a factor prompting Singapore to break away from the Malaysian Federation in 1965.

After the racial riots of May 1969, which left hundreds of Chinese dead, the government initiated the controversial New Economic Policy (NEP). This was aimed at increasing the economic share held by the indigenous 'bumiputras' – primarily, in practice, the Malays. This has sought, with only partial success, to promote Malay businesses and to empower Malay entrepreneurs. Inevitably, there have been well-founded accusations of racial favouritism, nepotism and outright corruption arising from this policy.

Other significant sources of potential racial tension include the presence of foreign workers, mostly Indonesian, who number up to 20% of the workforce. Approximately half this number are illegal immigrants.

Sporadic riots and individual outbreaks of racially motivated violence continue to lead to fatalities. In March 1998 and in March 2001, fighting broke out between Malays and Indians, the latter allegedly caused by an Indian funeral party encroaching onto the scene of a Malay wedding. Six people were reported killed in the latter incident.

The main parties of the *Barisan Nasional* (National Front or BN) ruling coalition all have a racially-based membership, with the three largest component parties, the United Malays National Organization (UMNO), the Malaysian Chinese Association (MCA), and the Malaysian Indian Congress (MIC) all being sectarian in nature. All have youth and other affiliate groups that are similarly racially based. Although a measure of unity is provided by the fact that these parties do operate in coalition, the likelihood of genuine inter-racial political institutions evolving in this climate is remote.

Recent ethnic unrest has centred on the closure or destruction of non-Muslim religious buildings. In November 2006, police opened fire on Chinese demonstrators protesting against the destruction of a Taoist temple on Penang. There have also been reports of violence surrounding the demolition of Indian Hindu temples.

Although the Malaysian constitution theoretically enshrines freedom of religion (and defines Malaysia as a secular state) its insistence that all ethnic Malays are Muslims in reality creates a climate of discrimination and persecution against followers of other faiths. All Muslims (and thus all ethnic Malays) are subject to Islamic *sharia* law, whether they are (or wish to be) active practitioners of Islam or not. Similarly, all Malays are identified as Muslims on their ID cards. Converts to Christianity face routine harassment. In May 2007 the highest Malaysian court upheld the view that conversions from Islam were inadmissible. Christian converts face the possibility of social exclusion by their families and the need to live a 'double life.'

Despite fears that the Asian Economic Crisis of 1997 onwards would trigger racial violence, this has largely been avoided in Malaysia, being deflected, perhaps consciously, by the willingness of most Malaysian parties to blame the economic crisis on foreign speculators rather than national factors. Longer term, the risk of a breakdown of racial (and religious) stability in Malaysia remains a significant concern.

# Indochina

**Principal protagonists**

Governments of Laos and Vietnam.

Laos: Hmong people; United Laos Liberation Front. Vietnam: Degar people; *Front Unifie de Lutte des Races Opprimees* (FULRO).

**Nature of conflict**

Laos: Military campaign against Hmong ethnic minority. Vietnam: Religious and cultural persecution of Degar minority.

- Genocide allegations levelled against Laotian government.
- Repression of Christians in Vietnam.
- Unknown. *(See text.)*
- Unknown. Accusations of mistreatment and forced repatriation of refugees have been made against Cambodia and Thailand.

**Population/ethnic composition**

Laos: 6.34m. Lao Loum 53%, Lao Theung 23%, Lao Tai 13%, Hmong c5%. Vietnam: Kinh (Vietnamese) 85%, Han Chinese 3.5%, Degar 1.9%.

**Territorial extent**

Primarily highland provinces of Laos and Central Highlands of Vietnam.

**Timeline**

22 Oct 1953: Laotian independence proclaimed.
21 Jul 1954: Formal division of Vietnam into northern and southern states under Geneva Accords.
20 Dec 1954: Cambodian independence recognized by France.
1959: Onset/escalation of Vietnam war.
1961 onwards: Hmong and Degar fighters recruited by CIA.
30 Apr 1975: Occupation of South Vietnam by North Vietnamese forces.
2 Dec 1975: Victory of Pathet Lao (Communist) forces.
1981: 'Easter uprising' by Degar in Vietnam.

**Current status**

Low-level insurgency by Hmong continues. Repression of Degar cultural and religious righs continues.

The hill tribes of Cambodia, Laos, and Vietnam include the remnants of the early Mon-Khmer and Malayo-Polynesian peoples who were among the aboriginal inhabitants of the region, before being displaced by subsequent waves of immigration and conquest. The hill tribes are sometimes collectively grouped under the French colonial term 'Montagnard', meaning 'from the mountain', although this name is generally taken to refer especially to the Degar people of Vietnam.

Famed for their warlike tendencies, the Hmong people of Laos staged a ferocious campaign against the French in the 1920s, after which episode they were largely left to their own devices by the colonial authorities. After the French withdrawal from Indochina in the mid-1950s and the start of the Vietnam War between the Communist North Vietnam and the pro-American South (a conflict which eventually spilled over into Laos and Cambodia) elements of the Hmong and Degar populations were recruited by the CIA to act alongside US and South Vietnamese special forces in operations against Communist insurgents. In both Laos and Vietnam, local forces drawn from the hill populations provided evasion routes for downed US pilots, acted as scouts, and interdicted Viet Cong supply routes along the Ho Chi Minh trail into South Vietnam. Around 40,000 Degars fought the Viet Cong, forming a significant element of the anti-Communist military effort in the Vietnamese Highlands.

The South Vietnamese government of the late 1950s initiated a programme of settling Kinh (Vietnamese) in the Highlands areas, prohibited the use of Degar tribal languages, and denied religious freedoms. In 1964 a number of pre-existing. Degar movements merged to form the *Front Unifie de Lutte des Races Opprimees* (FULRO). This strove for autonomy for the hill peoples and its relationship with the South Vietnamese government was initially hostile, despite US efforts to concentrate Montagnard efforts on the anti-Communist struggle. In 1964, up to 3,000 US-trained Degar special forces fighters briefly staged a revolt against South Vietnamese control over several Highland districts before a peace deal was negotiated by the Americans. Under US brokerage, relations between the Vietnamese and FULRO improved in later years, but US withdrawal from South Vietnam in 1975 precipitated the occupation of the whole of Vietnam by the North Vietnamese and the unification of the country, under Communist rule, in 1976.

Thousands of Montagnards fled to Cambodia after the fall of South Vietnam, rightly fearing that the new government would launch reprisals against them because of their alliance with the Americans. In the post-war era, the Vietnamese government resumed the policies of its 1950s predecessor, displacing Degar and other villagers from Vietnam's Central Highlands, to use the fertile land for coffee plantations and Kinh settlement. Total Degar numbers have declined from 3 million in the 1950s to around 750,000 today. The surviving Degar continue to suffer from land alienation, enforcement of the Kinh language in education, and from the repression of their religious beliefs – many of the Degar are Protestant Christians. In Easter 1981 the Degar rose briefly in full-scale revolt, and widespread protests, as well as government repression of religious and civil rights, continue to be regularly reported.

Following the victory of the Communist Pathet Lao forces in 1975, the Hmong were similarly abandoned by their American patrons, although a sizeable community – estimated at up to 300,000 – were able to emigrate to the United States. During the Vietnam war upwards of 20,000 Hmong are believed to have been killed, although it is not clear how many of these were combatants. The new Pathet Lao government vowed to track down the survivors "to the last root".

The remnants of the Hmong guerrilla forces retreated into the remote forest regions of Laos where they have continued low-intensity operations against the Laotian authorities in the face of massive military intervention. Although they deny targeting civilians, passenger buses have allegedly been attacked by the Hmong, and in 2004 some publicity was gained by threats (which did not materialize) to attack the ASEAN summit that was being held in Laos.

The death toll among the Hmong, and by extension the size of the surviving Hmong population, is disputed. Attacks by the Laotians, under the guise of rooting out the remaining insurgents, have been characterized as 'genocide' by the few Western observers and journalists who have been able to reach Hmong encampments, but this is hotly denied by the Laotian authorities. With a few exceptions, the plight of the Hmong has been largely ignored by the wider world. To Americans, they are, like the Degar and other anti-Communist Vietnamese, an embarrassing reminder of the US betrayal of its regional allies at the end of the Vietnam war, while to liberal 'human rights' organizations they are permanently compromised by their wartime complicity with the CIA.

In Cambodia, minority race relations have followed a different trajectory. In the 1960s the government sought the assimilation of the hill tribes, who are collectively known as the Khmer Loeu, including the compulsory teaching of the Khmer language. The policy backfired; the Khmer Loeu rose in revolt and were subsequently – unlike the hill peoples of Laos and Vietnam – courted and recruited by the Communists. As a legacy, overt discrimination against racial minorities is limited, although religious observance, particularly of Protestant Christianity, is severely restricted. There is, however, an undercurrent of racism against the Vietnamese minority, arising from resentment at historical Vietnamese domination. During the rule of the psychotic Khmer Rouge regime in the mid-1970s, possession of the 'dark skin' associated with the Vietnamese was sufficient, along with wearing spectacles, knowledge of French, and other signs of political unsoundness, to condemn the owner to the killing fields.

# Fiji

**Principal protagonists**

Fijian population.

Indian population.

**Nature of conflict**
Racial conflict over control of government. Land use also an issue.

🏃 Emigration of thousands of Indians following 1987 coup.

**Population/ethnic composition**
906,000 (2006). Fijian 52%, Indian 41.5%. (Indians a 51% majority until 1987.)

**Territorial extent**
Fiji: 18,270 km². 332 islands, of which around 110 inhabited.

**Timeline**
10 Oct 1874: Fiji becomes a British colony
1880s-1920s: Immigration of Indian indentured plantation labourers.
10 Oct 1970: Independence from Britain.
13 Apr 1987: Timoci Uluivuda Bavadra becomes Prime Minister.
14 May 1987: Coup staged by General Sitiveni Rabuka.
7 Oct 1987: Rabuka stages a follow-up coup. Republic of Fiji declared.
1990: New constitution introduced that enshrines Fijian political dominance.
1997: 1990 constitution revoked in favour of one which allows for multi-racial government.
19 May 2000: Coup staged in opposition to 1997 constitution.
6 Dec 2006: Military stage coup against government corruption and leniency shown to 2000 coup plotters.

**Current status**
Direct racial elements of dispute have declined somewhat, but political situation remains unstable and the country coup-prone, with generally weak governance.

Inhabited since around 1000 BC, the major ethnically related event in Fiji's recent history was the immigration of an estimated 60,000 Indian indentured labourers who moved to the island between the 1880s and 1920s to work the sugar plantations.

This altered the racial demographics of the islands, such that Indians, with their higher birthrate, came to be the majority population on the islands, with the original Fijians, who are largely an admixture of Melanesian and Polynesian stock, becoming a minority. Furthermore, the Indians were economically more successful than the Fijians, and their increasing demands for arable land (most of which had traditionally been communally owned by Fijian kinship groups) were a further source of conflict with the ethnic Fijians.

From independence in 1970 until the 1980s Fiji nevertheless avoided overt racial hostilities. An informal social contract pertained whereby Indians would retain their pre-eminence in business and commerce, while Fijians, although the minority, would retain control of government and the army. The election, in May 1987 of Timoci Uluivuda Bavadra, who, although an ethnic Fijian, headed a largely Indian-supported coalition, proved to be the flashpoint for the breakdown of this ethnic accommodation. Invoking the inevitable slogan 'Fiji for the Fijians', ethnic Fijian leaders staged a coup in May 1987. Consequent racial discrimination, and the introduction of a new constitution, which institutionalized Fijian political dominance, forced the emigration of thousands of Indians. As a result the ethnic balance tipped in favour of the Fijians, who today constitute the majority of the population.

Under increasing diplomatic and economic pressure, the 1990 constitution enshrining ethnic Fijian dominance was abandoned in 1997. On 19 May 2000 a further coup, led by a businessman, George Speight, saw the President, Mahendra Chaudhry, and other prominent politicians taken hostage. Speight's 'government' demanded that the 1990 constitution be restored.

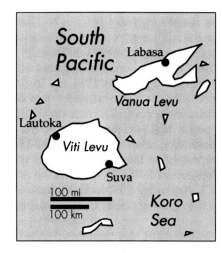

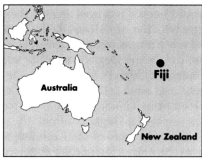

Speight and his co-conspirators were arrested in July 2000 and subsequently sentenced to death for treason, although the death sentences were later commuted.

Chaudhry was not returned to power after the failure of the 2000 coup. Instead, an 'interim' government consisting entirely of ethnic Fijians was appointed by the Great Council of Chiefs. Elections were held in 2001, but no party achieved a working majority and Fiji entered into a confused three-year period of political in-fighting. Yet another coup took place in December 2006. This was led by the military, whose grievances included perceived leniency towards the 2000 coup plotters as well as government corruption. Bizarrely, the military then placed a recruitment advertisement in the local press for 'people of good character' to fill Cabinet and other government posts. Fiji remains under an 'interim' administration. Ironically, the overtly racial elements to the conflict have receded, but the aftermath is a legacy of bitterness, weak government, and factionalism.

# Bougainville

**Principal protagonists**

Government of Papua New Guinea.

Bougainville Revolutionary Army and other separatist factions.

**Nature of conflict**

Resource allocation and self-determination. Full-scale regional war and economic blockade, 1988-1997.

☘ Up to 20,000 in fighting between 1988 and 1997.
♛ Copper mining and associated environmental damage a key issue. Also gold reserves.

**Population/ethnic composition**

175,000 (2000). Papuan 84%, Melanesian 15%.

**Territorial extent**

Bougainville: 8,500 km².

**Timeline**

1919: Bougainville comes, with Papua New Guinea, under Australian administration.
1 Sep 1975: Independence proclaimed as Republic of North Solomons.
16 Sep 1975. Papua New Guinea becomes independent of Australia.
9 Aug 1976. Bougainville incorporated into Papua New Guinea as autonomous Province of North Solomons.
1988-1997: Uprising by Bougainville Revolutionary Army descends into full scale war.
1989: Regional autonomy suspended.
10 Apr 1995: Transitional Government established, superseded (1 Jan 1999) by Reconciliation Government.
27 Mar 2002: Autonomy restored.
15 Jun 2005: Bougainville Autonomous Government elected.

**Current status**

Peace agreement generally holding.

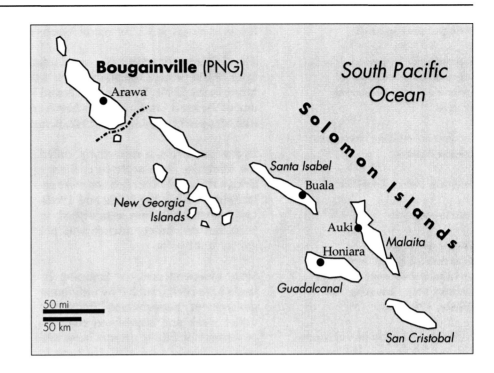

**Although geographically the northernmost (and largest) of the Solomon Islands, Bougainville is a province of Papua New Guinea.**

Local resentment at the remoteness of Papuan government and conflict over the exploitation of local resources has led to several attempts at secession. Prior even to formal Papuan independence from Australia on 16 September 1975, Bougainville declared itself separately independent (on 1 September) as the Republic of the North Solomons. This attempt at secession lasted until August 1976, when the island was accorded autonomous status within Papua New Guinea.

The Bougainville name for the island, Me'ekamui, means 'sacred island' and this reflects the close cultural significance that attaches to the land. By the late 1980s tensions over the ecological damage arising from the exploitation of the Panguna Copper Mine resulted in renewed clashes. At the time one of the largest copper mines in the world, Panguna supplied over 40% of Papua New Guinea's export earnings and was thus a vital resource to both parties. In 1989 the Bougainville Revolutionary Army rose in open revolt, demanding US$10 billion in compensation for environmental damage and loss of local revenues. The mining area was over-run and production halted. Papua responded by sending in troops and by terminating local autonomy. In May 1990 independence was once again proclaimed, as the Republic of Bougainville. A protracted jungle war then ensued which resulted in up to 20,000 deaths both through direct conflict and economic blockades imposed by Papua.

An uneasy peace was imposed in 1997, and a Bougainville Reconciliation Government inaugurated at the beginning of 1999. A 2001 treaty agreed renewed autonomy for the island, which was achieved in 2005. This settlement was rejected by elements of the Bougainville Revolutionary Army, including its leader, Francis Ona, who remained implacably hostile to the regional government until his death in 2005. Elections in 2005 resulted in the election of a separatist leader, Joseph Kabui, as president of Bougainville. The Panguna mine remains closed and environmental degradation is a key development issue.

# Solomon Islands

*See the map on page 6.27 for map of Solomon Islands.*

**Principal protagonists**

Government of the Solomon Islands. Australian-led Commonwealth intervention forces also actively engaged.

Guadalcanal residents; the Isatabu Freedom Fighters.

Melaitans; Malaita Eagle Force.

Chinese community.

**Nature of conflict**

Ethnic tensions fuelled by mass migration and weak governmental structures. Major inter-communal violence, 1997-2006.

☠ Unknown. Probably several hundred.
⚔ Up to 20,000 mostly Melaitans at height of disturbances. Several hundred Chinese in 2006.

**Population/ethnic composition**

552,000. Melanesian 93%, Polynesian 4%.

**Territorial extent**

Solomon Islands: 28,896 km².

**Timeline**

7 Jul 1978: Solomon Islands achieve independence from the UK.
1997: Violence erupts between Guadalcanal residents and Malaitan migrants.
1999: Commonwealth intervention. Peace accord signed, but unrest continues.
5 Jun 2002: Coup launched by Malaitan militants.
Jul 2003: Regional Assistance Mission to the Solomon Islands (Australian-led force) arrives to restore order.
Apr 2006: Severe rioting aimed against Chinese community.

**Current status**

Relatively calm under heavy Regional Assistance Mission influence. Underlying issues unresolved.

**The Solomon Islands have been inhabited by Melanesian populations for at least 30,000 years. Comprising over 1,000 islands, they became a British protectorate in the 1890s. During the Second World War, the island of Guadalcanal saw one of the most famous battles between the United States and the Japanese, who had occupied the islands in 1942. British rule was restored in 1945.**

In the late 1940s, a movement called the Marching Rule arose to challenge British rule, and other groups were established during the 1950s and 1960s. Limited self-rule was established in 1960, but full independence was not gained until 1978.

Since independence, the Solomon Islands have been troubled by indifferent government performance, frequently under weak and short-lived coalition governments. Ethnic groups have taken advantage of weak civil structures to press their own agendas.

In recent years, the key dispute has been between the inhabitants of Guadalcanal and migrants from Malaita islands, who have moved to Guadalcanal in considerable numbers. Resenting the presence of the newcomers, The Guadalcanal Revolutionary Army (later the Isatabu Freedom Fighters) was created to dislodge the immigrants. The Malaitans responded with the formation of their own militia, most notably the Malaitan Eagle Force.

By 1997, relations between the Malaitans and the Guadalcanal residents had descended into all-out conflict, which the central government appeared powerless to halt. As the crisis deepened, tens of thousands of Malaitans fled, under threat of Guadalcanal violence, into the capital, Honiara. Initially seeing the matter primarily as a law-and-order issue, the Solomon Islands government appealed to New Zealand and Australia for assistance, which was provided. Under Australian and New Zealand auspices, the Honiara Peace Accord was agreed on 28 June 1999, temporarily halting the fighting. A Commonwealth Multinational Police Peace Monitoring Force arrived in the islands in November 1999. The Solomon Islands have no regular military forces, although police had a paramilitary role until 2003. At the request of the Solomon Islands government itself, the Commissioner of Police has traditionally been either a New Zealander or Australian secondee. This has reflected the suspicion ethnic groups have towards local appointees.

Despite the peace accord, the situation in the Solomon Islands remained tense and unresolved. In 2000 attempts were initiated to develop a longer-term solution, with New Zealand and Australia again playing a facilitating role, including the use of warships as safe and neutral venues for talks. Despite these efforts, the security situation continued to deteriorate, with tit-for-tat retaliations. A new ceasefire in August 2000 failed and in June 2002, after yet another round of violence, the Malaita Eagle Force staged a coup which resulted in the detention and subsequent resignation of the then Prime Minister, Bartholomew Ulufa'alu. Guadalcanal militants retaliated and economic activity all but collapsed. In July 2003, a 2,200 strong Regional Assistance Mission to the Solomon Islands, led by Australian troops, effectively took over control of the country, restoring an uneasy calm.

In April 2006 mass rioting erupted in Honiara, aimed primarily at the Chinese business community. Most of the Chinatown district of the capital was destroyed and hundreds of Chinese were evacuated. The Solomon Islands maintains diplomatic relations with the Republic of China (Taiwan) but also receives significant inward investment from the Peoples' Republic. The use of Chinese business funds by the Prime Minister to bribe politicians was the immediate trigger for the violence. Once again, Australian and New Zealand forces intervened to restore order.

# Australia

**Principal protagonists**

Commonwealth of Australia; White population.

Aborigine population.

**Nature of conflict**

Race relations and equality issues.

☠ Potentially 200,000 Aborigine deaths (mostly through disease) since arrival of
European settlers in 1788.

🛒 Acquisition of Aboriginal land by Europeans a significant issue; legal disputes continue.

**Population/ethnic composition**

20.4m. White 91.4%, Asian 6.4%, Aborigines 1.5%. (Aborigine population between 300,000-470,000 depending on definition.)

**Territorial extent**

Commonwealth of Australia: 7,741,220 km².

**Timeline**

c50,000 BC: Commencement of human (Aborigine) settlement of Australia.

4 Mar 1606: Australia discovered by Dutch.

26 Jan 1788: First British colony (New South Wales) founded.

1788-1926: European diseases and massacres reduce Aborigine population from c350,000 to c160,000.

1803-1867: Eradication of Tazmanian population, largely through disease.

1 Jan 1901: British colonies in Australia united as Commonwealth of Australia.

27 May 1967: Federal government acquires right (following referendum) to legislate on behalf of Aborigines.

16 Dec 1976: First Aboriginal Land Rights Act passed.

**Current status**

Relationship between Europeans and Aborigines continues to be an active political issue.

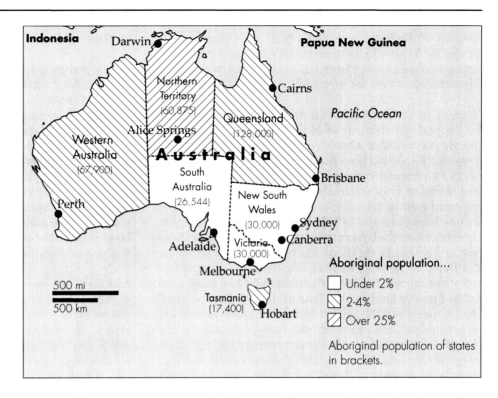

Although in recent years attention in Australian race relations has focused on tensions between the majority Anglo-Celtic population and relatively recent immigrants from Asia and Eastern Europe, the better known and more long standing ethnic question in Australian politics revolves around the relationship between the European population and the original Aboriginal population of the continent.

Human settlement in Australia is ancient, dating to at least 40,000 years ago and possibly much earlier. By the time of the first European settlement in the 18th century there were upwards of 300,000 inhabitants of Australia, organized into up to 750 linguistic or tribal groups, which collectively became known by Europeans as Aborigines. Geographical isolation and the often harsh climate meant that many of these communities operated barely above the subsistence level, nevertheless Aboriginal societies developed sophisticated visual arts, music and cosmology.

Permanent European settlement, by the British, commenced in 1788 and their arrival almost immediately had a deleterious effect on the Aborigine population. Aboriginal numbers declined catastrophically throughout the 19th century, largely as a result of exposure to diseases such as smallpox to which they had no immunity, but also as a result of forced re-settlement and outright massacre. 'Sporting' hunts of Aborigines by European settlers were a not uncommon phenomena in the early years of British settlement, although ostensibly these were in retaliation for thefts or livestock rustling. Most notorious, perhaps, was the 'extermination' of the Tasmanians, albeit largely through disease, whose numbers declined from 5,000 to 300 in the first three decades of the 18th century, the Tasmanians being declared extinct with the death of the last pure-blooded Tasmanian in 1876.

Organized massacres of Aborigines continued well into the 20th century, although in a limited and localized form. In 1926, in the 'Coniston Massacre', 32 Aborigines were killed by farmers in response to an attack by local Aborigines. A Court found their actions to be justified.

From the second half of the 19th century onward, the cultural assimilation of the Aborigines was vigorously pursued, not least by missionary groups. This policy included the removal of Aboriginal children from their families for rearing by Whites. The consequence of these practices, that continued in some forms until the 1960s, was severe cultural dislocation for many Aboriginal communities.

Changes to the Australian constitution in 1967 enabled the Federal government to legislate (for the first time) directly on behalf of Aborigines throughout the country. (Previously, this had been the prerogative of State governments.) This enabled the government to introduce measures aimed at improving Aboriginal education, employment and welfare benefits. In the 1970s land rights issues became important and in 1976 the Aboriginal Land Rights Act established the bases on which Aborigines could claim land and property rights on the grounds of historical or traditional ownership. In 1992, the Australian Courts formally overturned the view that Australia had been *terra nullius* ('empty land') at the time of the first European arrival. Throughout the 1990s moves were made to provide for greater political autonomy for recognized Aboriginal groups. Political autonomy has not necessarily led to better governance, however. In 2007 Federal authorities unilaterally intervened in desert tribal areas to tackle widespread child abuse and healthcare problems.

In recent decades, Aboriginal numbers have undergone a significant increase. This is due in part to organic growth – Aboriginal populations have twice the birth rate of the national average – re-classifications of the definition of 'Aboriginal' and the greater willingness of those of mixed-race ancestry to self-identify themselves as such.

In common with indigenous populations in other parts of the world, Aboriginal communities suffer disproportionately high levels of crime, depression, alcoholism, drug abuse and economic marginalization, which government interventions have only partially alleviated. Both the history of European/Aborigine race relations and their practical modern consequences remain live and controversial issues in contemporary Australia.

### Nuclear conflict in the Pacific

Political and geographical marginalization had led to the indigenous peoples of Australia and the Pacific Ocean region being subject to exploitation in a number of ways. The intensive exploitation of phosphate reserves on the island of Banaba (formerly Ocean Island and now part of Kiribati) resulted in widespread ecological degradation and the deportation of much of the population (by the British) in 1945. Mining continued until 1979, and although the Banabans won a long running legal battle against the British government, the Banabans continue for the most part to live abroad – only 200 of the estimated 6,000 total population have been able to return to the island. In recent years, Banaban activists have argued that the Kiribatan authorities have been using Banaban phosphate revenues for their own purposes, rather than for the development of the island.

From the 1950s onwards the United States, France and Britain conducted a series of hydrogen bomb tests in remote areas of Australia and the Pacific Islands. Little attempt appears to have been made to protect local inhabitants from the effects of radiation (although this may in part have been ignorance; Western soldiers and researchers were often similarly unprotected.) Long-term radiation damage both to land areas and to human populations have been claimed from Mouruoa and Fangataufa islands (scene of French tests) and from the British tests in Aboriginal areas at Maralinga, Australia. The original US hydrogen bomb tests at Bikini Atoll have resulted in land use loss and an alleged increase in radioactive Cesium levels among local populations.

French atomic bomb tests only ceased in the 1996, by which time 136 had been tested, including 41 atmospheric explosions. French claims that the tests were safe led activists to make the obvious rejoinder that, if so, could they not more conveniently be conducted in France itself? Following widespread worldwide protests and the controversy surrounding the 1985 destruction by French agents of the Greenpeace ship *Rainbow Warrior* (which had been monitoring the French tests), France officially abandoned its weapons testing programme following a final bomb test on Fangataufa in January 1996.

Various legal cases against the British, US and French governments on behalf of Aboriginal and island communities continue.

# Section 7: **Europe**

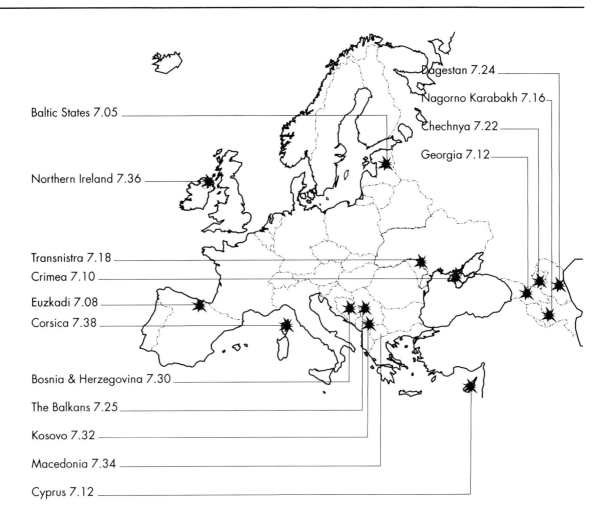

*Azeri separatists 7.17*
*Breakdown in Belgium? 7.04*
*Ethnic cleansing defined? 7.29*
*Europe's other minority (the Roma) 7.05*
*The Kaliningrad question 7.07*
*Ukraine's struggle for independence 7.11*

*Fields of Fire – An Atlas of Ethnic Conflict*

# Europe

## Key details

Principal Europe-wide organizations: North Atlantic Treaty Organization (NATO) (also includes USA and Canada); European Union (27 members); Council of Europe (46 members).

## Population/ethnic composition

c690m. (EU population: 492m.)
*(See panel opposite for ethnic composition of selected European nations.)*

## Territorial extent

c10.4m km². (EU area: 4,325,675 km².)

## Timeline

*(Since 1900.)*

28 Jul 1914-11 Nov 1918: First World War.
1917: Bolshevik revolution in Russia; Soviet Union formally established 1922.
30 Jan 1933: Nazi government elected in Germany.
1 Sep 1939: Start of Second World War in Europe.
8 May 1945: End of Second World War in Europe. Onset of Cold War.
4 Apr 1949: NATO founded.
1 May 1955: Warsaw Pact founded.
Oct-Nov 1956: Hungarian uprising against Communist rule.
25 Mar 1957: Treaty of Rome signed.
13 Aug 1961: Berlin Wall constructed.
9 Nov 1989: Berlin Wall falls. Popular revolutions remove Communist governments throughout Central Europe.
25 June 1991: Croatia and Slovenia declare independence from Yugoslavia, followed by other Yugoslav republics. Balkan conflict ensues as Yugoslav/Serbian forces attempt to prevent secession.
1 Jul 1991: Warsaw Pact dissolved.
26 Dec 1991: USSR formally dissolved.
14 Dec 1995: Dayton Accords halt conflict in Bosnia & Herzegovina.
1 Jan 1999: Single European currency, the euro, introduced.
24 Mar 1999: Kosovo war. NATO launches air assault on Serbia.
2005: Electorates in France and the Netherlands reject introduction of EU-wide constitution.

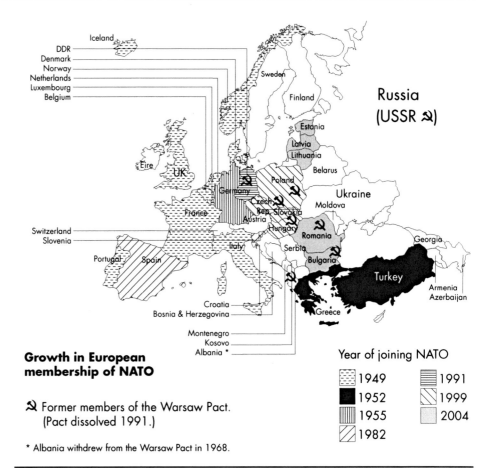

**Growth in European membership of NATO**

☭ Former members of the Warsaw Pact. (Pact dissolved 1991.)

* Albania withdrew from the Warsaw Pact in 1968.

Year of joining NATO
- 1949
- 1952
- 1955
- 1982
- 1991
- 1999
- 2004

**Growth in membership of the European Union**

€ States within the 'eurozone'.

Year of accession to European Union
- 1957
- 1973
- 1981
- 1986
- 1991
- 1995
- 2004
- 2007

As a main theatre of war in all four of the great global conflicts to beset our planet – the Napoleonic Wars of the 19th century, the First and Second World Wars, and the Cold War – Europe has rarely seen a sustained period of peace in its recent history. During the time of the Cold War, ethnic tensions both within and between European nations were largely kept in abeyance. Since 1989, however, ethnic conflict has re-emerged as a significant factor in south-eastern Europe and in parts of the former Soviet Union.

In contrast, overt and sustained ethnic conflict in Western Europe has been largely confined to regional trouble spots such as Northern Ireland, the Basque country, and Corsica. All these conflicts are largely contained at present. Secessionist movements elsewhere in Western Europe, for example in Scotland, have largely progressed along peaceful lines. Immigration and race relations issues also constitute an ongoing political problem for Western Europe. The post 9/11 rise in Islamic fundamentalism, with associated terrorist attacks against European targets, poses an unresolved threat.

The collapse of European Communism saw the disintegration of false multi-national states such as Yugoslavia, Czechoslovakia and the USSR that had been held together by socialist ideology and force of arms against the wishes of their peoples. One consequence of the collapse of the USSR was the creation of a number of 'aspirant' breakaway states – regions which are in some cases *de facto* independent, but that have neither been internationally recognized nor have reached an agreed settlement.

Europe has also witnessed the rise of multi-state government in the form of the European Union and its antecedents. Given that Franco-German rivalry had been central to the conflicts which had disfigured the continent since 1870, it was understandable that Europeans should reach for permanent solutions to this issue in the post-1945 environment. In 1957 the formation of the European Coal and Steel Community (the precursor to today's European Union [EU]) brought together six European states, including France and Germany, into an economic union intended to merge the political systems of the member states into, to quote the founding Treaty of Rome, "an ever closer union." The European Union's core historical aim – prevention of another war between Germany and France – was, in the event, a case of a solution to an obsolete problem. In the Cold War environment, with Europe effectively bisected into Soviet and US spheres of influence, the realistic prospect of inter-state warfare *within* the constituent parts of the two blocs was effectively zero.

In the 21st century, Europe faces four interlocking problems, three of

**Population/ethnic composition in selected European countries**

**France**
    61m. French 76.9%, North African 5%, Italian 1.9%, Portuguese 1.5%, Basque 1.3% (2000). Religious mix: Roman Catholic 82.3%, Muslim 7.1%, Protestant 3.7%, Orthodox 1.1%.

**Germany**
    82.4m. German 88.2%, Turkish 3.4% (2000).
    Religious mix: Protestant 35.6% (Lutheran 33.9%), Roman Catholic 33.5%, Other Christian 6.6%, Muslim 4.4%.

**Hungary**
    9.9m. Hungarian 84.4%, Roma 5.3%, Ruthenian 2.9%, German 2.4%, Romanian 1% (2006). Religious mix: Roman Catholic 51.9%, Calvinist 15.9%, Lutheran 3%, Greek Catholic 2.6%, other Christian 1%.

**Italy**
    58m. Italian 96%, North African Arab 0.9%, Italo-Albanian 0.8%. (2000) Religious mix: Roman Catholic 79.6%, Muslim 1.2%.

**Netherlands**
    16.5m. Dutch 81.6%, Indonesian 2.5%, Turkish 2.1%, German 2.5%, Surinamese 2%, Moroccan 1.8% (2002). Religious mix: Roman Catholic 31%, Dutch Reformed 13%, Calvinist 7%, Muslim 5.5%.

**Poland**
    38.5m. Polish 96.7% (2006).
    Religious mix: Roman Catholic 89.8%, Orthodox 1.3%.

**Russia**
    141.4m. Russian 80%, Tatar 3.8%, Ukrainian 2%, Bashkir 1.1%, Chuvash 1.1%, Chechen 0.9%, Armenian 0.9%. Numerous others. (2007). Religious mix: Orthodox 49.7%, Protestant 6.2%, Roman Catholic 1%, Muslim 7.6%.

**Spain**
    40.4m. Spaniard 44.9%, Catalonian 28%, Galician 8.2%, Basque 5.5%, Aragonese 5%, Extremaduran 2.8%, Roma 2%. (2000). Religious mix: Roman Catholic 92%, Muslim 0.5%.

**Sweden**
    9m. Swedish 88.5%, Finnish 2.2%, Asian 2.4%, Balkans 1.6% (2002). Religious mix: Church of Sweden (Lutheran) 86.5%, Muslim 2.3%, Roman Catholic 1.8%, Pentecostal 1.1%.

**United Kingdom**
    60m. British (including Irish) 92.1%, Black 2%; Indian/Pakistani/Bangladeshi 3.6% (2001). Religious mix: Anglican c60% (nominal observance), Roman Catholic 11%, Orthodox 0.9%, Muslim 2.7%, Hindu 1%, Sikh 0.6%.

which have a direct ethnic component. These are:

- A declining indigenous birthrate and an aging population in Western Europe;
- Immigration from outside the European Union;
- Intra-EU population movements;
- Long-term economic decline.

The lowering birthrate in many Western European counties means that this region is likely to experience major decline amongst indigenous groups in the coming decades. This has huge implications for pensions and social provision, as a declining working population seeks to support an aging population. On UN figures, Italy will experience a 32% decline in its working age population, Spain 26%, and Germany a 19% fall. Should this occur, it will be a decline unprecedented since the Black Death, but these figures pre-suppose, of course, no reversal of the birthrate decline among indigenous populations and no significant immigration. In stark contrast, figures published in November 2007 in the UK predicted a population *increase* to 70 million by 2031, largely fuelled by immigration.

Since 1945, Western Europe has experienced large-scale immigration from Asia, Africa and the Caribbean, initially largely fuelled by migration from the former colonies of the European powers (plus, in the case of Germany, from Turkey). Race relations in Western Europe have not, thus far, degenerated into wholesale ethnic conflict, with indigenous reaction to large-scale immigration being largely confined to support for often transient right-wing political parties. There have, however, been sporadic riots with a distinctive racial character in many Western European cities, although for political reasons politicians have sought to play up the socio-economic aspects of such flare ups rather than their racial dimension. The partial exception has been France, where repeated rioting in largely Muslim areas of French towns and cities comes close in scale to being classifiable as an ongoing ethnic conflict.

**Principal immigration/ migration routes in Europe**

---

**Breakdown in Belgium?**

Politics in Belgium is linguistically highly sectarian, with all major parties, even those that share broad socio-economic positions, divided between Flemish (Dutch) and Walloon (French) sections. In June 2007, the Prime Minister, Guy Verhofstadt, lost national parliamentary elections. In the ensuing horse trading, politicians failed to assemble a stable coalition, with the result that Belgium remained without a working central government for some six months until a partial solution in December 2007, when the King asked Verhofstadt to form an 'interim' administration.

Linguistic tensions and chauvinism have been a feature of Belgium's political landscape since the country was created in 1830, with the trend being towards the gradual accumulation of greater rights by the majority Flemish-speaking community. In many parts of the country the two communities have duplicate educational and utilities services; in one illustrative example, a Walloon community forced the diversion of a new sewerage system to avoid 'Flemish sewage' flowing though (or rather, under) their districts.

While a formal partition of Belgium is not currently likely, nationalists both in Belgium and abroad can point to the country's difficulties to highlight the problems of holding together, even in a democracy, what is essentially an artificial multi-national state. Supporters of European integration can, in contrast, argue that Belgium's continued functioning in the absence of a central government demonstrated the irrelevance and impotence of national governments in the supranational European Union environment. Meanwhile, secessionists in other parts of Western Europe will doubtless be observing events closely.

Post-9/11 attacks by Islamist terrorists in Western Europe have heightened concerns in all European states with appreciable Muslim minorities. The Islamist attack on the Madrid metro, suicide bombings by British-born Muslims, and the assassination of the Dutch film maker Theodor Van Gogh at the hands of an Islamic extremist, have highlighted the probability of on-going Islamist violence in Europe. Perhaps as worrying, evidence of increased social alienation amongst young Muslims suggests the failure both of the multicultural model favoured (until now) by governments such as Britain and the Netherlands, as well as the integrationist model favoured by France.

The accession of Central and Eastern European states to the EU and the open movement across the continent that this has facilitated has prompted significant east-west migration with, for example, an unprecedented 750,000 Polish workers moving to Britain. Such migrations have not, thus far, resulted in a significant rise in racial tensions.

In addition to intra-EU migration, large-scale overland/overseas migration into Europe occurs through the 'soft underbelly' route from North Africa and the so-called 'green route' of primarily Middle Eastern/Islamic immigration via the Balkans. An undercurrent to this process is that these routes can also be used for people trafficking, either for illegal immigration or the forced importation of women and girls for the vice trade.

The overall consequences of such large-scale migrations have yet to be evaluated. While, given Western Europe's low birthrate, population substitution by Central and Eastern European immigrants may appear advantageous, the loss of the most economically productive generation from Eastern Europe (estimated to be as high as 20% in countries such as Lithuania) is a potentially significant problem.

On the economic front, Europe faces other difficulties. The creation by the EU of a single European currency, the euro, was a programme largely driven by a political agenda. The 'one size fits all' economic model inherent in EU planning, and typified by the euro, has failed to promote lasting economic growth. The 'eurozone' single economy has historically had nearly twice the unemployment levels, and half the growth rates, of non-euro members such as the United Kingdom, and compares even less favourably with the United States or high-growth rate economies such as China or India. According to figures from the Organization for Economic Co-operation and Development (OECD), Europe faces the doleful prospect of its share of global trade and GDP halving over the next fifty years. Ironically, this may mitigate any negative effects of inward migration by making Europe a less attractive destination for immigrants, but the overall social and political consequences for Europe could be immense.

Europe's economic problems are closely bound in to its political structure. The centralizing political drive in the European Union is deeply counter-cultural to the drive towards greater political autonomy that has characterized recent history – not least in Europe itself, with the break-up of the Soviet Union, Yugoslavia and Czechoslovakia and the creation of devolved government institutions in Britain and Spain. There is no inherent reason why the EU should not be subject to similar centrifugal pressures, particularly if it continues to fail to deliver broad economic benefits. In 2005, voters in France and the Netherlands rejected the proposed EU Constitution. Virtually all the measures in the defeated constitution were, nevertheless, re-introduced in the 2007 EU Reform Treaty, but this was in turn rejected, this time by Ireland, in 2008. The failure of the EU to legitimize its constitutional process suggests that the popular limits to Europea integration have now been reached. The practical consequences of the EU experiment in political and economic centralization have doubtless not yet been fully played out.

---

**Europe's 'other' minority**

Numbering around 8 million, the Roma (Gypsies) are one of Europe's largest ethnic minority groups. Although commonly perceived as being nomadic, the Roma, who migrated to Europe from the Indian sub-continent a thousand years ago, are now largely settled. Only around 10% of the Roma population now follow their traditional migratory lifestyle.

Significant Roma populations exist in south-eastern Europe and Spain. The Roma have long been subjected to discrimination, whether official or unofficial and, occasionally, violence. Claims have been made of segregation in schools, forced evictions from housing, and denial of state benefits. Although there are widespread local variations, Roma characteristically live in depressed squatter settlements with high levels of unemployment and crime. Because of their marginal lifestyle, differences in language and culture, and perceived propensity towards criminality, there is generally a lack of mutual trust and integration between the Roma and mainstream host societies.

Roma populations are to be found in most European countries. The principal communities are:

| | |
|---|---|
| Romania | 2 million |
| Bulgaria | 800,000 |
| Hungary | 600,000 |
| Slovakia | 600,000 |
| Spain | 800,000 |
| Czech Rep. | 250,000 |
| Balkans | 250,000 |

Significant Roma communities also exist in Turkey, Brazil and Argentina.

# The Baltic states

**Principal protagonists**

Baltic states: Estonia, Latvia and Lithuania.

Russia; Russian minorities in Baltic states.

**Nature of conflict**

Potential political/ethnic conflict surrounding status of Russian minorities. Cyber-terrorist attacks on Estonia.

**Population/ethnic composition**

Estonia: 1.3m. Estonian 67.9%, Russian 25.6%; Latvia: 2.6m. Latvian 57.7%, Russian 29.6%; Lithuania: 3.5m. Lithuanian 83.4%, Polish 6.7%, Russian 6.3%.

**Territorial extent**

Estonia: 45,226 km²; Latvia: 64,589 km²; Lithuania: 65,200 km².

**Timeline**

1710: Estonia and Latvia annexed by Russia (from Sweden).

7 Jan 1795: Lithuania occupied by Russia.

Nov 1917: Republics of Estonia and Latvia declared.

11 Dec 1917: Lithuanian independence declared.

31 Mar 1940: Karilo-Finnish SSR created.

15-17 Jun 1940: Baltic states occupied by USSR.

3-6 Aug 1940: Baltic states incorporated into USSR.

16 Jul 1956: KFSSR downgraded to ASSR status.

11 Mar 1990: Lithuania declares restored independence.

20-21 Aug 1991: Estonia and Latvia declare independence.

6 Sep 1991: Independence recognized by USSR.

29 Mar 2004: Estonia, Latvia and Lithuania join NATO.

1 May 2004: Estonia, Latvia and Lithuania join European Union.

May 2007: Re-siting of Soviet war memorial in Tallinn sparks riots and concerted cyber-attacks on Estonia.

**Current status**

Potential exists for exploitation of Russian grievances leading to future conflicts.

**Historically and culturally orientated towards northern and central Europe, the political independence of the Baltic states has generally only been assured during periods of Russian weakness. The uneven relationship between the small Baltic nations and their eastern neighbour continues to be central to Baltic politics, while for Russia the issue has always been seen as a strategic one – protecting access to the Baltic sea and defending the approaches to St Petersburg.**

Annexed to Russia in the 18th century, the Baltic nations of Finland, Estonia, Latvia and Lithuania broke loose again in the aftermath of the Bolshevik revolution and the subsequent Russian civil war. Baltic independence was grudgingly recognized by the Soviets until the outbreak of the Second World War when, under the terms of the Molotov-Ribbentrop pact, the region was assigned to the Soviet sphere of influence. In June 1940 Estonia, Latvia and Lithuania were occupied by Soviet forces, and bogus Communist 'parliaments' in all three countries voted for incorporation into the USSR. In August, Moscow unsurprisingly acquiesced to this 'request'. Mass deportations of 'intellectuals' and 'bourgeous elements' followed almost immediately.

Finland proved more intractable. In March 1940 the Soviets created a Karilo-Finnish SSR (Karelia is the region immediately to Finland's east) transparently intending this as the political vehicle for the outright annexation of Finland. But Soviet troops were repelled in their attack of 1940, and although in 1944 Finland was forced to concede both territory and *de facto* Soviet tutelage (the process that became known in the Cold War as 'Finlandization'), Finnish independence was maintained. The rump SSR, having failing in its task, was discarded in 1956. Populations of Karelians displaced from their homeland exist in Finland and throughout the region.

In the immediate post-war period, 'Sovietization' of the Baltic states continued apace, as did the deportations of the Baltic populations and their displacement by Russian immigrants. Groups took to the forests to avoid the Soviet authorities, and although most were eventually rounded up, the last of these 'Forest Brothers' is believed to have held out in Estonia until 1979, when, as an old man, he flung himself into a freezing river and drowned to avoid capture.

Although their annexation was never formally acknowledged by the West, the three Baltic states continued as SSRs until the late 1980s, when (particularly in Lithuania) they came to the forefront of demands for the breakup of the USSR. Baltic independence was again achieved in 1990/1. In 2004 Estonia, Latvia and Lithuania became the first ex-Soviet states to join first NATO and then the European Union – an eastward expansion of Western institutions that inevitably triggered alarm bells in Moscow.

Ethnically, the key flashpoint is the presence of large Russian minorities, particularly in Estonia and Latvia. Displaced from their former Soviet-era positions of prominence, these populations are a very visible reminder to the indigenous population of the Soviet past. Ethnic Russians allege discrimination in the fields of naturalization, employment and housing. (Russian housing stock is characteristically of poor Soviet-era quality.) The Russian minority forms a potentially active pool of resentment that can be played upon by Moscow in attempts to apply political and economic pressure upon the small and exposed Baltic states.

Matters came to a head in Estonia in 2007. The prominent position, in the capital Tallinn, of a statue of a Soviet soldier 'liberating' Estonia had long been a point of contention. In May 2007, the Estonian government moved the statue to a less conspicuous position. This prompted demonstrations and riots by the Russian minority, threats of economic sanctions by Russia, and the stoning of the Estonian embassy in Moscow.

Potentially much more significantly, Estonia's banking, commercial and governmental internet system then came under sustained cyber-attack, which severely disrupted the country's e-commerce and communications infrastructure. Hackers used automated robot systems to hijack computers around the world to bombard Estonian sites with bogus information in what is termed a Distributed Denial of Access (DDoA) attack. Instructions on how to carry out a DDoA were allegedly posted on hundreds of Russian and other websites. The beauty of this form of attack, from the perpetrator's point of view, is that it is often impossible to identify the culprits. (In January 2008 a 20-year-old ethnic Russian Estonian became the first person to be convicted as a result of the May 2007 attacks.)

Estonia, through the adoption of strongly free market polities, is regarded as an economic success story; so much so that the tiny country is the only ex-Soviet state (with the exception of Russia itself) to have so far been invited to discuss joining the "rich nation's club", the Organization for Economic Co-operation and Development. As a modern, highly 'wired' economy, the cyber-attacks had a major economic effect. Estonia blamed Russia directly for the attacks, which soured scheduled EU/Russian talks in Samara later in the month. Tallinn also called for NATO and the EU to urgently establish ways to respond to what it termed 'cyber-terrorism.'

The internet has long been the forum for vigorous, and wholly unregulated debates on ethnicity and the validity of various national and religious claims. The medium has been put to positive effect by dispossessed and marginalized ethnic groups seeking to highlight their cases. But it has also been used by Islamist and other extremes both to promote their claims and for the practical planning of terrorist and other activities.

Although no-one was killed in the cyber-attack on Estonia it may well be a harbinger of future conflicts. It does not take too large a jump of the imagination to see how future attacks aimed at hospital computers or air traffic control systems could have a human as well as an economic cost. It may well be that cyberspace becomes a crucial theatre of war in future ethnic conflicts.

---

**The Kaliningrad question**

At the end of the Second World War the German province of East Prussia was occupied by the Red Army. Many of the German population fled in the closing days of the war, and the balance was deported. The only part of the erstwhile Third Reich to be annexed to the USSR, East Prussia, now an *oblast* of Russia, was renamed Kaliningrad, as was the capital, the historic Hanseatic port of Königsberg, perhaps best known as the birthplace of Kant. Königsberg was heavily damaged by Allied bombing during the war, and post-war reconstruction consisted largely of poor quality Soviet flats, a cityscape barely relieved by monumental 'Soviet realist' statuary.

During the Cold War, Kaliningrad, as the westernmost part of Russia, was heavily fortified and closed to foreign visitors. This continued until 1990 when the nature of Kaliningrad's isolation shifted – it now found itself surrounded by newly independent states rather than being contiguous with the USSR. Today, Kaliningrad continues as a detached outpost of the Russian Federation.

In the absence of a sizeable non-Russian minority in Kaliningrad, the possibility of ethnic conflict within the exclave is remote. Kaliningraders themselves, however, face a problematic future, cut off as they are from Russia proper and surrounded on all sizes by neighbours who are now members of NATO and the European Union. Raising the Kaliningrader's sense of isolation are increasing difficulties in getting visas for Poland and Lithuania now that these countries have joined the European Union.

A number of potential solutions for the Kaliningrad issue have been mooted. Some of these are, at best, aspirational – neither returning the region to Germany nor unifying it with Lithuania are serious political prospects. More realistic proposals have included the creation of a freeport area, allowing greater access of goods and people between Russia and the EU. Germany has funded the restoration of some pre-war monuments and some Kaliningraders have taken to calling their city by its former name. ('Kalinin' was a titular President of the USSR and had no connections to the region.) With relations between Russia and the West currently cool, however, the probability of meaningful developments appears regrettably low.

# Euzkadi (the Basque Country)

**Principal protagonists**

Basque separatists; *Euskadi Ta Askatasuna* (ETA).

Government of Spain.

**Nature of conflict**

Long-standing nationalist issue. Terrorist campaign by ETA, 1960 onwards.

☠ 900 in ETA attacks.

**Population/ethnic composition**

Basque Autonomous Community: 2,124,846. Navarre: 593,500. Parts of Pyrénées-Atlantique *département* (France): 600,000. c2.3m Basques in Spanish regions; 250,000 in French regions.

**Territorial extent**

Basque Autonomous Community: 7,234 km².
Navarre: 10,391 km².
Pyrénées-Atlantique *département*: 7,645 km².

**Timeline**

1521: Basque regions largely absorbed into Castilian kingdom. Northern areas absorbed by France.
1789: French provinces, including Basque regions, lose political status in aftermath of French revolution.
1836-1876: Political autonomy of Spanish Basque provinces abolished.
1895: *Eusko Alderdi Jeltzalea* formed.
1936: Basque Autonomous Government established.
17 Jul 1936-1 Apr 1939: Spanish Civil War. Basque autonomy suppressed following Francoist victory.
31 Jul 1959: ETA formed.
20 Nov 1975: Death of Franco.
25 Oct 1979: Referendum endorses creation of Basque Autonomous Community.

**Current status**

Partially resolved through autonomy for Basque region, but terrorist activity continues.

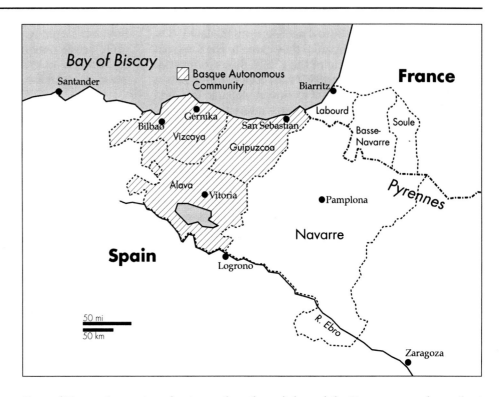

One of Europe's most ancient peoples, the origins of the Basque people are lost in the mists of time. They are generally accepted as a remnant of the Palaeolithic Franco-Cantabric inhabitants of Western Europe, who were already settled in the region by the time of the Roman Empire (and who were mentioned by Pliny and other Roman writers). In the Middle Ages, the Dukedom of Vasconia was centred on what is now the Basque Country, but after Muslim and Frankish invasions the territory was fragmented, subsequently coming together as the Kingdom of Pamplona (later Navarre) from the 9th century. Most of Navarre was annexed by Castile by 1521.

The 'Basque Country' is a composite term for the three Spanish provinces comprising the modern Basque Autonomous Community (Álava, Vizcaya [Biscay] and Guipúzcoa), the Navarran Autonomous Community and, in France, the old provinces of Labourd, Basse-Navarre and Soule that today form part of the Pyrénées-Atlantique *département*. (All French provinces lost their political status after the French revolution. Paris has rejected widely supported calls for a distinctively Basque *département*.) The four regions within Spain form *Hegoalde*, or 'Southern Basque Country', the French areas *Iparralde*, 'Northern Basque Country.' Basque nationalists are divided as to whether their aim is an independent state covering all seven regions or just those in Spain. Basque support for full independence varies regionally, rising to around a third in the Basque Autonomous Community, about 25% in Navarre, but only 15% in the French regions, where Basque separatism is not a significant political force.

Around a million people, including about 700,000 for whom it is their first language, speak the Basque language, Euskara. The roots of Euskara, which is not an Indo-European language, are obscure, and little of its history can be re-constructed by comparative methods. An extremely complex language (each noun is capable of 17 different forms of inflection) Euskara declined from the 1800s onwards, but has made a modest recovery in the Basque Autonomous Community where it has joint official status with Spanish. Within the Basque Autonomous Community the Basques enjoy extensive cultural, linguistic and political autonomy. The majority of schools in the region use Euskara as the main medium of instruction. In contrast, Euskara has no official standing in French Basque territories and is forbidden in schools and courts. Successive Navarre governments have sought to play up the distinctiveness of Navarre at the expense of any Basque identity, and the Basque language is much less widely accepted.

Historically, Basque autonomy was upheld by the *fueros*, charters granted by the kings of Castile that extended to the Basques a privileged position in terms of taxation, military service and legal autonomy. Modern Basque nationalism owes its roots to the Carlist period of Spanish history and the progressive loss of Basque autonomy. In 1836 and 1876 the historic *fueros* were abrogated by the Spanish state. In 1895 the first modern Basque nationalist party, the *Eusko Alderdi Jeltzalea (Partido Nacionalista Vasco* in Spanish) emerged against a backdrop of rapid industrialization in Spain, which was at the time still largely an agrarian society.

During the Spanish Civil War the EAJ-PNV-led Basque Autonomous Government, despite its Catholic leanings, supported the Republican side in order to preserve Basque autonomy. In 1937, however, the troops of the Basque Autonomous Government surrendered to the nationalists in a deal brokered by the Catholic church. (This capitulation is still known as the 'Treason of Santoña' to many left-wing Basques.) Pro-Franco Basque regions, such as Navarre, were rewarded by limited self-government following the Francoist victory. In general, however, large-scale immigration of non-Basque speakers and the suppression of the Basque language served to undermine Basque identity and culture, although the region flourished economically.

Under Francoism, Basque nationalism found a violent expression in the creation, in 1959, of *Euskadi Ta Askatasuna* (ETA). In contrast to the EAJ-PNV, ETA stressed the linguistic (rather than racial) roots of Basque nationalism and had a violent and more overtly left-wing agenda. The movement has also professed its support for European federalism. ETA carried out its first terrorist bombing, resulting in the death of a 22-month old child, in June 1960. Under Franco's regime, with non-violent forms of political and cultural expression tightly controlled, ETA gained a degree of domestic and international sympathy, particularly in 1970 when several ETA members were sentenced to death in the 'Trial of Burgos'. The most consequential of ETA's actions during the Franco period was the murder of Admiral Luis Carrero Blanco, Franco's intended successor, in 1973, indirectly contributing to the restoration of the monarchy, and thus of democracy, after Franco's death in 1975.

ETA violence continued, although with less support, in the post-Franco era. The 1978 Spanish constitution divided the country into 17 Autonomous Communities (and two enclaves) with varying degrees of autonomy. The Statute of Gernika established the Autonomous Community of the Basque Country in the three provinces of Álava, Vizcaya and Guipúzcoa. This was confirmed by a referendum on 25 October 1979 despite a boycott of more than 40% of the electorate, who sought greater autonomy and/or the inclusion of Navarre in the new region. The Navarre Autonomous Community, similarly created under the 1978 constitution, has (under the Statute of Gernika) the option of joining the Basque Autonomous Community, but has not thus far tested this in a referendum. The right of Basque self-determination was re-iterated by the Basque parliament, which defined the Basque region as 'a nation' in 2002 and 2006. The EAJ-PNV is the largest party in the Autonomous Community.

In recent decades, ETA has not commanded majority support even among Basque nationalists. The ETA political wing, Batasuma, has rarely commanded more than 15% support in the Basque regions. (Batasuma was outlawed in March 2003.) Increasingly, the general public saw ETA acts of terrorism as more akin to banditry than political action. From 1983-87 *Grupos Antiterroristas de Liberación* (GAL), anti-ETA groups covertly sponsored by the Spanish state, carried out a series of assassinations of ETA members and sympathizers. In 1986 *Gesto por la Paz* (Association for Peace) was formed. This organization convened mass silent demonstrations after any politically motivated killing. In 1988, all Basque parties (except for Batasuma) signed the Ajuria-Enea Pact aimed at halting political violence. ETA itself announced a ceasefire on 28 January 1988, but terrorist activities continued.

In 1997 ETA kidnapped and subsequently murdered Miguel Angel Blanco, a senior politician in the then opposition *Partido Popular*. This assassination backfired on ETA; the national wave of revulsion that swept the country saw more than 6 million Spaniards taking to the streets in protest. Massive demonstrations in the Basque regions themselves took place under the slogan 'Basques yes, ETA no'. In September 1998 ETA once more announced a ceasefire only to again resume violence in 2000. ETA was not implicated in the 11 March 2004 Islamist attacks on the Madrid metro, despite ill-conceived initial government claims to the contrary. On 22 March 2006 ETA announced a 'permanent ceasefire' but attacks continued, including the December 2006 bombing of Madrid airport, and on 6 June 2007 ETA formally abandoned its ceasefire. Subsequent attacks have seen 4 fatalities, and as of June 2008 ETA was vowing to continue its terror campaign, despite the arrest in France of its leader, Francisco Javier Lopez Pena. The very considerable sporting and cultural contributions made by Basques to the life of Europe may thus continue to be marred by the threat of terrorism.

# Crimea

**Principal protagonists**

Government of Ukraine; Autonomous Republic of Crimea.

Russian population.

Tartar population.

**Nature of conflict**

Potential secessionist conflict between Ukrainian government and Russian majority and/or with Tartar minority.

**Population/ethnic composition**

2.7m. Russian 63%, Ukrainian 24%, Tartars 10%.

**Territorial extent**

Crimea: 270,000 km².

**Timeline**

1 Jun 1475: Crimea annexed to Ottoman Empire.
1783: Annexed to Russia.
1854-56: Crimean War.
26 Dec 1917: Independence declared.
18 Oct 1921: Crimean Autonomous Soviet Socialist Republic proclaimed.
May 1944: Crimean Tartars deported to Siberia for alleged collaboration with the Nazis.
30 Jun 1945: Crimean status downgraded to that of an *oblast* within Russian FSSR.
19 Feb 1954: Crimea transferred from Russia to Ukraine.
12 Feb 1991: Crimean ASSR within Ukraine created.
24 Aug 1991: Ukraine declares independence.
26 Feb 1992: Crimean ASSR reconstituted as Crimean Republic.

**Current status**

Generally stable, although underlying potential for ethnic discontent remains.

**Geographically, Crimea is virtually an island, being joined to Ukraine proper by the Perekop Isthmus, which is only 7 km wide. To its east, the peninsula is separated from mainland Russian by the Strait of Kerch, which is barely 3 km wide at its narrowest point.**

Crimea was part of the Ottoman Empire from the 15th century in which the Turkic-speaking Crimean Tartars were the majority population. In 1783, Crimea was incorporated into the Russian Empire, and in the period from the start of the 19th century to the end of the 20th, significant demographic changes occurred, largely to the detriment of the Tartars. The Tsarist regime pursued a deliberately anti-Tartar policy, encouraging the inward migration of Russian speakers. Furthermore, the devastation of the Crimean War from 1853-56 forced the exodus of many Tartars.

Following the collapse of Tsarist rule in 1917, Crimea became a bastion of White Russian forces resisting the Bolsheviks. An independent Crimean state was proclaimed and a period of shifting loyalties and confused fighting continued until 1921, when the Bolsheviks definitively gained control. In 1921 a Crimean Autonomous Soviet Socialist Republic was proclaimed within the Russian Federated Soviet Socialist Republic. This was in keeping with the early Bolshevik policy that generally favoured the development of minority cultures. This policy was to be dramatically reversed under Stalin, whose regime developed openly racist policies towards 'politically unreliable' ethnic groups, including the Ukrainians and the Tartars. In May 1944 the entire Tartar population was deported for alleged collaboration with the Nazis, nearly half the population dying in the process. At the end of the Second World War the Crimean ASSR was downgraded in status, although remaining a part of the Russian republic. In 1954, however, Crimean jurisdiction was transferred from Russia to Ukraine.

This move, uncontroversial while the USSR existed, meant that, with the collapse of the Soviet system, Crimea became a part of Ukraine despite its Russian majority.

At the same time, exiled Tartars and their descendents returned from their Siberian exile, boosting their numbers, from around 38,000 in 1989, to approximately 270,000 today. Elements within the Tartar population commenced agitation for autonomy or even for independence. In December 1991, Tartar nationalists approved the draft of a constitution for a Crimean republic, apparently as a prelude to a bid for full independence. Under pressure from Ukrainian nationalists on the one hand, and Tartar demands on the other, the majority Russian population became increasingly concerned about its future as the USSR disintegrated.

The new Ukrainian republic was thus faced, from the outset of independence in 1991, with conflicting claims for self-determination by the Russian and Tartar communities, as well as the broader issue of conflict between Ukrainian and Russian interests. The latter was highlighted by the dispute over the ownership of the former USSR Black Sea Fleet, an issue which in the early 1990s threatened the possibility of serious conflict between Kiev and Moscow. (The issue was not conclusively resolved until 1997.)

In February 1991, the Ukrainian parliament granted Crimea autonomous status and this, combined with the narrow Crimean 'yes' vote in the 1 December 1991 Ukraine-wide referendum in support of Ukrainian independence, somewhat diffused the situation. Nevertheless, agitation for re-unification with Russia continued, gaining some support (including from non-Russian speakers) by the disparity in living standards between Crimea/Ukraine and Russia. In May 1992, the Russian Supreme Soviet attempted to annul the 1954 transfer of Crimea to Ukraine, but as the Soviet was itself in its dying days this resolution had no practical effect. In July 1993 the Russian parliament passed a resolution declaring Sevastopol a Russian city, again without practical result. The Tartars, who tend to regard Kiev as a better guarantor of their cultural rights than Moscow, remain generally opposed to Russian irredentist aspirations.

Crimea proclaimed self-government in May 1992, but the resolution stopped short of an outright declaration of independence, and was later rescinded in favour of continued autonomy within Ukraine. In 1995, changes were made, at Ukrainian behest, to the Crimean constitution, the effect of which was the abolition of the Crimean Presidency, which had been showing signs of separatist intent. Crimea is thus in the unusual position of being a republic that has no president.

Although Ukrainian is the sole official language throughout Ukraine, the constitution of the Autonomous Crimean Republic recognizes Russian as the language of the majority and guarantees its use in all spheres of public life.

**Ukraine's struggle for independence**

In the 10th century Ukraine was the centre of the powerful Kievan Rus state, which laid the foundation for the national identities both of modern Russians and Ukrainians. Gradually losing influence and independence, Ukraine came to be divided between the rival Russian and Austro-Hungarian empires. Following the Bolshevik revolution, Ukraine briefly claimed independence, but was incorporated into the USSR in 1922. In the 1930s Ukrainians suffered horribly under Stalin's collectivization policies, in which millions starved to death. In 1941, Ukraine again took advantage of Russian collapse (this time at the hands of the invading Germans) to claim independence. Again the attempt failed, although Ukrainian partisans continued to fight the Soviets until the 1950s.

In the post-war period, the Ukrainian SSR expanded through the acquisition of former Polish, Hungarian and Czechoslovak territories annexed to the USSR and by the transfer, in 1954, of Crimea from Russian to Ukrainian control. As part of the political compromise between the USSR and the Western powers that created the United Nations, the Ukrainian SSR became a founder member of the UN in 1945.

Ukraine's modern history has been dominated by the struggle for national identity and self-determination in the face of Russian/Soviet pressures. Ukraine is strategically the most important nation of the former USSR with the exception of Russia itself. Influencing the direction of Ukrainian foreign policy has been a significant post-Cold War concern both the West and for Moscow.

Much of the period of Ukrainian independence since 1991 has been characterized by periodic posturing on both sides underlain by Moscow's attempts to rein in Ukrainian independence. Ukraine has repeatedly challenged Russian geo-military ambitions, for example through the denial of Ukrainian airspace for Russian reinforcements to Kosovo, support for Moldova in its dispute with Moscow over Transnistra (see 7.18) and joint exercises with NATO. Russia in turn has threatened Ukraine with potentially crippling energy and other economic sanctions, and has sought to interfere in Ukrainian elections.

The potential ethnic dimension to this conflict stems from the sharp geographical distinction between the nationalist Ukrainian west, and the more Russophile east and south, including Crimea. The majority of Ukraine's 8.5 million Russians – who comprise around 17% of the total population – live in eastern districts. In Ukraine's controversial December 2004 general election, electorates in south and east Ukraine voted solidly for the 'pro-Moscow' Victor Yanukovich, raising temporary fears of secession when the more 'pro-Western' Yushchenko won the election.

Although these tensions have not thus far resulted in violence, the future possibility remains that domestic problems in either Ukraine or Russia may prompt Russian minorities – potentially stirred up by Moscow – to greater belligerence.

# Cyprus

### Principal protagonists

Greek Cypriots; Republic of Cyprus

Turkish Cypriots; Turkish Republic of Northern Cyprus. Turkish military actively engaged.

### Nature of conflict

Greek/Turkish ethnic conflict. Irredentism (Greek) and separatism (Turkish). Intercommunal violence, especially in 1965. Invasion of northern Cyprus by Turkey, 1975.

- Muslim/Christian conflict an underlying issue.
- Several hundred mostly Turkish deaths in 1965; 3,000 mostly Greek deaths in course of 1975 invasion.
- 200,000 Greek; 65,000 Turkish IDPs, mostly in 1975.

### Population/ethnic composition

Turkish population 264,172 out of Cypriot total of 835,000.

### Territorial extent

Cyprus: 9,250 km². Turkish controlled area: 3,355 km².

### Timeline

1571: Cyprus comes under Turkish rule.
1878: Cyprus ceded to Britain.
1955-60: Greek EOKA movement fights a guerrilla war against the British.
16 Aug 1960: Cypriot independence.
21 Dec 1963: Violence breaks out between Greek and Turkish communities.
15 Jul 1974: Coup attempt against Cypriot government.
20 Jul 1974: Turkey launches invasion of north. Ceasefire agreed 18 August.
13 Feb 1975: Turkish Cypriot Federated State proclaimed. (It becomes the Turkish Republic of Northern Cyprus 15 November 1983.)
24 Apr 2004: Proposed united republic agreed to by Turkish population, but rejected by Greeks.

### Current status

Currently largely peaceful, mainly due to the almost total separation of the two sides.

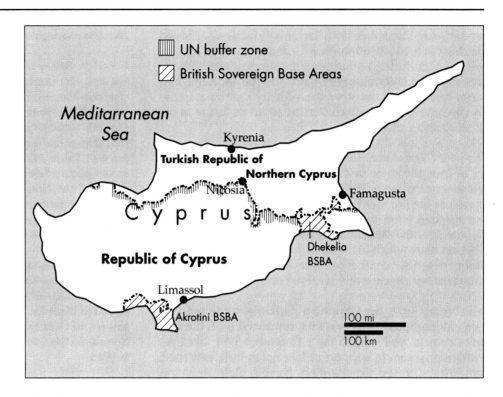

**The history of Cyprus has, for nearly half a millennium, been dominated by the hostility between the island's Greek and Turkish communities. This dispute shows no immediate signs of abating, and has resulted in the partition of the island into two states, the internationally recognized Republic of Cyprus in the south, and the Turkish Republic of Northern Cyprus, which is recognized only by Turkey.**

In modern times, the conflict between the Greeks and the Turks has crystallized into two conflicting demands. From the Greek side comes the call for '*enosis*', or full union with Greece. The Turkish equivalent is '*taksim*' – the partition of the island between Greece and Turkey. From 1955-60 Greek militants of the EOKA movement fought a guerrilla war against the British in support of *enosis*.

The creation of the modern Republic of Cyprus was itself a compromise between the aspirations of the Greek and Turkish populations. Granted independence from Britain in 1960, the new Cypriot constitution specified that the President be elected from among the Greek community while the Vice President was drawn from the Turkish population. The British retained full control over two Sovereign Base Areas in the south of the island. Under Article 4 of the treaty facilitating the establishment of an independent Cyprus, both Turkey and Greece retained the right to intervene if the independence, security, or territorial integrity of Cyprus were to be threatened.

In November 1963 President Makarios proposed a series of changes to the constitution that would have the effect of demoting the Turks from their status as co-founders of the Cypriot republic. Open conflict broke out between the Greek and Turkish populations in December, resulting in several hundred deaths, mostly of Turkish Cypriots. The constitutional changes were never formally implemented.

In April 1967, the "Colonels' Regime" seized power in Greece and began calling for the full integration of Cyprus into Greece. On 15 July 1974, the Athens regime encouraged a coup against Makarios by supporters of full *enosis*. Makarios himself escaped, but his government was replaced by a hard-line regime. Five days later, Turkey, citing the provisions of the 1960 treaty, landed Turkish regular forces at Kyrenia in the north of the island and swiftly occupied the largely Turkish inhabited northern portions of the island. A ceasefire was secured by the United Nations on 18 August, by which time approximately 37% of the island was in Turkish hands. In the aftermath of the Turkish invasion, the wholesale separation of the two populations took place, with an estimated 200,000 Greeks and 65,000 Turks leaving their homes. A buffer zone established by the United Nations severely restricted movement across what had become, in effect, a heavily policed international border. The capital city of Nicosia was similarly divided, a process that had in fact begun in 1965 with the creation of the 'green line' across the city. This became, after 1975, a permanent division reminiscent in some respects of the Berlin Wall, although less solid in construction. While prior to 1975 many Cypriot towns and villages had mixed communities (albeit with separate amenities) following the partition of the island virtually no mixed populations exist, with the exception of a number of closely controlled villages in the UN buffer zone and the British Sovereign Base Areas. An estimated 35,000 Turkish troops continue to be stationed in the north.

The Turkish Cypriot leader, Rauf Denktash, unilaterally proclaimed the formation of a Turkish Cypriot Federated State, which he envisaged as forming a component of a future Cypriot federal state, in February 1975. In 1983, Greece broke off negotiations and submitted the matter to the United Nations. Denktash responded by announcing, on 15 November 1983, the independence of the Turkish Republic of Northern Cyprus (TRNC). The new state failed to gain formal international recognition (except from Turkey itself). Nevertheless, the TRNC continued to function, albeit in isolation, and little was achieved to advance a solution. Regular demonstrations and protests by the Greek population, mainly focusing on the confiscation of their properties, were met with violence by the Turkish authorities. Greek Cypriots also sought, with only partial success, international legal recourse for land confiscations both against the new Turkish occupants and foreign nationals attracted by the low property prices in Northern Cyprus.

In January 2002, direct talks took place between the Greek Cypriot and Turkish Cypriot leadership under the auspices of the UN Secretary General Kofi Annan. The Cyprus issue came into sharper focus in 2003 with Cypriot negotiations for entry into the European Union. In April 2003, the Turkish Cypriot government relaxed broader controls between the two states. Full talks opened in October 2003, with a bare two month deadline being available prior to expected invitation by Brussels for the Republic of Cyprus (i.e., the Greek, southern portion of the island) to join the EU. Ankara threatened to annex the north if Cyprus was allowed to join the EU in the absence of a comprehensive agreement, while Athens in turn threatened to veto the accession of all new EU entrants (which at that time included nine ex-Communist Central and Eastern European states) if Cyprus was excluded from the EU.

Despite this unpromising context, progress on what came to be known as the 'Annan Plan' continued and by February 2004 the template had been drawn up for the creation of a United Cyprus Republic covering the whole island (except for the British territories). The plan envisaged a collective Presidency, a confederation between a Greek state and a Turkish state, and minimal central governmental powers. On 31 March 2004, with both sides still refusing to agree, Annan presented a proposed final settlement, and this was placed before a referendum of the two communities on 24 April 2004. The plan was accepted by 65% of the Turkish population, but rejected by over 75% of the Greek side. The Greek Cypriot government actively campaigned for the rejection of the settlement. Faced with this rejection, the planned re-unification of the island could not take place. The (Greek) Republic of Cyprus entered the EU on 1 May 2004, but the consensus view is that the Greek side has, diplomatically at least, lost ground through its rejection of the Annan Plan; UN officials being apparently infuriated at the Greek Cypriot government's 'betrayal' in campaigning openly for a 'no' vote in the referendum. Further border relaxations by the Turkish side have similarly tended to portray the Greeks as the more intransigent party.

In the aftermath of the collapse of the Annan Plan, no substantive proposals have been advanced for a permanent resolution of the Cyprus issue. The Cyprus conflict has long bedevilled relations between two nominal NATO allies, Greece and Turkey, and poses increasing problems for Ankara in its on-off negotiations to join the European Union. As matters stand, it is almost inevitable that both Greece and Cyprus would veto Turkish membership of the EU.

Given that Turkey has traditionally had to prop up the Turkish Cypriot state financially, the calculation may well be made in Ankara that whatever advantages existed for Turkey through intervention in the 1970s, these are no longer applicable more than thirty years later. Ankara may therefore conceivably jettison its Turkish Cypriot client state in favour of the perceived greater prize of EU membership. In view of the acceptance by the Turkish Cypriots of the principle of federation with the south (as demonstrated by the positive 2004 vote) the stumbling block to a final resolution may well remain the opposition of the Greek Cypriot community. This, coupled with Brussels' desire (at least officially) to see Turkey join the EU, is Ankara's remaining trump card. The possibility of Nicosia coming under pressure from the European Union to accept a federal structure as part of an overall deal to allow Turkey to join the EU cannot be ruled out. The question then remains of whether elements within the Greek Cypriot community would respond violently to what they would see as an EU-imposed settlement favourable to the Turks.

# Georgia

**Principal protagonists**

Government of Georgia.

Republic of South Ossetia; Republic of Abkhazia. Russian forces actively engaged.

**Nature of conflict**

Linguistic and separatist issues exacerbated by Russian geopolitical interests. Full scale wars, 1991-4. Low-level violence since.

- South Ossetia: 1,000 (1991-2); Abkhazia: 33,000 (1992-4).
- South Ossetia: 100,000 (1991); Abkhazia: 250,000 (1993-4).
- Geopolitical/military resources important to Russia.

**Population/ethnic composition**

South Ossetia: 72,000. Ossetian 66.4%, Georgian 28.2% (1989)
Abkhazia: c200,000. Georgian 29%, Abkhazian c45%. (Georgian population was 45.7% in 1989.)

**Territorial extent**

South Ossetia: 3,900 km$^2$.
Abkhazia: 8,600 km$^2$.

**Timeline**

1801: Georgia annexed to Russian (Tsarist) empire. Abkhazia annexed, 1864.
1921: Briefly independent Georgian republic annexed to Soviet Union.
9 Apr 1991: Georgia declares independence from the USSR.
28 Nov 1991: South Ossetia declares independence. Ceasefire 1992.
23 July 1992: Abkhazia declares independence. Ceasefire 1994.
Dec 2003: 'Rose Revolution' – popular uprising brings in 'pro-Western' government in Tbilisi.
Apr 2004: 'Second' Rose Revolution removes Adjarian separatist regime.
12 Nov 2006: South Ossetian referendum confirms independence.

**Current status**

Officially unresolved. South Ossetia and Abkhazia remain de facto independent.

**Separatism in Georgia is closely bound up with Russian ambitions in the region. Sponsorship of separatist movements is, for Moscow, an important tool in applying pressure on Georgia as well as facilitating the maintenance of Russian forces on Georgian soil, either in the form of peacekeeping troops or through the stationing of Russian garrison and naval forces with the agreement of separatist regimes.**

The Georgian government is currently not in full control of Georgian territory, with separatist states continuing to exist in South Ossetia and Abkhazia. A less well-founded separatist attempt in Adjaria has been effectively suppressed, however.

The Ossetians are descendents of a Persian-speaking Central Asia people, who migrated under Mongol pressure from their homeland in the Don region of Russia in the Middle Ages, and came to settle on both sides of the Caucasian mountains.. Today, the Ossetians live in two distinct populations, divided both by the Caucasian mountains and by politics. In 1921 the Soviets established a South Ossetian Autonomous Oblast and, in North Ossetia, an Autonomous Soviet Republic.

With Soviet disintegration in the late 1980s, demands for union between the two Ossetian populations re-surfaced, with the South Ossetian Supreme Soviet voting in November 1989 for union with North Ossetia. The Georgian government immediately repudiated the ruling and abolished South Ossetian autonomy. Following Georgian independence in 1991, South Ossetia declared separate independence, and fighting broke out between Georgian forces and Ossetian separatists. This resulted not only in a major refugee crisis within Georgia itself but also pushed the conflict over the border into North Ossetia and its neighbour, Ingushetia. Ossetian refugees from the south were settled in areas forcibly vacated by the Ingushetians and this led to a brief, but violent, ethnic war between Ossetians and Ingushetians.

Under Russian pressure, Georgia agreed a ceasefire in 1992, which effectively left most of South Ossetia outside of Georgian control. A Russian-dominated peacekeeping force has in practice maintained South Ossetian separation. Geopolitically, Russia has an interest in maintaining forces in the region to prevent transit of opposition forces to Chechnya and also for operations in the Pankisi

Gorge region, which the Russians believe is used as a base for Chechen operations.

The South Ossetian area is highly fragmented ethnically, with Georgian and Ossetian communities living side by side and in practice being ruled by their respective governments. (South Ossetia currently has two governments, the separatist regime in Tskhinvali and the Georgian administration of Shida Kartli, the official Georgian name for the region.) Mixed Ossetian and Russian villages exist throughout the territory, and intermarriage is not uncommon. When, on 12 November 2006, a poll was held (by the Ossetians) which confirmed South Ossetian independence by an overwhelming majority, a parallel poll in Georgian-administered areas produced exactly the opposite result.

Language is a significant area of contention in South Ossetia: both Russian and Ossetian were official languages in Soviet times, but upon independence the Georgian government insisted on Georgian as the language of government. Russian is the official language of the separatist regime in Tskhinvali. The current Georgian government advocates the sole official use of Georgian, an issue that also adversely affects Georgia's Armenian and Azeri minorities, who are under-represented in public life.

The Abkhazians are a Caucasian people whose language is a member of the North Caucasian group, very different to Georgian. Powerful Abkhazian kingdoms emerged from around 700 AD, and the Tsarists did not annex the region until 1864. Although a Soviet republic was briefly recognized after the Bolshevik revolution, Abkhazia was incorporated into Georgia in 1921, with its Union status being downgraded to Autonomous level in 1931. Despite the region's name, the Abkhazians do not represent the majority population, and until 1992 they were significantly outnumbered by Georgians and others. Subsequent Georgian emigration has altered the demography of the region, and the Abkhazians are today estimated to comprise 45% of the population. Although Abkhazians were actively discriminated against under Stalin, later Soviet policy reversed this process, with up to two-thirds of local government and Communist Party positions being assigned to Abkhazians, who therefore formed a pro-Moscow client group. The Abkhazian Supreme Soviet, in 1991, voted in favour of the maintenance of the Soviet Union, and, in 1992 (i.e., after Georgian independence) declared Abkhazia separate from Georgia – effectively a declaration of independence, although some sentiment in Abkhazia continues to favour union with Russia.

Georgia responded militarily to the threat of Abkhazian separatism and a year-long war ensued that ended, despite early Georgian successes, with Georgian expulsion from most of the region. Russian forces were undoubtedly involved in Abkhazian resistance, although their significance is disputed. *De facto* independence of Abkhazia was further reinforced by the establishment, in 1994, of a Russian-led peacekeeping force.

Most of Abkhazia remains outside Georgian control, although Georgia maintains a presence (and a shadow government) in Upper Abkhazia. As in South Ossetia, Russia has a geopolitical interest; a pro-Russian Abkhazia preserves Moscow's regional influence as well as directly applying pressure on Georgia over such issues as control of Georgia's Black Sea ports and oil pipelines running through Georgian territory.

Military considerations have similarly motivated Russian involvement in the south-western Georgian province of Adjaria, which borders NATO member Turkey and was traditionally a major garrison area for the USSR. Turkey only recognized Soviet sovereignty over the area in 1921, on the condition that Adjaria be given autonomy to protect the Turkish/Muslim minority. This suited the Soviets too, since it meant they could limit Georgian influence in the strategically important area. Pro-Moscow separatists seized control over the region in May 1991. The degree to which separatism was a genuinely popular movement is disputed: ethnic distinctions between Adjarians and other Georgians are not considerable, and subsequent events have tended to confirm the view that Adjarian separatism was largely an artificial creation.

Russian influence continued to be a significant factor in Adjaria until 2004, including its use as a vehicle for Russian ambitions in Georgia proper. These included Russian sponsorship of the Georgian opposition party, the Democratic Revival, led by Adjarian leader Aslan Abashidze, which favoured a pro-Russian position in preference to the more independent stance taken by the then Georgian leadership under Eduard Shevardnadze. In 2003, however, Georgia was plunged into the political crisis subsequently christened the 'Rose Revolution' and the election in January 2004 of a 'pro-Western' government committed to a more forceful assertion of Georgian independence from Moscow. One early consequence was a Georgian imposed settlement in Adjaria. In the 'Second Rose Revolution' of May 2004, Aslan Abasjidze was deposed as Adjarian leader in a popular uprising and the region re-incorporated into Georgia.

Tension between Russia and Georgia remains high. In August 2007 Georgian sources accused the Russian air force of dropping bombs inside Georgian territory and in November 2007 declared a state of emergency amid claims that Moscow was planning a coup. Following Kosovan independence, Russia lifted its trade blockade on Abkhazia, and both South Ossetia and Abkhazia made renewed calls for recognition, citing the 'Kosovo example.' (*See Kosovo, 7.22.*) Relations deteriorated further in April/May 2008 when a Russian jet shot down an unmanned Georgian reconnaissance drone over Abkhazia and the Russians deployed additional troops in Abkhazia – actions that the Georgians described and bringing the two countries "close to war". For Russia, manipulation of the South Ossetia and Abkhazia scenarios is emerging as a significant tactic by which Moscow can maintain political and military pressure on Georgia and, by extension, the West.

# Nagorno-Karabakh

**Principal protagonists**

Government of Azerbaijan.

Armenians of Nagorno-Karabakh (Artsakh). Regular Armenia forces also engaged.

**Nature of conflict**

Historical territorial issue. Regional war, 1991-4.

- Muslim/Christian conflict an issue.
- Up to 30,000.
- 238,000 Armenian IDPs. 700,000 Azeri IDPs.

**Population/ethnic composition**

145,000. Armenian 95%.

**Territorial extent**

Nagorno-Karabakh: 4,400 km². (Also Nakhichevan: 5,500 km².)

**Timeline**

1818-28: Transcaucasian region annexed by Russia.

1918-23: Territorial clashes between Armenians and Azeris. Soviet control established in 1923.

1923: Nagorno-Karabakh Autonomous Oblast created.

1936: Separate Armenian, Azeri and Georgian SSRs created.

20 Feb 1988: Armenian deputies in Nagorno-Karabakh vote for union with Armenia.

24 Feb 1988: Clashes between Armenians and Azeris in Nagorno-Karabakh.

23 Aug 1991: Armenia declares independence from USSR.

30 Aug 1991: Azerbaijan declares independence from USSR.

10 Dec 1991: Nagorno-Karabakh declares independence.

1994-present: Ceasefire leaves Nagorno-Karabakh (and surrounding tracts of Azeri land) in Armenian hands.

**Current status**

Unresolved. Nagorno-Karabakh remains *de facto* independent.

At its height under Tigranes the Great in the 1st century BC, Armenia occupied an extensive area covering most of modern Azerbaijan, Armenia, Nakhichevan, and parts of eastern Turkey. In 301 AD, Armenia became the first country in the world to adopt Christianity as its official state religion. In more recent times, Armenia has suffered through being on the natural invasion route between competing neighbours, most recently the Ottoman Turks and the Russians. Historical territorial claims, coupled with a tragic modern history – culminating in the Armenian Genocide of 1915 at the hands of the Turks – have made the modern Armenians highly vulnerable to fears of foreign domination and persecution.

Most of modern Armenia and Azerbaijan were annexed to Tsarist Russia between 1818-28. With the fall of the Tsar in 1917, both Armenians and Azeris attempted to establish independent states. Following the collapse of the short-lived Transcaucasian Democratic Federative Republic that united Armenia, Azerbaijan, and Georgia, Armenian and Azeri forces clashed over the status of the Nagorno-Karabakh region and of the Nakhichevan region between modern Armenia and Iran. By 1920 Armenia was also involved in a disastrous war with Turkey. The intervention of the Red Army was therefore regarded as a liberation (or at least a preferable outcome to Turkish occupation) in many Armenian quarters. Full Soviet control over the region was established by 1923, initially under the auspices of a Transcaucasian Soviet Federative Republic (TSFR) that, like its predecessor, combined Armenia with Azerbaijan and Georgia. Despite local sentiment (including some initial support from Azeri Soviet leaders) for the incorporation of Nagorno-Karabakh and/or Nakhichevan into Soviet Armenia, both districts were assigned to Azerbaijan. Nagorno-Karabakh, with its Armenian majority, became an Autonomous Oblast in 1923. In 1936 the TSFR was dissolved and separate Armenian, Azeri and Georgian Soviet Socialist Republics were created.

As the Soviet Union began to collapse in the late 1980s, Armenians were in the forefront of demanding independence from the USSR, becoming in August 1991, the first Soviet republic after the Baltic states to declare independence. Unfortunately, latent ethnic issues resurfaced at the same time, particularly over Nagorno-Karabakh where the Armenian majority agitated for separation from Azerbaijan and either independence or integration with Armenia. Armenian deputies to the National Council of Nagorno-Karabakh voted for incorporation into Armenia in February 1998 and days later armed clashes broke out in the region. Violence therefore started even before the formal dismemberment of the USSR. In 1989 the Azerbaijan SSR initiated an air and land blockade, which crippled the Armenian economy. Separately, elements in Nachichevan were also agitating for self-rule and closer links with Iran, where border posts were demolished in December 1989. (Nakhichevan became, in January 1990, the first Soviet territory to declare itself independent from the USSR.)

In December 1991 Nagorno-Karabakh voted for full independence and by 1992 Armenian regular and Nagorno-Karabakh forces were in a state of full-scale war with Azeri forces. By the end of 1992, Armenian forces held all of Nagorno-Karabakh and the territory between it and Armenia proper, including the vital Lachin corridor linking the two states. Fighting also spilled into Nakhichevan, which was shelled by Armenian forces in May 1992. Armenia also annexed the tiny Nakhichevan exclave of Karki, which was inside, and completely surrounded by, Armenian territory. The fighting resulted in a massive refugee crisis for both countries, particularly Azerbaijan, which has been reluctant to assimilate refugees for fear that this would represent a tacit acceptance of Armenian territorial gains. The status of the refugees (particularly former residents of Nagorno-Karabakh, who the Karabakh authorities would wish to see excluded from any future vote on the region's future) remains highly problematic.

By the time of a Russian-brokered ceasefire in 1994, Armenian forces were in control of an estimated 17,000 km$^2$ of territory including Nagorno-Karabakh itself, plus a significant portion of Azerbaijan proper. Despite periodic attempts at negotiation, no permanent peaceful solution to the issue is envisaged. Nagorno-Karabakh – known as 'Artsakh' to Armenians – remains independent, although unrecognized internationally. Although Azerbaijan has offered 'maximum autonomy' to Nagorno-Karabakh, this remains unacceptable to the Karabakh authorities, who favour a referendum on the territory's long-term status (which presumably would favour independence). In view of the disproportionate size of the Armenian and Azeri economies, with the latter benefiting from oil and natural gas exploitation, the possibility of a future Azeri leadership attempting a purely military solution remains high. Following Kosovan independence in March 2008, which co-incided with domestic political unrest in Armenia itself, Azerbaijan announced its willingness to resolve the Karabakh situation 'by force', while Yerevan, in return, threatened to recognize Nagorno Karabakh. The first serious clashes for many years between Armenian and Azeri forces left 18 dead. One possibility for resolution is that the Yerevan government, mindful of the economic and geographical weaknesses of Armenia proper, may put pressure on the Nagorno-Karabakh authorities to come to terms. Both Yerevan and Baku, however, remain alert to the possibility of violent domestic opposition to any 'sell out' over the Karabakh issue, and movement in Yerevan would require the marginalization of the 'Karabakh Committee' faction that currently dominates politics in Armenia proper.

**Azeri separatists**

The Lezghin, a Caucasian people, straddle the border between Dagestan (Russia) and Azerbaijan. As with the Ossetians, another people divided by the post-Communist division of the former USSR, there have been calls among the Lezghin for unity between the two communities. The Lezghin number some 189,000 in Dagestan, 158,000 in Azerbaijan, and a smaller community in Armenia. A Lezghin independence movement "Sadval" was established in Dagestan in 1990 and in 1991 it called for the establishment of an "independent Lezghistan" unifying Lezghins on both sides of the border. The organization was accused of terrorist acts, including an attack on the Baku metro, sabotage of economic installations, and participation in hostage-taking in Dagestan. In 1996 the Russian and Azeri authorities co-operated in the suppression of the Sadval movement. The remaining Lezghin activists have promoted peaceful autonomy since that date, although latent sentiments for unity and independence doubtless still exist.

In 1993, in a separate case, a short lived attempt was made to establish a Talysh-Mughan Autonomous Republic, in the extreme south-east of Azerbaijan, along the border with Iran. As with the Lezghins and other minorities, the Talysh claimed their culture was being undermined by integration into the Azeri state. Talysh nationalists, aided by local military elements (and with the tacit support of Russia) seized control of southern districts in June 1993. The insurgency was suppressed by August 1993, although autonomist sentiments continue.

*See the main text for discussion of the Nakhichevan exclave.*

# Transnistria

**Principal protagonists**

Transnistrian Moldovan Republic.

Republic of Moldova.

Russian forces, including peacekeepers.

Republic of Gagauzia (1990-4).

**Nature of conflict**

Linguistic and self-determination dispute.

☠ c500.
👥 100,000

**Population/ethnic composition**

Transnistria: 555,347 (2004).
Moldovan 31.9%, Russian 30.4%, Ukrainian 28.8%.

**Territorial extent**

Transnistria: 4,163 km².

**Timeline**

1812: Moldova annexed to Russia.

7 Feb 1918: Moldovan Republic proclaimed; subsequently joins Romania.

12 Oct 1924: Moldovan Autonomous Soviet Republic created.

28 Jun 1940: Bessarabia occupied by Soviet Union.

2 Aug 1940: Moldovan Soviet Socialist Republic proclaimed.

2 Sep 1990: Transnistrian Moldovan Republic declared.

2 Nov 1990: Clashes between Transnistrian and Moldovan forces.

27 Aug 1991: Moldova declares independence from the USSR.

1992: Fighting escalates between Transnistria and Moldova.

29 Jul 1992: CIS peacekeepers deployed.

**Current status**

Unresolved. Transnistria remains independent.

**As part of the ancient principality of Moldova, which also included parts of Romania, modern-day Moldova was under Ottoman rule until it was ceded, as Bessarabia, to the Russians in 1812. Following the Bolshevik revolution, an independent Moldovan Republic was proclaimed which in 1919 voted to join Romania.**

The Soviets never recognized the incorporation of Bessarabia into Romania and, the better to press their claim to sovereignty, carved a 'Moldovan Autonomous Soviet Republic' out of a strip of Ukrainian territory on the left bank of the Dniestr river in 1924.

Under the terms of the Molotov-Ribbentrop pact of 1940, Bessarabia was occupied by Soviet forces on 28 June 1940. Both Bessarabia and the Moldovan Autonomous Soviet Republic were then combined to form the new Moldovan Soviet Socialist Republic. Romania regained the territory during its participation in the German invasion of the USSR in 1941, but lost it again in 1944. In 1947, the Romanians were formally obliged to recognize the annexation of Bessarabia by the USSR.

In an attempt to distance the Republic from Romania, the Moldovan SSR experienced rapid and systematic 'Russification' in the years after the Second World War, and this policy included the replacement of Latin with Cyrillic script in the locally used Romanian language to create 'Moldovan.' With the disintegration of the USSR in the 1980s, a Popular Front emerged to challenge this tendency and, as a secondary goal, to seek re-unification with Romania. The Front became the dominant political force in parliamentary election in March 1990, but lost out in subsequent polls. During its time of prominence, however, the Popular Front was able to replace Moldova's Soviet-era flag with a new flag based on the Romanian colours, and to lead Moldova to independence, which was declared on 27 August 1991.

Minority groups, such as those in Transnistria and Gagauzia, were alarmed at these trends, in which they saw the prelude to absorption into Romania. The language law of 31 August 1989, making Latin-scripted Romanian an official language, was welcomed by huge demonstrations in Chisinau, but was opposed in counter-demonstrations in other parts of the country.

On 19 August 1990 (i.e., even before Moldovan independence) a Republic of Gagauzia was declared in the south, followed by the declaration, on 2 September 1990, of the Transnistrian Moldovan Republic, the latter having its capital in Tiraspol. Clashes broke out in November between Transnistrian and Moldovan authorities, and the welcoming by Tiraspol of the short-lived Soviet counter-coup in Moscow in August 1991 further soured relations. By March 1992, the security situation had deteriorated to the degree that a state of emergency was declared throughout Moldova. The fighting culminated in June 1992 when Transnistrian forces unsuccessfully attempted to seize the right bank city of Bendery. Following discussions between Commonwealth of Independent States (CIS) leaders in Moscow, a peace plan was evolved which lead to a ceasefire and the deployment of CIS peacekeeping forces in July 1992. This has effectively frozen the conflict, although sporadic clashes have taken place since.

On 9 September 1992, the Transnistrian authorities overturned Moldova's language legislation and re-instated Cyrillic for all uses, including educational purposes. In addition to Romanian speakers, Transnistria has a significant population of Slavic Russians and Ukrainians, who use Cyrillic/Russian as their main language.

Russian involvement in Transnistria has been ambiguous. Russian military forces were accused by the Moldovan authorities of aiding the separatists in 1991-2 and there is clear evidence that local Russian forces provided training, logistics and recruitment support to the creation of the Transnistra Republican Guard. On the other hand, Russia brokered the 1992 ceasefire and has largely been responsible for its enforcement. (Moldovans, of course, argue that this simply maintains the effective *status quo* of Transnistrian independence.) On the international stage, Moldova has accused Transnistria of being a 'rogue state', including accusation that Tirapol supplied weapons to Saddam Hussein's Iraq – although it is not entirely clear why, or how, Transnistria would have achieved this.

Although the Transnistrian dispute has a clear ethnic element, with language being the key distinguisher, it should be noted that the fighting of 1991-2 did not spread to other parts of Moldova, where three quarters of Moldova's Slavic population resides. Equally, ethnic Moldovans are represented in the Transnistrian government. Ideological differences, with the Transnistrian regime broadly favouring the old Soviet-style structures, and a general resistance to being governed from the centre, are factors in bolstering Transnistrian nationalism. The relative economic prosperity of Transnistria (35% of the GDP is produced in the region, despite it only having 17% of the population) is an additional factor in encouraging Transnistrians to think of themselves as a separate nationality rather than as 'Bessarabians'.

Resolution of the Gagauzia issue came in 1994 with the drafting of a law on special status for mainly Gagauzia regions. Part of the agreement included contingency for the Gagauzians to have a referendum on independence should Moldova opt to merge with another country (meaning Romania). Local language rights were also protected. The Gagauzia solution has been promoted as a possible template for resolution of the Transnistria issue, but thus far without significant progress being made.

In March 1994 Moldova held a referendum which voted overwhelmingly against seeking re-unification with Romania. The Moldovan government, previously committed to a unitary state, has also since conceded the principle of significant autonomy for Transnistria. While the effective disappearance of re-unification from the political agenda has removed one of the key fears of Transnistria, Tiraspol nevertheless remains committed to maintaining full independence, although it would compromise on a 'Moldovan Confederation' in which Transnistria and 'Bessarabia' would be equal parts.

# Tatarstan

**Principal protagonists**

Republic of Tatarstan.

Russian central government.

**Nature of conflict**

Self-determination and the relationship between central and regional government.

🟆 Significant reserves of natural gas, oil and gypsum.

**Population/ethnic composition**

3.8m. Tatars 52.9%, Russians 39.5%, Chuvash 3.4%.

**Territorial extent**

Republic of Tatarstan: 67,836 km².

**Timeline**

1236: Volga Bulgaria (precursor to Tatarstan) becomes part of Mongol Empire.
1550-52: Tatarstan annexed to Russian Tsarist empire.
27 May 1920: Tatarstan Autonomous Soviet Socialist Republic established.
30 Aug 1990: Tatarstan 'state sovereignty' declared.
12 Mar 1992: Referendum confirms majority support for independence.
15 Feb 1994: Treaty signed between Russia and Tatarstan.
2000: Amended Tatarstan constitution introduced.

**Current status**

Largely resolved through inter-governmental treaties.

Tatarstan is located in the centre of the great East European plain, around 800 km east of Moscow. Rich in natural resources, Tatarstan warrants inclusion in this volume largely because it has not, despite having many of the characteristics that lead to ethnic conflict, descended into inter-communal or inter-state violence. This is all the more remarkable when one considers the country's history and recent past, with both sides regarding the other as historical invaders and aggressors.

In the 13th century the Volga Bulgars, the ancestors of the Tatars, were invaded and conquered by the Mongol Golden Horde. The Mongols settled the region and incorporated many Tatars into their army. Accordingly, when the Mongols invaded Russia, which they largely occupied for 250 years from 1240, the Russians perceived their persecutors as being 'Tatars'.

Following the retreat of the Mongols and the re-assertion of Russian power, Tatarstan was annexed to Russia by the troops of Ivan the Terrible in the early 1550s. Harsh repression of the Islamic religion was only eased in the 1770s. In the 19th century Tatarstan became a centre of the Jadidist Islamic sect, which preached tolerance of other religions. Jadidist influence continues to inform Tatarstan's generally moderate interpretation of Islam. Following the Bolshevik revolution, attempts were made to establish an independent Idel-Ural State. This was suppressed by the Red Army and instead a Tatar Autonomous Soviet Socialist Republic was established on 27 May 1920.

The Soviet Union recognized a hierarchy of states, headed by Soviet Socialist Republics (such as Armenia, Ukraine, and Kazakhstan), followed by Autonomous Soviet Socialist Republics (ASSRs) of which Chechnya and Tatarstan were examples, and other constitutionally lesser regions. Whether a region became an SSR or an ASSR was always something of a lottery, and was motivated primarily by the geopolitical needs of the day and the political reliability, or otherwise, of the regional ethnic groups. In the modern era, however, the distinction became crucial as the SSRs advanced towards recognized independence upon the collapse of the Soviet Union whereas the ASSRs did not.

With their long history of independence in mind, Tatarstan opened negotiations in 1990 with the Soviet government aimed at achieving full Union republic status. Under the Soviet constitution, SSRs were theoretically permitted to secede from the USSR. This constitutional fiction became a reality with the collapse of Soviet power in the early 1990s, and had Tatarstan achieved Union status, it is likely that it would, as with the other Soviet republics, have achieved internationally recognized independence. As it was, Soviet authority disintegrated before negotiations could reach a conclusion. On 30 August 1990 Tatarstan declared itself a 'sovereign state' and no longer part either of the USSR or Russia. Significantly, however, the declaration fell short of declaring 'independence.'

The precipitous collapse of the USSR in 1991 left the new Russian government of Boris Yeltsin with no clear policy regarding the relationship between Moscow and the constituent parts of the new Russian republic. Boris Yeltsin's attitude towards regional autonomy was ambiguous. During the period of his struggle with Mikhail Gorbachev and the decaying Communist regime, Yeltsin visited Tatarstan (amongst other regions) and urged them to "take as much sovereignty as you can swallow." He was supportive, if only for tactical reasons, of the dissolution of the USSR through Union states gaining independence, but the secession of Russian autonomous regions – which threatened the future geographical integrity of Russia proper – proved to be a different matter for the Moscow leadership.

In April 1993, Yeltsin won a popular referendum (against the opposition of the Russian Parliament) for his economic reform programme. In July 1993, the Constitutional Conference that Yeltsin established, again in defiance of the Russian parliament, allowed the constituent republics of

**Republics of the Russian Federation**

the putative Russian Federation the right to adopt their own constitutions, flags, anthems and other trappings of sovereignty. However, the reaction to this liberal policy, from a number of republics, was renewed attempts to proclaim full independence. Nevertheless, the Constitutional Conference overwhelmingly adopted a new constitution for the federation. This in turn led to the constitutional confrontation of September/October 1993 which lead to the storming of the Russian Parliament by troops loyal to Boris Yeltsin and the effective imposition of the new constitution by force.

Meanwhile, from 1990-4, Tatarstan was to all practical purposes an independent state; one which, moreover, entered into treaty obligations as between equals with Moscow. In March 1992 Tatarstan became, with Chechnya, one of two Russian republics to refuse to sign the Uniform Federal Treaty defining the relationship between Moscow and the republics.

On 15 February 1994 a carefully worded agreement was signed between Kazan and Moscow. Entitled 'The Treaty on Delimitation of Jurisdictional Subjects and Mutual Delegation of Authority between the State Bodies of the Russian Federation and the State Bodies of the Republic of Tatarstan', the treaty used deliberately ambiguous language with respect to issues relating to sovereignty. From 1994 Tatarstan became, by its own lights at least, a state 'voluntarily associated with Russia on a confederal basis'. The Tatarstan constitution of 2000 further codified the position between Tatarstan and Russia. It described Tatarstan as a state 'associated' with the Russian Federation while at the same time allowing Moscow to claim that Tatarstan was a constituent republic of the Federation.

Although the 'acid test' of sovereignty – internationally recognized independence leading to a seat at the United Nations – has not been achieved in the case of Tatarstan, the country does nevertheless enjoy many of the trappings of independence, including, crucially, full autonomy in the exploitation of natural resources. (Tatarstan has an estimated billion tons of oil.) Kazan is also, unusually, enabled to conclude international treaties with foreign governments. Although these are limited to the economic sphere, the ability to make international treaties is a characteristic more generally associated with fully independent states.

A number of explanations may be advanced as to why Tatarstan escaped the violence which has disfigured other ethnic disputes, not least in the former USSR itself. Tatarstan's relatively strong economic infrastructure, its multi-party system, strong legal base, and effective civic society, are all contributor factors. A comparatively moderate government, realistic in its aspirations, is also significant, as is the absence of Islamic extremism. From the Russian perspective, avoiding outright Tatarstan secession (which might precipitate a domino effect of confrontations with a string of far-eastern regions) was the crucial issue. The calculation was probably that it was better to have a widely autonomous Tatarstan at least nominally within the Russian space than run the risk of formal Tatarstan secession encouraging other breakaway regions. Equally, Tatarstan's remoteness and lack of geopolitical dimension (when compared to, for example, Chechnya) may have led Moscow to believe that a quasi-independent Tatarstan was less of a threat to the overall integrity of the Russian federation.

Further revisions to the Tatarstan constitution in 2002 and a further inter-state agreement in October 2006 have been criticised as eroding Tatarstan state sovereignty. The insistence within the institutions of the Russian Federation that Cyrillic must be the only official script is a source of considerable discontent within Tatarstan. Notwithstanding these problems, The 'Model of Tatarstan' stands as an example of how complex disputes can be resolved or at least mitigated, and is held up – not least by the Tatarstan government itself – as a template for the relationship between central governments and regional states seeking autonomy.

# Chechnya

**Principal protagonists**

Chechen separatists; Chechen Republic of Ichkeria.

Russian authorities; Republic of Chechnya authorities.

**Nature of conflict**
1994-6: Secessionist war between independent Chechen state and Russia.
1999-present: War between separatist forces and Russian forces/Russian sponsored local government.

- Reprisals against civilians by both sides regularly reported.
- Islamism an issue, particularly in internationalization of conflict.
- Up to 100,000.
- Up to 260,000; numbers vary with intensity of fighting.

**Population/ethnic composition**
c1 million. Chechens 93.5%, Russians 3.7%. Most Chechens are Sunni Muslims.

**Territorial extent**
Chechnya: 15,300 km². Conflict overspill into neighbouring republics. (See Dagestan 7.24.)

**Timeline**
12 Oct 1813: Chechnya nominally ceded to Russia by Persia. Not effectively incorporated into Russia until 1859.
5 Dec 1936: Chechen-Ingush ASSR established.
1 Nov 1991: Independence of Chechen Republic of Ichkeria proclaimed.
11 Dec 1994-31 Aug 1996: First Chechen war.
7 Aug-14 Sep 1999: Incursions into Dagestan.
30 Sep 1999: Second Chechen war: Russia begins re-occupation.
6 Feb 2000: Grozny occupied.
2 Apr 2003: Republic of Chechnya re-constituted as a republic within the Russian Federation.

**Current status**
Fighting with separatist forces continues.

Inhabiting the central part of the volatile north Caucasus region, the Chechens have a long history of active resistance to outside rule. The term 'Chechen' is in fact a Russian designation – the Chechen people refer to themselves as 'Nokhchii'. The country's mountainous geography and the clan-based structure of Chechen society has made them difficult to conquer and, because traditionally there is no overall leader, it has also been difficult for invaders to co-opt elite groups.

Incorporated into Tsarist Russia in 1859, Chechnya saw uprisings in the 1870s, 1920s and in the 1940s – the latter resulting in the wholesale deportation of the population for allegedly collaborating with the Nazis. In the post-Soviet era, Chechnya has been the scene of two full-scale wars and continuing violence.

The surviving exiles from the 1944 deportations were allowed to return to the Chechen-Ingush Autonomous Soviet Socialist Republic (ASSR) in the late 1950s, but a policy of Russification, including the use of Cyrillic script, continued throughout the Soviet era. Furthermore, as an ASSR, the Chechen-Ingush republic did not have the constitutional right of secession enjoyed by full Union SSRs like Georgia or Azerbaijan. This was to have crucial consequences when the USSR broke up in the early 1990s. As the Soviet Union disintegrated, the individual Union republics gained international recognition as independent states, but not one of the numerous former ASSRs achieved recognized sovereignty despite, in some cases, representing national minorities at least as historically distinctive as those of the SSRs.

In Chechnya, as elsewhere, local nationalists started agitating either for full recognition within the USSR and for a formal separation from Russia. Claims to the legitimacy of Chechen independence stem from an ordnance by Mikhail Gorbachev on 26 April 1990 making ASSRs full subjects of the USSR, including – according to nationalists – having the right to secede. Separatists also point to Boris Yeltsin's urging of the republics to "take as much sovereignty as you can stomach" (See Tatarstan, 7.20), while pointing out also the basic historical injustice of other small nations, such as Armenia and Estonia, being allowed to achieve an independence denied to others largely through accidents of Soviet politics and constitutional history.

In October 1990 Dzhokhar Dudaev won a landslide election in Chechnya on a nationalist platform and declared the independence of the Chechen Republic of Ichkeria a year later following the final breakdown of the Soviet Union. The next day, however, Moscow declared this announcement unlawful and a week later Russian special forces moved into the territory in an unsuccessful attempt to arrest the government. At this point the former Chechen-Ingush ASSR formally split, with Ingushetia opting to remain a constituent part of the Russian federation.

Russian concerns centred on Chechnya's strategic significance to the country's oil industry and also that Chechen independence would set a precedent for other restive regions, such as Tatarstan. These prompted Moscow to seek a wholesale military solution to the problem in 1994 which was, however, unsuccessful. After two years of fierce fighting, Moscow was obliged to sign a ceasefire that left Chechen independence intact but unrecognized. The overall effect on the Chechen economy was devastating, with an estimated 80% of its economic infrastructure destroyed and a mass exodus (or expulsion) taking place of non-Chechen minorities, mostly Russians.

A May 1997 peace treaty was followed by the election of Aslan Maskhadov, who steered Chechnya towards a more radical Islamic policy, for example introducing elements of *sharia* law. Relations with Moscow gradually deteriorated, with the final trigger for renewed conflict being Chechen involvement in a failed Islamic insurgency in August 1999 in neighbouring Dagestan. *(See 7.24.)* This sparked the second Chechen war. On this occasion, the Russian forces were better prepared and were able to occupy most of the country, capturing Grozny in February 2000 and installing a pro-Moscow government. In October 2003 Akhmad Kadyrov, a former rebel, was elected President of the Moscow-leaning government of the re-constituted Chechen republic. Maskhadov and other separatists for the most part fled into the mountains, where they started a guerrilla war that continues to the present day.

Personalities play a key role in Chechen politics and it is not surprising that both sides have resorted to political assassinations. Kadyrov, regarded as a traitor by hard-line nationalists, was assassinated in May 2004. Maskhadov was killed by Russian forces in March 2005, to be replaced as President of the now nebulous Chechen Republic of Ichkeria by Abdul Khalim Saidullayev, who was himself killed by loyalist Chechen special forces in June 2006. In February 2007 Kadyrov's son, Ramzan, another former rebel, was appointed President of the Chechen Republic despite (or because of) an unsavoury human rights record.

Throughout the Chechen conflict, and particularly in the post-9/11 environment, Moscow has sought to portray Chechen separatists as extreme 'Wahabbi' Islamists. Some credence has been given to this view by the appearance of Chechen fighters in Islamist '*jihadist*' conflicts as far apart as Bosnia, Afghanistan and Iraq. Chechnya has also been highlighted as a key Islamist grievance in broadcasts by Al Qaeda and its associates. In January 2000 the Taliban regime in Afghanistan recognized Chechen independence and established a short-lived diplomatic presence in Grozny. The degree of Islamist penetration of Chechen society itself is debateable, however. Chechen Islam is heavily influenced by a Sufi mysticism that, with its veneration of saints and icons, is regarded as highly suspect by fundamentalists. The acephalous nature of Chechen society means that the widespread infiltration of society by any one group or faction is likely to be limited.

From 2002 onwards, the conflict entered a new stage, with the overwhelming Russian presence in Chechnya effectively obliging insurgents to seek softer targets outside Chechen borders. In addition to 'mainstream' insurgencies, a number of high profile acts of terrorism were carried out, including bombings in Moscow, the Moscow theatre siege of 23 October 2002, and the September 2004 occupation of the Beslan Secondary School No.1 in North Ossetia. In both these latter two incidents, Russian special forces bungled their assaults resulting in widespread casualties among the hostages, including the 186 children killed at Beslan. In 2004 and again in 2005, fighting also spilled over into the increasing unstable republic of Kabardino-Balkaria, with clashes in the capital, Nalchik, between Islamists and local security forces. Hostage taking and suicide bombings continue to be a regular occurrence in Dagestan and Ingushetia, as well as in Chechnya itself where an insurgency looks set to continue for the foreseeable future.

# Dagestan

**Principal protagonists**

Russian authorities; Dagestan authorities.

Dagestan Islamists; Shariat Jamaat movement; 'Shura of Dagestan'; Chechen insurgents.

**Nature of conflict**

Chechen insurgency exacerbating local religious/nationalist issues. Localized Islamist terrorism.

- Islamism a key issue.
- c700.
- c4,000 at peak in 1999.

**Population/ethnic composition**

2.5m. Avars 29.4%, Dargins 16.5%, Lezghins 13.1%, Russians 5%. 90% of the population is Sunni Muslim.

**Territorial extent**

Republic of Dagestan: 50,300 km².

**Timeline**

24 Oct 1803: Region becomes Russian province. Resistance to Russian rule continues until 1877.

11 May 1918: Mountainous Republic of the Northern Caucasus established. Occupied by USSR 1920.

31 Mar 1992: Republic of Dagestan established as a part of the Russian Federation.

7 Aug 1999: Insurgency by Chechen Islamists in support of local Islamic 'Shura of Dagestan', which declares Dagestan an independent Islamic state.

14 Sep 1999: Chechen-led insurgency suppressed.

**Current status**

Ongoing low-level insurgency.

See page 7.22 for map of Dagestan.

**Dagestan, the largest of the north Caucasian republics, is home to over 30 mostly clan-based hill peoples who are principally Sunni Muslims. Unusually for a Russian republic, the name 'Dagestan' (which means 'Land of the Mountains') does not refer to a specific ethnic group.**

The Dagestanis adopted Islam under Arab influence from the 7th century onwards. From the 13th century, central Dagestan came under the Avar Khanate, which maintained a degree of independence until the 19th century. In common with other Caucasian peoples, the Dagestani tribes were fiercely resistant to outside governance. Dagestan came, at least nominally, under a number of rulers until Russia gained the territory from Persia following the Treaty of Gulistan that ended the First Russo-Persian War in 1818. Resistance to Russian rule continued until 1859 and flared again in 1877 when Russian forces were engaged in the Crimean War. In 1918, after the collapse of Tsarist rule, a Mountainous Republic of the Northern Caucasus was established embracing Dagestan, Chechnya, Ingushestia and North Ossetia. The Republic was suppressed by the Soviets in 1920 and Dagestan became an Autonomous Soviet Socialist Republic in 1921.

Unlike its Chechen neighbour, Dagestan did not seek full independence upon the break up of the USSR and signed the 1992 Uniform Federal Treaty, making it a constituent part of the new Russian federation. In Chechnya a full-scale secessionist war broke out in 1994 which was ended, in 1996, on terms favourable to the Chechens. (See 7.22.)

In 1998 a group of militants calling themselves the Russian Union of Muslims stormed a government building in the Dagestani capital, Makhachkala, and briefly announced the creation of an Islamic state before being overpowered by the local authorities. Despite this incident, Dagestan remained relatively quiescent until August 1999 when up to 2,000 Chechen-based militants seized a number of villages in the Botlikh border region between Dagestan and Chechnya. In the name of the 'Islamic Shura of Dagestan' they proclaimed the formation of an Islamic Dagestani state.

Russia called the insurgency an 'invasion' claiming that it was entirely the creation of Chechen Islamic expansionists who had no significant support in Dagestan. Weight appears to be given to this view by the fact that the prominent leaders of the *Shura* (council) were known Chechen warlords. Leader of the insurgency was Shamyl Basayev, who had been Prime Minister of the independent Chechnya for a six months in 1998 and who had subsequently been involved in a number of other high-profile attacks in Russia, including the Budennovsk hospital crisis in 1995 in which 1,000 were held hostage. Basayev was later to be responsible for the 2004 Beslan school siege, before being killed by Russian special forces in 2006.

Whatever the underlying nature of the incursion, it rapidly became clear that the insurgents had overplayed their hand. Responding with air power, including bombing raids both by fixed wing aircraft and helicopter gunships, Russia rapidly regained the initiative and the incursion gave the Russians the perfect pretext for resuming the conflict in Chechnya, which resulted in the establishment of a pliant pro-Moscow regime in Grozny.

Electoral reforms in 2006 sought to end ethnically predicated polling districts in Dagestan, but acts of sabotage and terrorism continue to plague both Dagestan and Ingushestia. Bombings, assassinations and gun battles between Islamic militants and members of the Russian security forces, including in Makhachkala, are regularly reported, as are armed attacks on transport and government installations.

# The Balkans

**Principal protagonists**

Primarily Serbian forces supporting continued Yugoslav/Serb regional hegemony.

Nationalist movements in former Yugoslav republics.

**Nature of conflict**

Self-determination by national groups opposed by Yugoslav/Serb hegemonists.

⚑ Human rights abuses by official and paramilitary forces on all sides.
☦ Catholic/Orthodox and Christian/Muslim conflicts are issues.
☠ c200,000.
👥 c2 million; numbers varying at different stages in the conflicts.

**Population/ethnic composition**

Yugoslavia: 22.4m in 1981. Serbs 36.3%, Croats 19.7%, Muslims 8.9%, Slovenes 7.8%, Albanians 7.7%, Macedonians 6.0%, Yugoslavs 5.4%, Montenegrins 2.6%, Magyars 1.9%. (See graph on following page for ethnic composition of individual republics.)

**Territorial extent**

Former Yugoslav total: 250,790 km².

**Timeline**

1 Dec 1918: Kingdom of Yugoslavia proclaimed.
Apr 1941: Occupied by Germany.
29 Nov 1943: Socialist 'second Yugoslavia' proclaimed.
4 May 1980: Death of Tito.
Early 1990s: Collapse of Yugoslavia. (See individual country sections for details.)
27 Apr 1992: Federation of Yugoslavia, comprising Serbia and Montenegro, created.
24 Mar 1999: Start of NATO attack on Kosovo/Yugoslavia.
3 June 2006: Montenegro votes for independence. Final dissolution of Yugoslavia.
17 Feb 2008: Kosovo declares independence.

**Current status**

See text and individual country sections.

From the outset, the state of Yugoslavia was always entirely a political creation which never arose out of any shared nationalism or common interest among its peoples. The first Yugoslavia, from 1918 to 1941 was reluctantly supported by Croats and Slovenes as a bulwark against possible Italian or Hungarian aggression and failed to withstand the stresses placed upon it by the Second World War. The second Yugoslavia, founded after the war, was held together largely by the Communist ideology of its founders and the force of character and purpose of its leader, Josip Broz Tito. Under his rule, Yugoslavia was divided into six republics, Serbia, Bosnia & Herzegovina, Croatia, Slovenia, Macedonia and Montenegro, as well as two autonomous regions, Kosovo and Vojvodina.

Although ethnicity, in line with Marxist ideology, was officially declared a non-issue in Tito's Yugoslavia, censuses dutifully recorded the ethnic make-up of the country, while the republics themselves (not least in their names) remained potential nationalist vehicles in the making. Unsurprisingly, ethnic consciousness remained strong throughout the region, with only a small minority, usually from the deracinated urban classes, identifying themselves as 'Yugoslav' in census returns.

Following Tito's death in 1980 an unwieldy rotating presidential system was put in place that sought to balance regional ethnic differences in the face of gradual economic collapse. In its early days, Communist Yugoslavia's experiment in independent socialism bore favourable comparison with conditions in the Soviet-dominated Eastern European bloc. However, as the 1980s progressed, the underlying economic weaknesses in the socialist model became ever more apparent, particularly in comparison with standards

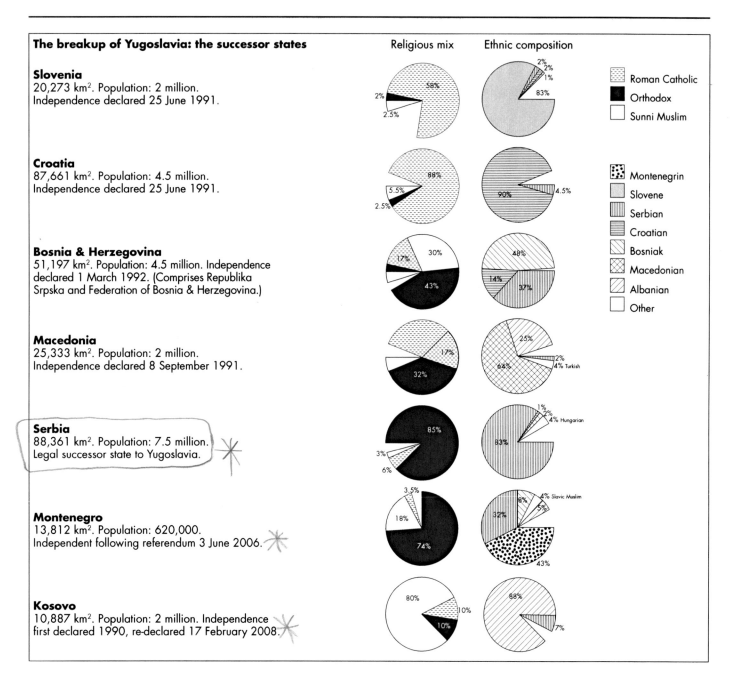

**The breakup of Yugoslavia: the successor states**

**Slovenia**
20,273 km². Population: 2 million.
Independence declared 25 June 1991.

**Croatia**
87,661 km². Population: 4.5 million.
Independence declared 25 June 1991.

**Bosnia & Herzegovina**
51,197 km². Population: 4.5 million. Independence declared 1 March 1992. (Comprises Republika Srpska and Federation of Bosnia & Herzegovina.)

**Macedonia**
25,333 km². Population: 2 million.
Independence declared 8 September 1991.

**Serbia**
88,361 km². Population: 7.5 million.
Legal successor state to Yugoslavia.

**Montenegro**
13,812 km². Population: 620,000.
Independent following referendum 3 June 2006.

**Kosovo**
10,887 km². Population: 2 million. Independence first declared 1990, re-declared 17 February 2008.

of living in Western Europe. Against this background, traditional ethnic rivalries – centring on the economic, military and political status of the Serb majority vis-à-vis other groups, rapidly gathered momentum.

The key year in the disintegration of Yugoslavia is 1988, when Slobodan Milošević first rose to prominence on the back of an openly xenophobic Serbian political agenda. One of Milošević's early demands was that the provinces of Kosovo and Vojvodina lose their autonomy and be fully incorporated into Serbia. On 20 October 1988, the Politburo of the Yugoslav Communist Party voted down Milošević's proposals in favour of a continuance of the looser arrangements inherited from Tito. This Milošević would not accept and, in November, following a series of mass demonstrations, he engineered the resignation of the Party leaders in Kosovo. In January 1989 he turned his attention to Montenegro and on the 11th, again using mass Serb demonstrations as his instrument, he forced the resignation of the entire Montenegrin government and its replacement with Milošević appointees. Milošević now, in effect, controlled all of Serbia and Montenegro. The battleline between the more economically advanced, liberal and westernized republics of Slovenia and Croatia, and the Serbian bloc was now established.

Against this deteriorating political situation, the economic collapse of Yugoslavia continued, with inflation hitting 250%, forcing the resignation of the federal government at the end of 1988. The new government, headed by Ante Markovic, attempted economic reform, but in the face of intransigence by the Serbian/Communist bloc this was impossible and in 1989 Serbia initiated an economic blockade of Slovenia.

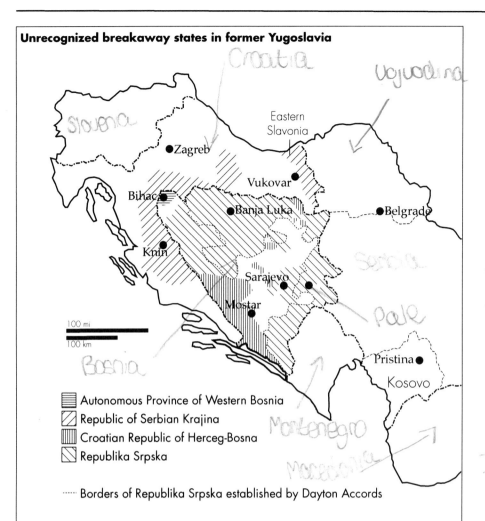

**Unrecognized breakaway states in former Yugoslavia**

- ▤ Autonomous Province of Western Bosnia
- ▨ Republic of Serbian Krajina
- ▦ Croatian Republic of Herceg-Bosna
- ▧ Republika Srpska

····· Borders of Republika Srpska established by Dayton Accords

### Autonomous Province of Western Bosnia

Bosnian Muslim enclave proclaimed in 1993 by local businessman Fikret Abdic. Later aligned to Serbian Krajina. Absorbed into Bosnia & Herzegovina after Croatian occupation of Krajina in August 1995.

### Republic of Serbian Krajina

Independence declared 19 December 1991. Attempted union with Republika Srpska in 1995 but was occupied by Croatia on 7 August 1995. (East Slavonia incorporated into Croatia 15 January 1998.)

### Croatian Republic of Herceg-Bosna

Independence declared 28 August 1993. Joined Federation of Bosnia & Herzegovina 31 May 1994 and officially dissolved 17 December 1996, although continued to function *de facto* for some years afterwards.

### Republika Srpska

Declared independence 7 April 1992 and at one stage occupied over 70% of Bosnia. Since 1996 one of the two official 'entities' comprising Bosnia & Herzegovina.

### Kosovo

Unoffical Kosovan parliament declared independence 2 July 1990. After the NATO/Yugoslav war of 1999 Kosovo was placed under international administration. *(See Kosovo, 7.32.)*

In December 1989, the Communist Parties in both Croatia and Slovenia voted to hold free elections the next year, abandoning the Communist Party's 'leading role' in society. On 20 January 1990, a national Communist Party convention broke up in disarray, when the Slovene delegation walked out. The Slovenes, and their Croatian, Macedonian and Bosnian allies, had demanded basic constitutional guarantees, such as freedom of speech and free elections. They had been defeated, however, by the Serb/Montenegrin block vote. Most commentators believe the break-up of Yugoslavia was, from this point on, inevitable. The resulting territorial wars were framed in ethnic terms rather than on regional, ideological or class bases.

In April and May 1990 non-Communist governments were elected in Slovenia and Croatia respectively. Both republics affirmed their 'sovereignty'. Slovenia and Croatia formally declared independence on 25 June 1991. The Serb response was war. Within days of Slovenia's independence, the Slovene capital, Lubjanja, came under air attack from the Yugoslav Air Force, the first European capital to be bombed from the air since 1945. Yugoslav military activity was largely confined to air activity because of two factors: Croatia denied Yugoslav National Army (JNA) forces passage across its territory and secondly the "mother's revolt" saw many parents collecting their conscript sons from Slovenia and taking them home. It should be borne in mind that Slovenia had no appreciable Serb population, so little justification can be offered for the Yugoslav action, other than a desire to hold together the collapsing Federation.

With Slovenia lost, the Krajina region in Croatia emerged as pivotal in the thinking of the JNA and its political allies in Belgrade. Krajina, which means 'borderland', had always been the transitional area between what is now Croatia and Bosnia, and had been settled by Serbs in antiquity as a bulwark against Austro-Hungarian expansionism. The Serbian settlement was centred on the historic town of Knin, which now found itself in Croatia. In December 1991, Serbs in Krajina declared independence from Croatia, becoming the first of a series of ethnically-based microstates in former Yugoslavia to seek either independence and/or a redrawing of the Yugoslav republics' pre-war borders.

Krajina's geographical position meant that, in 1991, it was central to any aspiration held by the JNA/Serbs of preserving Yugoslavia in anything approaching its pre-1990 borders. Because of Croatia's odd 'U' shaped geography (with Krajina at the base of the 'U') control of an expanded Krajina was used to cut Croatia in two, crucially denying Zagreb access to the vital Dalmatian coastal region. Secondly, Krajina was the logical jumping off point for any assault against Zagreb – the aim being to install a pliant regime in the Croatian capital. Lastly, and most ambitiously, were Yugoslavia to have any chance of regaining Slovenia this could only be done once Croatia had been neutralized.

The JNA offensive against Croatia, ostensibly carried out at the behest of the oppressed Serbs of Krajina was, in reality, informed by these military and political objectives. Croats were ruthlessly expelled from the expanding 'Krajina' and a new term *etničko čišćenje* – 'ethnic cleansing' was coined by the Serbs themselves to describe the process. *(See 7.29.)* Eventually, a two-pronged assault on Zagreb developed, which was halted by the Croatian forces outside the provincial towns of Karlovacs and Sisak, both about 35km from Zagreb. Meanwhile, Serbia opened a second front against Eastern Slavonia, where Croatia directly borders Serbia. This too was halted, at the town of Vukovar, which saw the fiercest and most protracted ground fighting in Europe since 1945. Although Vukovar eventually fell, the JNA offensive was effectively exhausted. The Serb atrocities which followed the fall of the town, including the murder of wounded of all nationalities in the hospital at Vukovar, are well documented.

Thirdly, the JNA and the Yugoslav Navy took the opportunity to systematically bombard the historic and virtually undefended city of Dubrovnik, which had neither an appreciable Serb population nor any strategic significance. Although this had the effect of crippling the Croatian tourist industry, this backfired on Serbia in propaganda terms, as it brought home to the world the aggressive nature of Serb intentions. Nevertheless, official Western policy appeared to be largely informed by the simplistic notion that Yugoslavia's problems could be blamed on largely incomprehensible and intractable 'tribal' conflicts rather than on the reality of territorial aggression in support of the creation of a 'Greater Serbia.' *(See 7.30.)* Depicting the Balkan conflict as a tribally-driven civil war between morally equivalent factions served to obscure the reality of the situation on the ground and correctly reinforce the perception in Belgrade that the enforced continuance of some form of Yugoslav state was the preferred option of the European Union and the broader 'international community.'

By the end of 1991, with the Serb forces halted outside Zagreb, an uneasy ceasefire ensued, and subsequently attention focused on Bosnia, which experienced some of the most horrific inter-ethnic violence of the entire series of conflicts. Western intervention finally followed in Bosnia, and this led to the signing, in December 1995, of the Dayton Accords which brought a halt to the fighting in Bosnia by creating an internationally-bolstered administration. *(See 7.30.)*

In August 1995 in 'Operation Storm', Croatian forces launched a rapid offensive that recovered Krajina in 48 hours. Serb supporters claim that the West turned a blind eye to this assault, which undoubtedly resulted in the largest population movement of Serbs since the conflict began – although this has to be set against the far greater numbers of Croats and Bosnians driven from their homes in Serbian offensives. However, an equally compelling reason for the collapse of Krajina was the withdrawal of support by the JNA and the Belgrade politicians. By August 1995, Milošević desperately wanted the Dayton Accord process to succeed, because this would effectively legitimize Serb gains in Bosnia and relieve the economic pressure being applied against Serbia proper. The price for Croat support for Dayton was a free hand in Krajina.

Yet another war was to follow, however, when fighting broke out in the largely Albanian-inhabited province of Kosovo in 1999. *(See 7.32.)* In sharp contrast to the Western prevarication in Bosnia, a massive NATO bombing campaign was launched in March 1999, which eventually led to the withdraw of the Serbian forces and the establishment of another international protectorate, which became independent in 2008.

The collapse of Yugoslavia suggests that conflict becomes almost inevitable when different ethnic groups are forcibly integrated in a single state for any length of time. In Yugoslavia, the triggers for this explosion were the deepening economic crisis which beset the country in the late 1980s, the loss of the unifying figure (and iron hand) of Tito, attempts by Serbian factions to impose an overtly Serb political hegemony on the entire country, and reciprocal attempts by democrats in Slovenia and Croatia to achieve independence. The six former Yugoslav republics have followed different trajectories since attaining independence. Slovenia and Croatia have established functioning multi-party democracies, and Slovenia joined the European Union on 2004. Bosnia & Herzegovina continues to be under international supervision, and its long term future has to be regarded as uncertain. Macedonia left Yugoslavia without initial bloodshed, but experienced conflict with its Muslim minority later, as well as suffering overspill problems from the Kosovo war. Montenegro, the only republic not to break away in 1991-2, remained tied in gradually loosening federation with its larger Serbian neighbour, and consequently suffered both by association, the practical effects of sanctions against Belgrade, and the direct damage of NATO military action against Montenegrin targets during the Kosovo war. Despite opposition from the European Union, Montenegro voted for full independence in June 2006.

For Serbia, the core republic in the old federation, and the state which sought to dominate any successor republic, the consequences in territorial and political terms of four lost wars has been disastrous. Belgrade has lost control not only over what was once Yugoslavia, but has also lost, in Kosovo, territory regarded as integral to the Serbian state itself. The process of attack and defeat by outsiders has inevitably tended to reinforce the Serb self-view as a people at best misunderstood, and at worst actively persecuted, by the rest of the world.

---

**Ethnic cleansing defined?**

The term 'ethnic cleansing' entered the political lexicon in the early 1990s. It first came to prominence as a translation of the Serbian *'ethniko ciscenje'* which was used as a term *of approval* for Serbian actions in clearing the Croat populations of areas such as the Krajina region. Albanian militants appear, however, to have used the term somewhat earlier to describe the expulsion of Serbs from Kosovo, and the phrase may be derived from Yugoslav military doctrine which talks of 'cleaning' an area of the enemy.

The term ethnic cleansing has since been 'retro-fitted' to earlier massacres, such as the Jewish Holocaust and the Armenian Genocide, as well as to later events like the Rwandan Genocide. The term has no defined meaning in international law, although the United Nations expressly recognizes it as a form of genocide, a crime subject to international sanction.

To avoid the term being devalued and applied to any massacre of one ethnic group by another, a number of criteria may be helpful in classifying an event as 'ethnic cleansing.' The first is that there must be a systematic element to the process, with some degree of conscious planning in the initiation or instigation of the attack. The second is that it is directed against the target population as a whole, including – often especially – women and children. Specifically, the use of rape as a deliberate weapon of war will go beyond that expected 'in the heat of battle.' Systematic rape demoralizes the target population by inflicting guilt on the men and shame on the women, particularly when it leads to involuntary pregnancies that can be seen (by either side) as the biological conquest of the target population.

The aim of ethnic cleansing is frequently *not* the wholesale extermination of the target population, but the creation of an environment of terror and intimidation in which a mass exodus is achieved. Thereafter members of the attacking group will generally occupy the individual houses, towns and territory of the 'cleansed' group.

A further characteristic is the distorted view of history that is used to justify the attacks. This is accompanied by the re-naming of settlements and the appropriation (or destruction) of religious and cultural monuments. The one-sided view of history will be fuelled by extreme propaganda and demonization of the target population, whipping up a killing enthusiasm among the attackers. From the point of view of the organizers of ethnic cleansing, the demonization of the enemy, as well as the actual violence of the cleansing, will reinforce the determination of the attacking community to resist any peaceful future accommodation with the target group. Attitudes on both sides are hardened, to the benefit of political and military elites, purposefully making conflict resolution more difficult to achieve.

# Bosnia & Herzegovina

**Principal protagonists**

Republic of Bosnia & Herzegovina; Federation of Bosnia & Herzegovina; UN High Representative. NATO forces actively engaged 1994-5; security currently provided by European Union force.

Republika Srpska.

**Nature of conflict**

Territorial ethnic conflict between Muslims (Bosniaks), Croats and Serbs. Full-scale war 1991-5.

- Muslim/Christian and Catholic/Orthodox conflicts are issues.
- 110,000 in war of 1991-6.
- 1.8 million, 1991-6.

**Population/ethnic composition**

Federation: c3m. Serb 2%, Bosniaks 80%, Croats 17%. Republika Srpska: c1.5m. Serb 88%, Bosniaks 11%.

**Territorial extent**

Bosnia & Herzegovina total: 51,197 km².
Federation: 26,110 km².
Republika Srpska: 25,053 km².

**Timeline**

29 Feb 1992: Referendum held on independence.
1 Mar 1992: Bosnia & Herzegovina declares independence from Yugoslavia.
7 Apr 1992: Republika Srpska declares independence.
28 Feb 1994: First NATO combat action (air/air combat against Serbian planes).
18 Mar 1994: Muslim/Croat Federation of Bosnia & Herzegovina created.
6-11 Jul 1995: Srebrenica massacre.
30 Aug 1995: Start of NATO airstrikes.
14 Dec 1995: Dayton Accords signed.
20 Dec 1995: NATO peacekeeping force deployed.

**Current status**

Partially resolved through Dayton Accords, but deep divisions remain.

In 1918, shortly before the creation of the first Yugoslav state, Serb nationalists produced maps purporting to show the Greater Serbia. These were neither traditional areas of Serb occupancy, nor even areas in which Serbs were the majority – they simply drew a line around all the areas in which Serbs lived.

This view of 'Greater Serbia', as including all areas in which there was any Serbian settlement, was to a degree sublimated through Serbian participation in Yugoslavia, in which Serbs were the largest group. Confusion over the definition and demarcation of any future Serbian state re-surfaced disastrously during the break-up of Yugoslavia, and nowhere more so than in the central republic of Bosnia & Herzegovina. Bosnia faced particularly problems in independent nation forming. Although home to the majority of Yugoslavia's Muslims, it also had sizable Croat and Serb populations. Any geographical division of Bosnia into Muslim, Croat or Serb areas was always going to be complicated by the intermingling of the population groups, which permeated down to the familial level – up to 40% of Bosnian families were estimated to be 'mixed'. However, under the Yugoslav census, although it was possible to identify oneself as a 'Yugoslav' the category of 'Bosnian' was not included. (The term 'Bosniak' is generally used to indicate a Muslim citizen, as opposed to 'Bosnian' which is any citizen of Bosnia & Herzegovina.) The 'nationality' of a child was patrilineal – and recorded on ID cards. As underlying hatreds surfaced, this proved to be a potent factor. The absence of a 'Bosnian' option in the census enabled both Serbs and Croats to claim that there was no such people, and that 'Bosniaks' were merely Croats or Serbs who had converted to Islam.

Elections in 1990 had produced Bosnia's first post-Communist government, but although the largest political parties agreed to work together in government, all were ethnically based. The collapse of Yugoslavia and the declarations of independence in Slovenia and Croatia in mid-1991 split opinion in Bosnia along ethnic lines. Serbs favoured remaining within what was left of Yugoslavia, while Muslims and Croats strongly supported independence. On 9 January 1992 a Republic of the Serb people of Bosnia & Herzegovina (later simply Republika Srpska) was proclaimed by the Bosnian Serb Assembly and declared to be a part of the Yugoslav federation. A national referendum on independence held in

February 1992 – which was boycotted by most Serbs – produced virtual unanimity on independence, but did so on a turnout of only 63.7% – crucially, below the two-thirds majority necessary to change the constitution. Bosnian independence was nevertheless declared on 1 March 1992, by which time fighting had already broken out between the Muslim and Croat communities and the Serbs. Serbian forces, backed by strong elements of the Yugoslav National Army (JNA) initially gained the upper hand, coming to occupy some 70% of the territory of Bosnia & Herzegovina and placing the capital, Sarajevo, under siege.

Croats, too, set up their own state – 'Herceg-Bosna' – in Herzegovina (the south-eastern region of the country) which became to all practical purposes an extension of Croatia proper. It is widely believed that the Presidents of Serbia and Croatia (Slobodan Milošević and Franjo Tudjman respectively) while bitter enemies elsewhere, envisaged the partition of Bosnia & Herzegovina into Serbian/Croatian spheres of influence as the solution to the Bosnian 'problem'. By 1993 the population pressures imposed by refugees fleeing the conflict led to fighting between Croats and Muslims, as well as with the Serbs. The conflict thus became triangular.

International horror at the scale and ferocity of the conflict gradually forced Western governments to take a more interventionist stance. In April 1993, three Bosniak enclaves, Gorazde, Srebrenica and Zepa, which were being besieged by Serb forces, were declared United Nations 'safe areas'. The impotence of this policy, which arguably simply turned the enclaves into informal concentration camps for the thousands of refugees who congregated there, was demonstrated when the Serbs launched a series of offensives against the 'safe areas' from April 1994 onwards. The UN simply withdrew or stood aside, allowing the 'safe areas' to be over-run with horrendous civilian casualties. In July 1995 Serb forces committed the 'Srebrenica massacre' – the murder of over 8,000 civilians following the fall of the Srebrenica 'safe area'. This was the largest massacre of civilians in Europe since the Second World War. Zepa also fell in July 1995, leaving Gorazde as the only significant Bosniak-inhabited town in eastern Bosnia.

The failure of the UN 'intervention' did at least finally provoke a meaningful Western military response, the final breaking point being the second of the two 'Markale (market) Massacres' when Serb forces mortar bombed Sarajevo market in August 1995. Against a background of gradually hardening Bosnian government resistance to Serb attacks, decisive NATO air strikes from 30 August 1995 – 'Operation Deliberate Force' – enabled the Bosnian government to halt the advances of the Republika Srpska and force all sides to the negotiating table.

The resulting Dayton Agreement was signed on 14 December 1995. This recognized three ethnicities – Bosniak, Serb and Croat. Under Dayton, a complex system of consociational checks and balances was introduced with the overall security and governance of Bosnia falling under the international supervision of a High Representative. Under the Dayton Agreement, Bosnia was divided into two 'entities', Republika Srpska and the Federation of Bosnia & Herzegovina, the latter itself divided between Muslim and Croat 'components'. Bosnia & Herzegovina was further regionally divided into ten cantons assigned to one or other of the 'entities'. (One territory, Brčko District is an anomaly, in that it belongs to both 'entities' in an apparent, although pragmatic, breach of the Dayton agreement). The partition of Bosnia has been criticised as legitimizing Serbian war gains, and Republika Srpska, moreover, occupies the most fertile and industrially productive regions of the country.

The degree of lasting success the Dayton Agreement has achieved is questionable. A resumption of general hostilities has been avoided, but largely through the continued presence of NATO (later EU) troops. Effective efforts at genuine national building have been limited; Republika Srpska and, to a lesser extent, the Croatian region of the Muslim-Croat federation, still operate as independent states in all but name. Many of the central institutions of the Bosnian state exist only on paper or are propped up by international participants. It is likely that Kosovan independence will prompt renewed demands for Republika Srpska's independence (or union with Serbia) both as 'compensation' for the loss of Kosovo and on the argument that if the partition of Serbia into ethnically-predicated states is acceptable in the case of Kosovo the same right of secession cannot legitimately be denied to the Bosnian Serbs. *(See Kosovo, 7.32.)* Objectively, it is likely at present that Bosnia & Herzegovina would descent rapidly into renewed violence and 'failed state' status should international support be withdrawn.

# Kosovo

**Principal protagonists**

Albanian community; Kosovo separatists.

Republic of Serbia; Serb community.

NATO-led Kosovo Force (KFOR).

**Nature of conflict**

Inter-ethnic conflict and self-determination issue. NATO intervention 1999.

Muslim/Christian conflict an issue.
10,000, 1998-9.
125,000, 1999

**Population/ethnic composition**

2m. Albanians 88%, Serbs 7%.

**Territorial extent**

Kosovo: 10,887 km².

**Timeline**

28 June 1389: Serbs defeated at Kosovo Polje by Turks.
1912: Kosovo annexed by Serbia.
1945: Kosovo established as a separate province within Serbia.
5 Jun 1990: Kosovan autonomy officially terminated by Serbia.
2 Jul 1990: Unofficial Kosovo parliament declares independence.
1996-99: Conflict between Serbian and KLA forces.
6 Feb-18 Mar 1999: Rambouillet talks end with Serbian rejection of Western proposals, triggering Kosovo war.
24 Mar-10 Jun 1999: Kosovo war. UN/NATO occupation of Kosovo.
10 Dec 2007: UN Security Council fails to agree on Kosovo's future status.
17 Feb 2008: Kosovan parliament declares Kosovo independent.

**Current status**

Kosovan independence declared in 2008, despite opposition from Serbia and Russia.

**In June 1389, at the Battle of Kosovo Polje – the Field of Blackbirds – an army of Serbs and their allies was decisively defeated by the Ottoman Turks. Although a defeat, the event is still regarded by Serbs as symbolic of the origins of Serb unity in the face of outside persecution. Accordingly, the status of Kosovo as the birthplace of the Serbian nation has an emotional appeal far beyond other political or strategic considerations.**

Annexed by Serbia during the 1912-3 Balkan War, Kosovo became an autonomous province of Serbia (within Yugoslavia) in 1945. Since the 1940s, Kosovo has seen a significant increase in its Muslim/Albanian population, both by immigration from Albania and through a higher Albanian birthrate than that of the Serbian population. As a consequence, Albanians now significantly outnumber Serbs and other minorities within the province. The historic roots of the conflict have thus become inflamed with more recent demands and population pressures, including irredentist claims by Albanians supporting union with Albania, as well as more general calls for independent statehood.

The 1974 constitution for the autonomous province of Kosovo enabled Albanians to tighten their grip on the regional government at the expense of non-Albanians. Popular support for outright independence became manifest in a series of student demonstrations in the early 1980s that were violently suppressed by the Yugoslav authorities. As the Yugoslav state itself began to unravel in the mid 1980s, many Serbs became concerned about its future direction, and in particular of the future for the Serb people. In 1986 the Serbian Academy of Sciences and Arts produced the 'SANU Memorandum', subsequently leaked to the media, which accurately predicted the disintegration of Yugoslavia into warring ethnic states. These concerns were seized upon by a rising Serbian politician, Slobodan Milošević, who became President of Serbia in May 1989. In an impassioned speech to 100,000 listeners in Kosovo on the 600th anniversary of the Battle of Kosovo Polje, Milošević pledged himself to the unconditional defence of the Serb nation. Many commentators see this speech as the first step towards the abandonment by Serbs of the Titoist vision of a superficially non-ethnic state in favour of the creation of a 'Greater Serbia.' Later in 1989, Milošević engineered a dramatic reduction in the autonomy of the Kosovan regional government, whose powers were formally abolished a year later.

Following the conclusion of the Bosnian war in 1995, ethnic Albanians organized the Kosovo Liberation Army (KLA) and commenced guerrilla-style hit-and-run attacks against Serbian targets – both civilian and military – throughout the province. Serbian reprisals were characteristically brutal and the security situation rapidly deteriorated. In 1998 a partial ceasefire was forced upon Serbia (but not the KLA) by the Western powers, but this did little to halt the killing. Following the Racak Massacre of 16 January 1999, in which 45 Albanian civilians died, Serbia was pressurized into participation in the Rambouillet conference, at which Serbia (supported by Russia) refused to support an agreement that would have permitted NATO forces access not only to Kosovo but to Serbia proper.

Controversy continues over responsibility for the ethnic conflict in Kosovo. The conventional view, shared by most Western governments and media, is that the violence was essentially a continuation of the Serbian government-sponsored ethnic cleansing programmes seen in Croatia and Bosnia in previous Balkan wars. By this interpretation, Serbs were the main aggressors and Muslims the main victims. An alternative, albeit more conspiratorial, interpretation is that the KLA was well aware of the collective Western guilt over its late intervention in Bosnia and were adroit enough to recognize that KLA attacks on Serbs, which would solicit a disproportionately violent response both from informal militia and the authorities, would trigger Western intervention on their behalf. In this latter scenario, moral complicity for the considerable loss of Muslim life becomes more complex. Whether intentional or not, the KLA was correct in its analysis. Following Serbia's rejection of Western demands at Rambouillet, NATO commenced, on 24 March 1999, a massive aerial bombardment of military and industrial targets across Kosovo, Serbia proper, and Montenegro (the latter being, at the time, in federation with Serbia). The attack was estimated to take no more than four days. In the event, 79 days of continuous bombing followed before Serbia capitulated and allowed NATO forces to occupy Kosovo. Kosovo was placed under a transitional UN administration backed militarily by NATO forces. The post-war period was marred by widespread reprisals by Albanians against the Serb minority, culminating in major inter-ethnic riots in March 2004. Increasingly, the international forces found themselves protecting the Serbs from the Albanians rather than the reverse.

A general election of 2004 saw the election of a new governing coalition of the Democratic League of Kosovo (LDK) and the Alliance for the Future of Kosovo (AAK). Serbian candidates declined to take their seats in the new assembly. In 2006, negotiations, chaired by UN Special Envoy Martti Ahtisaari, were started to determine a final dispensation for Kosovo. The resulting draft proposal, published on 2 February 2007, fell short of using the word 'independent' in describing Kosovo's future status, but did propose for the new entity all the trappings normally associated with full sovereignty, including national symbols, citizenship, and the right to join international organizations. Serbia almost immediately rejected the proposals.

Further negotiations aimed at securing a workable compromise over Kosovo's future status broke up without agreement in December 2007, with Russia vetoing proposals that would have led to Kosovan sovereignty. With the European Union determined to press ahead with Kosovan independence, the proposal was then tabled that Kosovo would be permitted to declare independence in a 'co-ordinated procedure' with the EU. Ironically, this diplomatic formula has its roots in Montenegrin independence, which the EU vigorously opposed. The EU 'took note' of Montenegrin independence, but left the decision to establish formal diplomatic links up to individual governments. This procedure sidestepped the objections to Kosovan independence from a number of smaller EU member states, including Romania and Cyprus – the latter naturally being concerned about a precedent being set in Northern Cyprus.

On 17 February 2008, Kosovo's parliament unanimously declared Kosovo independent. This was recognized the next day by the United States, Turkey, and a number of EU states including Britain, Germany, Italy and France. Russia condemned the move and blocked UN Security Council moves to admit Kosovo to the United Nations. Clashes between Serbs and UN forces broke out in Serb-majority areas in Kosovo, most notably the town of Mitrovica, following the independence declaration. The diplomatic snub both to Russia and Serbia runs the risk of contributing to a further cooling of relations between Moscow and the West as well as fuelling Serbian xenophobia.

Furthermore, Kosovan independence sets an important and potentially dangerous precedent in that, for the first time, a new state would emerge from the breakup of the USSR/Yugoslavia that previously only had provincial, rather than full republic, status. Logically, it could be difficult on this basis to deny sovereignty to Nagorno-Karabakh, Republika Srpksa, Chechnya, and any number of other claimant nations – not least the Serbian majority northern districts of Kosovo itself which may seek separate 'independence' or union with Serbia.

# Macedonia

**Principal protagonists**

Republic of Macedonia.

Albanian community; Albanian irredentists.

**Nature of conflict**

Autonomist/irredentist demands by Albanian community. Exacerbated by mass refugee influx from Kosovo, 1999.

☠ 200.
⚐ 540,000 Albanian refugees from Kosovo in 1999.

**Population/ethnic composition**

2m. Macedonian 64.2%, Albanian 25.2%, Turkish 3.8%, Roma 2.7%, Serbian 1.8%.

**Territorial extent**

Primarily north/west regions of Macedonia. Total Macedonia area: 25,333 km².

**Timeline**

1893: Internal Macedonian Revolutionary Organization (IMRO) created.
2 Aug 1903: 'Ilinden-Preobrazhenie uprising'.
1912-13: Balkan wars.
1919: Yugoslavia created.
1945: Socialist Republic of Macedonia created within re-constituted Yugoslavia.
8 Sep 1991: Macedonia declares independence.
8 Apr 1993: Macedonia internationally recognized as 'Former Yugoslav Republic of Macedonia'.
Dec 1992-Feb 1999: UN mission deployed.
23 Mar 1999: Kosovo war breaks out. Albanian refugees flood into Macedonia.
21 Jan 2001: Fighting breaks out between Albanian and Macedonian forces.
Jul 2001: Ceasefire agreed.
13 Aug 2001: Peace deal formally agreed.
21 Aug-26 Sep 2001: NATO force deployed.

**Current status**

2001 peace agreement generally holding, but tensions persist.

Macedonia presents an example of a nation in the process of 'ethnogenesis' or self-formation. *(See 1.04.)* A modern Macedonia national consciousness started to emerge in the 19th century, with the development of the Macedonian language and the appearance of political nationalism. In 1893 the Internal Macedonian Revolutionary Organization (IMRO) was formed to press for the creation of an autonomous Macedonia within a Balkan federation. In 1903, IMRO launched an insurgency, the 'Ilinden-Preobrazhenie Uprising', which, although crushed, contributed considerably to the development of a distinctive Macedonian identity. However, it is only really since the Balkan Wars of 1912-3 and particularly in the latter half of the 20th century that Macedonians started to think of themselves as such, rather than as 'South Serbs' or 'West Bulgars.'

Even today, there is a sentiment in Bulgaria that regards the Macedonian language as a dialect of Bulgarian, and as the Macedonians themselves as essentially Bulgarian. Whether this view crystallizes into organized irredentist sentiment remains to be seen.

As a political entity, modern Macedonia has only existed since 1945, when Tito created the Macedonian Socialist Republic as one of the six republics in his re-constituted Yugoslavia, thus recognizing the Macedonian ethnicity officially for the first time. Part of his motive for doing so was to reduce the overall power of Serbs in the new federation. Macedonia remained something of a backwater in Yugoslavia, largely agrarian and under-developed, until the collapse of Yugoslavia in the early 1990s. Macedonia declared itself independent, without fuss, on 8 September 1991, becoming the only Yugoslav republic (until Montenegro, in 2006) to secede without violence. Despite this peaceful transition to independence, Macedonia was initially denied the international recognition that was its due because of protests by Greece, which claimed that the use of the name 'Macedonia' implied an irredentist claim on parts of Greece. This was partially resolved when Macedonia agreed to alter national symbols, including its flag, and to accept recognition under the clumsy title 'Former Yugoslav Republic of Macedonia' (FYROM). The 'FYROM' name is never used in Macedonia, nor by an increasing number of countries having dealings with Macedonia, including the United States.

Macedonia largely escaped the violence and upheavals that accompanied the collapse of Yugoslavia until 1992, when relations deteriorated between the Macedonian majority and the country's Albanian minority, which is largely concentrated in the west and north-west. Some of the Albanian-majority districts had, in fact, been part of Albania at various times in the past, a number being transferred by Albania to Yugoslavia after the Second World War as a goodwill gesture between the two Communist states. Albanian political representation had been secured through the participation of the Democratic Party of Albanians in coalition governments, but this party itself only represented a minority of Albanian voters. The main Albanian grievances centred on their lack of formal proportional representation in government and related issues such as language use and the wording of the 1990 constitution that changed the definition of Macedonia from "a state of the Macedonian people and the Albanian and Turkish nationalities" to a "national state of the Macedonian people". Autonomist and irredentist sentiments also began to make themselves heard. In January 1992, Albanians sought to organize a referendum on greater autonomy, which was condemned by the government as seeking to split the country.

By December 1992, the situation had deteriorated to the extent that a United Nations force of soldiers and policemen was deployed, with the agreement of the Macedonian government. This force worked to maintain calm in the border regions until February 1999, when it was abruptly withdrawn. The People's Republic of China vetoed the continuation of the mission in the UN Security Council because Macedonia had recognized the Republic of China (Taiwan). The timing of the mission's withdrawal was disastrous as it coincided with the outbreak of hostilities in neighbouring Kosovo. *(See 7.32.)* In March 1999 a mass influx of Albanians into Macedonia took place and fighting broke out between Albanian guerrilla groups and Macedonian forces in January 2001. The Albanian insurgents – who called themselves the National Liberation Army – were closely linked to, if not synonymous with, the Kosovo Liberation Army forces fighting in Kosovo. Albanian/Kosovan tactics generally featured rapid hit-and-run raids on Macedonian villages around strategic towns and highways. As in Kosovo, the intention appears to have been to provoke the authorities into a heavy-handed counter response, including the forcible occupation of Albanian-majority towns and villages that would serve to further mobilize the Albanian population. This strategy largely failed, in part, ironically, because of the tactical weakness of the Macedonian forces in responding to the attacks.

In April 2001, the Macedonian authorities initiated a political dialogue aimed at reducing ethnic tensions, but the main Albanian opposition party, the Party for Democratic Prosperity, boycotted talks. A broadened coalition was, nevertheless, created in July following heavy international pressure on both sides. A formal halt to the fighting was negotiated under the Ohrid Framework Agreement in August, and a NATO force arrived to ensure order. The NLA was disbanded under the agreement and handed over its weapons, some of which were found to date from the First World War, having been handed down through the generations. In August 2004, Macedonia's parliament passed legislation redrawing local boundaries and giving greater local autonomy to Albanians in areas where they constitute the majority. Areas of tension persist but there has been no wholesale return to violence, although conflict surrounding the independence of Kosovo may serve to re-inflame the situation.

# Northern Ireland (Ulster)

**Principal protagonists**

Mainly Protestant Unionists/Loyalists; Democratic Unionist Party; various other political parties and paramilitary groups.

Mainly Catholic Nationalists/Republicans (supporters of unification with Republic of Ireland); Irish Republican Army/Sinn Féin; various other political parties and paramilitary groups.

**Nature of conflict**

Long standing historical conflict; irredentist claims by Irish republicans. Terrorist war.

† Protestant/Catholic conflict.
☠ 3,500.

**Population/ethnic composition**

1.7m. Protestants 53.1%, Roman Catholics 43.8%.

**Territorial extent**

Northern Ireland: 14,139 km². (The term 'Ulster', often used as synonymous with Northern Ireland, refers to one of the four traditional provinces of Ireland. In addition to the six Northern Irish counties, Ulster also includes Cavan, Donegal, and Monaghan in the Republic of Ireland.)

**Timeline**

1172: Henry II (of England) conquers Ireland.
Jun 1541: Kingdom of Ireland in personal union with England.
1 Jan 1801: Act of Union creates United Kingdom of Great Britain and Ireland.
18 Jun 1922: Independence of southern counties as Irish Free State; Northern Ireland opts to remain British.
30 Mar 1972: Direct rule imposed on Northern Ireland by London.
10 Apr 1998: Good Friday Agreement signed. Later ratified by referendums in both Northern Ireland and the Republic of Ireland.
7 May 2007: Devolved government restored.

**Current status**

Peace agreements generally holding.

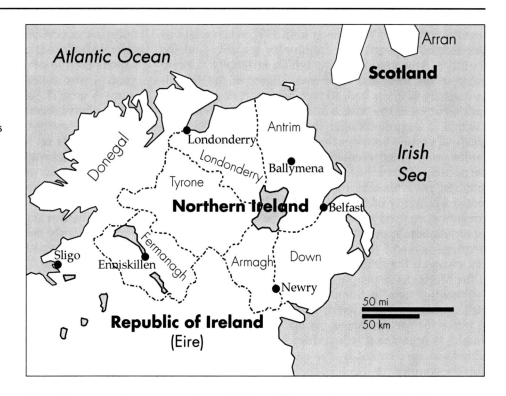

**One of Europe's longest running ethnic conflicts, and one of the few in Western Europe to descend into sustained violence, Northern Ireland has long bedevilled attempts at a solution. Part of the reason for the difficulty in resolving the conflict is its sheer longevity, with historical opinions and myths entrenched on both sides, although prospects for a lasting settlement are currently reasonably high.**

The Northern Ireland conflict operates on a number of interlocking levels. First, the dispute is a continuation of the uneven centuries-old conflict between Ireland and its dominant English/British neighbour. In 1172, Ireland was conquered by the English king, Henry II, who instigated the settlement of his Anglo-Norman supporters into the country. In 1366 the Statute of Kilkenny forbade intermarriage between the English and the Irish. In 1541 Henry VIII declared himself King of Ireland and in 1801 Great Britain (comprising England, Scotland, and Wales) was formally unified with Ireland to create the United Kingdom of Great Britain and Ireland. In the mid-1840s the Irish potato famine caused massive hardships and mass emigration to America. The British authorities are still held by many in Ireland (and America) to be responsible for the extent of this tragedy.

The second cleavage is religious. Northern Ireland is now the only region in the world in which conflict between Protestant and Catholic Christians is a significant cause of violence. The persecution of Catholics dates from Henry VIII's split with the Roman Catholic Church in 1534. In 1607 James VI (James I of England) started the plantation of Scottish and English Protestant settlers into Ulster, thus creating the fundamental division between Ulster and the rest of Ireland. In 1641, some 30,000 Protestants were massacred in Ulster, but in 1649 the Catholics were themselves comprehensively crushed by Oliver Cromwell. In 1690, the Catholic King James II was comprehensively defeated, on Ulster soil, at the Battle of the Boyne by William of Orange.

The third division is between those who wish to retain the constitutional link with the United Kingdom – Unionists or Loyalists – and those seeking unification with the Republic of Ireland – Nationalists or Republicans. (As a generalization, Loyalists and Republicans are terms used to indicate the more extreme – including paramilitary – wings of their respective positions.) Those seeking unification essentially view the issue as one of 'unfinished business' arising from Ireland's long struggle for independence from Britain. Modern Irish nationalism dates from the formation, in 1905, of the Sinn Féin party and the paramilitary National Volunteer Force. Following the failed 1916 Easter Uprising in Dublin, Sinn Féin members of the British parliament established their own Irish parliament and declared independence in 1919. Following two years of guerrilla warfare, an Anglo-Irish Treaty was signed in 1922. This established an Irish Free State, but the six north-eastern counties of Ireland opted to remain British, becoming Northern Ireland. Civil war then broke out in the south between the National Volunteer Force – later renamed the Irish Republican Army (IRA) – and the 'Free Staters' in which the latter prevailed in 1923. The IRA never accepted the division of Ireland and terrorist violence flared intermittently until the early 1970s when, exploiting Catholic grievances at poor housing, lower employment rates and political marginalization, the IRA and its various offshoots initiated a terrorist bombing and shooting campaign that was to last more than thirty years and claim over 3,000 lives. Northern Ireland continued to be governed by a devolved assembly in Belfast until 1972 when London imposed direct rule in response to the worsening security situation.

It should be noted at this point that the religious and political cleavages in Northern Ireland are not wholly contiguous. Although almost all Protestants favour the maintenance of the union with Great Britain, not all Catholics favour unification with the republic. A secondary issue facing Northern Ireland is that the political parties are essentially sectarian head-counts. This is not entirely a self-inflicted wound; until comparatively recently the mainstream parties of the UK (which, like most parties in Western democracies are essentially aligned on socio-economic grounds) refused to organize in Northern Ireland or even to accept members from the province. As a related point, many 'UK-wide' bodies, including trades unions, charities and financial institutions, do not in practice operate in Northern Ireland, while Irish bodies similarly do not operate in the north, or, if they do, are unacceptable to the unionist majority as representing a tacit acceptance of integration with the Irish Republic. Thus civil society in Northern Ireland generally is comparatively weak. An additional issue is intra-communal violence and coercion, with paramilitary groups on both sides using the threat of violence to extort benefits from their host communities.

From the 1970s onward the violence continued in varying degrees of intensity until the 1990s. Repeated attempts at dialogue and the restoration of devolved government all failed. Terrorist violence was largely confined to Northern Ireland itself, although the IRA did commit a number of 'spectaculars' on mainland Britain, including a nearly successful assassination attempt on Prime Minister Margaret Thatcher and her cabinet in 1984. In 1985 an Anglo-Irish Agreement was signed, giving the Irish government a limited consultative role in the affairs of Northern Ireland, but this failed to stop the killing. Finally, after many false starts, a ceasefire by the IRA and most (although not all) of the other republican and loyalist paramilitary groups came into force in 1994. Although sporadic bombing attacks continued to be committed by 'dissident' republican groups, the general improvement in the security situation, and the gradual move by the IRA and its Sinn Féin political proxy towards democratic dialogue, facilitated the Good Friday Peace Agreement of 1998. This was ratified by referendums in both parts of Ireland. In the north, voters agreed to a power sharing agreement and the involvement of nationalists in civic institutions. In the south, the electorate agreed changes to the Irish constitution, dropping its long-standing territorial claim to Northern Ireland. A complex, and at times intermittent, process of 'decommissioning' under independent auspices was agreed by the IRA. In October 2006 it was confirmed by the decommissioning commission that the majority of IRA arms had been surrendered.

One unforeseen consequence of the Good Friday Agreement has been the political polarization of both communities, with Catholics migrating away from the 'moderate' Social Democratic Labour Party in favour of Sinn Féin, and the 'hard-line' Democratic Unionist Party supplanting the once dominant Ulster Unionist Party on the Protestant side. Nevertheless, on 7 May 2007, devolution was once again restored to Northern Ireland under an arrangement which saw the Democratic Unionists and Sinn Féin sharing power.

Various paramilitary factions continue to exert pressure within their communities, whether for political or criminal purposes. However, at present the prospects for a lasting, if imperfect, peace appear higher than for many years.

# Corsica

**Principal protagonists**

Government of France.

Corsican separatists; *Fronte de Liberazione Naziunale di a Corsica* (FLNC).

**Nature of conflict**

Self-determination and linguistic conflict.

☠ c10.

**Population/ethnic composition**

279,000. Corsican speaking population around 100,000.

**Territorial extent**

Corsica: 8,680 km².

**Timeline**

30 Nov 1789: Corsica, formally Genoese, is officially annexed to France.
2 Mar 1982: Declared a Special Status Region with a directly elected Regional Assembly.
13 May 1991: Declared a *collectivité territoriale*, with a directly elected Corsican Assembly and an Executive Council.
6 Jul 2003: Proposals for further autonomy narrowly rejected in referendum.

**Current status**

Rejection of autonomy deal in referendum of 2003 effectively leaves the issue unresolved but in abeyance, with no new political initiatives proposed. Sporadic terrorist bombing campaign continues.

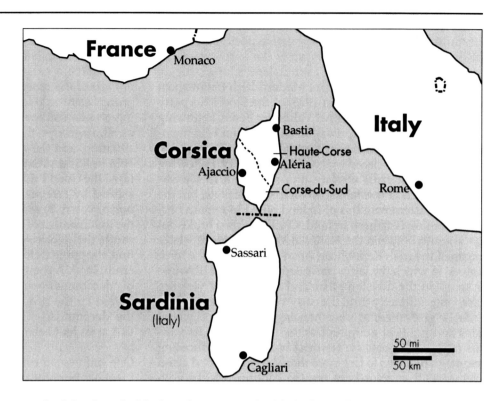

**In the island probably best known as the birthplace of Napoleon, sections of the rugged and individualistic Corsican people have been pressing for greater autonomy from France for many years. Although the violence of the conflict has never approached that of Northern Ireland or the Basque Country, Corsica has nevertheless been witness to hundreds of bombings and a number of politically motivated murders since the 1970s.**

The Corsican language has traditionally been the main focus of Corsican culture, but the trigger for the current round of conflict was immigration. After Algerian independence, around 100,000 French-Algerian settlers of Corsican origin established themselves around the eastern town of Aléria. Native Corsicans resented the favouritism allegedly shown towards the settlers and in August 1975 militants occupied a wine farm near Aléria, where they were later raided by the police. Two policemen and a wine grower were killed. In 1996 a number of groups merged to form the *Fronte di Liberazione Naziunale di a Corsica* (FLNC) which, over the next two decades, was responsible for a series of bomb attacks against French governmental and other targets. The organization's greatest 'achievement' was the assassination, in 1996, of Claude Erignac, who, as Prefect of Corsica, was the senior representative of the French government on the island.

The FNLC, which has been prone to splits over its history, is a political amalgam, combining elements of Marxist rhetoric with populist views on immigration, free-market measures (such as the creation of a tax-free zone) and reactionary conservatism (women are excluded from membership). In December 1999 (and again in 2003) the main FNLC faction declared a ceasefire, but sporadic bombings have continued to the present day.

The French state is ideologically incapable of easily accommodating regional distinctions, arguing instead in favour of the universality of French culture and the French language within the Republic. (Ironically for Corsica this is in part the legacy of their most famous son, Bonaparte.) Nevertheless, in 2000 Prime Minister Lionel Jospin, who had negotiated the 1999 ceasefire, proposed greater autonomy for the island. In a referendum in July 2003, however, Corsicans rejected the autonomy proposal by 51% to 49%, effectively leaving the 'Corsican Question' largely dormant if unresolved.

# Index

14 March Coalition  4.05
9/11 attacks  2.33, 3.16, 5.07, 4.05, 4.11, 4.14, 5.22, 5.23, 5.24, 7.03, 7.17
Abbas, Mahmoud  4.18
Abkhazia  7.14, 7.15
Aborigines (Australian)  6.26, 6.29, 6.30
Accra  2.45, 2.47
Aceh  6.08, 6.09
Acholi  2.29, 2.30
Adagez  2.50
Adalet ve Kalkinma Partiyi (AKP)  4.03
Adjaria  7.14, 7.15
Afewerki, Issavas  2.18
Afghanistan  4.11, 4.15, 5.17, 5.22, 5.23, 5.24, 5.25
Africa (overview)  1.02, 2.02, 2.03, 2.04
African National Congress  2.54, 2.55
African Union  2.13, 2.21, 2.34, 2.35, 2.36
Africa's 'first world war'  1.02, 2.28
Afrikaans  2.55, 2.59
Afro-Asian (ethnic group)  2.02
Afro-Guyanese  3.12
Afro-Shiraz Party (ASP)  2.52, 2.53
Ahtisaari, Martti  6.08, 7.33
al Anfal campaign  4.10, 4.11
al Medhi Army  4.10, 4.11, 4.12
al Qaeda  2.07, 2.51, 4.10, 4.15, 4.16, 5.23, 5.24, 6.07, 6.19
al Qaeda in the Islamic Maghreb  2.06, 2.07
al Sadr, Muqtada  4.11
Alaska  3.15
Albania, Albanians  7.32, 7.34
Algeria  2.04, 2.06, 2.07, 2.33, 2.34, 2.35, 2.50, 2.51, 7.38
Algers  2.07
Amazonia  3.03
'Ambazonia'  2.39
American Indians  3.14, 3.15
American Revolutionary War  3.14
Americo-Liberians  1.09, 2.40, 2.41
Amerindians  3.02, 3.03, 3.06, 3.07, 3.11 See also individual Latin America country sections
Amin, Idi  2.30
Amritsar  5.11
Andhar Pradesh  5.08
Anglo-Burmese Wars  6.02
Anglo-Irish Agreement (1985)  7.37
Angola  1.01, 2.04, 2.25, 2.28, 2.29, 2.60 See also Cabinda
Annan, Kofi  7.13
Aoun, Michel  4.05
Aozou strip  2.11
apartheid  1.04, 1.09, 2.38, 2.54, 2.55
Arabs  2.14, 2.32, 2.34. 2.52, 4.10
Arabs, Israeli  4.06

Arafat, Yasser  4.18
Aramaic  4.06
Argentina  3.03
Armed Forces Revolutionary Council  2.43
Armenia, Armenians  4.02, 7.16 See also genocide, Armenian
Artsakh  See Nagorno-Karabakh
Arunachal Pradesh  5.13
Arusha Peace Accords  2.24
Assam  5.12, 5.13
assimilation  1.03, 1.04, 1.09
Ataturk, Mustafa  4.02
Atlas Mountains  2.07
Atomic tests, French  6.30
Auma, Alice  2.3
Australia  6.07, 6.27, 6.29, 6.30
Autonomous Region of Muslim Mindanao  6.19
Autonomous Soviet Socialist Republics (ASSRs)  7.11, 7.14, 7.16, 7.20, 7.22, 7.24
Avar Khanate  7.24
Azerbaijan  7.11, 7.16
Azeri separatists  7.17
Aztecs  3.02
Ba Cruu  2.35
Baghdad  4.10
Bakassi peninsula  2.38
Baker II Plan  2.34
Baker, James  2.34
Baker-Hamilton Report  4.12
Balfour Declaration  4.17
Bali  6.11
Balkan War (1912-3)  7.32
Balkans  1.02, 7.25, 7.26, 7.27, 7.28, 7.29 See also sections on individual former Yugoslav republics
Balochistan  5.24, 5.25, 5.26
Baltic states  7.06, 7.07
Bamiyan Buddhas  5.23
Banaba  6.30
Bangladesh  5.12
Bantu population group  2.27
bantustans  2.93, 2.54, 2.55, 2.59
Banyamulenge  2.25, 2.27, 2.29 See also Tutsis
Barotseland  2.59
Barre, Siad  2.20
Basayev, Shamyl  7.24
Basque Country  See Euzkadi
Basra  4.12
Basters, Rehoboth  2.58, 2.59
Bedie, Henri  2.48, 2.49
Bedouin  2.34
Beirut  4.04
Beja  2.13
Bekaa Valley  4.05
Belgium  2.24, 2.26, 2.28, 7.04
Belize  3.11

Bella, Ben  2.07
Bemba (ethnic group)  2.28
Bemba, Jean-Pierre  2.29
Benedict XVI, HH  2.37
Berbers  2.06, 2.07, 2.32, 2.34
Beslan school seige  7.23, 7.24
Bessarabia  7.18
Bethlehem  4.06
Beydane  2.32, 2.32, 2.33
Bhutan  5.19
Bhutto, Benazir  5.26
Biafra  2.03, 2.36
Bikini Atoll  6.30
Bin Laden, Osama  2.13, 4.11, 4.14, 5.23, 5.24, 6.07
Birao  2.17
Bishkek  5.07
Black Americans  3.15, 3.16
Black Economic Empowerment  2.55
'Black Hawk Down'  2.20
Black Sea Fleet  7.11
Boers  2.54
Bokassa, Jean-Bedel  2.16
Bonn Process  5.23
Bophuthatswana  2.55
borders, colonial  2.03, 2.22, 2.18, 2.36, 2.38 See also Scramble for Africa
Borneo  See Kalimantan
Bosnia & Herzegovina  2.25, 4.11, 7.25, 7.26, 7.27, 7.28, 7.30, 7.31
Bosnians, Bosniaks  See Bosnia & Herzegovina
Botlikh  7.24
Bougainville  6.27
Bozize, Francois  2.17
Brazil  3.03
Brcko District  7.31
Breton  1.03
Britain, British  2.14, 2.21, 2.22, 2.38, 2,43, 2.44, 2.54, 3.03, 3.12, 3.13, 3.14, 3.15, 3.16, 4.12, 4.17, 5.04, 5.12, 5.17, 5.20, 5.23, 5.27, 6.28, 6.29, 7.03 7.12, 7.36
British Indian Ocean Territory  See Chagos Islands
British Sovereign Base Areas  7.13
Buddhism  5.04, 5.08, 5.20, 6.05
Budennovsk hospital crisis  7.24
Bulgaria  7.34
Burkina Faso  2.40, 2.41, 2.44, 2.46, 2.50
Burma, Burmese  5.12, 6.02, 6.24
Burnham, Forbes  3.12, 3.13
Burundi  2.04, 2.26, 2.27, 2.28, 2.29
Bush Negroes  3.03, 3.06, 3.07
Bush, George (snr)  4.11
Bush, George W  4.11
Cabinda  1.08, 2.04, 2.60
Caliphate, Islamic  2.06, 4.10, 4.14, 4.15

Cambodia  6.24, 6.25
Cameroon  2.17, 2.36, 2.38
Cameroons, Northern  2.38
Cameroons, Southern  2.04, 2.38
Canada  3.14, 3.15
cannibalism  6.10
Cape Colony  2.54
Caprivi Strip  2.58, 2.59
Caribbean  2.02, 3.03, 3.12
Carnation Revolution  6.12
Casamance  2.08, 2.09
caste system, in Hinduism  5.09
Central African Republic  2.11, 2.16, 2.17, 2.31
Central Asia  1.04, 5.07
Central Intelligence Agency (CIA)  6.24, 6.25
Chad  1.09, 2.10, 2.11, 2.13, 2,14, 2.16, 2.17, 2.51
Chagos Islands  5.17
Chagossians  5.17
Chaldeans  4.06
Chama Cha Mapinduzi (CCM)  2.53
Chauchan, Jaggit Singh  5.11
Chechens  1.01
Chechnya  7.22, 7.21, 7.23, 7.24
Chiapas  3.04, 3.05
Chin  6.24
China, People's Republic of  1.01, 2.04, 2.11, 3.03, 5.04, 5.05, 5.06, 5.07, 5.13, 5.14, 5.15
China, Republic of (Taiwan)  2.11, 5.04, 6.28, 7.36
Chinese (as ethnic group)  6.06, 6.22, 6.28 See also Han (Chinese)
Chins  6.02
Choco region  3.07
Christianity, in China  5.07
Christianity, in India  5.12
Christianity, in Malaysia  6.22
Christianity, Middle Eastern  4.06
Christians, Zionist  4.06
Ciskei  2.55
Civic United Front (Zanzibar)  2.52, 2.53
Civil Defence Forces (Sierra Leone)  2.44
civil rights conflicts  1.08, 2,54, 3.14
civil war, American  3.15
civil war, Iraqi  4.12
civil war, Irish  7.37
civil war, Lebanese  4.04
coca  3.03, 3.07
coffee  3.03
Cold War  1.01, 2.39, 4.10, 5.17, 6.07, 7.03, 7.06 See also Soviet Union
Colombia  3.06, 3.07
colonial conflicts  1.08 See also Cabinda, East Timor, West Papua, Western Sahara
Coloureds (South African ethnic group)  2.55, 2.59

Commonwealth of Nations  2.38, 2.39, 3.12
Commonwealth of Independent States (CIS)  7.19
Communism  6.24, 7.03, 7.21 See also Soviet Union
Comoro Islands  2.52
Confederate States of America  3.15
confessionalism  1.09, 4.04
conflict interlock  2.04, 2.05
conflict resolution, types of  1.09
Congo Free State  2.28
Congo, Democratic Republic of  1.02, 2.04, 2.25, 2.26, 2.28, 2.31, 2.36, 2.60
Conseil National pour la Defense de la Democratie-Forces de Defense de la Democratie (CNDD-FDD)  2.26
constitution, EU  7.05
constitution, Indian  5.11
Conte, Lansana  2.44
copper  2.28, 6.27
Coptic church  4.06
Corsica  7.03, 7.38
Costa Rica  3.02
Cote d'Ivoire  2.26, 2.40, 2.41, 2.42, 2.44, 2.48, 2.49
coups d'etat  1.08, 2.06, 2.33, 3.10, 4.10, 7.12
Creoles  2.43
Crimea  7.10, 7.11
Croatia, Croats  7.25, 7.26, 7.27, 7.28
Cuba  3.11
Cuban missiles crisis  1.01
Cultural Revolution  5.05
Cyprus  1.09, 4.02, 4.06, 7.03, 7.12, 7.13
Cyrillic script  See Russification
Czech Republic  5.24
Dacco, David  2.16
Daddah, Ould  2.33
Dagbon Traditional Area  2.47
Dagestan  7.23, 7.24
Dagestan, Islamic Shura of  7.24
Dagomba  2.47
Dalai Lama, HH  5.04, 5.05
Dalit  5.09
Darfur  2.04, 2.11, 2.12, 2.13, 2.17
Darien Gap  3.07
Dayaks  6.06, 6.10, 6.11
Dayton Accords  4.11, 7.28, 7.31
Deby, Idriss  2.10, 2.17
decommissioning (of IRA weapons)  7.37
Degar  6.24, 6.25
Delta Region (of Nigeria)  2.37
Democratic Turnhalle Alliance (DTA)  2.59
Denial of Access attack  7.07
Derg, The  2.20, 2.23
desertification  2.33

dhimmi  4.02
diamonds as conflict issue  2.17, 2.40, 2.41, 2.43
diaspora, African  2.02
Diego Garcia  5.17
Dinka  2.17
Diola  2.08
Dioula  2.46
Djibouti  2.19, 2.20, 2.23
Dniestr River  7.18
Doe, Samuel  2.41
drought  2.33
Druze  4.04
Dubrovnik  7.28
Dudaev, Dzhokhar  7.23
Durant Line  5.23, 5.25
Durban  2.55
Dutch  3.12, 3.13, 6.06, 6.08, 6.10
East Timor  See Timor Leste
Easter Uprising (Irish)  7.37
Eastern Front (Sudan)  2.13
Economic Community of West African States (ECOWAS)  2.33, 2.41, 2.42
Economic Community of West African States Monitoring Group (ECOMOG)  2.41, 2.43
Egypt  2.14, 4.06, 4.13, 4.17 See also Sinai
El Salvador  1.01
'end of history'  See Fukuyama, Francis
English (language)  3.11, 3.12
'entities' (Bosnian)  7.31
Eritrea  2.03, 2.13, 2.18, 2.21
Eritrean Peoples' Liberation Front  2.18
Ethiopia  2.18, 2.22, 2.23
Ethiopian Peoples' Revolutionary Democratic Front  2.18
ethnic cleansing  1.09, 6.07, 7.28, 7.29
ethnic diversity  1.03
ethnic rebellions  1.06, 1.08, 1.09
ethnicity, as concept  1.03
Ethniki Organosis Kyprion Agoniston (EOKA)  7.12
ethnogenesis  1.04
etnicko ciscenje  See ethnic cleansing
euro (currency)  7.04
Europe (overview)  7.03, 7.04, 7.05, 7.06
European Coal and Steel Community  7.03
European Union (EU)  2.03, 2.35, 7.04, 7.05, 7.07, 7.13, 7.28, 7.29, 7.31, 7.33
Euskadi Ta Askatasuna (ETA)  7.09
Eusko Alderdi Jeltzalea  7.09
Euzkadi  7.08, 7.09
extermination order (Herero)  2.58
Falkland Islands  3.03
Fatah  4.18
Federally Administered Tribal Areas  5.23
Fifth Brigade (Zimbabwe)  2.56

Fiji, Fijians  6.26
Finland  7.06
Firestone Corporation  2.41
first Gulf War  *See* Gulf War(s)
First Nations Peoples  3.14, 3.15
First World War  2.38, 4.10, 4.14, 4.17, 7.03
Flanders  7.04
Flemish (language)  7.04
Forces Nouvelles  2.48, 2.49
Former Yugoslav Republic of Macedonia (FYROM)  1.04, 7.34
France, French  1.03, 2.06, 2.08, 2.10, 2.11, 2.16, 2.22, 2.24, 2.38, 2.48, 2.49, 2.50, 6.24, 7.03, 7.04, 7.08, 7.36
Franco, Francisco  7.09
Free Patriotic Movement (Lebanon)  4.04
Freetown  2.43
French (language)  3.14, 3.16, 7.04
Frente de Libertacoo de Mocambique (FRELIMO)  2.04
Frente de Libertacao do Enclave de Cabinda (FLEC)  2.60
Frente Popular de Liberacion de Saguía el Hamra y Río de Oro (POLISARIO)  2.33, 2.34, 2.35
Frente Revolucionária de Timor-Leste Independente (FRETILIN)  6.12, 6.13
Front de liberation Nationale (FLN)  2.06
Front Islamique de Salut (FIS)  2.06
Front Populaire Ivorien  2.48
Front Unifie de LUtte des Races Opprimees (FULRO)  6.24
Fuerzas Armadas Revolucionarias de Colombia (FARC)  3.06, 3.07
Fukuyama, Francis  1.01
Fulani  2.45
Fur  2.14
Gabon  2.36
Gaddafi  2.40. 2.51
Gagauzia  7.18, 7.19
Gambia  2.08
Garang, John  2.17
Gatumba  2.29
Gaza strip  4.06, 4.14, 4.17, 4.18
Gbagbo, Laurent  2.48, 2.49
Gbaya  2.16, 2.17
Gemayel, Pierre  4.05
genocide  1.09
genocide, Armenian  4.06, 7.16, 7.29
genocide, Herero  2.24, 2.25, 2.55
genocide, Rwandan  1.02, 2.25
Georgia  7.14, 7.15
Gerakan Aceh Merdeka (GAM)  6.08, 6.09
Germany, Germans  2.24, 2.26, 2.27, 2.38, 2.30, 2.58, 3.03
Ghana  2.45, 2.47

Ghandi, Indira  5.09. 5.11
Ghandi, Mahatma  5.09
Ghandi, Rajiv  5.21
Gio (ethnic group)  2.41
Global Positioning System  5.17
globalization  1.01, 3.05
Golan Heights  4.17
Golden Temple  5.11
Good Friday Agreement  7.37
Gorazde  7.31
Gorbachev, Mikhail  7.22
Great Lakes Region (Africa)  2.27, 2.29
'Greater Somalia'  2.23
Greece, Greeks  1.04, 7.12, 7.13, 7.34
Greek Cypriots  *See* Cyprus
Green Line (Cyprus)  1.09, 7.13
Green March (Moroccan)  2.34
Groupe Islamique Arme (GIA)  2.07
Groupe Salatiste pour la Prediction et la Combat (GSPC)  2.07
Grozny  7.16
Guadacanal  6.28
Guatemala  3.10, 3.11
Guerza  2.44, 2.46
Guinea  2.40, 2.41, 2.43. 2.44, 2.45
Guinea Bissau  2.08, 2.09
'Guinea Fowl War'  2.47
Gulf states  4.06
Gulf war(s)  4.09, 4.11, 4.14, 5.17
Guyana  1.09, 3.03, 3.12, 3.13
Guzman, Abimael  3.08, 3.09
Gypsies  *See* Roma
Habibie, Rudy  6.09
Habre, Hissene  2.11
Habyarimana, Juvenal  2.24
haciendas  3.03
Haiti  2.36
Hamas  4.06, 4.18
Hamitic population group  2.27
Han (Chinese)  5.05, 5.06
Harar  2.22
Haratines  2.32
Hariri, Rafik  4.05
Haryana  5.11
Hausa  2.36
Herceg-Bosna  7.27
Herero  2.24, 2.58, 2.59
Hill Tribes (Indian)  5.13
Hill Tribes (Nepalese)  5.19
Himachal Pradesh  5.11
Hindi (language)  5.08, 5.19
Hinduism  5.08, 5.18, 5.20
Hitler, Adolf  1.01, 4.17
Hizb ut-Tahrir  4.15, 6.07
Hizbollah  4.04
Hmong  6.24, 6.25
Ho Chi Minh trail  6.24
Holy Spirit Mobile Units  2.30
Horn of Africa  2.20, 2.22

Houphouet-Boigny, Felix  2.41, 2.48
Human Genome Project  1.01
humanitarian relief  2.37
Hungary  5.24, 7.03
Hussein, Saddam  4.10, 4.11, 4.15
Hutu  2.24, 2.26, 2.27, 2.28
hydroelectricity  2.40
hydrogen bomb tests  6.30
Ickeria, Chechyn Republic of  7.23
Igbo (Ibo)  2.36
Ilois  5.17
immigration  1.02
immigration, into Europe  7.04
Incas  3.02. 3.08
India, Indians  1.01,1.02, 5.04, 5.08, 5.09, 5.10, 5.14, 5.15, 5.20, 6.22, 6.26 *See also* Kashmir, Punjab, Seven Sisters States
Indian Wars (US)  3.15
Indians (South African)  2.55
Indo-Guyanese  3.12
Indochina  6.24
Indonesia  6.06, 6.07, 6.08 *See also* Aceh, Moluccas, West Papua, Timor Leste
Ingushetia, Ingushetians  7.14, 7.22, 7.23, 7.24
Institutional Revolutionary Party  3.05
integration  *See* assimilation
Inter Governmental Authority on Development (Sudan)  2.14
Interahamwe  2.25
Inter-communal violence  1.06, 1.08, 1.09
Internal Macedonia Revolutionary Organization  7.34
International Court of Justice  2.34
International Criminal Court  2.31
International Security Assistance Force (ISAF)  5.24
internet  3.05, 7.07 *See also* Denial of Access Attack
inter-state warfare  1.04, 2.18
intervention, international  1.04
intifada  4.17, 4.18
Iran  4.06, 4.07, 4.08, 4.09, 4.10, 4.15, 5.25, 5.26, 7.24
Iran/Iraq war  4.10
Iraq  4.06, 4.08, 4.09, 4.10, 4.11, 4.12, 4.15, 7.19
Ireland, Irish  7.36
Irish Free State  7.37
Irish Republican Army (IRA)  7.37
Islam, in Chechnya  7.23
Islam, in Europe  7.04
Islam, in Thailand  6.20
Islam, in Africa  2.02, 2.03, 2.32, 2.36
Islam, in Malaysia  6.22
Islam, in Turkey  4.02
Islamists  1.01, 2.06, 2.51, 4.14, 4.15, 6.07 *See also* Taliban, Al Qaeda

Israel  4.04, 4.05, 4.06, 4.13, 4.15, 4.16, 4.18
Italy  2.22, 3.03, 7.03
Ituri  2.29
Jadidists  7.20
Jaffna  5.21
Jagan, Cheddi  3.12, 3.13
Jakarta  6.07
Jamial-e-Ullema  5.24, 5.25
Jammu & Kashmir  *See* Kashmir
Janatha Vimukthi Peramuna  5.21
Janjaweed  2.11, 2.14
Japanese  3.03, 6.06, 6.08
Java, Javanese  6.06, 6.11
Jerusalem  4.17
Jews  1.01, 4.16, 4.17
Jim Crow laws  3.16
Johnson, Prince Yormie  2.41
Jordan  4.06
Kabardino-Balkaria  7.23
Kabbah, Tejan  2.43
Kabila, Joseph  2.29
Kabila, Laurent  2.25, 2.29
Kabylie  2.07
Kachin  6.02
Kadyrov, Ramzan  7.23
Kagame, Paul  2.25
Kalashnikov economy  2.3
Kalat, Khanate of  5.25
Kalimantan  1.08, 6.06, 6.10, 6.11
Kaliningrad  7.07
Kampala  2.31
Karamojong  2.31
Karbardino-Balkaria  7.23
Karelians  7.06
Karen  6.02
Karenni  6.02
Karzai, Hamid  5.23
Kashmir  1.02, 5.08, 5.11, 5,14, 5.15, 5.16
Katanga  2.28
Kawtholei  6.03, 6.04
Kazan  7.21
Kenya  1.09, 2.14, 2.20, 2.61, 2.62
Khalistan  5.10, 5.11
Khmer Rouge  6.25
Khoi-San (language group)  2.02
Khoisians  2.59
kidnapping (as political tactic)  7.09
Kigali  2.24
Kikulu  7.04
Kinh (Vietnamese)  6.25
Kinshasa  2.28, 2.29
Kiribati  6.30
Kirkuk  4.09
Kivu (Congo)  2.29
Knin  7.27
Koenigsberg  *See* Kaliningrad
Konkomba  2.47

Kony, Joseph  2.30
Korea, North  2.56
Kosovo  1.04, 7.25, 7.26, 7.27, 7.28, 7.29, 7.31, 7.32, 7.33
Kosovo Liberation Army  7.33
Krahn  2.41
Krajina  7.27, 7.28, 7.29
Krio  2.43
Kurdistan, Kurds  4.02, 4.03, 4.08, 4.09, 4.10, 4.11
Kuwait  4.11
KwaZulu Natal  2.55
Kyi, Aung San Suu  6.02
Kyrenia  7.13
Lachin corridor  7.17
Lagos  2.36
Lakwena  2.3
land alienation  2.57, 2.58, 2.59, 3.10, 6.30
land ownership disputes  2.33, 2.45
language, as ethnic marker  1.03
Laos  6.02, 6.24, 6.25
Lashkar-e-Tarba  5.16
latifunda  3.03
Latindo (ethnic group)  3.03, 3.10, 3.11
Latino (US ethnic group)  3.16
Latvia  7.06
League of Nations  2.24, 2.26, 2.38. 2.59, 4.17
Lebanon  1.09, 4.04, 4.05, 4.06
Leopold, King of the Belgians  2.28
Lezghin  7.17
Lhasa  5.04
Liberation Tigers of Tamil Eelam  *See* Tamil Tigers
Liberia  1.09, 2.40, 2.41, 2.43, 2.44, 2.46
Liberians United for Reconcilliation & Development (LURD)  2.43, 2.44, 2.45
Libya  2.07, 2.40
Limba  2.43
Line of Control (Kashmir)  5.14, 5.15
Lingali  2.29
Lithuania  7.04, 7.06. 7.07
Lord's Resistance Army  2.17, 2.29, 2.30, 2.31
Los Angeles riots  3.16
Loya Jirga  5.23
Loyalists (Ulster)  7.36
Lozi  2.59
Lubjanja  7.25
Luo  7.04
Luzon  6.19
Macedonia  1.04, 7.25, 7.26, 7.34, 7.35
Macenta  2.45
Machar, Riek  2.31
Machel, Samora  2.04
Madhesi  5.18, 5.19
madrassas  5.22

Madrid Accord  2.34
Madurese  6.06, 6.10, 6.11
Maghalaza  5.12
Mai-Mai  2.29
Makhachkala  7.24
Malaita  6.28
Malaysia  6.22, 6.24
Mali  2.50, 2.51
Malinke  2.46
Mandela, Nelson  2.54, 2.55
Mandinko  2.08, 2.41, 2.42
Manipur  5.12
Mano River region  2.40, 2.41
Maoist insurgents  3.03, 3.08, 5.09, 5.18, 5.19
Maronites  4.04. 4.06
Marxism  1.01, 2.04, 3.03, 3.08, 4.06
*See also* Communism
Mashona  2.55, 2.57
Matabele  2.56, 2.57
Mauritania  2.32, 2.33, 2.34
Mayans  3.02, 3.04, 3.10, 3.11
Mbeki, Thabo  2.55
M'bororo  2.16, 2.17
Medellin cartel  3.07
Melanesians  6.06, 6.07, 6.26, 6.28
'melting pot'  1.09
Mende  2.43
Mesopotamia  4.10
Messianic Jews  4.06
Mestizos  3.03, 3.04, 3.06
Mexico  3.04, 3.05
Middle East  2.02
Milosevic, Slobadan  7.26, 7.28, 7.29, 7.31, 7.32
Mindanao  6.18, 6.19
'Minority Majority' states  3.16
Miss World Contest (riots over)  2.37
Mission de l'Organisation des Nations-Unies au Congo (MONUC)  2.28, 2.29
Mississippi  3.15
Mizo  5.13
Mizoram  5.13
Mobuto, Sese Seku  2.25, 2.28
Moldova  7.18, 7.19
Molotov-Ribbentrop Pact  7.06, 7.18
Moluccas  6.07
Mon  6.04, 6.18
Mong  *See* Hmong
Mongols  5.07, 7.20
Monrovia  2.41, 2.42
Montagnard  6.24
Montenegro  7.25, 7.26, 7.27, 7.28, 7.33
Moro National Liberation Front  6.18, 6.19
Morocco  2.07, 2.34, 2.35
Moscow theatre seige  7.23
Mouvement des forces democratiques de la Casamance  2.09

Mouvement pour la liberation du Congo (MLC)  2.29
Movement for Democratic Change (MDC) (Zimbabwe)  2.57
Movement for the Emancipation of the Niger Delta  2.37
Mozambique  2.04, 2.38, 2.39, 2.57
Mugabe, Robert  2.56, 2.57
multiculturalism  1.03, 3.16, 7.04
Musevani, Yoweri  2.30, 2.30
Musharraf, Pervez  5.26
Muslim League (Indian)  5.09
Muslims  2.41, 2.42, 2.45, 2.48, 2.52
See also Islam
Mussolini, Benito  2.22
Muzorewa, Bishop Abel  2.56
Mwai Kibaki, Mwai  7.04
Myanmar  See Burma
Nackichevan  7.17
Nagaland  5.13
Nagas  5.13
Nagorno-Karabakh  7.16, 7.17, 7.33
Nama  2.58, 2.59
Namibia  2.02, 2.24, 2.28, 2.57
Napoleon, Bonaparte  1.01, 7.38
Napoleonic wars  7.03
narcoterrorism  3.06, 3.07
Natal  2.54
National Congress (Indian)  5.09
National Islamic Front  2.17
National Liberation Army (Macedonia)  7.35
National Patriotic Front of Liberia  2.41
National Resistance Army (Uganda)  2.3
National Patriotic Fund of Liberia  2.41
Navarre  7.08
Ndadaye, Melchoir  2.26
negritude  2.04
Nepal  5.18, 5.19
Nepalgunj  5.19
Netherlands  7.03
New Economic Policy  6.22
New Zealand  6.28
Niger  2.50, 2.51
Niger Delta Region  2.36
Niger-Congo (ethnic group)  2.02
Nigeria  2.36, 2.37, 2.38, 2.39, 2.41. 2.42, 2.43
Nilotic (ethnic group)  2.27
Nilo-Saharan (ethnic group)  2.02
Nkomo, Joshua  2.57
Nkurunziza, Pierre  2.26
Nomads  2.45
North America  3.14, 3.15 See also United States
North American Free Trade Area (NAFTA)  3.04, 3.05

North Atlantic Treaty Organization (NATO)  1.04, 4.15, 5.23, 5.24, 7.02, 7.07, 7.11, 7.29, 7.31, 7.33, 7.35
North West Froniter Province  5.23
Northern Areas (Kashmir)  5.14
Northern Ireland  1.09, 7.03, 7.36, 7.37, 7.38
Northern Ireland Women's Peace Movement  1.09
Ntaryamira, Cyprien  2.26
Nuba  2.17
Nukah (ethnic group)  3.07
Nunavat  3.15
Obote, Milton  2.3
Occitan  1.03
Ocean Island  See Banaba
Odinga, Raila  7.04
Ogaden  2.22, 2.23
Ogaden National Liberation Front  2.20, 2.21, 2.23
Ohrid Framework  7.35
oil as conflict issue  2.11, 2.17, 2.36, 2.37, 2.39, 2.60, 4.10
Olympic Games  5.04, 5.05
Oman  2.52
Omar, Mullah Mohammed  5.22, 5.23, 5.24
Operation Storm  7.28
Operation Turquoise  2.25
opium  5.23
Orange Free State  2.54
Organization of African Unity  See African Union
Organization of Islamic Conferences  2.53
Oromo  2.23
Orwell, George  1.01
Oslo Accords  4.18
Ossetia (North and South)  7.14, 7.24
Ottoman empire  4.02, 4.03, 4.08. 4.14, 4.17
Ovambo  2.03, 2.58, 2.59
Pacific islands  6.26, 6.30
Pakistan  1.02, 5.14, 5.15, 5.16, 5.22, 5.23, 5.24, 5.09, 5.10, 5.11, 5.25, 5.26
Palestine Liberation Organization (PLO)  4.04, 4.16, 4.17, 4.18
Palestine, Palestinians  4.04, 4.06, 4.13, 4.15, 4.16, 4.17, 4.18
Palestinian Authority  4.17, 4.18
Panchan Lama  5.05
Papua New Guinea  6.27
Paraguay  3.03
Parti Quebecois  3.16
Partiya Demokrata Kurdistan (PDK))  4.09
Partiya Karkeren Kurdistan (PKK)  4.09
Pashtuns  5.22, 5.23, 5.24, 5.25, 5.26
Patasse, Ange-Felix  2.17
Pathet Lao  6.24

patronage, political  2.33
Pattani  6.20, 6.21
peacekeeping forces  2.28
Pemba  2.52, 2.53
People's Liberation Army (PLA)  5.04
Peoples National Congress (Guyana)  3.12, 3.13
Peoples Progressive Party (Guyana)  3.12, 3.13
Persia  See Iran
Peru  3.03, 3.08, 3.09
peshmerga  4.09
Phalange (Lebanese)  4.04
Philippines  5.24, 6.18, 6.19
phosphates  2.34, 6.30
plebiscites  2.19, 2.34, 2.35, 2.39, 6.27, 7.03, 7.09, 7.19. 7.20, 7.31, 7.38
Poland, Poles  1.01, 5.24, 7.03
Polynesians  6.26
Portugal, Portuguese  2.02, 2.08, 2.60, 6.12, 6.13
Portuguese (language)  3.02, 3.05
power sharing  1.09
Princely States  5.12, 5.14
Protestanism  7.37
Punjab  5.08, 5.10, 5.11
Quebec  3.16
Quechua  3.08
Racak Massacre  7.33
Race, as ethnic marker  1.03
Rakhines  6.04, 6.05
Rambouillet conference  7.33
Rassemblement conglais pour democratie  2.29
referendums  See plebiscites
refugees, refugee camps  2.29, 2.35, 2.44, 2.45, 2.56, 2.57
religion, as ethnic marker  1.03
Republicans (Northern Ireland)  7.36
Republika Srpska  7.30, 7.31, 7.33
Revolutionary United Front (RUF)  2.41, 2.43, 2.44, 2.45, 2.46
Rhodes, Cecil  2.56
Rhodesia, Rhodesians  2.56, 2.57
Rio de Oro  2.34
Rohingyas  6.04, 6.05
Roma  7.05
Roman Catholicism  2.09, 2.46, 2.48, 3.10, 3.16, 7.37
Romania  7.05, 7.18, 7.19
Rose Revolution  7.15
Royal Navy  2.52
rubber  2.41
Russia, Russians  1.01, 7.06, 7.07, 7.10, 7.11, 7.19, 7.20, 7.24, 7.33
Russian Union of Muslims  7.24
Russification  1.04, 7.16, 7.18, 7.21
Rwanda  1.02, 1.04, 2.04, 2.24, 2.34, 2.26, 2.27, 2.28, 2.29, 2.30

Rwandan Patriotic Front (RPF)  2.24, 2.28, 2.29
Sabah  6.22
Sahara Arab Democratic Republic (SADR)  2.34, 2.35
Sahara desert  2.02, 2.51
Saharawis  2.34
Sankoh, Foday  2.40, 2.43
Sao Tome & Principe  2.36, 2.37
Sarawak  6.22
Saudi Arabia  2.33, 4.11, 4.15, 5.22
Scotland  7.03
Scramble for Africa  2.02, 2.28
Seattle riots  3.16
secessionist conflicts  1.04, 1.06, 1.08, 1.09
second Gulf War  See Gulf War(s)
Second World War  1.01, 2.04, 2.38, 6.06, 6.08, 6.18, 7.03, 7.06, 7.10, 7.16, 7.35
Sendero Luminosa  See Shining Path
Senegal  2.08, 2.09, 2.32, 2.33 See also Casamance
Serbia, Serbs  7.25, 7.26, 7.27, 7.28, 7.29, 7.30, 7.32, 7.33
'Seven Sisters States'  5.08, 5.12, 5.13
Sevres, Treaty of  4.02
sharia law  1.04, 2.14, 2.36, 2.37, 6.22
Shias  4.04, 4.06. 4.12, 4.14, 4.10, 4.11
Shining Path  3.03, 3.08, 3.09
Shiraz (ethnic group)  2.52, 2.53
Siachen Glacier  5.15
Sierra Leone  2.40, 2.41, 2.42, 2.45, 2.43
Sikhism  5.08, 5.09. 5.10, 5.11
Silk Route  5.06
Simulambuco, Treaty of  2.60
Sinai  4.13, 4.17
Singapore  6.22
Sinhalese  5.20, 5.21
Sinn Fein  7.37
slavery  2.02, 2.14, 2.32, 2.41, 2.49, 2.52, 3.02, 3.12, 3.15
Slavs  1.01
Slovenia, Slovenes  7.25, 7.26, 7.27, 7.28
Smassides  2.33
Smith, Ian  2.56
Solomon Islands  6.28, 6.29
Somalia, Somalis  1.02, 2.20, 2.22 See also Ogaden
Somaliland  2.04, 2.21
South Africa  2.02, 2.25, 2.54, 2.55, 2.56, 2.67, 2.58
South Kasai  2.28
South Lebanese Army  4.05
South Sudan  2.14, 2.31 See also Sudan
South West Africa  See Namibia

South West African Peoples Organization (SWAPO)  2.58, 2.59
Soviet Union  1.02, 2.04, 2.20, 5.07, 7.03, 7.06, 7.16, 7.17, 7.20, 7.22, 7.23
'Sovietization'  7.06 See also 'Russification'
Spain  2.34, 3.04, 3.06, 3.08, 3.10, 3.13, 7.03, 7.08
Spanish (language)  3.02, 3.03, 3.10, 3.14
Speight, George  6.26
Srebrenica  7.31
Sri Lanka  5.20, 5.21
St Petersburg  7.06
Stalin, Josef  1.01
State Peace & Development Council  6.02
Stone Town  2.52
Sub-Saharan region  2.02
Sudan  1.02, 2.04, 2.10, 2.11, 2.14, 2.13, 2.31
Sudan Peoples Liberation Army  2.14
Sufism  5.09
sugar plantations  6.26
Suharto  6.07
suicide bombers  5.21
Sukarno  6.06
Sukarnoputri, Megawati  6.07
Sulawesi  6.11
Sumatra  6.08, 6.11
Sunnis  4.10, 4.11, 4.14
Suriname  3.13
Swahili  2.29
Sweden  7.03
Syria  4.04, 4.06, 4.09, 4.11, 4.12, 4.17
Taiwan  See China, Republic of
Taliban  4.11, 5.07, 5.15, 5.22, 5.23, 5.24, 5.25
Talysh  7.17
Tamasheq  2.50
Tamil Eelam  5.20, 5.21
Tamil Nadu  5.20
Tamil Tigers  5.21
Tamils  5.20, 5.21
Tanganyika  See Tanzania
Tanzania  2.36, 2.52. 2.53
Tartars (Crimean)  1.01, 7.10
Tasmanians  6.29
Tatars (of Tatarstan)  7.20
Tatarstan  7.20, 7.21
Taya, Ould  2.33
Taylor, Charles  2.36, 2.40, 2.41, 2.43, 2.45
Temne  2.43
Terai  5.18
terra nullius  6.30
terrorism  1.08, 5.09, 6.07, 7.09, 7.37, 7.38 See also 9/11 attacks
Thailand  6.02, 6.18, 6.19, 6.20, 6.21, 6.24

Thatcher, Margaret  7.37
Tibet  5.04, 5.05
Tibetan Autonomous Region  5.04
Tigrayans  2.18, 2,19
Timbuktu  2.50
Timor Leste  1.08, 6.07, 6.09, 6.12, 613
Tito, Josip Broz  7.25
Tlaxala  3.04
Togo  2.47
Transcaucasian Soviet Federative Republic  7.16

Transitional Federal Government (TFG) (Somalia)  2.21. 2.23
Transkei  2.55
Transmigration policy (Indonesia)  6.06, 6.10, 6.11
Transnistria  7.18, 7.19
transport infrastructures  2.02
Transvaal  2.54
Tripuna  5.12
tsunami  6.08
Tuareg  2.50, 2.51
Tuareg Mouvement Nigeriens pour la Justice  2.51
Tunisia  2.07
Turkana  2.31
Turkey, Turks  4.02, 4.06, 4.08, 4.09, 7.12, 7.13, 7.15, 7.16, 7.32
Turkish Cypriots  See Cyprus
Turkish Republic of Northern Cyprus  See Cyprus
Tutsis  2.04, 2.24, 2.25, 2.26, 2.27, 2.28, 2.29
Tutu, Archbishop Desmond  2.55
Twa  2.26, 2.27
Uganda  2.05, 2.14, 2.16, 2.17, 2.21, 2.24, 2.25, 2.27, 2.29, 2.30
Uganda National Liberation Army  2,28
Ukraine  7.10, 7.11, 7.18
Ulster  See Northern Ireland
União Nacional para a Independência Total de Angola (UNITA)  2.04, 2.28, 2.29, 2.58, 2.60
Uniform Federal Treaty  7.21, 7.24
Union des Forces Democratiques pour le Rassemblement  2.16, 2.17
Union of Soviet Socialist Republics (USSR)  See Soviet Union, also Russia
Unionists (Ulster)  7.36
United Arab Emirates  5.22
United Islamic Courts (Somalia)  2.21
United Nations  1.04, 2.07, 2.13, 2.18, 2.20, 2.24, 2.28, 2.29, 2.35, 2.39, 2.41, 2.44, 3.11, 4.13, 5.14, 5.18, 7.13, 7.31, 7.35
United Nations Assistance Mission in Sierra Leone (UNAMSIL)  2.43, 2.44

United Nations Mission in Liberia (UNMIL) 2.42
United Nations Operations in Cote d'Ivorie (UNOCI) 2.48, 2.49
United States of America 2.20, 2.33, 2.41, 3.11, 3.13, 3.14, 4.09, 4.10, 4.11, 4.15, 5.17, 5.24, 2.51, 2.59, 6.18, 6,24, 6.25
United Wo States Army 6.04
untouchables 5.18 See also Dalit
Uribe, Alvara 3.06, 3.07
Uruguay 3.02, 3.03
Uyghurstan See Xinjiang
Venda 2.55
Venezuela 3.13
Vhavenda 2.55
Viet Cong 6.24
Vietnam 1.01, 6.24, 6.25
Vietnam War 6.24, 6.25
Vojvodina 7.25
Vukovar 7.28
Wade, Abdoulage 2.09
Wahid, Abdurrahman 6.07
Wallonia 7.04
Walloon (language) 7.04
'war on terror' 4.11, 4.15, 5.16, 6.05 See also 9/11 attacks
Warsaw Pact 7.02
Waziristan, Islamic Emirate of 5.24
Weapons of Mass Destruction (WMD) 4.11
West Bank 4.06, 4.17, 4.18
West Papua 6.07, 6.13, 6.16, 6.17
Western Bosnia, Autonomous Republic of 7.27
Western Sahara 1.08, 2.33, 2.34
Whites (ethnic group) 2.03
Whites (of South Africa) 2.54, 2.55
Whites (of Zimbabwe) 2.56, 2.57
Windhoek 2.59
Wolof 2.32
Xhosa 2.54, 2.55
Xinjiang 5.06, 5.07
Yakomo 2.16, 2.17
Yawi (language) 6.20, 6.21
Yeltsin, Boris 7.16, 7.20, 7.21
Yekiti Nistimani Kurdistan 7.09
Yemen 4.07
Yoroba 2.36
Yucatan 3.04
Yugoslav National Army (JNA) 7.27, 7.28
Yugoslavia See Balkans
Zaghara 1.09, 2.10, 2.11, 2.14
Zagreb 7.28
Zaire See Congo
Zambia 2.28, 2.36, 2.59
Zanzibar 2.51
Zapatistas 3.04, 3.05

Zaydiyyah, Zaydis 4.07
Zimbabwe 2.25, 2.28, 2.29, 2.54, 2.55
Zimbabwe African National Liberation Army (ZANLA) 2.56
Zimbabwe African National Union - Patriotic Front (ZANU-PF) 2.55, 2.57
Zimbabwe African Peoples Union (ZAPU) 2.56
Zimbabwe Peoples Revolutionary Army (ZIPRA) 2.56
Zimbabwe-Rhodesia 2.56
Zinguinchor 2.08
Zionism 4.16, 4.17
Zulus 2.54, 2.55
Zuma, Jacob 2.55

Lightning Source UK Ltd.
Milton Keynes UK
UKOW02f0648280114

225405UK00003B/293/P